THE NEW NATUR

A SURVEY OF BRITISH

C000215353

G O W

The aim of this series is to interest the general reader in the wildlife
of Britain by recapturing the enquiring spirit of the old naturalists.
The editors believe that the natural pride of the British public
in the native flora, fauna and fungi, to which must be added
concern for their conservation, is best fostered
by maintaining a high standard of accuracy
combined with clarity of exposition
in presenting the results
of modern scientific
research.

THE NEW NATURALIST LIBRARY

GOWER

JONATHAN MULLARD

Collins

This edition published in 2006 by Collins,
an imprint of HarperCollins Publishers

HarperCollins Publishers
77–85 Fulham Palace Road
London w6 8jb

www.collins.co.uk

First published 2006
Reprinted 2006
Reprinted 2007

A cip catalogue record for this book is available
from the British Library

Set in ff Nexus by
Rowland Phototypesetting Ltd,
Bury St Edmunds, Suffolk

Printed in China by Imago
Reprographics by Saxon Photolitho, Norwich

Hardback
isbn-13 978-0-00-716067-9
isbn-10 0-00-716067-4

Paperback
isbn-13 978-0-00-716066-2
isbn-10 0-00-716066-6

To Gower naturalists, past, present and future.

And it would seem a weird and unnatural thing for a man to pursue what is called 'Truth', either by strictly scientific, or by the more imaginative philosophical method if this pursuit was not in itself attended by happiness or at least presumed to result in happiness.

John Cowper Powys, *The Art of Happiness*

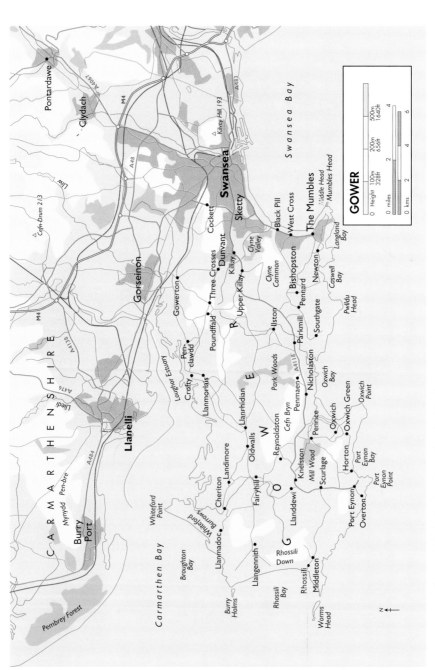

FRONTISPIECE. Gower: with the key locations described in the text.

Contents

Editors' Preface

Regional volumes have long been an important and distinctive element of the New Naturalist library. Most of these have focused on the National Parks, from *Snowdonia* by F. J. North, Bruce Campbell and Richenda Scott, published in the early days of the series 57 years ago (in the very same year that the National Parks and Access to the Countryside Act created our first National Parks), to the most recent, Angus Lunn's *Northumberland*, which appeared in 2004. With *Gower*, however, we break new ground in that this famous part of South Wales is not a National Park but an Area of Outstanding Natural Beauty. AONBs were established by the same far-sighted piece of post-war legislation that set up the National Parks – but seemingly as not much more than an afterthought, as they are buried right at the end in the section headed 'General, Financial and Supplementary'!

Gower was the first AONB to be created and 2006 is its fiftieth birthday. We are proud to present this new addition to the New Naturalist series to mark both its jubilee year and half a century of designation of some of the most beautiful landscapes in England and Wales. Gower has long been famed among naturalists for its geology and wildlife. Protruding into the Bristol Channel from the belly of South Wales and bounded by Carmarthen Bay to the west and Swansea Bay to the east, it is a land of astonishing diversity and rich cultural history that has withstood the advance of industry and development that have been such a marked feature of neighbouring parts of South Wales over the last two hundred years.

Jonathan Mullard is especially well qualified to present this account of the natural history of Gower. A professional ecologist and all-round naturalist, he was appointed Gower Countryside Officer in 1990, the first senior AONB officer to be appointed in the UK. For ten years he was responsible for the policy and management of the AONB, during which time he developed a unique insight into the complex interactions between the land and its people that have crafted this beautiful and special place. Although he has since moved northwards and is currently Director of Park Management for the Northumberland National Park Authority, he is still researching and recording the wildlife of the peninsula.

An area such as Gower poses a particular challenge to the author. With such a marvellous variety of landscape and habitat within a relatively small area the task is daunting. From the heathlands of Rhossili Down and Llanmadoc Hill to the great wide lonely spaces of the Burry Inlet, from the famed limestone cliffs of the south Gower coast to the dunes of Whiteford Burrows, Gower has one of the richest wildlife heritages in Britain. Inevitably regional volumes often reveal something of the author's own particular enthusiasms and prejudices, but anyone attempting such insights in *Gower* is likely to be frustrated. Archaeology, birds and geology; plants, insects and rocky shores; caves, lichens and mosses on dung are all treated with equal felicity and authority. It is with pleasure that we welcome this our first account of the natural history of an Area of Outstanding Natural Beauty.

Author's Foreword and Acknowledgements

T HE NATURAL and cultural riches of Gower attract millions of visitors each year and quite a few naturalists. Many are looking for a detailed guide to the wildlife of the area, but none exists. The aim of this book is therefore to fill the gap. It contains in one place, for the first time, all of the currently available information on the natural history of the peninsula. As the stated aim of the New Naturalist series is to recapture 'the enquiring spirit of the old naturalists' I have also highlighted opportunities for the reader interested in taking things further, either alone or in conjunction with the appropriate organisation.

The book has as its underlying theme the evolving landscape, and seascape, and the effect that the associated changes have had, and indeed are having, on species and habitats. These changes are now accelerating and their causes are in future going to be global rather than local and, as such, will be very difficult to control. The natural world seems, more than ever before, to be in a state of flux due to the increasingly warm climate – and Gower is not immune from these influences. By the year 2080 the climate in Wales is expected to be warmer all year round by up to 3.5°C, wetter in winter by 7–24 per cent and drier in summer by 7–14 per cent. The areas that are currently suitable for many species are therefore likely to alter, and it is unclear whether the plants and animals and the habitats on which they depend will be able to keep pace with this change. If current trends continue the peninsula is going to be an extremely different place in a hundred years' time. Yet I hope that something of its very special atmosphere will remain and that this overview of Gower at the beginning of the twenty-first century will still have some relevance, if only as a historic record.

In May 1996 I organised a national conference in Swansea to celebrate Gower's fortieth anniversary as the UK's first Area of Outstanding Natural Beauty (AONB). In comparison to National Parks the AONB designation had, at that time, little attention or resources. The conference succeeded beyond my wildest expectations and I little thought when addressing the audience on the need for new legislation that only four years later this objective would be realised in the Countryside and Rights of Way Act. What I also could not have anticipated was the opportunity to celebrate the fiftieth anniversary of the designation by producing a volume in the New Naturalist series, the book that you now hold in your hands. Throughout my career in conservation the series has been, and continues to be, a constant source of inspiration to me. Finding a copy of William Condry's book on the natural history of Wales on a Cardiff bookshop shelf in 1984 was a special experience – though I would, of course, claim that he did not give enough attention to Gower! Following in his footsteps has been an interesting exercise.

I have structured the book around the main habitats present in the peninsula, but given the nature of Gower, and its incredible diversity, these divisions are sometimes arbitrary, especially as many habitats blend into one another. To give a single example, a short half-hour walk south from Green Cwm to Three Cliff Bay would involve passing through the subjects covered by at least four separate chapters. Everyone who knows the area has their own favourite places, plants and animals, but it has been my intention to provide a balanced overview of the peninsula and its wildlife. Inevitably, though there has not been the space to explore some topics in detail. In any case to do this would have radically altered the style of the book and taken it away from a general readership.

The Ordnance Survey Explorer Map 164, *Gower/Gwyr*, at a scale of 1:25,000, is a useful companion to this volume and shows clearly many of the sites that I have described. Names of places and features are mainly taken from this map, even though the spelling may differ from that which is locally accepted. The book is not, however, intended as a field guide and, although a considerable area of Gower is accessible to the public, the description or mention of any site does not necessarily imply that there is access to it, or that a right of way exists. An account of an area or site, or its appearance on a photograph or map, should not therefore be taken as an invitation to visit.

ACKNOWLEDGEMENTS

A particularly enjoyable part of writing the book has been the contacts I have made, or re-established, with a large number of people. Given the richness of Gower and its natural history it would have been impossible to have completed the task without their help. Without doubt I must start by thanking Harold Grenfell, an eminent Gower naturalist and photographer, who has supported me enthusiastically throughout the process. His dry humour has kept me going when due to other pressures the project might have suffered. In addition to helping select the final list of photographs Harold has generously donated many of his own pictures and this volume would be poorer without them. He has also read and provided detailed and constructive observations on the majority of chapters.

Many staff of the Countryside Council for Wales have also contributed material, advice and encouraging words. In particular I would like to thank Michael Hughes, David Painter, Brian Pawson and Rebecca Wright in the Swansea office, all of whom I have worked closely with over the years. I must also record the contribution that Tony Jenkins, former District Officer for West Glamorgan, has made both to the conservation of the peninsula and to the early stages of preparing this book – although he may not have realised it at the time. Other staff too have been enthusiastic about the project. Mike Howe especially has provided assistance with invertebrate records and kindly read a number of chapters. Sid Howells amended the sections relating to geology and geomorphology. Rohan Holt provided information on sea caves. The acquisition of much of these data would have been infinitely more difficult without the help of Ruth Parr, who supplied me with copies of numerous reports and surveys, sometimes at short notice.

Malcolm and Ruth Ridge of the Gower Society have again supported the project from the beginning, helping me to contact a number of people and contributing a unique photograph of Phil Tanner from the archives. In addition the chapter on commons has benefited from the input of Edward Harris, while Bernard Morris has helpfully read and commented on the sections relating to the influence of people. I must also thank Diane Williams of Cadw and Robert Young, Northumberland National Park Archaeologist, for their useful advice and guidance on this chapter. David Leighton allowed me to use the results of his extensive researches into Parc le Breos.

My former colleagues in the City and County of Swansea, Steve Parry and Richard Beale, have refreshed my memory on the activities of the Gower Countryside Service, while Bernice Cardy of Swansea Museum has expertly pointed me in the direction of sources on the early naturalists, located photographs and ensured that I did not confuse the Dillwyns.

Andrew Mackie at the National Museums and Galleries of Wales and Andy Woolmer at the University of Swansea added an extra dimension to the text by providing essential information on the marine environment. In the same vein I must also thank another New Naturalist author, Peter Hayward, again from the

University, for ensuring accuracy in the sections on the seashore. It is a tribute to
the peninsula's rich shore life that so many of the photographs in his book were
of Gower. Graeme Hays supplied data on marine turtles.

Quentin Kay has read and commented on the main botanical sections, while
Joe Sutton of Plantlife International and Tim Rich of the National Museums
added further useful information on plant conservation. The latter's colleagues in
the Department of Biodiversity and Systematic Biology, Alan Orange and Adrian
Plant, advised on the sections relating to lichens and flies respectively. Dai Jermyn
of the Vincent Wildlife Trust assisted with mammal records. Jon Winder of
the Woodland Trust supplied the most recent information on Common Wood.
Andy Wills of Forestry Commission Wales gave me access to material on the
Gower woodlands managed by that organisation. Mike and Pam Evans from the
Glamorgan Badger Group updated my knowledge on the status of the species in
the peninsula. Similarly Tom McOwat has shared the results of his extensive and
perceptive analysis of bat populations in the area and the issues facing them. Mike
Powell and Barry Stewart of the Glamorgan Moth Recording Group have helped
with records. Nigel Ajax-Lewis of the Wildlife Trust of South and West Wales
provided a range of useful information and assembled a current list of nature
reserves. Paul Llewellyn donated material on barn owls and provided contacts.
Lionel Kellaway explained the details of adder populations. Sîon Brackenbury of
the Gower Commons Initiative supplied information on the achievements of the
project. Mark Winder helped with data on arachnids. Bob Burn gave me the
benefit of his experience derived from many years of educational work in the
peninsula. Elaine Arthurs, Collections Officer at the Steam Library in Swindon,
kindly spent some time researching the origin of the paint colours used in the
GWR liveries.

The memories of Iorwerth (Iorrie) Rees, former Assistant Regional Officer for
the Nature Conservancy, have been invaluable in helping to establish the early
history of the Conservancy, and its successor the Nature Conservancy Council,
in Gower. Likewise Winnie Weston provided the background on the formation
of the Wildlife Trust and the Gower Field Education Project, and in addition gave
me support at a crucial stage in the proceedings.

Finally, and certainly not least, I must thank my wife Melanie, who diligently
read the various drafts, and my daughters Caitlin and Bethan for their help and
encouragement and for putting up with uncounted weekends at home while I
wrote this book.

Text and Picture Credits

THE QUOTATIONS, illustrations and photographs in this book are reproduced with the kind permission of the following organisations and individuals who hold the copyright, have supplied material which is out of copyright, or have provided their own material. The author has made all reasonable efforts to contact the relevant copyright holders and apologises to any that may have been omitted.

David Higham Associates for permission to quote from the writings of Dylan Thomas; Robert Hale Ltd for sections from *Portrait of Gower* by Wynford Vaughan-Thomas; the Gower Society for items by Horatio Tucker and others; Cadw Welsh Historic Monuments for the extract from *Gower*; HarperCollins for material from *The Common Lands of England and Wales* and *The Natural History of Wales*; Christopher Sinclair-Stevenson for the piece from *The Art of Happiness* by John Cowper Powys.

David Painter for Figures 13, 16, 41, 43, 48, 49, 51, 68, 71, 73, 74, 76, 78, 79, 80, 83, 84, 85, 88, 98, 103, 115 and 144; the author for Figures 7, 24, 25, 33, 36, 50, 58, 91, 97, 99, 106, 116, 120, 123, 133, 136, 165 and 167; West Glamorgan Archive Service for Figures 1, 96, 128, 138, 142 and 157; Margaret Hodge for Figures 42, 59, 60, 63, 64 and 66; the Countryside Council for Wales for Figures 131, 132, 168, 169 and 171; Swansea Museum for Figures 8, 9, 12 and 26; Peter R. Douglas-Jones for Figures 11, 40 and 102; Paul Kay for Figures 61, 62 and 65; Royal Commission on the Ancient and Historical Monuments of Wales for Figures 32, 34 and 100; Barry Stewart for Figures 82, 119 and 146; Peter Francis for Figures 156 and 164; the Gower Society for Figures 6 and 15; the Joint Nature Conservation Committee for the use of Figures 125 and 160 from *Karst and Caves of Great Britain*; the City and County of Swansea for Figure 172; the Department of Geology, National Museums and Galleries of

Wales for Figure 158; the Estate of Evan Evans for Figure 105; the Gower Commons Initiative for Figure 173; Melvin Grey for Figure 161; David Leighton for Figure 30; Paul Llewellyn for Figure 67; Colin Matheson for Figure 69; the Natural History Museum for Figure 104. All other figures are by Harold Grenfell.

Note on Species Names

VERY ATTEMPT has been made to use the most up-to-date scientific names for species, but there are estimated to be six times more scientific names for species in the British Isles than actual species. This creates obvious difficulties for naturalists identifying, naming and working with them. An example of this occurred when I commissioned the picture of the Gower money spider from the Natural History Museum. As the only species actually named after the peninsula it was felt to be essential to include a photograph in the book, but initial searches for a specimen produced a blank and it was only after more research that it became apparent that it previously had a different scientific name. Using this the specimen was easily located and the photograph taken. To solve this problem the Museum has launched an online species directory at www.nhm.ac.uk/nbn that aims to bring all the common and scientific names of British wildlife into one place. Where possible this resource has been used to check the scientific names for animals used in this book. Names, both scientific and common, given in quotations have not, however, been altered. It should also be noted that many species have no common name.

Plant names, for the most part, follow those used in the *New Flora of the British Isles* (Stace, 1995), although they have been updated as necessary. Where the English common names are not those generally used in South Wales the more familiar versions have been substituted. The names of marine species are based on those in *The Species Directory of the Marine Fauna and Flora of the British Isles and Surrounding Seas* (Howson and Picton, 1997). Common names for fungi are derived from the *List of Recommended English Names for Fungi* produced by the British Mycological Society (2003) on behalf of a consortium of conservation bodies, including the Countryside Council for Wales. Bird names are based on the *British List* (British

Ornithologists' Union, 2005), but I have not followed all the recently recom-
mended changes that have resulted, for example, in the chough *Pyrrhocorax pyrrhocorax* being renamed the 'red-billed chough'. Any errors in species names that remain are my own responsibility.

PART I

A Separate and Special Place

CHAPTER 1

A Land Set Apart

Gower is a land set apart from the rest of South Wales. It is a peninsula heading out into
the Bristol Channel owing allegiance to neither east nor west Wales. And yet it is a region
of contrasts, boasting much of the topographical diversity of Wales in miniature.

Diane Williams, *Gower*

GOWER IS INDEED a land apart. Separated from the rest of Wales by the sprawling urban area of Swansea, it retains its own identity, despite being only a short drive from the city centre. The broadcaster Wynford Vaughan-Thomas called it a 'rare patch of the Earth's surface' and went on to say, 'No one born in Swansea or the peninsula ever calls it The Gower. And after all the original name was Gwyr and not Y Gwyr. People do not take kindly to this practice.' The hated definite article was once included in the title of the new metric series of Ordnance Survey maps, and caused a lot of anger. After a strong campaign by the Gower Society the error was corrected in subsequent editions. So the title of this book is simply *Gower*. To Isaac Hamon, steward of the manor of Bishopston in the seventeenth century, it was 'Gowersland', although he records that the peninsula was 'in Welsh called formly Tyr Gywr and Cwmwd Gwyr'. In contrast, the spelling of individual place names in the peninsula has always been inconsistent, and Rhossili is a notorious example. 'It seems to be spelt differently in the church-porch, the post-office, the signposts, on the car-park ticket and on the maps. Is it Rhossili, Rhossily, Rhosili, Rhossilly, or Rhosily?' asked Vaughan-Thomas.

Historically there have always been two Gowers. Following the Norman invasion the medieval Lordship of Gower, which extended beyond the peninsula into mainland South Wales, was divided into English Gower, Gower Anglicana, and Welsh Gower, Gower Wallicana. To the south and west of the dividing line compact rural settlements were created and English was spoken. To the north and east of the dividing line single farms and hamlets were the dominant elements in the settlement pattern and Welsh was spoken. From this it is clear that the Normans took the land with the better soils and climate for their own use. The cultural boundary, still evident today, therefore has its origins in the geological boundary and was the reason why the area was once known as 'Little England beyond Glamorgan'. In this Gower has much in common with south Pembroke-shire, which was known as 'Little England beyond Wales', referring to the invisible divide known as the Landsker line that was created there between the English and the Welsh during the Norman period.

This account is concerned mainly with the natural history of peninsular Gower (Fig. 1), an area that is slightly larger than the present-day boundary of the Area of Outstanding Natural Beauty (AONB). The small, formerly industrialised, northeast section of the peninsula around Crofty and Pen-clawdd was excluded from the designated area, an omission that does not make sense today. Gower is approximately 25 kilometres in length and between 5 and 10 kilometres wide, covering an area of around 200 square kilometres. It is bounded on the south by the Bristol Channel, on the west by Carmarthen Bay, on the north by the Burry Inlet and Loughor Estuary and on the east by Swansea Bay and the valleys of

FIG 1. Gower, as shown on Christopher Saxton's map of Glamorgan, c.1610. (West Glamorgan Archive Service)

FIG 2. Rhossili Bay looking north from the Coastguard Cottages, one of the classic views of the Gower coast. (Harold Grenfell)

the Clyne River and Gors-fawr brook, which run from Blackpill to Gowerton.

Ever since the sixteenth century people who have visited the area have gone away claiming that they have found a land of remarkable beauty. It is not surprising therefore that in 1956 Gower was the first place in the UK to be designated an AONB. The complex geology of the peninsula produces a correspondingly wide variety of scenery, ranging from the superb limestone cliffs of the south coast to the salt marshes and sand-dune systems in the north. These spectacular coastal landscapes and sea views contribute significantly to the area's sense of identity and in 1973 they were also defined as a Heritage Coast. Many of the classic views of Gower, such as Rhossili Bay (Fig. 2) and Three Cliff Bay, feature the coastline and the sea beyond. In a poll of the readers of Country Life magazine in 2002 the view of Three Cliff Bay, with the wide sweep of the sands contrasting with the distinctive cliffs, was voted one of the five best views in Britain (Fig. 3). Similarly, Worms Head has been voted the eighth most spectacular location for sunsets in the whole of the United Kingdom. Almost the entire coastline is in the protective ownership of the City and County of Swansea, the Countryside Council for Wales, the National Trust, or the Wildlife Trust of South and West Wales. Inland, the most prominent features are the large areas of common, dominated by sandstone heath ridges, including the prominent crest of Cefn Bryn.

In addition to the varied geology, Gower also contains an extremely large

FIG 3. Three Cliff Bay, voted 'one of the five best views in Britain' by the readers of *Country Life* magazine. (Harold Grenfell)

number of archaeological and historical sites of all periods. In the *Register of Landscapes of Outstanding Historic Interest in Wales* (Cadw, 1998) the area is described as 'an unrivalled microcosm of Wales's historic wealth'. The sites range from caves occupied in the Palaeolithic period, through to medieval castles, eighteenth-century parkland landscapes and nineteenth-century industrial monuments. The peninsula also has a continuous tradition of mixed farming, including both cereal cultivation and large-scale production of vegetable crops, as well as dairying, stock raising and sheep farming (Fig. 4). The details that have been lost elsewhere in the countryside still survive in Gower, and hedges, banks, ponds, small woods and marshy areas remain part of the landscape.

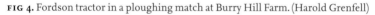

The weather is also benign and Gower avoids most extremes of heat or cold. Mild winters and cool summers combine to produce a long growing season of over 320 days per year. The closeness to the sea is important as it acts like a blanket in winter, keeping the coast milder than inland, with sea temperatures ranging from an average of 9°C in February to 17°C in July. The shelter from cold northerly winds offered by the coalfield plateau, the Carmarthen Fans and the Brecon Beacons means there is little snowfall over Gower. When snow does fall it seldom covers the ground, and when it does fall thick enough and long enough to settle, it lasts no longer than a day or two. Rain is a different matter, however, and Swansea is reputed to have a higher rainfall than Manchester. As a local saying goes, 'If you

FIG 4. Fordson tractor in a ploughing match at Burry Hill Farm. (Harold Grenfell)

can see Mumbles lighthouse, it is going to rain. If you can't see it, it is raining.' Despite this the peninsula, and indeed South Wales as a whole, has a high number of recorded sunshine hours in comparison with the rest of Britain, with the best sunshine in May and June.

As a result of all these factors the peninsula is unique in terms of the variety of habitats and species that occur in and around its relatively small boundary. Along with an extensive list of plants there are 'attractive insects like butterflies and bumble bees ... song birds in the hedges and woods, skylarks rising above the fields, seagulls and rooks following the tractor and wintering flocks of starlings, seagulls, fieldfares and redwings wheeling against the sky' (Kay 1997a). The inlet and estuary in particular, the largest wholly within Wales, is one of the country's great wildlife spectacles, especially in winter when large flocks of overwintering birds sweep across the area. The commons too are rich in wildlife and are particularly important for invertebrates (Fig. 5). Many of the species described in this book, however, are not immediately obvious and naturalists visiting for a day will have only a brief glimpse of what the peninsula has to offer.

To Horatio Tucker, one of the most eloquent chroniclers of Gower in the first half of the twentieth century, the apparently unchanging natural world of the peninsula was a source of great comfort. He was a man who as he walked along the cliffs was able to give a 'continuous commentary' on what he passed, 'the common and scientific names of plants, the identification of fungi, the little cliff butterflies, the types of cloud, the rock formations, birds.' In *Gower Gleanings* (1951) Tucker writes:

> *The villages, the churches, and the castles now studding the countryside, are but transient; the things not made with hands will endure.*
>
> *The sun will rise each morning, uncaring for the woes of mankind; the sunlight will drench the bays, the cliffs and the moorland. In the evening, shadowy fingers will creep over the landscape and melt into the thickening dusk; the rain will lash the clifftops and brim the streams; the lavender will colour the salt marshes and blench in the sun as it has always done; snipe will rocket out of the sedge and weave into the distance; widgeon and teal will feed on the water's edge, and, unheedingly, approach the shore with the incoming tide; nature's flautists, the oystercatchers, will wheel and flash over the breaking wave-tops; ravens will tumble and seagulls will glide over Thurba as they have done for ten thousand years; kestrels will be quartering the moorland; lobsters and crabs will return to their weed-fringed pools as has been their wont since the ice-age; the featureless Downs will retain their ancient silhouettes, and still harbour the lapwing and the curlew; the ripples on the golden sands will not cease to be reshuffled by the ebb and flow of the waves.*

FIG 5. Pengwern Common, near Llethrid, in early May. A key habitat rich in invertebrates, such as marsh fritillary, green and purple hairstreak butterflies, dotted beefly and beechafer. (Harold Grenfell)

The lapwing *Vanellus vanellus* and curlew *Numenius arquata* may have gone from the Downs, but Gower still has a greater density of conservation designations than almost anywhere else in Britain. There are three National Nature Reserves, three Local Nature Reserves, five Special Areas of Conservation and over twenty-five Sites of Special Scientific Interest. There are also nineteen Geological Conservation Review Sites, of national and international importance to earth science, on the coast alone. It is difficult to find a part of the peninsula that does not carry at least one designation.

Most of these sites and the associated species are also easy to reach, one of the significant features of Gower being the amount of access land, consisting of registered common land and land owned by the National Trust and Forestry Commission. In total these holdings amount to 2,470 hectares or 12 per cent of the AONB. This area was considerably increased when the Access Maps were published under the Countryside and Rights of Way Act 2000. It remains to be seen what impact this improved legal access will have on the number of visitors to Gower, given that there was already *de facto* access over most of the peninsula.

Because of these attractions over three million people visit Gower each year, the peninsula being a major water-sports and family holiday destination for urban South Wales and indeed much further afield. Many of these visitors are drawn to the area by the extensive sandy beaches, which range from the popular and easily accessible beaches such as Limeslade and Caswell, to larger beaches such as Oxwich and Rhossili. In addition, for the past fifty years Gower has been a popular area for schools and colleges undertaking environmental field work, as it is close to the large urban populations in Swansea and Neath and there is a sufficient supply of suitable residential accommodation for groups of students visiting from outside the local area. Over the past ten years there has been a significant increase in particular in the number of youth groups carrying out organised and challenging adventure and leisure activities on the cliffs and inshore waters.

Gower was not always so accessible, however, and the peninsula was isolated from the rest of Wales, both geographically and socially, for centuries. Although it may be hard to appreciate today, before the Edwardian period it was not an easy area to cross. The roads were so uneven that until about 1830 wheeled carts were not utilised, packhorses being used instead. Even in the late nineteenth century, when horse-buses first ran from Port-Eynon to Swansea, the journey would take about four hours, the roads that existed being poorly surfaced and badly affected by weather. The passengers were not able to ride all the way: they had to get out and walk up the steeper hills. Only in the 1920s were the roads improved sufficiently to allow motorised vehicles into the peninsula. The area, however, was not as remote as this description would suggest, as for centuries there was a busy trade in limestone, dairy goods and livestock across the Bristol Channel to North Devon, and at one time it is said that there were stepping-stones from Whiteford across the inlet to Carmarthenshire. As late as the nineteenth century there was more trade with Cornwall than with Swansea. Even so the majority of the population never travelled very far from home and led much the same lives as their ancestors. C. J. O. Evans in 1953 noted, 'It has always been an inaccessible district and has suffered in many ways for its isolation.'

Lady Blythswood, the owner of the Penrice Estate from 1920 until 1949, who has been described as a 'benevolent despot of two-thirds of the Gower landscape', saw no reason to change the situation. It was only after her death and that of Admiral Heneage-Vivian in 1952 that the large estates of Penrice, Clyne and Le Breos were broken up. One of the founders of the Gower Society, David Rees, recalled that in the 1950s 'the peninsula was in general isolated and deserted in a way that seems almost unimaginable today'. Gower therefore remained unspoilt well into the twentieth century, not because of any positive moves to conserve the peninsula, but because of a deliberate policy of stagnation by the major landowners.

Despite the many pressures on Gower half a century later, and the large number of visitors, it still manages to retain an atmosphere of isolation and remoteness. The area had a major influence on Dylan Thomas and he often spent whole days 'walking alone over the very desolate Gower cliffs, communing with the cold and the quietness'. In the two years between his job as a local journalist and his move to London he re-explored much of 'one of the loveliest sea-coast stretches in the whole of Britain', which he had known as a boy. Gower's spectacular landscape and seascape permeates his early writing, especially the two stories *Extraordinary Little Cough* and *Who Do You Wish Was With Us?* Rhossili in particular was a favourite destination. His friend Vernon Watkins lived at Pennard for much of his life and wrote many poems about the peninsula. His lines 'I have been taught the script of the stones, And know the tongue of the wave' are quoted on a small memorial tablet on the west side of nearby Hunt's Bay.

One of the peninsula's supreme cultural assets was undoubtedly the last 'Zinger' of Gower, Phil Tanner, who died in February 1950 (Fig. 6). Tanner was 'one of these islands' greatest traditional folk singers' and was once, in 1948, noted as singing 88 songs, one after the other without hesitation. Only a handful of these were recorded by the BBC, a great loss for traditional music. He was also the guardian of what remained of the local customs and rituals. Llangennith, his home village, was famous throughout the peninsula for its 'Mapsant' (saint's day festival) on 5 July, St Cenydd's Day, which was a great occasion for dancing and singing. By 1900 this traditional custom, and others such as the 'Horse's Head'

FIG 6. Phil Tanner, the last 'Zinger' of Gower, at work with his dog. (Gower Society)

ceremony had ceased, but Tanner kept the tradition of wassailing alive as long as he was able.

The 'English' of Gower was once a virtually impenetrable dialect to people from outside the peninsula. Today it has almost disappeared; but true natives, as in Phil Tanner's time, will still describe themselves not as English or Welsh, but as 'Gowerian'. Local names for plants and animals were still in common use in the 1930s, when Jack Phillips nested on the sands, the fernowl laid its marbled eggs in the bracken and the lundibirds nested on the sea cliffs, while oakwibs 'pinged against the lamp-lit windows' along with witches. Today these names are a dusty memory in old books.

Perhaps the best, and most evocative, expression of the attraction of the peninsula for the naturalist is that set out by D. E. Grandfield in *Pryer's Gower Directory & Holiday Guide*, published in 1952:

> The land of Gower … is a land for which the inhabitants and visitors foster the most jealous regard. Gower … fills forever the memory with thoughts of green hills and valleys and gentle countryside, summer scents of bracken and sweet gorse, and always the wonderful clear skies and the running tide … For many there is the added enjoyment of 'place' in that satisfaction which comes with the acquisition of one or more of the many facets which make up this jewel. It may be an understanding of the birds whose habitat Gower is, or the fish in the sea, or the flora of the cliffs and moors. For some it is a deeper knowledge of the histories of Gower's many castles and churches, and other ancient things. Others find their love of place enriched by an understanding of the significance of Gower from the earliest times – the times of the first men; the very earliest men, who left in Gower so many unique evidences of their existence and their cultures. Surely there are few places so complete for the pursuit of studies or of thought, or so kindly to those who come overburdened by the weight of either.

CHAPTER 2

Naturalists and Visitors

*Summer visitors to Gower in the years past will have treasured memories of sultry days
amidst the golden gorse in the slades, when the oppressive noontide calm was broken only
by the monotonous chant of the yellowhammer; memories of cloudless skies and
shimmering blue water lapping gently on the stippled sands, of many coloured anemones
in crystal clear rock-pools, of seagulls circling lazily over the sun-baked cliffs.*

Horatio Tucker, *Gower Gleanings*

OR SOME OF the earliest information on the natural history of Gower
we have to thank Edward Lhuyd, Keeper of the Ashmolean Museum in
Oxford, or more accurately his correspondents. Appointed Keeper in
1691, Lhuyd was a polymath who made important contributions to the emerging
disciplines of botany, geology, antiquities and philology. He was part of the new
order of experimental science, scorning the earlier naturalists 'who, til this last
century contented themselves with bare reading and scribbling paper'. This
approach committed him to first-hand observation whenever possible and also,
as he was revising the Welsh sections of Camden's *Britannia* (1586), to creating a
network of correspondents throughout Wales. Despite this antiquarian work he
considered himself to be a naturalist, not an archaeologist, and commented that
'I was obliged to undertake ye Antiquities for ye sake of encouragement, not
that I delight in ye study so much as in Nat. History'.

Lhuyd's need for local information was greatest in the south of the country
and this is probably the reason for his connections with no fewer than four people
within the bounds of the Marcher Lordship of Gower. Although only two of these
were in the peninsula – Gower as we know it today – the area features prominently
in Lhuyd's collections for his survey of Wales. The first of these informants was

John Williams of Swansea. As with most of his contacts, Williams was a native of the area about which he wrote and was able to write with authority. Although Williams' Gower correspondence is limited to thirteen letters written between 1693 and 1696 he responded amongst other things to Lhuyd's enquires about the megalith known as Arthur's Stone, surveyed the blow-hole at Worms Head, reported on local belief in the curiosities known as *maen magal* or *glain neidr* (the latter translating literally as 'jewel snake') and supplied Lhuyd with a wide range of these fossils. Unfortunately the two men later became bitter opponents over the question of whether fossils were of organic or inorganic origin.

Lhuyd's most prolific correspondent, however, was Isaac Hamon. When or how they were introduced is not clear, but they met at least once when Lhuyd reached Swansea in 1697 at the beginning of five years of travels to collect information. Lhuyd had previously visited Gower in the autumn of 1693 and again in 1696, and it is likely that in 1697 Hamon took him to see some of the sites he had described. Hamon's account of Gower, prepared for Lhuyd, provides a valuable description of the area as it was at the close of the seventeenth century. Covering the 23 parishes of the Lordship of Gower, it represents a substantial part of the known response to Lhuyd's *Parochial Queries* (1696), a set of 31 questions dealing with the geography, antiquities and natural history of Wales. Hamon's knowledge was most detailed and certain within the area where he lived and worked, a radius of some 6 miles (9.7 kilometres) from Bishopston. He made no claim to first-hand knowledge of West Gower – 'I am not very well acquainted there, therefore I have but hinted some things' – and because of his honesty he is regarded as an accurate observer.

Hamon set out to describe Gower as he knew it and provides a direct account, almost certainly the first compilation of its kind. The report covers, among other things, the natural character of the peninsula, the distribution of the English language, evidence of early settlement, economic geography and natural features. In covering the last subject he exceeded the questions asked by Lhuyd and provided a list of plants common in Gower instead of just the rarities. His 1697 list of 42 plants is the first Gower flora. The relevant section appears under the heading of 'The Sea Cost', where he states:

> The South pt of Gowersland (being Swanzey hundd) being in length from Swanzey to Worms head about 12 miles ... with store of limestones, & limestone cleeves, wherin are many great holes or caves ... here are these sorts of sea hearbes, as scurvie grasse, Sampire & lavar ... of Rock herbs, Cetrack, maiden hair, walrue, & in the pishes of Bishopstown, Pennard, & Oystermouth there is plenty of juniper & some buckthorn.
>
> Of field herbs (especially in the said 3 pishes) Agrimony, wild carret, mullein,

Dandelyon, Pelamountain, mallows, Burdock, Tutsan, Eybright, Bettony, Elecampane,
Foxfingers, yellow and blue Kay-roses, Rames or Ramsey, Centry, Yarrow, Adders
tongue, vervain, St John's wort, Canker wort, Devilles bit, Ragwort, mugwort,
Breakestone-psley, Larks bill, plantane, Pimpnell, Fumitory, Burnet, Botchwort.
  of hearbs in some waterie places, as water cresses, Rosa solis, Lungwort, Liver wort.

A list of these plants together with the likely current scientific and common
names is given in Appendix 1. Among the plants for which Hamon used colloquial
names are the cowslip *Primula veris* and cultivated polyanthus, 'yellow and blue
Kay-roses', and ramsons *Allium ursinum*, 'Rames or Ramsey'. 'Larks bill' is probably
larkspur *Consolida ajacis*, while 'Breakestone-psley' is probably parsley piert
Aphanes arvensis.

The *Flora of Glamorgan* notes that after Lhuyd's visit 'a long night seems to have
settled on botanising in the county' and that until the end of the eighteenth
century very few other botanists visited the area. Resident botanists at this period
seem to have been nonexistent.

The travels and tours, which were such a feature of life for educated people in
the eighteenth century, did not include Gower, or for the most part even Wales.
The government secret agent and author Daniel Defoe made it to Swansea in 1722,
but avoided the peninsula. Only two of the tourists, Henry Wigstead and Henry
Skrine, son of the celebrated Richard Skrine of Cobham in Surrey, ventured from
Swansea into Gower. Wigstead himself got no further than Caswell Bay, which he
noted, was 'the finest sandy beach I ever saw'. Skrine ventured further, although
he found Gower 'in general a rocky and uninteresting district except where the
sea views enliven it', and a 'bleak peninsula'. Between 1739 and 1790 John Wesley
visited Oxwich frequently on his preaching tours through Wales (Fig. 7), and
recorded that 'Gower is a large tract of land, bounded by [Glamorgan] on the
north-east, the sea on the south-west and rivers on the other sides. Here all the
people talk English and are in general the most plain, loving people in Wales'
(Davies, 1996). After 1800, with the French revolutionary and Napoleonic wars in
Europe inhibiting the grand European tour, the number of tourists who came to
seek wild and romantic scenery in Wales increased and the natural history of
Gower began to be recorded more fully.

The most notable resident scholar in Glamorgan during the late eighteenth
and early nineteenth century was Edward Williams (1746–1826). Williams, better
known by his bardic name of Iolo Morganwg, spent most of his life as a stone-
mason, living in the Vale of Glamorgan, but travelled widely throughout the
county, including Gower. He had many interests but his reputation was unfortunately tainted by numerous literary and historical forgeries that he produced

FIG 7. The 'Wesley' cottage in Oxwich, frequently used by John Wesley on his preaching tours in the eighteenth century. (Jonathan Mullard)

with the intention of enhancing the history and culture of his native county. Because of his forgeries, the prevailing view until recently has been that anything written by him must be ignored. This interpretation is now being challenged and there is every reason to suggest that Williams was in fact Wales's greatest Romantic scholar. Included amongst the 88 volumes of literary manuscripts in the National Library of Wales there is a vast collection of notes on Glamorgan. A preliminary analysis of the archaeological information contained in these has shown not only that he produced field records of quality and accuracy, but also that his work was far superior to that of the contemporaries who ridiculed him. The same high standards apply to his notes on agriculture, botany and topography, although they have never been properly analysed. It is likely that there are many references to the natural history of the peninsula contained within these, but to find them would be a major academic undertaking.

The Romantic Revival epitomised by Williams was accompanied by an increasing interest in botany and a new era began, that of the production of a variety of local lists and floras. The first such list to include Gower plants, although his main interest was the study of shells, was produced by Dr William Turton for the first edition of the *Swansea Guide*, produced in 1802 by the Reverend John Oldisworth,

Master of the Free Grammar School. Unfortunately, while Turton's collection
of shells, including some from the peninsula, was well regarded and is now at the
United States National Museum in Washington, his botanical records were not
always accurate. The guide also included a checklist of birds by John Lucas of
Stouthall, which includes a remarkable 146 species. This list, however, requires
careful interpretation and many of the names such as 'black and white gull',
'greater tern' and 'Welsh sandpiper', a 'new' species 'recently discovered by
G. Montague, Esq. F.L.S.' will not be recognised by today's naturalists. A revised
volume of the *Swansea Guide* was published in 1823.

In July of the same year that Oldisworth produced his guide, Gower was
visited by Edward Donovan, the celebrated author of *British Zoology*, an enormous
work published in 20 volumes. He recorded his visit in a two-volume account of
his travels in South Wales entitled *Descriptive Excursions Through South Wales and
Monmouthshire in the Year 1804 and Four Preceding Summers*, with a certain amount
of understatement:

> *Before we left Swansea, this tract of country was represented to us as an inhospitable
> region, black, barren, and rocky; thin of inhabitants and destitute of accommodation for
> the stranger. A statement we have since observed to be not perfectly correct in every
> particular, although in a certain meaning true … Upon the lofty rocky verge of the shore
> to the left, the fogs arising from the sea rolled heavily; the air was cold, and the rains
> beating violently in our faces from the westward in the space of an hour after we first set
> out, had nearly drenched us to the skin. Under these circumstances we evidently surveyed
> the country to a lamentable disadvantage.*

Despite the evidently appalling weather Donovan and his party did get to
Pennard castle, and he goes on to record that he collected specimens of yellow
whitlowgrass *Draba aizoides*. In the second volume there are also a number of
references to marine molluscs at Oystermouth and Oxwich.

One of the rarest plants in the British flora, small restharrow *Ononis reclinata*,
was discovered by Daniel Sharpe 'on rocks at Port-Eynon' in 1828. Sharpe was a
very able and observant geologist, who was President of the Geological Society in
1856, but died in London, as the result of an accident, in the same year. It seems
likely that the site that he discovered, at the age of 22, would have been the one
immediately west of, and above, Culver Hole cave on the seaward face of Port-
Eynon Point. The original specimen was sent to Joseph Woods, the famous
architect and botanist, and was incorporated into his herbarium. Small restharrow
still exists in four localities, between Port-Eynon Point and Worms Head, the two
western locations only being discovered recently. It is difficult to find, though, as

the number of plants and the period in which they flower varies noticeably from year to year.

John Gutch, who lived in Swansea for a number of years in the early nineteenth century, maintained Swansea's first reliable weather records and published two local lists of plants, the first in the pamphlet *The Medical Topography, Statistics, Climatology and Natural History of Swansea*. In it Gutch remarks, 'I am well aware that the foregoing list is comparatively of no value without the insertion of the various habitats.' This defect was rectified in his second list, entitled simply *A list of plants met with in the neighbourhood of Swansea, Glamorganshire*, which was published in the first volume of *The Phytologist* in 1841. Gutch's list of some 550 plants is of great interest, containing as it does references to stinking iris *Iris foetidissima*, a familiar plant of the limestone coast, hoary rock-rose *Helianthemum oelandicum* and sea campion *Silene uniflora*.

By this time natural history had become the favoured activity of a number of the local gentry, in particular the landowner Lewis Weston Dillwyn (1778–1855) (Fig. 8). Dillwyn had come from London to live in Swansea in 1802 when he was 24 to manage the Cambrian Pottery on the banks of the River Tawe, and was an enthusiastic naturalist. Indeed he managed to link his two interests by specialising in natural-history designs on pottery. He became an important figure in the county, being High Sheriff in 1818 and a Member of Parliament from 1832 to 1841. In 1805, with Dawson Turner, he produced a *Botanist's Guide Through England and Wales*, but is particularly remembered for producing one of the first systematic works on algae, *British Confervae*, in 1809. Using only simple lenses that gave small magnifications, he described and illustrated a large number of marine and freshwater species, many of them collected in Gower. Dillwyn followed this in 1829 with *Memoranda Relating to Coleopterus Insects Found in the Neighbourhood of Swansea* and in 1840 he privately printed his *Contributions Towards a History of Swansea*, which included a list of the rarer flowering plants that had been found within 20 miles (32 kilometres) of the town. The list was apparently compiled in great haste and 300 copies were printed for sale at a bazaar in aid of Swansea Infirmary. As Carter (1952) noted, 'Perhaps this is the only occasion upon which a Flora has been compiled with such a charitable end in view.'

In 1848 the British Association held its annual meeting in Swansea and Dillwyn, who was Chair of the Natural History Section, privately published his *Materials for a Fauna and Flora of Swansea*. The botanical section of this was an expansion of his 1840 list and included localities for 267 species of flowering plants, ferns and stoneworts. Gower plants recorded in the book include stinking hellebore *Helleborus foetidus* from Parkmill, where it still grows, and herb-paris *Paris quadrifolia*, which is recorded from a number of woods including

FIG 8. Lewis Weston Dillwyn (1778–1855), an inspiring local naturalist who encouraged and supported many others. (Swansea Museum)

Nicholaston. Also included was a list of 93 bird species, and this relatively small total reflects the limitations of his contacts and their interests. Interestingly the book also contains a short list of beetles collected by Alfred Russel Wallace, the celebrated naturalist, evolutionist, geographer and anthropologist, who at that time was engaged in helping his brother survey the ground for the new railway line through the Neath valley. It is not clear if any of the beetles collected were from Gower.

Dillwyn was a close friend of scientists such as Michael Faraday and Humphry Davy and introduced Joseph Banks and other eminent naturalists to the attractions of Gower and the Swansea area. Banks was the British explorer and naturalist who, as long-time President of the Royal Society, London, became known for his promotion of science. In particular Dillwyn had a special interest in geology and went on geological expeditions whenever possible, often stopping in Oxford with his very good friend William Buckland. Buckland was also a frequent visitor to Swansea, staying with Dillwyn, and with other colleagues he excavated a number of

Gower caves, including most famously the rich deposits in Goat's Hole (Paviland Cave). There is no doubt that Dillwyn took part in these excavations.

He also seems to have inspired other local landowners in various ways, as this note on the nightingale *Luscinia megarhynchos* indicates:

> My late friend, Thomas Penrice, Esq., completely failed in an attempt to introduce this lovely songster, by bringing several cages of them from Norfolk, and turning them out in his woods at Kilvrough, which are warmly situated by the sea-side, about eight miles to the westward of Swansea.

A pair did, however, eventually breed at Hillend in 1944, but while nightingales were annual summer visitors to the Vale of Glamorgan during the nineteenth century, Gower was close to the northern and western limits of its distribution in Britain. The species is now confined mostly to southeast England and there have been no further records for the peninsula.

Dillwyn communicated his enthusiasm for natural history to his sons, notably John Dillwyn-Llewelyn (Fig. 9), who inherited an interest in botany and became a pioneer of the new photographic techniques, taking many photographs of Gower, especially the coast. He was a relative by marriage of the pioneer photographer Henry Fox Talbot. Dillwyn's other son, Lewis Llewelyn Dillwyn, a 'competent geologist', married a daughter of the noted geologist Sir Henry Thomas de la Beche, founder of the Geological Survey of Great Britain. De la Beche's explorations in Gower resulted in some of the earliest geological surveys.

Seemingly not content with all this activity, Dillwyn was also President of the Royal Institution of South Wales from its foundation in 1835 until he died in 1855 and acted as mentor for an ever-widening circle of naturalists who explored Gower and the Swansea area in some detail. In particular, Dillwyn encouraged John Gwyn Jeffreys to collect shells along the Gower coastline. Jeffreys later became extremely well known with the publication between 1862 and 1869 of the five volumes of *British Conchology*, a landmark publication that is still consulted today for its precise descriptions of shells. Jeffreys was born in Swansea where he followed the family tradition and worked as a solicitor until 1856 when he was called to the bar, after which he lived in London for the rest of his life. He was introduced to natural history at Swansea Grammar School through a Naturalists' Society organised by Llewellyn John, a noted field naturalist.

During the nineteenth century the number of naturalists who lived in the Swansea area, or visited Gower and recorded their finds, increased substantially. It is not possible to list them all here; indeed their exploits and finds would form

FIG 9. John Dillwyn-Llewelyn and his photographic equipment. (Swansea Museum)

a book in themselves. The more notable personalities include Charles Babington, Professor of Botany at Cambridge, who arrived at Mumbles in August 1839 having crossed from Devon 'by the mail steamer at 5pm arriving at the Mumbles Lighthouse at about 9pm. As the tide was low we had to land at the Mumbles and walk to Swansea a distance of five miles'. On 6 August he wrote in his diary, 'Called on Mr Flower, who was in lodgings, and he went with me to Pennard Castle where we saw plenty of the *Draba aizoides* on the walls and rocks near the castle and *Sinapis cheiranthus* [wallflower cabbage *Coincya monensis* ssp. *recurvata*] on the steep side of the sandhills.'

The famous diarist the Reverend Francis Kilvert visited Gower in April 1872, staying with friends at Ilston Rectory, and noted that it was the 'cleanest coast I ever saw – no seaweed, no pebbles, hardly a shell – not a speck for miles along the shining sand, and scarcely even any scent of the sea'. He did notice, however, that 'the rocks were covered with millions of barnacles, mussels, limpets and sea snails, and there were sea anemones in the little pools above the rocks'. On the coast path between Langland and Caswell Bay he records that 'a flock of strange and beautiful black and white birds flew along the rock faces below us towards the lighthouse piping mournfully. They were I suppose some kind of gull but they seemed to me like the spirits of the shipwrecked folk seeking and mourning for their bodies.' Kilvert was well aware of the dangers of the Gower coast. The 300-ton steamship *Hazard*, wrecked when it struck the rocks at Port-Eynon on 11 January, a few months before his visit, is only one of nearly 360 vessels recorded as lost in the area and there are probably many others. The birds Kilvert noted were without doubt oystercatchers *Haematopus ostralegus*, a highly vocal bird with loud piping calls which often flies low along the shoreline, exactly as Kilvert describes (Fig. 10). Their courtship display is one of the noisiest of any British bird and has been called the 'piping display'. It consists of several birds walking

FIG 10. Oystercatchers off the Gower shore, as recorded by the Reverend Francis Kilvert. (Harold Grenfell)

around in an agitated manner uttering a chorus usually described as 'kleep-kleep-kleep'. In flight the note, as Kilvert found, is a shorter 'pic-pic'.

Probably the most prolific painter of the local scene was Edward Duncan, who spent almost every summer between 1865 and his death in 1882 in Gower. His paintings and sketches provide an unrivalled record of the peninsula at this time and were produced in prodigious numbers (Fig. 11). In March 1885, for example, Christie's auction house held a three-day sale of his 'remaining works' and another sale two years later lists nearly 2,000 sketches and paintings. Among the hundreds of watercolour paintings exhibited in London during his lifetime were 'The Bury Holmes, Rhossili Bay', 'The Worms Head, South Wales', 'Worm's Head, Rhossili Bay' and 'Oyster dredgers off Mumbles'. In the last three years of his life the Royal Watercolour Society exhibited 'Oyster boats leaving with the turn of the tide', 'On the shore at Porteynon' and 'A Gower cottage, Llanrhidian'. Many of these are now in the great national collections.

The Swansea Scientific Society (Fig. 12) was set up about 1890 and its reports, included in those of the Royal Institution of South Wales, contain many short papers on Gower, which are mainly reports of papers read at field meetings of the Society by the Reverend J. Jackett between 1891 and 1897. They are of a popular nature and include 'On the wild flowers of the district' (Sand dunes at Port-Eynon), 'Notes on the botany of Clyne and Killay districts' and 'The botany of Gower'.

FIG 11. Detail of 'Rhossili Bay' by Edward Duncan, a prolific and nationally known nineteenth-century painter of the Gower scene. (Peter R. Douglas-Jones)

FIG 12. A field meeting of the Swansea Scientific Society in the 1890s, probably at Oxwich. Note the horse-bus and the thatched roofs of the cottages. (Swansea Museum)

There is a record of a large party going by horse-drawn brake to Rhossili in June 1890. In 1893 Colonel Morgan, a leading member of the Scientific Society, led a team which excavated a prehistoric tomb on Penmaen Burrows. Numerous women were involved and as early as 1889 there were 18 female members.

By the early twentieth century the focus of the Society had moved away from natural history, but there was still felt to be a need for an organisation devoted to natural history. In June 1906 therefore a group of local naturalists formed the Swansea Field Naturalists' Society, its area of interest being defined as the 15 mile radius from Swansea castle. As a separate organisation it lasted for 14 years until in 1920 the Scientific Society asked to merge with the Naturalists as 'they had been hit much worse by the war', that is, most of their members had been killed in the First World War and they were no longer a viable organisation. Despite some initial resistance from the naturalists the two organisations merged and became the Swansea Scientific and Field Naturalists' Society. The Society organised itself into four branches, botany, zoology, geology and archaeology, the latter in defer-ence to the remaining members of the Scientific Society. By 1925 Gower had been fairly well covered by both organisations and a large amount of information on the natural history of Gower resides in the proceedings of the two organisations. A thorough analysis of the contents of their journals is long overdue.

A *Flora of Glamorganshire* by H. J. Riddelsdell appeared in 1907 as an 88-page supplement to the *Journal of Botany*. He divided the county into nine districts, including Gower, basing his division on the drainage areas of the principal rivers rather than geological divisions. Riddelsdell continued to contribute many records to the journal after the publication of his county flora, including, in 1911, a paper on the flora of Worms Head. By coincidence there were actually two floras of Glamorgan published in 1907, the second by A. H. Trow, Professor of Botany at Cardiff. Perhaps a combined effort would have been more effective. The two men certainly knew each other, as Riddelsdell was one of the chief recorders for the volume edited by Trow, contributing 482 records, many of them from Gower.

Our knowledge of the Gower insect fauna at this time would have been very poor if it were not for the contribution of one man, Henry Mortimer Hallett, who began to study the aculeates (bees, wasps and ants) of Glamorgan (and, to a lesser extent, Monmouthshire) in 1909. For the next 26 years, until he moved to Herefordshire in 1935, he collected extensively in east Glamorgan and made frequent collecting trips to the west of the county. His vice-county compilation of Glamorgan in 1928 provides an invaluable insight into the state of the aculeate fauna of South Wales in the first half of the twentieth century. Unfortunately, he did not publish his review of the Welsh fauna, *The Hymenoptera Aculeata of Wales*, before his death in 1958, although he donated the manuscript to the National Museum of Wales, where it may be consulted in the Department of Zoology.

A substantial advance in bird recording was made in 1889 when the Reverend Digby S. W. Nicholl's notes on the birds of Glamorgan were published. This was the first attempt at a countywide avifauna for Glamorgan; it was inspired by one published earlier for Somerset and included 218 species. In the same year Harry Rowland Wakefield came to Swansea as Chief Science Demonstrator for the Swansea School Board. A founder member of the Scientific and Field Naturalists' Society, he became life president in 1931. He was a keen naturalist with a particular interest in beetles and molluscs, recording in particular 1,083 species of beetle, many of these in Gower. Other conchologists active in the area included John le Brockton Tomlin (1864–1954), who accumulated one of the world's major collections of shells, leaving over 200,000 specimens to the National Museum of Wales. He was also interested in beetles and left a collection of 82,000 of these as well. Collecting specimens on this scale can no longer be condoned, but the collections now form an important reference source. Conservation was not, however, an issue in those days. Tomlin was also a close friend of Wakefield and they had many joint excursions to find beetles in Gower.

In 1948 J. E. Lousley, the outstanding field botanist of his generation, visited the Gower cliffs with Miss E. Vachell and Mr D. McClintock for the purpose of checking the section on Gower for his New Naturalist volume *Wild Flowers of Chalk and Limestone* (1950). In the book he notes that:

For many years I expected that someone would find Hair-leaved Goldilocks, Crinitaria
linosyris in Gower. It grows in Somerset and North Wales on the Carboniferous
Limestone and there are plenty of suitable habitats on this coast. My expectation has
proved to be well justified ... There were only a few plants, but they grew in a wild place
far from houses in limestone turf and are undoubtedly native.

Now known as goldilocks aster *Aster linosyris* (Fig. 13), its presence in Gower, as
Lousley surmised, is 'geographically and ecologically unsurprising' (Wade *et al.*,
1994). The plant is very rare, however, being known from only eight sites between
Port-Eynon and Mewslade Bay. The largest population occupies an area of about
40 square metres in low gorse *Ulex europaeus*. Lousley also records that he had 'seen
Stinking Hellebore near Park Mill and Gladdon and Caper Spurge (*Euphorbia*
lathyris) at Nicholaston'.

FIG 13. Goldilocks
aster, the 'hair-leaved
goldilocks' sought by
J. E. Lousley. (David
Painter)

Another notable, but local, botanist in the first half of the twentieth century was John Arthur Webb, a Swansea schoolmaster, who during school holidays and after his retirement travelled widely throughout Wales recording and collecting specimens, which he sent to the National Museum of Wales. The first specimens arrived in 1921 and the last in 1956 when he was over 70 years old. In collaboration with Arthur Wade of the Museum, Webb wrote a number of manuscript floras including a partial copy for Gower that was discovered in the library of Swansea University in the mid-1990s. The first and only published part of this Gower flora was produced as a supplement to the *Proceedings of the Swansea Scientific and Field Naturalists' Society* in 1956. Following the launch of the *Gower Society Journal* in 1948 Webb contributed numerous articles, including some very useful pieces on the development of natural history in Gower, which have been used as guidance in this chapter.

One more important publication, *The Natural History of Gower* by Mary Gillham, was published in 1977. Gillham, who came to Cardiff in 1961 to work for the Extramural Department of University College Cardiff, was a founder member of what was then the Glamorgan Naturalists' Trust. Having previously written a number of travel books on Antarctica and New Zealand, she was asked to edit a book on the natural history of Glamorgan. Despite making contact with numerous researchers there were no contributions forthcoming, so she was asked to write the book herself. Given her previous research background on seabird islands Gillham started at the western end of the county with Gower, 'the gem as far as I was concerned'. In the end so much information was collected that there was enough material for a book on the peninsula alone. Following the publication of the Gower volume she has single-handedly worked her way eastwards through the former county, producing another nine local publications, including a number for the Glamorgan Heritage Coast, and has finally completed the series, and the original aspiration, with a book on Cardiff and the Taff corridor.

Bird recording in Gower was greatly improved by the formation of the Gower Ornithological Society in 1956 and the publication of checked and authenticated bird records by successive records secretaries. One of the earliest secretaries was Robert (Bob) Howells, who has to be one the most dedicated of the present-day Gower naturalists (Fig. 14). Although it is difficult, and certainly controversial, to single out any contemporary naturalist for attention, Howells has painstakingly counted the birds off Blackpill and in the inlet and estuary for over a third of a century; in a magazine article in 1991 he calculated that he had seen 5 million wildfowl, 17 million waders and 4 million gulls. On one day in 1989 he counted 13,000 dunlin *Calidris alpina*. Howells has braved all weathers, including the deep snow of the 1962/3 winter, in order to carry out his surveys. This dedication has

FIG 14. Robert (Bob) Howells, perhaps one of the most dedicated of present-day Gower naturalists, birdwatching at Llanrhidian. (Harold Grenfell)

enabled him to produce a comprehensive account of the species using the area, and because of his work it is now known to be the most important estuary in Wales for birds. A full list of current naturalists would also include, amongst many others, Harold Grenfell and Derek Thomas for their work on birds, Quentin Kay, who has added thousands of new plant records for Gower, Tom McOwat for his studies of bats and Barry Stewart for his research on moths. Perhaps one day their history and exploits will be covered in more detail.

Since people have been exploring Gower for well over 300 years it may seem that there is nothing new for the present-day naturalist to discover. This is not the case, however: as this book makes clear, changes in plant and animal distribution are continuous. Even in botany there are discoveries, the latest as recently as 1987 when western clover *Trifolium occidentale*, a new record for Wales, was found by Jo Dunn, an Oxfordshire botanist, growing in the clifftop red fescue *Festuca rubra* turf near Tears Point. Later searches showed that the clover grew not only on the Point but also on similar south-facing cliffs between Fall Bay and Mewslade. It is not an easy plant to find and might yet turn up elsewhere. One of the best times to search is during April, as it flowers earlier than white clover *Trifolium repens*. The plant is largely restricted to exposed sites liable to soaking by salt-laden winds, often growing around rock outcrops or on stabilised sand. Rock and sand, indeed, form the basis of the Gower landscape. Before returning to the flora and fauna, therefore, it is important to understand their origins and the features that they have created.

PART II

The Evolving Landscape

CHAPTER 3

The Peninsula Emerges

... all these beloved and enduring things, which combine to make the real Gower which we have inherited, and which our children's children will enjoy until the time when the glaciers flow south again, perhaps to envelop and disfigure our peninsula ...

Horatio Tucker, *Gower Gleanings*

DESPITE THE apparently unchanging nature of the earth, the continents are in constant motion, travelling enormous distances over great periods of geological time. The continental plate of which Gower is part has been situated on, and even to the south of, the equator and has drifted slowly northwards over the past 425 million years. The rocks that make up the peninsula today have therefore been deposited under widely varying conditions, such as subtropical seas rich in corals, arid deserts and coastal swamps. The distinctive landscape, with its rocky coastal cliffs, sandy bays and rolling hills, is a direct result of the exposed solid rocks and the processes that have affected them during this long and complex history. Some of the rocks contain large numbers of fossil plants and these provide not only evidence of past plant communities, but also important information about plant evolution. In geological terms the present-day flora is only a passing phase in the area's long history.

Gower is formed from very ancient rocks (Fig. 15, Table 1), and rocks younger than 290 million years ago are hardly represented. All were deposited as sediments, as sands, gravels and other fine-grained deposits in horizontal layers known as beds or strata, and were themselves the result of existing rocks being eroded, or of accumulations of organic remains. Small breaks in the deposition, or changes in the sediment type, can cause the beds to be visibly separated from

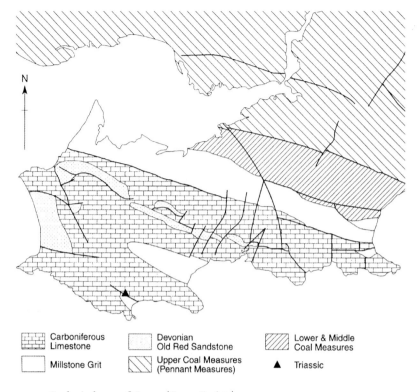

Carboniferous
Limestone

Millstone Grit

Devonian
Old Red Sandstone

Upper Coal Measures
(Pennant Measures)

Lower & Middle
Coal Measures

▲ Triassic

FIG 15. Geological map of Gower. (Gower Society)

each other. This interface between one bed and another is known as the 'bedding plane' and shows clearly when rocks have been folded due to earth movements. Folds where the bedding planes have been bent into an arch are known as 'anticlines' and downward folds are known as 'synclines'. When erosion cuts across these folds anticlines show the oldest rocks at their axis, whereas younger rocks are present at the centre of synclines.

THE RECORD OF THE ROCKS

The oldest rocks exposed in Gower are characteristically red in colour and are known as Old Red Sandstone. They were laid down in the Devonian period, from 390 to 360 million years ago (although there appears to have been a lengthy gap in deposition) and occur only in the cores of major anticlines. The nature of any

TABLE 1. Rock types exposed in Gower, related to simplified geological time divisions. Age in millions of years before present. (Adapted from Aldhouse-Green, 2000)

PERIOD	AGE (BP)	ROCKS PRESENT IN GOWER
Quaternary	1.8–0	Various glacial and postglacial drift deposits
Neogene	23–1.8	
Paleogene	65–23	
Cretaceous	142–65	
Jurassic	206–142	(Found offshore on seabed to the south)
Triassic	248–206	Remnant terrestrial deposits near Port-Eynon and rare fissure-fills within older rocks
Permian	290–248	
Carboniferous	354–290	Coal Measures in northeast Gower; Millstone Grit; Carboniferous Limestone
Devonian	417–354	Old Red Sandstone
Silurian	443–417	
Ordovician	495–443	
Cambrian	545–495	

underlying 'basement' rocks is not clear. At this time the area lay in a region of sediment-laden rivers that crossed a wide plain between mountains to the north and the sea to the south, which lay over what is now Devon, the county giving its name to this period of the earth's history. The climate at this time was tropical, with monsoon weather, and vast rivers carried sediment resulting from the intense erosion that was taking place in the mountains. These rivers deposited large amounts of material as they flowed to the sea and this eventually formed the sandstone rocks. A period of uplift and erosion in mid-Devonian times temporarily stopped this sedimentation. Although the Devonian is sometimes referred to as 'the Age of Fishes', other animals were present too, including insects, sharks, lungfishes and amphibians, the latter being the first vertebrates to walk on the land. They looked like large newts or salamanders. Increasing numbers of plants were also appearing on the land at this time and they were growing bigger and more complex than the first terrestrial plants.

The tough, coarse sandstones and even coarser conglomerates form the high ground of Cefn Bryn, Llanmadoc Hill and Rhossili Down. Since it is only in the cores of major anticlines that these rocks are brought to the surface all the hills on the peninsula coincide with upfolds in the rocks underneath. Although it is not a general geological rule, in Gower anticlines always form hills and synclines always form valleys. This results from the fact that the older rocks are hard and the younger rocks are soft.

Around 360 million years ago at the beginning of the Carboniferous period there was a major rise in sea level, which covered almost all of what is now Wales, and the wide coastal plains of the Devonian landscape were drowned. After an initial period when mainly muddy sediments were deposited, the water became clearer, the amount of detritus reaching the area from the land reduced and limestones began to form. What is now Gower was then passing across the equator. Even today it is principally in such equatorial regions, where there is little sediment being deposited from the land, that limestone is formed. In the warm water lime (calcium carbonate) can be precipitated, and accumulates together with the remains of marine animals that secrete shells and skeletons. Without the sediment from the land to dilute them, these shells can form rocks on their own, although many limestones are composed of microscopic particles of lime, known as lime mud.

The Carboniferous Limestone in Gower is approximately 800 metres thick, with fine exposures in the southern cliffs, but northwards the sequence becomes gradually thinner and there may also be some parts missing. This suggests that the sea further north, as it was nearer the land, was shallower. The limestone consists of many different types, each with a different texture, thickness and group of fossils. Recent studies have shown that the deposition was controlled by a worldwide rise or fall in the sea level and not by a local or regional subsidence or elevation of the land. There were several advances and retreats of the sea from the south and layers of carbonates gradually built up under a very shallow sea that was rich in corals and brachiopods, sedentary shelled animals with feathery appendages to waft food particles to the mouth. The uppermost part of the Carboniferous sequence in Gower consists of marine shales and the muddy limestones of the Oystermouth Beds. These contain the widespread limestone fauna of brachiopods and corals, together with the rare trilobite *Griffithsides* spp. Brachiopods are the most abundant fossils, especially *Martinia* spp. and *Spirifer* spp. One of the *Spirifer* species is named *Spirifer oystermouthensis* after Oystermouth village, where it is found in Clements Quarry, the so-called 'Black Lias Quarry', named due to the alternations of dark, muddy limestones (which weather to white) with thin dark, calcareous shales. There are many theories about how this regular pattern was produced, but there is a strong possibility that it had some seasonal or climatic cause. Also present in the quarry, which is easy to access as it is currently used as a car park, is the small cornet-shaped shell *Zaphentis oystermouthensis*.

From time to time the carbonates were above sea level and there is evidence of erosion and of plant roots. Unusual breccias (rocks composed of angular fragments) suggest the presence of salts formed by the evaporation of sea water in a hot climate. Other deposits suggest lagoons and oolite, a limestone composed of small grains, comparable with those forming today in shoals around the Bahamas. In some levels there are algal tufts and mats that formed as calcareous layers built up by lime-secreting algae that favoured shallow, warm seas. These varying conditions produced different types of limestone, and six main rock units can be identified, all named after areas on the peninsula (Table 2).

During the Carboniferous period forces that were eventually to fold and fault the Gower rocks were beginning to bend the earth's crust upwards. This increased the runoff from the land, which in turn resulted in river deltas swamping the limestone sea with sediment. In comparison to other areas of Glamorgan, where the rocks show that there were alternating periods of non-marine and marine conditions, the sea over Gower at this time, some 320 million years ago,

TABLE 2. Simplified stratigraphy of Gower limestone. (Adapted from Lowe, 1989)

AGE (BP)	ROCK UNITS THICKNESS	SUB UNITS	OTHER TERMS
290 my	Oystermouth Beds 30 m		Upper Limestone Shales
	Oxwich Head Limestone 50 m		
	——thin coal seam——		
	Oxwich Head Limestone 50 m		
	Hunts Bay Oolite 160–250 m		Main Limestone
	High Tor Limestone to 100 m		
	Caswell Bay Mudstone		
	Caswell Bay Oolite 40 m		
	Penmaen Burrows Limestone to 300 m	Langland Dolomite Tears Point Limestone Shipway Limestone	
354 my	Cefn Bryn Shale		Lower Limestone Shales

was comparatively deep, and fine shales were deposited with marine animals preserved within them. This fine material, known as Namurian Shales, is relatively soft and was subsequently eroded to form the bays of Oystermouth, Oxwich and Port-Eynon. The best section through the Namurian rocks occurs along Barland Common Stream, near Bishopston, where the rock sequence contains a number of bands with marine fossils. The section is of historical interest as it was originally recorded by de la Beche and described in the first Geological Survey Memoir published in 1846.

The environmental conditions of the Namurian continued into the latter part of the Carboniferous period, with the formation of the Coal Measures. The coal seams originated as peat formed in low-lying swamps on the coastal plains, and coal formation may be linked to changes in sea level. The Coal Measures consist of sandstones, shales and coals arranged in a repeated sequence, indicating that forests grew, were buried by shales as the land subsided and then by sands as the rivers deposited sediments. On top of the river sand soil developed and eventually the forest became established again. In the northeast of the peninsula coal occurs in seams running diagonally from Blackpill to Llanrhidian.

The freshwater and brackish swamps, marshes and lagoons of this period of Gower's history supported rich forests and there were large numbers of fern-like plants, the seed ferns, together with the true ferns that occur today. One of the most conspicuous features of the flora at this time was the presence of large tree-sized ferns in groups that are now only represented by small herbaceous types, the most spectacular being the horsetails and lycopods. Such plants inevitably broke up and fossil fragments consisting of discrete pieces of roots, stem and leaves are common.

The great coalfield basin dominates the geology of South Wales and Gower forms part of the southern rim of the massive South Wales Coalfield syncline. The peninsula should therefore consist of strata that dip northwards and become progressively older towards the south. This is not the case, because the structure of the southern part of the coalfield is much more complex than it appears to be from the outcrop pattern, and on the southern limb of the syncline there is a series of tight folds. The axes of these folds lie roughly east–west, like the axis of the coalfield itself, and this shows that the pressure that created these folds was coming from the south. One of the best places to see the structures formed during these earth movements is at Bracelet Bay, where a plunging anticlinal fold has been eroded by the sea to create a gently curving pattern of limestone beds in the wave-cut platform. This fold, known as the Langland anticline, and associated structures such as faults and veins, can also be seen in the cliffs on the eastern side of Caswell Bay.

Rocks of the latter part of the Carboniferous period are not present in Gower. Around this time a prolonged period of uplift and erosion, lasting for some 80 million years, affected much of what is now Wales and adjacent regions. During this time, through the Permian and well into the Triassic period, the Coal Measures and older strata were folded into the present coalfield basin.

Life flourished during the Carboniferous and Permian. Crinoids, ammonites, corals and fish diversified in the seas, while amphibians and reptiles continued their invasion of the land. After more than 100 million years of relative stability, however, the end of the Permian (248 million years ago) saw the largest extinction event in the earth's history, an event far more devastating than the later and much more famous Cretaceous extinction, when the dinosaurs died out. Around 75 per cent of known species of land animals and 96 per cent of marine animals disappeared forever, together with early corals and trilobites. Many causes have been suggested for the Permian extinctions including fluctuations in sea level, a change in the salinity of the ocean, and volcanic activity. The most important factor, however, seems to have been climate change.

By the end of the Triassic period Gower lay in northern tropical latitudes and the climate was hot and semi-arid. The Triassic was a fresh beginning for life on earth and new species evolved to fill the gaps left by the Permian extinction, with the first dinosaurs evolving towards the end of this period. Throughout the Triassic, river systems running south across what is now Glamorgan drained into a lake or lakes whose northern shore lay close to the present Bristol Channel. From about 220 to 210 million years ago a complex of mudstones and evaporates was deposited as a result of the rapid evaporation of these lakes. In some areas these sediments have penetrated and filled fissures in the Carboniferous Limestone. The lakes appear to have been surrounded by an arid treeless hinterland, since there are few fossils of plants and insects. Only one small area and a few infilled fissures near Port-Eynon remain as evidence of a similar Triassic cover in the peninsula. In the 1690s this 'red ochre' deposit from the age of the early dinosaurs was discovered by John Lucas of Port-Eynon, who considered it a 'seam or deposit of paint material'. Lucas 'employed men to dig therefore to the great well being and benefit to himself and to the men and he possessed much wealth in moneys, and did buy skiff at Swainsey and Bristol to beare ye paint material away to number of five ...' This source of material was exploited for centuries and the skiffs carried it to Cardiff for sale. According to the accounts of the Penrice Estates the use of this paint was the origin of the Great Western Railway livery of brown and ochre. The 1938 edition of the company magazine recording that they used 10,000 pounds (4,536 kilograms) of 'levigated raw ochre' a year for their paints.

Marine conditions gradually returned some 210 million years ago, reaching their full extent in the early Jurassic period. The seas were full of life, including ammonites and marine reptiles such as ichthyosaurs and plesiosaurs. During this period the early Jurassic sea surrounded islands of Carboniferous Limestone, such as Gower, and the Blue Lias Limestone was deposited as muds and lime muds in a relatively quiet sea, the beds now covering much of the Vale of Glamorgan. Purer and lighter limestones originating in shallow water then succeeded the Blue Lias. It has long been claimed that thick layers of younger Jurassic rocks, plus succeeding deposits from the Cretaceous period, including the chalk, originally covered the whole of Wales. No evidence of these younger rocks remains, but it does seem likely that the chalk, formed mainly from the remains of microscopic plankton called coccoliths, may have covered much of the country, with the exception perhaps of small areas of Mid and North Wales. It appears that this late Cretaceous deposit was removed by erosion shortly after it was formed. No Jurassic or Cretaceous rocks remain in Gower today, although Jurassic strata have been found offshore to the south of the peninsula and they also occur to the east in the Vale of Glamorgan.

THE SHAPE OF GOWER

The general topography of Gower has developed since the beginning of the Tertiary period when Wales was subjected to a long period of periodic uplift. As a result, around Swansea and in the Vale of Glamorgan there is a series of stepped, but highly dissected, coastal platforms at 60, 90, 120 and 180 metres, which are considered to be remnants of marine erosion surfaces, or 'wave-cut platforms'. Like similar planation surfaces in the uplands they truncate pre-existing geological structures. Remnants of the 180m surface are represented in Gower by the Old Red Sandstone ridges of Cefn Bryn, Llanmadoc Hill and Rhossili Down. Much of the peninsula is at a lower level and like the Vale of Glamorgan extends to a little over 120 metres. This 120m platform is not very clear, but can be seen near Pen-clawdd, Three Crosses and Clyne Common. The southern cliffs represent the lowest platform, later erosion along fault lines producing the dry valleys known locally as 'slades'. The general appearance of the peninsula is therefore a series of plateaus with occasional hills rising above the surface.

The general shape of the south Gower coast is determined by a number of pitching folds (folds with tilted axes) in the Carboniferous Limestone that result in anticlinal headlands with cliffs and synclinal bays with sandy beaches. The anticlines occur at Mumbles Head, Pwlldu Head and Oxwich Point, while synclines form the major bays of Oxwich and Port-Eynon (Fig. 16). The many smaller bays such as Limeslade and Bracelet have, in contrast, generally been formed by erosion along faults running north–south (Table 3).

In some locations on the peninsula displacement of the rocks has occurred along a reverse fault, a break in the rock where one mass of rock has pushed up over another. Such faults tend to run parallel with the axis of the folds and are called 'thrusts' in Gower, although this is strictly not the correct use of the term. One such thrust occurs on Cefn Bryn where it is marked by a hollow on the north side and crest of the anticline that is followed by the road from Cilibion to Reynoldston. Because both the anticlines and the thrusts in Gower were formed by pressure from the south they tend to lie parallel to one another. The peninsula owes much of its shape to geological faults. Professor Neville George, Senior Lecturer in Geology at the University of Swansea, noted in 1933 that 'Almost every bay, inlet, gully, mere, cave or sound is eroded along a joint or a fault or a fold or a soft bed.' Faulting has, for instance, resulted in the small coves and bays at Langland, Caswell, Pwlldu and Limeslade (Fig. 17). Other faults run between the tidal islands of the Mumbles. Each island is also bisected by a smaller fault. The faults may contain interrupted iron veins, which indicate incremental openings of the fault or fissure.

FIG 16. The anticlinal headland of Oxwich Point and the synclinal Oxwich Bay. (David Painter)

TABLE 3. The four key factors in Gower geology. (Adapted from Bridges, 1997)

FACTOR	EXAMPLES
1. East–west anticlines and synclines.	Mumbles Head Port-Eynon Bay
2. Anticlines producing hills and synclines producing wide valleys.	Llanmadoc Hill Oxwich Bay
3. East–west thrust faults where one mass of rock has pushed up over another.	Cefn Bryn
4. North–south faults, which may give rise to typically narrow bays where they meet the coast.	Limeslade Bay Three Cliff Bay Western scarp of Rhossili Down

Iron is an important characteristic of many faults in Gower, and mineral veins associated with them usually contain calcite and haematite. The blood-red haematite ore was probably derived from the underlying Old Red Sandstone by the action of the hydrothermal solutions from which the vein minerals were crystallised. One of the larger faults, which runs across Mumbles Hill and whose southern end forms Limeslade Bay, was mined for iron from the Roman period until the nineteenth century. Between 1845 and 1899 the remaining iron ore was blasted out, broken into fragments and barrowed to small ships that took it across Swansea Bay to Swansea and Briton Ferry. The *Swansea Guide* of 1851 notes that 'a valuable vein of iron ore ... has been worked, much to the disfigurement of this romantic spot.' A narrow trench, known as 'the Cut', was left across the hill. It was almost completely backfilled with rock hollowed out of Mumbles Hill when an underground sewage works was constructed in the 1930s. The remaining part of the trench can be clearly seen today from the viewpoint at the top of the hill, near the coastguard radio mast.

Rhossili Down is a rather exceptional feature; unlike the other high points on the peninsula the axis of the anticline is aligned north–south rather than east–west. This is because the rocks that make up the ridge were rotated along the line of the Llangennith fault. The west-facing scarp of Rhossili Down is formed along the Broughton fault and the Port-Eynon thrust lies to the south. It is therefore surrounded on three sides by faults, the steep slopes on the west, south and east being fault faces.

This then is the sequence of the Gower rocks and the forces that have shaped them into the peninsula. Because it is the oldest rocks, the Old Red Sandstone,

FIG 17. Rocky shore near Pwll Du showing a cross-section of a fold. (Harold Grenfell)

that are now exposed on high ground at Cefn Bryn, Llanmadoc Hill and Rhossili Down it is clear that in these places the combined thickness of the Carboniferous Limestone, Millstone Grit and Coal Measures has been removed over the last 280 million years. The action of wind and water, assisted by plant roots, chemical breakdown and glaciers, has taken away an incredible 4,600 metres of rock.

GLACIATION

The whole of Gower was affected by ice on numerous occasions although, as in many places, the current shape of the land can only be related to the last two glaciations. Despite this the peninsula has one of the most complete glacial records in Britain and is therefore critical to the understanding of the Quaternary period. Advances and retreats of the polar ice caps were interrupted by interglacial periods lasting many thousands of years during which the climate was much milder, in many cases even warmer than it is today. Most of the ice in the penultimate glaciation appears to have been derived from source areas in the mountains of central and southern Wales. However, the ice in western Gower, along with that in Pembrokeshire and the Vale of Glamorgan, formed part of a very extensive ice sheet that encroached inland from the southern Irish Sea. This is clearly indicated by the glacial debris, which north of Cefn Bryn contains a greater amount of material originating from the South Wales coalfield while south of the ridge the rock types suggests an Irish Sea origin.

As the ice melted during what is known as the Ipswichian interglacial period, between 130,00 and 120,000 years ago, sea levels rose about 6 to 9 metres above present levels. Subsequent falls in sea level left behind beach deposits cemented with calcium carbonate, which are known as 'raised' beaches but should not be confused with the true raised beaches found in Scotland. Although the beaches and their platforms have been eroded since their formation their origin is shown by the rounded shingle and the shells they contain. At Foxhole, near Southgate, for example, at the foot of the low cliff, there is an elevated platform on the Carboniferous Limestone. On this wave-cut platform is preserved one of the best examples of the 'Patella beach', which is composed of sand, rounded limestone fragments and fossils of the common limpet *Patella vulgata*, held together by calcareous cement (Fig. 18). In Gower this deposit of shelly shingle (in which periwinkles and dog-whelks *Nucella lapillus* are also very common) is widespread and is normally cemented into a hard conglomerate, which rests on a narrow, wave-cut platform.

Many of the Gower caves open onto the platform of the raised beach,

FIG 18. The 'Patella beach' at Foxhole, near Southgate. (Harold Grenfell)

and it is probable that they were enlarged by wave action at the same time as the platform was created. Associated with the beach deposits are the well-known cave deposits, which have yielded bones of animals such as straight-tusked elephant *Palaeoloxodon antiquus*, hippopotamus *Hippopotamus amphibius* and soft-nosed rhinoceros *Dicerorhinus hemitoechus*, showing that the climate was much warmer than that of today. The importance of these deposits lies in their relationship to the raised beaches and the information this provides on the climatic changes in the late Devensian. Minchin Hole at Pennard contains a particularly important sequence of deposits and is regarded as the 'type site' for the Patella beach, which has been commonly used as a 'marker horizon' throughout southwest Britain. The cave is also unique in South Wales in containing two raised beaches of different ages superimposed in a single section. Investigations in the 1980s suggested that these beaches represent two separate interglacial periods, and because of this Minchin Hole is a nationally important site for studies of the Pleistocene (Fig. 19).

The last glaciation, known as the Devensian, which reached a maximum about 18,000 years ago, destroyed many of the features created by the previous glaciation and is responsible for most of the glacial landforms preserved in Gower today (Table 4). This time all of the ice was derived from Wales and large glaciers occupied Carmarthen and Swansea bays. Mammals typical of the Devensian period include mammoth *Mammuthus primigenius*, woolly rhino *Coelodonta*

FIG 19. Minchin Hole, a nationally important site for studies of the Pleistocene. (Harold Grenfell)

antiquitatis, horse *Equus caballus*, reindeer *Rangifer tarandus*, arctic fox *Alopex lagopus*, spotted hyena *Crocuta crocuta* and abundant small mammals such as arctic lemming *Dicrostonyx torquatus*.

The limit of this last glaciation in South Wales has been the subject of much debate. By about 22,000 years ago, much of Wales had been overrun by ice, and

TABLE 4. The development of the Gower landform. (Adapted from Bridges, 1997)

EPOCH	AGE	YEARS AGO	FEATURES
	Historical period		Sand blown inland. Development of coastal dune systems.
Holocene	Flandrian	From 10,000	Rising sea levels drowning estuaries and causing aggradation in rivers with redistribution of fluvioglacial debris. Renewed cliff cutting.
Pleistocene	Late Devensian	18,500	Glacial cover over north Gower and in Swansea Bay. Periglacial conditions and solifluction over remainder of the area. Sea levels over 40m lower than present.
	Early Devensian		Periglacial conditions, sludging of former red soils and drift material partly over raised beaches. Ipswichian sea cliffs degraded.
	Ipswichian	125,000	Sea levels at this period about 5m higher than today, flooding low-lying areas and producing wave-cut platforms that were subsequently abandoned.
	Wolstonian	450,000	Complete cover of ice from Irish Sea and Black Mountain areas leaves behind till over much of Gower. Meltwater modification of drainage as ice cover disappears.
Tertiary		Around 50 million	Initiation of present drainage systems as plains of marine abrasion were cut and sea level fell relative to land. In-situ development of thick clays (including 'terra rosso' on limestone) in climate similar to Mediterranean conditions.

large glaciers occupied Carmarthen and Swansea bays. Much of south Gower, however, lay beyond the limits of the ice sheet and the deposits found above the raised beach sediments at Worms Head record these cold conditions. These 'head' deposits consist of angular limestone fragments prised from the slopes and cliffs above by the action of frost. During this cold period much of the ground would have been permanently frozen (permafrost) – only the upper layers would have thawed out, and during such thaws, soil and other loose materials would have slipped down the slope (solifluction) to lie with the broken limestone fragments above the raised beach deposits. These different types of sediment make Worms Head an outstanding site for scientists studying the ice ages and the way climatic changes occur through time. The evidence from Worms Head complements that obtained from Rhossili Bay, where there is more direct evidence for glacial activity during this period.

The narrow strip of land below the scarp of Rhossili Down is the prime example of a 'solifluction bench' formed by large quantities of surface material sliding down the scarp at the end of the last glaciation (Fig. 20). This formed an apron which the sea has now eroded, forming a low cliff of loose material. Similar examples occur at the foot of the limestone cliffs between Slade and Oxwich Point. The slopes of the other Gower hills also have the appearance of having been affected by solifluction, with a smooth flowing shape and few rock outcrops. On the south-facing outcrops of the Carboniferous Limestone, frost shattering and scree formation occurred and some glacial debris was deposited.

While it is clear that the ice covered the northeast of the peninsula, doubts remain about the precise limit of ice in west Gower. Most of the available evidence comes from the northern end of Rhossili Down where a large exposure of shelly gravels occurs. This material is thought to be the 'outwash' of an ice sheet in Carmarthen Bay. Whiteford Point is a shingle ridge that may have originated as

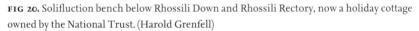

FIG 20. Solifluction bench below Rhossili Down and Rhossili Rectory, now a holiday cottage owned by the National Trust. (Harold Grenfell)

the remnants of the terminal moraine, a continuous line of debris left by the glacier that occupied the Loughor valley. This glacier greatly modified the landscape by providing an abundant supply of silts, clays, sands and boulders that have been reworked during the subsequent rise in sea level to form the basis of the marshes today. It is also likely that ice reached the coastal cliffs on the north shore, clearing frost-shattered debris and solifluction material. Ice sheets and glaciers also brought many large rocks into the peninsula, the most obvious of which is Arthur's Stone. Utilised in the Neolithic period to form a chambered tomb, the 24-tonne conglomerate capstone contains brown clay-ironstone, coal fragments and traces of fossil plants, which do not occur in the Devonian conglomerates elsewhere in the peninsula. This confirms that the capstone was derived from the northern outcrop of the Millstone Grit and carried to Gower by the ice.

After the glaciations the sea level rose again and at its maximum extent low cliffs were cut in Oxwich and Swansea bays. Since then sediments accumulating in front of these low cliffs has isolated them from the sea and sand dunes have formed. Present marine activity is restricted to a limited zone at the foot of the soft cliffs. In contrast the limestone cliffs were largely shaped in the Pleistocene when sea levels were high. The north Gower cliffs, which are now some distance from the sea, are in the main 'fossil' cliffs, while those on the south coast are best described as 'relict' because although they were largely shaped at the same period as those of north Gower in places they are still subject to erosion by the sea. Periglacial conditions were also present immediately following the last glaciation, but the retreat of the ice was rapid and much of the peninsula is thought to have been ice-free by 14,000 to 15,000 years ago. There is no reason to believe, however, that the ice will not return. Despite global warming, the present conditions represent only a brief respite in a predominantly glacial age.

At the end of the Pleistocene period, 10,000 years ago, sea levels were well below the present, probably at least 22.5 metres lower. Early in the postglacial period the area of the present-day Bristol Channel would have been occupied by a large river in the middle of a wide plain of birch tundra. From the end of the last glaciation to the early Neolithic, about 5,700 years ago, sea levels in Britain rose steadily as the water which had been locked up in the ice sheets was slowly released and covered these coastal woodlands. Offshore from Rhossili are drowned river valleys, the channels of which, although partially infilled with sediment, are generally 5 metres deeper than the adjacent seabed. The general trend therefore has been for low-lying coastal margins to become inundated, as shown by the submerged peat beds in areas along the coast. In some cases tree remains are also found, the so-called 'submerged forests'. Describing Oystermouth in Swansea

Bay at the end of the seventeenth century, Isaac Hamon wrote 'The sea hath encroached upon a great part of the low grounds of this parish, as appears by the roots of trees, and whole trees that lyes in the sands and other tokens.' Other remains of the forest have also been uncovered in the past in Port-Eynon and Broughton bays.

Comparatively little research has been carried out on the remains of this past habitat, much of the interest being centred on the geology and animal fossils present. As Neville George (1930) remarked, 'it cannot be too strongly emphasised that much of the interest of the Forest rests in its being a forest, and that a considerable portion of the material consists of an abundant and varied flora; an investigation by some competent botanist of this rich and practically untouched assemblage could not fail to prove exceedingly illuminating.' Species recorded include silver birch *Betula pendula*, hazel *Corylus avellana*, alder *Alnus glutinosa*, elder *Sambucus nigra*, deergrass *Trichophorum cespitosum*, rushes *Juncus* spp., irises *Iris* spp. and spurges *Euphorbia* spp. Leaves of pedunculate oak *Quercus robur* have also been found. This group of plants is characteristic of low-lying wet habitats with dry land nearby and represents a similar habitat to that existing today in parts of Oxwich marsh. Insect remains include the wing-cases of beetles such as the dung beetle *Geotrupes vernalis*, which appears to have been fairly common and was probably associated with the presence of larger animals, including roe deer *Capreolus caprea*, red deer *Cervus elaphus* and ox *Bos taurus*.

THE CREATION AND DISTRIBUTION OF SAND

The grinding action of ice flow and glaciers, when the majority of northwest Europe lay under thick ice sheets, formed sands and gravels. After the last glaciation, some 6,000 to 8,000 years ago, a period of global warming produced large volumes of meltwater, which transported these materials into the river systems and near coastal waters. When the sea level rose it reworked these sands and gravels and pushed them shorewards, until they lay at or near the heads of bays. These sediments are not being significantly renewed by natural processes and are therefore a finite resource. Although the Bristol Channel once contained vast reserves of this 'glacial outwash' research has shown that there is a long-term and generally westward transport of sand out of the area, leaving behind a largely rocky seabed with a sparse covering of sediment.

The high tidal range of the Bristol Channel results in wide expanses of sand being exposed at low water, and when conditions were suitable some of this was blown inland, leading to the development of coastal dune systems. Near the northwestern end of Whiteford Point peat, containing leaves, roots and other plant material, is exposed just below the high-tide level and represents a former land surface. It has not been dated, but Bronze Age remains have been recorded on top of the clay and beneath the dunes that fringe Broughton Bay, with Roman remains on the overlying sand. This indicates that sand began to move inland in significant quantities in the Iron Age, around the first millennium BC. This process continued for centuries, although there was a considerable increase in storminess in northwest Europe from AD 1200, which continued after a slight improvement in the fifteenth and early sixteenth centuries into the seventeenth and eighteenth centuries. The seventeenth and eighteenth centuries have been described as the 'Little Ice Age' because of the increase in the size of the European mountain glaciers that took place during this time. The environmental evidence is backed up by documents that record devastating sand movements between the thirteenth and fifteenth centuries, corresponding with the period of climatic deterioration. In addition, studies of tidal levels show that the general level of the tide was steadily increasing during the twelfth and thirteenth centuries, with a peak around 1433, and that it remained very high during the two following centuries before diminishing. This combination of increasingly stormy weather and higher tides played a significant part in determining the fate of many coastal settlements in South Wales.

Incursions of sand are thought to be responsible for settlements at Rhossili, Penmaen and Pennard being abandoned during the thirteenth and fourteenth centuries, although it appears that their abandonment was more the result of a loss of interest in maintaining them, rather than a result of the settlements being rapidly submerged beneath deep sand. Sand movement is usually sufficiently gradual for land to remain in use if necessary. At Rhossili, for example, there seems to be evidence for the abandonment of the lower village on economic grounds alone, land on the plateau being about twice as productive as that on the solifluction bench where the deserted settlement was located. The presence of a strip field in the medieval field complex adjacent to the medieval village called 'Sandylands' suggests that windblown sand affected both parts of the manor and not just the area below Rhossili Down. The besanding of settlements such as these, on cliff tops situated well above sea level, is not a common phenomenon, but studies have shown that winds of sufficient speed to carry sand up to the top of cliffs can be expected to occur about eighty times a year, even in today's climate. Once sand is airborne it remains so until it is caught by a suitable surface, or the local wind speed falls below a critical velocity, which is dependent on particle size. In this situation it is the local topography that determines where the deposition of sand takes place (Table 5).

TABLE 5. Besanded sites in Gower. (Adapted and simplified from Toft, 1988)

PLACE	SITE	SITE SITUATION DESCRIPTION	BEACH LOCATION
Nicholaston Burrows	Church and suspected settlement	In steep valley, 0.4 km from beach	South of site
Penmaen Burrows	Church and ringwork	On cliff top above beach	Below headland
Pennard Burrows	Church, castle and house	In valley and on plateau 0.65 km from beach	Valley orientated south-southwest
Rhossili Warren	Church and house	On platform below 200 m high hill and beside 61 m cliff	Below cliff

There are two documents relating to sand at Pennard (Fig. 21), one from the fourteenth century and another 200 years later. The first, from 1317, has been generally accepted as marking the beginning of the advance of the sand. In the document William de Breos III granted hunting rights on the 'sandy waste at Pennard'. Excavations at a medieval house site close to Pennard Castle, however, revealed that sand was present long before the fourteenth century. The second document is preserved among the archives of All Souls College, Oxford and is a petition written in 1535 by Harry Hopkin, the vicar of Pennard, to the king's commissioners at Swansea. The commissioners were engaged in compiling a comprehensive valuation of ecclesiastical benefices to provide the Crown with an up-to-date assessment of their income as a basis both for imposing on them a perpetual tax (amounting to one-tenth of their annual net incomes) and also for levying the whole income of every benefice for the first year following the appointment of a new vicar.

It was this valuation in the deanery of Gower that prompted Hopkin to submit the petition, because the encroachment of drift sands that affected Pennard and some other coastal areas of South Wales at this time had substantially reduced the value of the benefice. Indeed the advance of drift sand along the coast of Glamorgan was sufficiently serious to be the subject of an Act of Parliament of 1554 (*An Acte touchynge the Sea Sandes in Glamorganshyere*) and its contribution to the decline of the coastal borough of Kenfig is well documented. The sand had seriously affected the parish for many years before the petition was written.

Because of the sand tenants had had their rent reduced in 1478, and in 1517 the church was excused its royal levy. Eventually it was abandoned during the 1520s in favour of a new site 2 kilometres to the east, along with the 'mansion house' appertaining to it, by which Hopkin presumably meant the priest's house or vicarage. The glebe lands belonging to the church had also been covered over together with many other tenements. All this is described in the first part of the petition:

> To the kinge's comysshionerz nowe being at Swansey.
>
> In his humble wyse shewyth unto your masterships your oratour Sir Harry Hopkin, vicar of Penarth in the denery of Gower within the dyosys of Saint David, that where the said churche and the vicaraige with all the glebe landes to the same belonging or appertaynyng is utterly and clerly destroyd and overgon with the dryfe sandes of the see. And not only the said church with the mansion house and the glebe landes whyche to the same appertained, but also diverz and many other tenements whyche were within the said paryshe be in like wyse destroyed and decayed by reason of the said dryfte sandes, in such wyse the proffites of the said churche is gratly decayed ...

FIG 21. Pennard Castle, a site 'besanded' during the thirteenth and fourteenth centuries. (Harold Grenfell)

Records, including further Acts of Parliament concerned with coastal protection, show that the stormy conditions and subsequent drifting of sand continued until the eighteenth century.

SOILS

Soil formation in Britain began as the ice cover diminished, and it is continuing today. An earlier origin has been proposed for the red clay-rich material that lies on top of the Gower limestone, but in most cases this appears to have been produced by glacial 'smearing', or by solifluction. The soils (Table 6) broadly reflect the distribution of the underlying geology of Carboniferous Limestone, Millstone Grit and the Coal Measures, but are more locally influenced by a covering of glacial, or periglacial, deposits. South and west Gower is covered with gravely loams, while finer-textured soil is widespread in the northeast. Brown earths are the main soils in the complex till and glaciofluvial deposits that occur in south and west Gower. These soils, which cover most of the peninsula, are agriculturally important and are deep and loamy with rounded stones throughout the soil profile. Although they are derived from relatively acidic Carboniferous rocks, with a pH of around 5.0, their acidity has been lowered by the application of lime 'manure' and basic slag.

It was a common practice for Gower farmers to mix lime with proportions of earth to produce what was termed 'marl'. Lime making was one of the earliest industrial activities in the peninsula, the material being produced by heating limestone in kilns and then treating it with water to form calcium hydroxide. The Oxwich jurors wrote in 1632 that it was their right 'to digge lime-stones for to repair ... and to burn lime', while at Landimore in 1639 it was recorded that 'there be Quarries of Limestones where Tenants time out of mind have used to burn their Lime for the composting of their lands'. Most of the surviving limekilns were constructed largely in the period between 1750 and 1850 to burn limestone in order to make lime for local use: to spread on the fields as a soil improver, to make mortar for construction, lime-wash for painting buildings and for many other uses. Lime burning had all but died out by the turn of the twentieth century and the kilns (Fig. 22) were abandoned. Walter Davies described the application of lime in the first volume of his book, a *General View of the Agriculture and Domestic Economy of South Wales* (1814–15):

> In Gower, west of Swansea, sound soil on limestone; some rich land near the Mumbles, letting for 3 1., 3 1. 10s., and 4 1. per acre. The Duke of Beaufort grants three lives' leases,

esteemed here the best preservatives of land, 'as the farmer finds a warmer interest in the
soil' ... Course of leaseholders for three lives: 1. Wheat on fallow, limed on the first
ploughing with from 50 to 100 stacks or horse-loads (150 to 300 bushels) per acre, and as
much dung on the third tilth; 2. Barley; 3. Oats; 4. Barley, with dung and coal-ashes, and
lay down for four years without seeds ... Course of tenants at will, in the same tract:
1. Wheat on fallow, with half the above quantity of lime and dung, or less than that;
2. Barley; 3. Oats; 4. Barley; and lay down for four years; or as some do, 5. Oats, and oats
as long as any can be had.

Despite the details of the application rate it is difficult to estimate how much
lime was actually applied. The imperial bushel, legally established in Great Britain
in 1826, was a dry measure of 8 gallons (36 litres) used principally for grain and
fruit, but it also had a great variety of other values in local use, varying not only
from place to place but in the same place according to the kind or quality of the
commodity in question. Frequently it was no longer a measure of capacity, but a
weight of flour, wheat, oats or potatoes.

On the Coal Measures in the northeast of the peninsula the soils are heavy
and impermeable and this, together with gentle slopes and the humid climate,
causes these soils to be wet for much of the year. Unimproved soils are extremely

FIG 22. Limekiln at Mewslade. Lime making was one of the earliest industrial activities in
the area. (Harold Grenfell)

TABLE 6. The soils of Gower. (Adapted and simplified from Wade *et al.*, 1994)

UNDERLYING ROCK OR OTHER PARENT MATERIAL	DOMINANT SOIL GROUP	SOIL CHARACTERISTICS
Dune sand	Raw sands	Calcareous windblown sand; thin humic topsoils only present on stabilised dunes and frequently buried. Gleyed soils and peat in hollows.
Limestone and Triassic 'gash' breccia	Brown earths	Well-drained loamy, or loamy over clayey soils, shallow in places, especially on steep slopes and crests with '*rendzina*' in rocky areas.
Fluvioglacial sands and gravels	Brown earths	Deep well-drained loamy soils.
Millstone Grit and Coal Measures	Brown podzolic soils	Well-drained loamy soils over sandstone, usually on steep slopes. Heavy clays on shales – slowly permeable, seasonally waterlogged soils with a peaty surface, usually on valley floors.
Devonian conglomerate and sandstone	Podzols	Well-drained, very acid sandy soils with a bleached subsurface horizon over conglomerate. Associated with less acid well-drained reddish loamy soils over sandstone and siltstone.
Till	Stagnohumic gley soils	Heavy stony clays – very acid, slowly permeable seasonally waterlogged loamy soils with a peaty surface horizon.
Estuarine alluvium	Alluvial gley soils	Loamy alluvial soils with high groundwater. Saline and partially anoxic in marshes. Sand or soft mud on intertidal flats.

acidic with pH values around 4.0. On improved land the values are higher, commonly around 5.5 to 6.5.

The soils on the ridges of the Old Red Sandstone outcrops are mainly rocky, coarse loamy podzols. They are found under heathland vegetation and below a surface accumulation of acid plant debris there is a thick bleached sandy horizon which overlies a dark zone of humus, iron and aluminium accumulation. This passes to a yellowish red horizon enriched with hydroxides of iron and aluminium. The associated fine loamy brown earths and brown podzolic soils lie mainly under grassland with associated bracken *Pteridium aquilinum* and their distribution is related to the underlying rocks. The podzols are very acidic with pH values less than 4.0, while the associated brown earths and brown podzolic soils are only slightly less acid, with pH values around 4.5.

Well-drained fine loamy and silty brown earths occur along the south Gower coast and are commonly shallower than 30 centimetres on the cliffs themselves. The calcareous material and the relatively low rainfall, together with additions of lime and basic slag on the agricultural land, result in these soils having a near-neutral pH of 6.5 to 7.0. Brown podzolic soils are well-drained coarse loamy soils that can be distinguished from the duller-coloured brown earths by layers of bright orange-brown subsoil, which contain larger proportions of iron and aluminium hydroxide.

All the soils on the salt marshes are affected by the high water table and are classed as alluvial gley soils. They have different profiles depending on slight differences in elevation and there are four types recognised, each with a distinctive vegetation community. At the lowest point on the shore there is an extensive area of common saltmarsh-grass *Puccinellia maritima* and the upper 20cm of the soils show some structural development. On the mid-shore under red fescue the subsoil structures are well developed and the upper 20cm is almost completely decalcified. The highest zone of the marsh, on the landward edge with sea rush *Juncus maritimus*, the soils are completely decalcified with a pH value of 5.5 in the upper 50cm.

The raw sands of the dunes are composed largely of quartz grains and shell fragments and except on the inland areas where they have been fixed by vegetation they are unstable and there is no visible structure below the top few centimetres. As the dune surfaces are very unstable fresh sand frequently buries old topsoils causing layering. On fixed dunes there can be more than 5cm of topsoil. In dune slacks humic-sandy gley soils form, with surface layers rich in organic matter, overlying gleyed sand. Stabilised dunes on cliff tops such as those at Pennard, where there is little accretion of fresh sand, are sometimes decalcified below 30 cm and the soils are non-calcareous, resulting in an interesting flora.

PLANT COMMUNITIES

The plant life of every area, including Gower, is characteristic of the rock, soil and climate. Plants can change their growth patterns relatively quickly, but because changes in the soil occur over long periods there must be an equivalent slow change in plant growth. Plants adapted, for example, to growing on the coarse loamy podzols of the commons may not be able to survive on the brown earths covering the limestone. Some plants, however, can grow equally well on both acid and neutral soils if there is reduced competition. Many existing habitats in the peninsula have been largely formed by human activity, but they are so old and so traditional that they have come to be regarded as natural. So commons and heathlands are described in this book as plant communities, even though they need constant management to exist in their accepted form. The intervention of people is the subject of the next chapter.

CHAPTER 4

The Influence of People

… that interesting peninsula of Gower, an English-speaking district in the heart of
Wales, bristling with castles and ancient camps, and full of interest to the archaeologist.
Alfred Watkins, *Pigeon Houses in Herefordshire and Gower*

I N ORDER TO appreciate the present natural history of the peninsula it is important to understand the influence that people have had on the area over the past ten thousand years. The many important sites include Longhole and Paviland caves, Bronze and Iron Age settlements, the medieval strip field system at Rhossili known as the Viel and the saltworks at Port-Eynon. In addition, Cefn Bryn Common in central Gower is one of the richest archaeological areas in South Wales, with dense concentrations of monuments on the crest and slopes of the ridge that provide evidence of human activity from at least the fourth or third millennium BC. Elsewhere there are the extensive remains of a medieval deer park, and four historic parks and gardens are identified in the *Register of Landscapes* (Cadw, 2000): Clyne Castle, Kilvrough Manor, Stouthall and Fairyhill. Each has its own distinct character. Penrice Castle and the adjoining estate also have many similar characteristics and make a major contribution to the landscape and rich wildlife of the area.

In contrast the domestic buildings in the peninsula have suffered badly from the blight of 'modernisation' and there have been few attempts to retain the vernacular architecture of the area. Many important buildings have been demolished, or altered beyond recognition. Even as late as the 1950s two significant cottages in Port-Eynon, Chestnut Cottage and the Abbey, were demolished. When pulled down in 1952 the latter was reputed to be 800 years old.

There are, of course, no dividing lines in history and one period merges unnoticeably into the next. Although the following account is therefore in broad chronological order, it sometimes reaches back, or moves forward, in order to describe how the peninsula emerged from the glaciations and developed into the place we know today.

THE BEGINNINGS

The earliest sign of people in Gower is a flint handaxe that was found at Rhossili and is now in the National Museums and Galleries of Wales. It dates from around 125,000 years ago, when the peninsula was in an interglacial period. It is not until nearly 100,000 years later that evidence for the presence of people is again recorded, principally from cave sites such as Cathole. Just before the final advance of the ice sheets some 28,000 years ago, in the early upper Palaeolithic, a young man was buried in what is probably the most well-known cave, Goat's Hole, Paviland (Fig. 23). Mistaken for a female skeleton, the so-called 'Red Lady' was discovered by the Reverend William Buckland in 1823. The body was buried with ivory bracelets and wands and perforated sea shells, all of which were covered with ochre that stained the bones red. Goat's Hole is the largest and the most imposing of all the Welsh caves occupied in the Palaeolithic, though not the largest and

FIG 23. Goat's Hole, better known as Paviland Cave, the most important of the Welsh Palaeolithic caves. (Harold Grenfell)

most impressive cave in Gower, and it has been argued that it was a place of spiritual importance and perhaps pilgrimage.

Today the cave can only be reached from the cliff above at low tide, but when it was occupied it would have overlooked, not the sea, but a coastal plain rich in game animals. Over 5,000 finds, of flint, chert, bone and antler, together with the remains of a rich fauna, have been recovered from the cave. Unfortunately, as described in Chapter 13, the finds were all made before the age of scientific exploration and most of the remaining archaeological deposits have since been swept out of the cave by the sea. At the time of the excavations Buckland was the first Professor of Geology at Oxford and as a result the 'Red Lady' is now on display at the Oxford University Natural History Museum. It is one of many important cultural artefacts that have been removed from Wales and the museums in Cardiff and Swansea only have replicas. A campaign was started in 2004 to bring the skeletal remains back to the area, with the intention of displaying them in Swansea.

For around 15,000 years after the burial in Goat's Hole Gower was too cold for human habitation, but as the climate became warmer again around 13,000 years ago people returned and the cave sites were reoccupied by hunter–gather groups whose presence is indicated by tools, made from flint and bone, found at Cathole and Goat's Hole. The tools are probably indicative of hunting parties right in front of the ice. These early people had little or no influence on the natural environment, as populations were very small. In any case this was a world of herbs, grasses, dwarf shrubs and no trees. There were probably fewer than 5,000 people in Britain as a whole at this time and as few as 50 people in Wales. A population of this size would have consisted of no more than one or two extended families. Indeed it has been suggested that Palaeolithic people might sometimes have walked for two weeks without meeting another human, except for members of their own immediate group.

Once the ice had finally disappeared, around 10,000 years ago, plant communities dominated by grass and sedge spread north. Many of the plants that are now found in Gower, in the heathland or limestone grassland, grew in these open communities, but woodland plants rapidly replaced them as forests also moved north. By about 8,500 years ago forests of oak *Quercus* spp., pine *Pinus* spp., birch *Betula* spp. and elm *Ulmus* spp., with an understorey of hazel, probably covered most of the peninsula. The spread of trees was assisted by a climate that was warmer than at present. Some ecologists think that there were no clearings, as many of the large browsing or grazing animals present in earlier warm periods had disappeared. Others have suggested that these forests were in fact pasture-woodlands with many glades and open areas created by native herbivores, including bison *Bison bonasus*, auroch *Bos primigenius* and the wild horse or tarpan *Equus ferus*. There is also the intriguing possibility that, since the early hunters contributed to the extinction of many of the large grazing animals, they may have actually assisted the development of forests.

Whatever the vegetation inland, coastal habitats were an attractive location, favoured by the Mesolithic groups that are known to have fished and gathered shellfish. During this period the sea level was rising rapidly and was only 15 to 20 metres below its present level, with the shoreline only a few kilometres beyond its present position. Although Mesolithic people were only present in Gower in small numbers they probably influenced the vegetation significantly, mainly through the use of fire to create clearings around their campsites, to clear underbrush and to drive game animals. Repeated burning of the forests would have led to an increase in fire-resistant species such as pine and hazel, and it has been suggested that the known abundance of hazel during this period occurred as a result, possibly benefiting people by increasing the crop of hazel nuts. The pollen records from Gower are not continuous, but evidence from the Glamorgan uplands suggests that during the Mesolithic period there were fairly large areas of heathland. Certainly the existence of a Mesolithic flint-working site on Burry Holms, close to Rhossili Down and Llanmadoc Hill, and the similarity in soils, topography and vegetation between these hills and the uplands, suggests that clearances using fires could have allowed heathland vegetation to spread to these areas from its refuges on exposed coastal sites. It may be that parts of Rhossili Down have remained as heathland for over 8,000 years.

THE INTRODUCTION OF FARMING

Around 6,000 years ago, following the introduction of farming from the continent, Neolithic communities arrived in Gower, accidentally bringing with them harvest mice *Micromys minutus*. The species is predominantly eastern in its distribution and while it spread naturally into eastern Europe in postglacial times there is evidence to show that the animal's subsequent spread into western Europe is due to the movements of people and clearance of woodlands. The removal of this habitat was necessary for the introduction of domesticated plants and animals, which themselves required a more settled existence. These clearances by Neolithic people were assisted by the open heathland created in the Mesolithic period. There is little surviving evidence of domestic activity in this period other than a scattering of flint tools, fragments of pottery and animal bones, and Gower is no exception in this respect. One of the most characteristic artefacts of the Neolithic period is, however, the polished stone axe, examples of which have been found at Paviland, Oystermouth and Barland. With this tool the Neolithic farmers were able to efficiently and permanently clear the forest covering the fertile soils. It is unlikely, however, that they would have felled the forest of oak, birch and alder that grew on the poorly drained and infertile soils which are now commons, when better land was available in other parts of the peninsula. Limestone woodland probably remained on the steeper and poorer soils where it survives today.

In the small cornfields created in cleared areas arable plants such as dead nettles *Lamium* spp., charlock *Sinapis arvensis* and poppies *Papaver* spp. probably became established after being introduced with crop seed, with docks *Rumex* spp. and plantains *Plantago* spp. occurring on areas of fallow land and in pastures. The sea level was close to its present state during the Neolithic and sand dunes and salt marsh were probably present in both Oxwich and Swansea bays. Salt marsh may have also extended along Pennard Valley. These are naturally open habitats and they probably provided excellent grazing for both cattle and deer in the winter when there was little food available in the forest.

Most finds and monuments of prehistoric date occur in the west and south of the peninsula. Near the boundary separating the freely drained and poorly drained soils Neolithic communities constructed a variety of megalithic monuments. Only six megalithic chambered tombs survive, and they can be divided into two groups based partly on their location and partly on their construction. The first group in the west includes the two Sweyne's Howes (the megalithic tombs on Rhossili Down; Fig. 24), Arthur's Stone and Nicholaston tomb, while the second group in the southeast consists of Penmaen Burrows and the Parc le Breos tomb (the Giant's Grave) in Green Cwm. The age of Sweyne's Howes is uncertain, but Parc le Breos probably dates from the middle of the Neolithic period, between 4,800 and 5,200 years ago.

The type and the number of domestic animals kept by prehistoric farmers is an important indicator of the character of the landscape. Forests can support quite high numbers of pigs, but few cattle, while more cattle can survive on grassland and sheep are unable to live in woodland. Large numbers of cattle bones, particularly when they are found alongside sheep bones, therefore indicate the presence of a significant amount of open grazing land. Unfortunately while the animal bones recovered from Parc le Breos included those of pig, sheep, goat and cattle, the numbers involved were too small to undertake a proper analysis. Alongside the remains of domesticated animals, however, were bones of wild animals such as red deer, wild cat *Felis catus*, fox *Vulpes vulpes* and badger *Meles meles*, which would seem to indicate that the area was at least partially wooded at this time.

FIG 24. Sweyne's Howes on the eastern slope of Rhossili Down, traditionally the burial place of Sweyn, who may have given his name to Swansea. (Jonathan Mullard)

FIG 25. Arthur's Stone, or Maen Ceti, situated on Cefn Bryn Common and overlooking the inlet and estuary. (Jonathan Mullard)

The megalithic tomb known as Arthur's Stone, or Maen Ceti, is dramatically situated on a 'false crest' on Cefn Bryn (Fig. 25). Both the English and Welsh names refer to the massive glacial erratic which serves as a capstone and covers two chambers encircled by the remains of a round cairn. It is likely that the tomb was constructed by excavating under the capstone and inserting the uprights beneath it. The Welsh name is first mentioned in a Triad of the sixteenth century in which the raising of the stone is listed as one of the 'three mighty achievements of the Isle of Britain'. The English name mentioned by Lhuyd as being used 'by the common people' is probably of equal age and originates in the recurrent legend of a pebble from a giant's shoe. In this version it was said to have been thrown from Llanelli by King Arthur. As well as Arthur's Stone there is a remarkable concentration of standing stones in west Gower. Apart from the eight that still survive, the best known of which is Samson's Jack, there are reliable records of another single stone, a group of two or three and another group of four. In addition one of the existing stones is linked with the name Stone Park, and two other menhirs, both named Long Stone, are known to have existed. Some fourteen other field names also imply the presence of an upright stone.

THE DIVISION OF THE LANDSCAPE

The Bronze Age saw a return of a warmer and drier climate. The concentrations of barrows and cairns on the ridge of Cefn Bryn and on Rhossili Down and Llanmadoc Hill suggests that these areas had been cleared by the end of the Neolithic period, or at least by the early Bronze Age, some 4,000 years ago. The siting of barrows, in locations where they are clearly visible from the ground below, also implies that the landscape was open when the barrows were built. It is often stated that people in the Bronze Age were primarily nomadic shepherds, with herds of cattle and sheep, who also hunted for food, but they are also likely to have grown cereal crops in lowland areas such as Gower.

The later Bronze Age, about 3,500 years ago, is notable for the formal demarcation of the landscape, with a dispersed pattern of small open settlements set within field systems. Bronze Age artefacts have been found in Gower (Fig. 26), but if the people who made them were farming the peninsula then the field systems they created are unrecognised or have been removed by later cultivation. It is quite possible, however, that fragments of the boundaries of Bronze Age field systems survive to the present day. Around the fringes of Dartmoor, for example, some hedges still continue the boundaries (reaves) of Bronze Age field systems. In looking for evidence in the peninsula it would be worth investigating the original

FIG 26. A bronze socketed axe found in Cathole, with the rim from a fourth-century storage jar and a piece of Roman Samian ware from Gower. (Swansea Museum)

limits of the commons as they are certainly amongst the oldest surviving boundaries. A prehistoric date has also been suggested for a linear wall of sandstone blocks, some 1.7 metres wide and 0.2 to 0.3 metres high, which runs for some 400 metres across the ridge of Rhossili Down. It is likely that the wall marked territory, perhaps for the regulation of grazing. The division of the landscape and a possible nearby settlement enclosure do seem to reflect the agricultural exploitation of the area at an early date. The structure could nevertheless have been constructed at any time during the later prehistoric or early historic periods.

THE INTRODUCTION OF IRON

Iron working was introduced to Wales some 2,600 years ago and the availability of iron implements gradually transformed agriculture. Until the late Bronze Age bronze was scarce and expensive, being used mainly for weapons, and agricultural implements seem to have been made mainly of wood or stone, as they were in the Neolithic period. As described in the previous chapter, iron ore is widely distributed in Gower and wood and charcoal for smelting was readily available. A number of samples of iron ore, which appear to have been partially melted, have been recovered from the site of the submerged forest in Port-Eynon Bay. With improved implements, clearance of woodland was now much easier and it was possible to cultivate the heavy but fertile soils. The pollen record shows that there were extensive clearances on a much larger scale than in previous periods. At Harding's Down hillfort, for instance, which is situated nearly 150 metres above sea level, pollen found beneath the rampart indicates that oak forest with ferns *Polypodium* spp. dominated the site prior to clearance and construction of the ramparts, while grass was unimportant. Grassland subsequently replaced the forest and has dominated the area since, although birch has been present throughout the history of this site, except during very recent times.

The finest hillfort is Cil Ifor (Fig. 27), which consists of three large ramparts and ditches enclosing the steep-sided hill, but there are other prominent hillforts such as the Bulwark on Llanmadoc Hill. The patterns of small enclosed fields near villages and the shared grazing on common land may also date from this period, despite being modified by the partial imposition of the manorial system and later enclosures.

Iron Age society was primarily agricultural, and small farmsteads supported dispersed communities. Many of these small farmsteads were marked with a circular bank and ditch enclosure and surrounded by linear ditch systems that formed small rectangular fields radiating out from the farm itself, but as yet no evidence for such field boundaries has been found in Gower. Animals provided meat, functioned as draught or pack animals and as symbolic wealth, as raw materials for clothing, as providers of dairy produce and manure and as aids to herding and hunting. Plants provided staple foods, fuel, bedding and roofing material, while managed woodland provided resources for building, fencing and carts. The best-known of the cereals grown in prehistory is emmer wheat *Triticum dioccum*, which was grown extensively in Britain during the late Iron Age and the Roman period along with spelt wheat *Triticum spelta*. Besides the cereals a number of legumes were grown including peas, vetches and beans.

FIG 27. Cil Ifor, the finest hillfort in Gower, from the southwest. (Harold Grenfell)

THE ROMAN INFLUENCE

The Roman invasion of Wales took place just under 2,000 years ago, in AD 50, with the Roman army defeating the dominant Iron Age tribe the Silures, whose territory probably covered Gower. Although there was fierce resistance, the conquest of South Wales was completed and by AD 78 the Romans had established a series of military roads and forts. The Roman fort at Loughor lies below the medieval castle and there was a Roman building at Oystermouth, where fragments of mosaic are on view in the church. Isaac Hamon noted that 'part of the church-yard was formerly paved with small bricks like dices, but something larger, of divers colours as red, white, yellow &c, which lies scattered abt still, The people called it The Saints pavemt.' Above the quarry at Barland, pottery, glass, charcoal and ironwork have also been found, indicating that another Roman settlement was located nearby in the second century.

Despite the introduction of towns, Roman Britain was still essentially a rural society, with the vast majority of the population living in farms and small settlements away from the urban centres. Most settlements in Gower are likely to have operated a mixed farming economy, with sheep, pigs and cattle being the main species, although there is known to have been an increase in the numbers of cattle during this period. Other domesticated animals included goats, chickens, ducks and geese.

As it is likely that Gower already contained extensive field systems in the late Iron Age, the impact of the Roman conquest would not necessarily have been to increase the amount of land used for cultivation. The Romans themselves had a long tradition of hedging and there is some evidence, elsewhere in Britain, of a system of small fields bounded by ditches, which had been hedged with hawthorn *Crataegus monogyna*. The basic units of land tenure were not always altered by the Roman conquest. There was also continuity in farming methods, with a similar type of iron ploughshare being found at both Iron Age and Romano-British sites, although the range of cereals grown increased noticeably through this period.

Enormous quantities of oysters and other shellfish were also eaten, to judge by the numbers of shells found at most Roman sites. British oysters were a delicacy in Rome, indicating that they were regularly exported. Sea fish would also have been an important part of the diet for many people in Gower. Fishing with nets and fixed baskets were the main methods, but fishing hooks and tridents for spearing fish have been recovered from sites elsewhere.

Apart from agriculture it is known that a wide range of activities occurred in rural areas such as Gower, from mining and manufacturing to hunting and fishing. Hunting with dogs was particularly popular, and indeed there were specially bred animals that were regularly exported from Britain during both the Iron Age and Roman period. Brown hares *Lepus europaeus* were probably introduced in this period, since there is no evidence of their presence in Britain before Roman times, and these may have been hunted, but the reasons for their introduction are not clear. Some bones have, nonetheless, been found in Iron Age deposits, which may indicate an earlier introduction. This argument is supported by the note that Julius Caesar wrote on arriving in Britain around AD 44, 'These Britons think it wrong to eat hare and fowl, rather they keep them as pets.' But this may have referred to the smaller native mountain hares *Lepus timidus*. Whatever the exact date of introduction, as they spread into lowland farming districts like Gower, brown hares would have displaced any mountain hares that may have previously inhabited these areas. In Ireland, where the brown hare is absent, mountain hares are found in lowland districts to the present day. Because of predation and hunting for food, brown hares were possibly never very abundant until the eighteenth and nineteenth centuries when the combination of land enclosure, agricultural improvement and predator control allowed populations to rise.

The Romans also introduced a number of important tree species to Britain such as the cultivated sweet cherry *Prunus avium*, medlar *Mespilus germanica*, fig *Ficus carica*, walnut *Juglans regia*, sweet chestnut *Castanea sativa* and possibly also the horse chestnut *Aesculus hippocastanum* and holm oak *Quercus ilex*. Sycamore *Acer pseudoplatanus*, which is sometimes thought to have been brought into the country in this period, is probably a later introduction.

THE AGE OF SAINTS

When, around AD 400, Rome abandoned Britain, South Wales reverted to the Iron Age pattern of small independent kingdoms. From the seventh to the ninth century 'Guhir' formed part of the 'Seisyllwg' of ancient De Heubarth, which by the tenth century was under the rule of the famous lawmaker, Hywel Dda, or Howell the Good. This post-Roman period has often been referred to as 'the Age of Saints' and it has been argued that there was an early Welsh church unique in character. Unfortunately there is little real evidence, in Gower at least, for a Celtic church with its own structures and practices, but nevertheless there are a number of important sites. At Llanmadoc church, for example, a Christian tombstone survives from around AD 500, while Llangennith was the site of a small monastery founded by St Cenydd in the sixth century and destroyed by Viking raiders. In the porch of Llanrhidian church there is a carved stone block known as the Leper

FIG 28. Llanrhidian Church, location of the 'Leper Stone'. (Harold Grenfell)

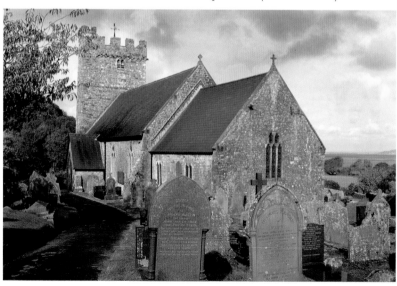

Stone. This is a massive block of stone, bearing simple representations of human figures and stylised animals, that is believed to date from the ninth or tenth century (Fig. 28).

THE NORMAN INVASION

The small kingdoms survived for over 700 years until the Norman invasion of Britain in 1066. About 35 years later, soon after 1100, Gower had been annexed and was a Marcher Lordship with the new town of Swansea created as its fortress, complete with castle. The Norman possession of Gower was disputed and many attempts were made by the rulers of the Welsh states of Cardigan and the Vale of Towy to drive out the invaders. At least six times, between 1113 and 1217, the Welsh burned the turf and timber castles and devastated the countryside, but failed to retake the peninsula. The Reverend Latimer Davies in his book *Pennard and West Gower*, published in 1928, recorded that according to the *Annales of Winchcomb* in 1136 'packs of wolves descended from the Welsh mountains, and found their way into Gower, and devoured the bodies of a large number of men slain in battle between the Normans and Welsh.'

Towards the end of the thirteenth century the earlier structures were replaced by the strong stone castles present today, at locations such as Oxwich, Penrice, and Pennard. Although some of the castles were damaged during Owain Glyn Dŵr's revolt between 1400 and 1413, their construction marked the end of Welsh resistance. One result of the Norman Conquest was that English settlers from the West Country crossed the Bristol Channel, and this was a major force in creating the distinctive character of the people and the peninsula.

In this period all land was owned by the Lord Signeur and held under him by the lords of the various manors. It was worked by the local people, mainly in large open fields. In Gower there were important and extensive manors, which were part of the Seignory (the lordship) of Gower. The Lord Signeur held the two principal demesne manors of *Gower Anglicana* and *Gower Wallicana*. The departure of the last resident lord in the 1320s marked the beginning of a long period of uncertainty over its rulership, and the later lords hardly visited the peninsula.

CULVER HOLE

Located in a natural cleft some 420 metres west of Port-Eynon Point, the impressive medieval pigeon house of Culver Hole (Fig. 29) is thought to represent the last remains of Port-Eynon Castle that may have previously existed on the cliff top above and which was mentioned in lawsuit records in 1353. The massive 18 metre high masonry wall, pierced with windows, seems to have been used as a columbarium, or dovecote, where pigeons were bred for food. On the inner face of the wall, and reached by a rough stone stairway, are hundreds of L-shaped nest holes, typical of pigeon houses. Popular legends maintain that it was a smugglers' retreat, but the fact that the Old English for pigeon is *culver* almost certainly proves the matter. One of the mysteries of Gower is why a dovecote came to be built in such a remote location. Local tradition records that Culver Hole was built by the same family who built Oxwich Castle, which possesses a more normal dovecote. Alfred Watkins, the extraordinary Victorian country gentleman best known for his ley theory, who visited the site and undertook 'a rather difficult climb' up the inside of the wall, also considered the matter in his 1891 article on 'pigeon houses in Herefordshire and Gower':

> But why should a dovecote be constructed in this lonely and unusual situation? (high tides wash the floor of the cave). This was a puzzle until I remembered that the wild rock dove still inhabits this coast line, that in former times they were far more plentiful, that they nest in the numerous caves and clefts, and that all our domestic pigeons are direct descendants of, and will interbreed with these wild doves (Columba livia). Here, then, is the inevitable conclusion I arrived at; that in castle-building times, a dovecote was built in the cliff with the evident intention of enticing and perhaps partly domesticating the wild pigeons. With what success will probably be never known.

There is another Culver Hole near Three Chimneys at the western end of Broughton Bay, which is a cave used as a burial place during the Bronze Age. It too was obviously used by pigeons at one stage in its history.

THE GREAT DEER PARK

With the Normans came an interest in deer management and the creation of deer parks. These are much rarer in Wales than in England, but Gower has one of the best examples at Parc le Breos (Fig. 30). The deer park enclosed a sizable part of the

FIG 29. The impressive medieval pigeon house of Culver Hole. (Harold Grenfell)

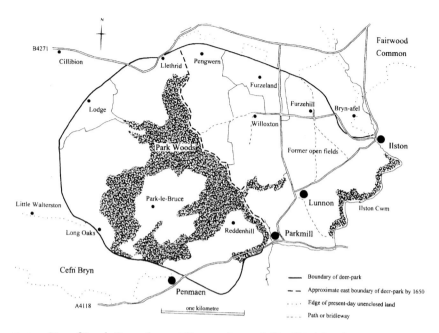

FIG 30. Map of Parc le Breos, the great Norman deer park. (David Leighton)

Gower landscape and it is the only definite example to have been established in the medieval lordship. The park, which surrounds the house of Parc le Breos, is exceptionally large and consists of an oval area of about 800 hectares that encloses the valleys of the Green / Llethrid Cwm and Ilston Cwm. The purpose of a deer park was to supply venison, other meat, wood and timber. The Normans introduced fallow deer *Dama dama*, probably at the same time as rabbits *Oryctolagus cuniculus*, and for many centuries they were semi-agricultural animals, which did not roam the countryside, but which were enclosed in parks or protected in forests. The deer shared the park with sheep or cattle, the grazing rights being let to local farmers. Deer were probably released from the park onto the Forest of Fairwood, Lunnon Moor or Cefn Bryn for the chase when required. Retaining deer the rest of the time ensured a supply of venison throughout the year.

What is remarkable about Parc le Breos is that, despite having undergone many changes over several centuries, its identity has remained intact. The park boundary is still clearly visible on Ordnance Survey maps and on air photographs and once consisted, for the most part, of a dyke formed from an earthen bank with a core of stones, varying in scale and preservation, but normally between 3 and 6 metres wide and 1 metre high. In many places the line is followed by modern hedgerows and is very overgrown, while in other sections the dyke has disappeared and its place has been taken by a narrow lane. The main expense of a park was the 'pale', a fence of cleft oak stakes set individually in the ground and nailed to a rail. This was supported by a bank formed by excavating a ditch on the inside. The pale had to be of sufficient size to contain the deer and deter trespassers. There were two types of parks, 'uncompartmented' parks, which were accessible to the deer at all times, and 'compartmented' parks, where the trees and grazing were separated. Park Le Breos seems to have been a compartmented park.

Even though evidence of the park has survived for centuries, there are very few historical records and it remains an enigma. It is not known if deer parks were set up in Gower before the thirteenth century, but it is unlikely. The history of the lordship throughout the twelfth and early thirteenth centuries was one of great instability and, as the frequent attacks by the Welsh are known to have delayed the construction of the castles, it is likely that costly schemes such as deer parks were also deferred. This seems to be confirmed by the fact that the earliest reference to the 'silva de Bruiz', the great medieval deer park, is in 1230. There is also a mention of the 'Park-de-Breoz' in 1306 and the 'parcus de Bruz' in 1319. Although it is traditional to assign the creation of the park to William de Breos, documentary evidence suggests it is more likely to be the work of his son John. In 1439 it was described as 'a Park side called ye Park of Prys', but some time during the fifteenth century it was 'disparked' and divided into fields and closes. In the 1580s, for example, Rice Merrick, the Elizabethan chronicler of Glamorgan, described it as 'an ancient lodge house called Park y Price ... sometime emparked with a wall and pale but long time past dis-parked' (James, 1983). A disused park usually reverted to being a wood and often permanently acquired the name 'Park Wood', or in this case 'Park Woods'.

Whatever the sporting value of the area, deer parks also had a number of economic uses and this seems to have been the case at Parc le Breos. Several financial accounts for the lordship are available, the earliest relating to 1337/8 when the park was included in the account for Lunnon; there is also one for 1366/7 when the park had a separate account. The pasture of livestock, or 'agistment', was clearly important as it constituted most of the income in 1367, for example. There are also entries for pannage (the pasture of pigs in oak woods in the autumn for winter fattening) and for the sale of wild honey and ferns. Almost as important was the sale of timber, and the recorded sale of underwood implies the management of trees for the purpose of providing a regular crop. While pollarding and lopping may have taken place, direct evidence has survived for a coppicing tradition in what is now Park Woods. Although today they comprise a single expanse of woodland, they once consisted of several individual woods, each of which was separately enclosed. This arrangement is characteristic of coppices, where rotational cutting required new growth to be protected, and was a well-documented feature of deer parks, where the production of timber was maximised by keeping it separate from pasture. Because of the importance of timber for fuel and building, coppice rotation, once established, usually continued for several centuries. The compartmented nature of Park Woods was still noticeable in the nineteenth century.

In the medieval period the supervision of felling and removal of forest products by the appointed foresters was an important feature and the rules concerning such activities were explicit. For example, in the charter of William de Breos to the people of Gower in 1306, wood could be taken under the watch of the forester, but if the forester was not present the applicant had to blow a horn three times, or if they had no horn, strike a tree three times with an axe and await the arrival of the forester. If the forester did not arrive in a reasonable time, the necessary wood could be taken without obstruction. The Book of Llandaff, written in the second half of the twelfth century to underline the diocesan claim to territory and privileges, mentions many woods, but names only a few, including Luhin Latron, Thieves Wood, Gower, which is thought to refer to Clyne Wood, or woodland near Three Crosses.

As hunting and deer husbandry declined in importance, partial 'disparkment' took place in the eastern portion to make way for cultivation. It is not entirely clear when this reduction of the park took place, but around Lunnon a pattern of elongated and rectilinear fields represents the remains of a strip field system created, probably, in the thirteenth century. The economy at the beginning of the fourteenth century was weak. Bad weather had resulted in poor harvests, there had been a series of animal plagues and the Black Death, in the second quarter of the century, decimated the human population. Although there are no details of the Black Death in Gower, evidence of its effects can still be seen today. A significant proportion of the population was lost, fields were untended, farms became vacant and food prices unstable. Gower was also not spared the devastation that followed, and in less than a century had been severely affected by war, famine and pestilence.

Despite these pressures, the western portion of the deer park continued to function until the end of the fourteenth century, as suggested by a record of repairs made to the pale from fallen oak trees in 1400. It is not clear when the keeping of deer finally ceased, but after the demise of the de Breos family in the 1320s the need for them would have gradually diminished. By 1650 the Cromwellian survey named the owner as the Earl of Worcester and the land was divided into three farms: Longoaks, Park Price and Llethrid. Oliver Cromwell subsequently became Lord of Gower. In 1845 the Tithe Maps show woodland in almost the same areas as today, with the Duke of Beaufort as landowner. Around 1850, however, the whole of the woodland was clear-felled and replanted with the oak trees that now dominate the area. In this period Hussey Vivian bought the estate and the Vivian family owned the area until 1952 when Admiral Heneage-Vivian died. Following his death the farms were sold to the tenants and the Forestry Commission bought the woodland. In the early 1990s, with the increased awareness of the benefits of multi-purpose forestry, Park Woods was recognised as being particularly valuable in terms of amenity, recreation and conservation and the Commission stopped treating the area as a site for timber production.

It is usually stated that there are no deer in Gower today, the urban areas of Swansea and Gowerton forming an effective barrier across the neck of the peninsula, but this is probably no longer correct. There are now more deer in Britain than since the time of the Domesday Book, compiled in 1086. They have been increasing in numbers and spreading over the past three or four decades, primarily because of the increase in new woodlands and forests, which provide cover and food. Roe deer have recently reappeared in Wales around Llandrindod Wells and at the current rates of expansion it will not be long before animals reach the peninsula. Urban areas are no barrier for this species. They were once common in Glamorgan and Neville George recorded a pair of antlers that were found, in the clay near the low water mark, in the submerged forest in Port-Eynon Bay. Chinese muntjac *Muntiacus reevesi* are also present along most of the South Wales coast. The species is not gregarious and most of the records are of scattered individuals, the total population in Wales being around 250 adult animals. Muntjac are essentially small forest-dwelling animals and are extremely shy and secretive, with a preference for thick cover such as bramble *Rubus fruticosus* agg., gorse and rhododendron *Rhododendron ponticum* bushes. It is likely, therefore, that one or two animals are present in Gower, having made their way along the edge of the estuary.

RABBIT WARRENS

The medieval rabbit was not the same animal as those that occur today. It was a delicate creature, which needed protection, and at first it could not dig its own burrow. The changes from the tender animal of the twelfth century to the robust rabbit of today (Fig. 31) are almost certainly due to genetic change and adaptation to the British climate. Earthworks were made to encourage burrowing, and these can be identified as the rectangular flat-topped mounds known by archaeologists as pillow-mounds. Only one pillow-mound is known in Gower, at Penmaen, where

FIG 31. Rabbit at Cwm Ivy. (Harold Grenfell)

there is an isolated mound about 20 metres long that tapers from a width of 6.4 metres at the south end to 4.4 metres at the north. There are very shallow ditches along its flanks, but these do not run around the ends. Many of the warrens would never have required pillow-mounds as they were sited in sand dunes where the easy burrowing provided shelter for the rabbits. Indeed this is probably the reason why nearly all the sand-dune systems in Gower are known as 'burrows'.

William de Breos, by a charter of around 1317, granted to William, his hunts-man, the right to hunt, at certain times, hares, foxes and rabbits, and other wild animals and birds, throughout the whole of his warren of Pennard, except in his cuniculary, or rabbit warren, of Pennard in the sand-burrows (*cuniculario nostro de Pennarth in la Sanborghwys*). It seems, therefore, that there was a specially managed enclave, where the lord reserved the rabbiting for himself. The warren must have been located in Pennard Burrows immediately south of the castle and church. There were also warrens at Oxwich, Rhossili and Llanmadoc. Isaac Hamon recording that 'Here is a warren in Oxwich one at Rossilly and another at Lanmadock in West Gower'. It is impossible to estimate when the Oxwich warren was set up, but in 1703 it is recorded that there was a lease of 'ground and burrows called warren of Oxwich with liberty to kill rabbits' and a further lease in 1708 concerned 'Oxwich Castle with warrens and boroughs rabbits and coneys'. The warren still existed in 1741, but, as with its origin, it is impossible to say when it fell out of use. The location of the Llanmadoc warren is indicated by the place name, 'The Conygaer', at the south end of Whiteford Burrows. The site of the 'Rhossili' warren was probably at Hillend Burrows. There is also an eighteenth-century Welsh field name closely related to cwningar, meaning warren, near Willoxton. This may be circumstantial evidence for another early warren, although there is no trace of it on the ground.

There was no substantial increase in wild rabbit populations until the middle of the eighteenth century, when changes in agricultural practice created favourable habitats and an increased interest in game led to intensive predator control. The natural spread of rabbit populations can be quite slow. In the middle of the nineteenth century, however, they began to increase dramatically until they became major agricultural pests. Their increase was partly due to the large-scale planting of hedgerows, which provided rabbits with shelter and an opportunity to burrow in loosened soil. This rapid expansion was bought to an abrupt halt in the early 1950s when myxomatosis occurred in Britain and within two years 99 per cent of the population had died. The disease has since become less virulent and rabbits are developing resistance, but outbreaks still occur. The population is still, however, well below that recorded before myxomatosis. Interestingly pre-myxomatosis populations were highest in Wales and southwest England whereas Wales now has one of the lowest rabbit populations in Britain.

What did Gower habitats look like before the arrival of the rabbit? It is an interesting question, but not one that can easily be answered due to the lack of detailed records. Grazing by rabbits can be very beneficial to maintain the diversity of habitats such as limestone grassland, heathland and sand dunes, preventing, or at least slowing, natural succession. When the numbers crashed following the introduction of myxomatosis, many grassland habitats changed to scrub, with a loss of associated wildlife. At Oxwich, for example, brambles, shrubs and small trees started to colonise the fixed dunes and dune slacks. Before the arrival of rabbits it is likely the land had been just as heavily grazed, but by sheep and other domestic animals.

THE WHITE MONKS

The development and management of the monastic estates was also a great influence on the landscape and wildlife of Gower. Founded in 1130 by monks from Savigny in France, the monks of Neath Abbey later merged with the Cistercians, eventually creating what has been described as the 'fairest abbey in all Wales'. The lands granted to the Cistercians in Wales lay originally in undeveloped and well-wooded locations, but they then proceeded to colonise these areas by clearing woods, draining marshes, reclaiming 'waste' and developing sheep farming. They were noted 'changers of landscape' and there is no doubt that they had a significant impact in the peninsula. The basis of the Cistercian economy and their skill as agriculturalists lay in their possession of large tracts of both arable and pasture land. The order organised much of its property into a series of farms called granges, which were supposed to be within a day's journey of the 'mother-house'. In the case of their lands in Gower this was the monastery at Neath, which had holdings at Paviland, Walterston, Berry and Cilibion.

The Taxation of Pope Nicholas IV of 1291 includes the grange of 'Pamlond' consisting of one 'carucate' of arable and two mills, one of which appears to have been a water mill and the other a windmill. The grange is represented today by the seventeenth-century farmhouse of Paviland. Although no monastic buildings survive, four small square fields lying east and northeast of the house bounded by banks 2.5 to 3.0 metres wide and 0.3 to 1.3 metres high are perhaps a relic of the medieval economy. The presence of the Cistercians is remembered in the farm known as Monksland, near Scurlage village, which lies at the northeast extremity of the former grange. Towards the end of the twelfth century William de Barri granted the monks of Neath '30 acres of land in Guer, between the hill of Kevenbrin and the way which leads through the wood of Bruiz [Parc le Breos] to the vill of Penmain'. Around 1220 he completed the transfer of land to the monks by exchanging the whole fee of Walterston for 100 acres (40.5 hectares) of the abbey's land in Somerset. The site of the grange was probably at one or other of the modern farms at Walterston on the north slope of Cefn Bryn. At Cilibion the abbey's ownership of the manor meant that its land in this part of Gower extended to the boundaries of Welshmoor. In Berry the boundary of the monastic land is uncertain, but it probably formed a continuous strip, which connected to Paviland Grange.

Gower was not always an ideal place for farming, however. A note made by a monk in the twelfth century records that the abbey's holdings in the peninsula were considered to be of low value because whenever a lord of Gower died the lordship was overrun and devastated by the Welsh. Despite these setbacks there is evidence for corn production shown by the monastic possession of barns and mills. The Cistercians were great sheep farmers and, as this required suitable pastures, it is likely that Neath had common rights in the area. As Cistercians never ate flesh, at least in the early days of the order, fish was a very important source of fresh food and there were fish weirs on the coast at Paviland.

Coal, known as carbon stone, was also worked by the monks in South Wales. There was a thriving trade in Gower coal, which depended on the proximity of coal to tidal water, the collieries being principally at Clyne and Wernffrwd in Higher Llanrhidian. Neath had three mines in Gower which lay in 'clay and slime ground' and they were 'maintained and upholden with timber'. The veins of coal they contained were called the 'pit coal', 'stone coal' and 'sea coal'. A 'Coalway' crossed the lands of the monastery to the north of Walterston and the line of this is today followed closely by the 'red road' across Cefn Bryn Common from Cilibion to Reynoldston. By the Elizabethan period there was a growing export trade in coal from Gower. This sea coal came from small pits in the parishes of Upper Llanrhidian and Loughor, sited as close as possible to tidal water. One Llanrhidian farmer, who died in 1609, possessed £5 in 'coales above the gound alredy wrought', and 'one Vayne of coles where upon there is two pitts open'. The scale of working was ambitious for the period, with coal exports from north Gower in 1699 amounting to 7,848 tonnes.

THE VIEL

Between Worms Head and the villages of Rhossili and Middleton lies the remarkable fossilised medieval strip field system known as the Viel (Fig. 32). The name 'viel' is thought to have derived from the Old English word *gefilde* meaning a field or plain, the *f* being pronounced as *v*. 'Land y vile' was also used as a strip name in the Oystermouth area. The Viel is a unique survival and, as such, it is of national importance. Groups of strips still retain distinctive names such as Sandyland, Priest Hay, Bramble Bush and Stonyland. The latter, adjoining Rhossili village, is on the southern limit of glacial drift deposits. The field system contributed to an economy based partly on agriculture and partly on the products of the sea. The fields are still communally occupied and cover an average of 1.5 acres (0.6 hectares), being enclosed by drystone walls near the cliffs and earth banks near the villages. Within these field boundaries the unenclosed strips are separated by narrow unploughed ridges known as landshares. Holdings are spread over the groups of strips. A plan of 1780 shows the land of one farmer, John

FIG 32. The fossilised medieval field system known as the Viel. (Royal Commission on the Ancient and Historical Monuments of Wales)

Griffith, which amounted to 32 acres (13 hectares), as 21 separate parcels, most consisting of unenclosed strips within the Viel. Such land was passed on as part of the farm holding when tenancies changed and some Rhossili and Middleton families have farmed the same strips for many generations. Since the sale of this part of the Penrice Estate in the 1950s the strip holdings are privately owned, but there have been few changes. A few wire fences have been erected along the landshares, however, and they have occasionally been ploughed out.

Another characteristic of open fields is that they are subject to common rights and uses. In particular it was the custom to graze livestock over the fields and furlongs that were lying fallow in a given year. The stubble fields could also be freely used after the crop had been harvested. There are no memories of communal grazing on the Viel, though grazing of strips by supervised cattle was a feature several generations ago. Fortunately a document has survived which proves beyond doubt that the fields were once managed in this way. Interestingly it also tells us that the area was then known as the Great Field, or sometimes as Rhossili Field. Drawn up by a group of 13 local men in the summer of 1731 at a 'Court Leet & Baron ... held at the dwelling house of John William in the village of Reynoldston', the aim of the document was to set out new regulations for the equitable use of common grazing on the Viel. Each man was a tenant of that part of the manor of Landimore at Rhossili, the 'homage of Rosilly' as they called it, which was then owned by Lord Mansel. It appears that some tenants had put an excessive number of cattle and horses on the Viel 'to the great Detriment, prejudice and losse of several of the tenants there' while others had turned livestock loose 'when several of the Tenants have their Corn on the Ground' (i.e. they were in the middle of harvest). This had 'often been the occasion of a great deal of disturbance and like to end in Law suites for divers Trespasses committed there'. It was therefore decided that there were to be restrictions, a 'Stint', on the number of animals and when common grazing was permitted. It is interesting that there is no mention of sheep in the document. Gower farmers in the eighteenth century certainly kept plenty of sheep, but they were evidently not folded on the Viel, being kept instead on the open commons of the cliffs.

If the tenant had one acre of fallow unploughed land he was allowed to graze a horse and two oxen, or two mature cattle, or six young cattle. If he had an acre under crops he could graze an ox, one mature and two young cattle, but no horse. The tenant, however, could only exercise these rights at agreed times. He must not put out his animals until every man had harvested his crops and he had to remove them again on St Andrew's Day (30 November). Between then and Candlemas (2 February) animals were not allowed on the Viel, to allow the sowing of wheat *Triticum* spp., barley *Hordeum* spp. and other crops. How successful these regulations were in practice is, unfortunately, not recorded, but it is to be hoped that they did 'for hereafter be a Custome to be observed and kept by the present and all other future tenants'.

Surviving field patterns, tithe surveys and manorial records show that other Gower manors were also once communally managed in a similar way, some surviving until the nineteenth century. With the exception of the Viel, however, all are now enclosed. In the southern half of Bishopston manor, for example, the numerous narrow strips which covered the arable area in 1844 are still noticeable, and their landshares have not entirely disappeared. The field patterns here would have resembled those at Rhossili. Pennard with its besanded lands had small groups of strips called Forge Field, Great Field and Bush Moor. Lunnon, north of Pennard, had the remains of Middle, Great and High Grove Fields in fenced or unfenced landshares. The five Lunnon farmers also had various landshares in Llethrid Common Meadow, which lies in Parc le Breos Cwm. Similarly a map of the local estates of Thomas Mansel Talbot made by John Williams in 1780 shows that the Penrice lands and those of several others were often unfenced and were grouped under names such as Hoarstone, East Field, Great Park, Furzehill and the extremely descriptive Great Longfield.

CORN AND CHEESE

Farming has always been the major land use in the area, whether it involves the use of the extensive common grazing or the cultivation of individual fields. It is not until the sixteenth century, however, that records become available and it is possible to reconstruct farming practices in some detail. At this time west Gower was well known as a corn-growing region and Camden described it as 'more noted for Corn than Towns'. Camden was headmaster of Westminster School, but in his free time he travelled the country and eventually published *Britannia*, a geographical survey, in 1586. His description is supported by an account of the Welsh coastlands made in 1562 when Gower was recorded as 'the Countrey full of corne'. In contrast to this rather fragmentary evidence for arable farming, the pastoral element is fully recorded and from various wills and leases it is possible to draw a detailed picture of the number and kind of livestock kept by Gower farmers in the late sixteenth century. In general the farmers relied heavily on the open commons and the acreages of their farms were mostly arable. A Horton lease of 1551, which included 15 acres of arable land with 13 of rough ground, was not unusual.

All the farmers kept cows, both for the purposes of breeding and the production of milk. Dairy herds yielded a good profit in cheese and butter and many farmers had enough dairy produce to bequeath it in their wills. At the height of the season (in June 1611), for example, William David Morgan of Loughor left his daughter 'all my chees and butter which I have in my house or shalbe due unto me between this and All Saynts next'. Some idea of the amount of tithe cheese rendered by the farmers of Ilston, an average-sized parish, can be had from the deceased Rector's inventory in December 1605, which states that he owned 40 stones (290 kilograms) of cheese. (The 'cheese stone' equated to 16 pounds, or 7.26 kilograms, instead of the usual 14 pounds or 6.35 kilograms.) Dairy produce was shipped to the West Country from Swansea and particularly from smaller ports in Gower, like Oxwich and Port-Eynon, whose mariners' accounts often refer to butter and cheese. One of the most typical farmhouses is Kennexstone, which was built in 1610 and moved to the Museum of Welsh Life in 1963 (Fig.33). Painted a vivid red colour with ox blood and lime, it is one of the most iconic buildings at the museum. The colour of the walls was thought to protect the house against evil spirits, as was the rowan tree *Sorbus aucuparia*, a specimen of which has been planted in the garden nearby.

FIG 33. Kennexstone Farmhouse, built in 1610 at Kennexstone and re-erected at the Museum of Welsh Life at St Fagans in 1963. (Jonathan Mullard)

THE PRODUCTION OF SALT

On the west side of Port-Eynon Bay are what appears to be the ruined remains of two cottages (Fig. 34). Below them, on the same level as the beach, are a number of stone-lined reservoirs surrounded by a modern concrete sea wall. In operation for about a hundred years between about 1550 and 1650, Port-Eynon Salthouse is an early example of the industrial production of salt by the open-pan process. Sea water was transferred by a simple wooden pump, from the stone-lined saltwater cisterns that still remain, to a panhouse on a vanished upper floor of a building, where it would have been evaporated in metal pans set over flues heated by a coal-fired furnace. The cisterns, which are the most noticeable features of the remaining complex, had flagged floors and lime-plastered walls and were formerly vaulted. Above the cisterns on a low cliff is a range of buildings, those at the southern end being domestic accommodation, while the more extensive buildings to the north served as workshops, or storage facilities. In the seventeenth century a fortified extension was added, with a series of musket loops, and it was later converted into a dwelling before being abandoned in the 1870s. It is perhaps not surprising that the salthouse was fortified. Salt was of great importance and subject to taxation and customs duties, while its value is shown by records of its illicit production and smuggling.

FIG 34. Port-Eynon Salthouse, on the western side of the bay. (Royal Commission on the Ancient and Historical Monuments of Wales)

The site was saved from erosion by the sea and consolidated by the Glamorgan–Gwent Archaeological Trust and the local authority, which owns the site, in the early 1990s. It was not the only salthouse in the peninsula, however, the site of the second structure being commemorated in the place name of Salthouse Point near Crofty.

THE AGRICULTURAL REVOLUTION

Agricultural practices remained more or less the same until the seventeenth and early eighteenth centuries, when Welsh farmers responded positively to the introduction of new techniques. In the latter century in particular the enclosure of most of the open fields in Gower required considerable amounts of fencing, and this usually caused a decline of woodland in thinly wooded areas such as the peninsula. A surge in demand for fencing materials provided the finance to clear woods for farming, instead of retaining them for coppice. It has been estimated that the creation of enclosure fields required between 400 and 500 poles, usually oak, per mile (1.6 kilometres) of fencing.

One of the most important innovations affecting these newly enclosed fields was the introduction of crops that gave the farmer a much richer yield for feeding livestock. Among the plants available, broad red clover *Trifolium pratense* var. *sativum*, sainfoin *Onobrychis viciifolia* and perennial rye-grass *Lolium perenne* were of special interest. Broad red clover, which is early flowering, is used for forage, fresh or dried fodder (in hay), for silage or as a green manure. It was, at the latest, being grown in Gower by the 1690s and fields were rapidly converted to the new system. Isaac Hamon stated that there was 'much clover grass and seed' being sown. He added that the cultivation of clover was particularly prevalent in the Bishopston area. This evidence is probably correct, because Hamon was for many years the steward of the estate in which most of the Bishopston farms lay. Sainfoin was also a valuable new fodder crop for the Gower farmers and was used particularly for sheep.

One of the first people to introduce clover was Mr Lucas of Stouthall, who was a noted improver. Farmers began by preparing a summer fallow in one of their fields and sowing the clover in August or September. If the animals were kept off during the winter then, by the following spring, the field provided a rich crop, much heavier than the normal sward. If cut for hay twice during the summer, clover would last for three or four years before giving way to the natural grasses. This autumn sowing, which was one of two recommended methods of cultivation at that time, was followed until 1739, when, as Walter Davies (1814–15) noted, 'the great frost of that winter destroyed it on Mr. Lucas's farm at Stout-hall. Mr. Lucas was deemed one of the first agriculturists of his time; not willing to forego his clover crop for a whole year, he made an experiment to sow it with barley in the spring; it of course succeeded.' Lucas's neighbours followed his example and clover began to be generally sown with spring crops, barley, oats *Avena* spp. and sometimes with beans.

Apart from these developments the pattern of farming remained unchanged. Traditionally both horses and oxen worked side by side in the fields. In 1840 a Gower farmer recorded in his journal that his spring ploughing was done by 'four Cattle and two Horses in one plow, and six cattle and a horse in the other'. The absence of transport produced a system where the animals were walked to market and batches of fat cattle and sheep were driven to Swansea every Saturday throughout the winter. The summer in contrast was spent in producing and storing crops for feeding the stock in winter.

WATER MILLS

Although the volume of water flowing along the Gower streams is relatively small it is constant, and this influenced the locations of the early settlements (Fig. 35). Water mills were once common in the peninsula and according to Rice Merrick, writing in 1584, there were 'upon Burry ... seven grist mills builded within a mile space'. It seems likely that the original water-powered grist mills were built at the same time as the Norman castles. There were undoubtedly water mills in Gower before this period, but it was the Normans who established the manorial system and set up their 'custom' mills in or near their manors. These mills were a profitable source of income and all tenants were obliged to grind their corn at the mill and to assist in its maintenance. The Survey of the Manor of Priorstown in 1642 states these responsibilities clearly:

> *Tenants ... dwelling in the said Lordship ought to grind all such corn growing in the said Lordship and are to scoure and cleanse the mill ditch and water courses that runneth to turn the same ... they are to yield and pay the miller for the time being, the twentieth part of the bushel or of any other quantity of wheat, rye or barley in meal ... and they are to repair and keep the head of the mill house as often as need shall require of thatch, so that the timber be sufficient to hold the same.*

FIG 35. Fields near Cheriton, alongside the wooded course of the Burry Pill. (Harold Grenfell)

FIG 36. Llanrhidian Mill, which once had the largest waterwheel in Gower and is now a private residence. (Jonathan Mullard)

Up to 1750, it was common practice for mills to be built of wattle and daub, with perhaps the gable end in stone. There were, however, many innovations and developments in the late eighteenth century and, as a result, many mills were redesigned or rebuilt. Almost every Gower parish had its weavers and there were water-powered looms. However, the repeal of the Corn Laws in 1846 and the advent of steam roller mills and cheap flour from imported corn sealed the fate of the grist mills, as did the mass production of cloth which put the local weavers out of business. In order to feed water to the mills, certainly for the larger wheels, leats and millponds were created, the best surviving example of a millpond being that at Lower Mill, Llanrhidian (Fig. 36). The mill, built in 1803, once had the largest waterwheel in Gower, measuring 18 feet by 3 feet (5.5 by 0.9 metres), but by the 1960s the wheel had been removed along with the machinery. The building is now a private house.

LIMESTONE

The main export from the two coastal villages of Oxwich and Port-Eynon in the eighteenth and nineteenth centuries was limestone, which was shipped to north Devon as the raw material of agricultural lime. Surprisingly large amounts were quarried, Isaac Hamon recording that 'they do transport much limestones . . . along this coast'. At Oxwich alone, for instance, between April and August 1708, according to manuscripts from the Penrice estate, there were shipments amounting to 1,698 tonnes. The cliffs stretching out from Oxwich Bay to the Point have been quarried for their limestone since 'time out of mind', though the industry did not really develop until the early part of the nineteenth century, reaching its peak in about 1850. In the early days the limestone was broken away from the cliff using hammers and wedges, but later explosives were used and the 'shot holes' for placing the charges can still be seen. For about a mile out towards the point the cliffs are still a mass of quarry faces and artificial scree slides. The land is still unstable with huge blocks occasionally becoming detached, the last in 1985. The broken rock was piled up on the beach and small sailing ships holding between 50 and 100 tonnes would come alongside these piles at high tide.

Most of the limestone was shipped across the Bristol Channel to Devon where it was converted into lime for use on the acid soils of north Devon and Cornwall. The 'alien stones' found on the beach below the quarries are igneous rocks picked up from the Devon beaches and used as ballast. The lower part of Crawley Bluff also bears the scars of commercial quarrying. Similarly on Mumbles Hill during the 1850s some 3,000 to 4,000 tonnes of limestone were quarried every year, the activity employing nearly 40 men. At Pwlldu there was a large community that worked the quarry, the remains of which can be seen in the parallel bands and ditches which run down the steep slopes of the headland to the west of the bay. Once there were two public houses to cater for the thirsty workers, but today these are private residences. The overgrown and derelict remains of many of the workers' cottages can be found in the nearby woodland.

LANDSCAPED PARKS

In the late eighteenth century there was a fashion for developing landscaped parks around grand houses, which was driven by the developments at Woodstock in Oxfordshire and the activities of professional park designers such as Lancelot 'Capability' Brown. Even a relatively isolated area such as Gower was not immune to this trend and in the 22 years between 1776 and 1798 a number of substantial mansions were built, or extended, and an extensive area of ground set aside for development. Parklands have a typical structure that consists of large, open-grown or high forest trees at various densities in a matrix of grazed grassland and woodland communities. These provide a number of specialist habitats for a variety of animals, including bats, birds and saproxylic (wood eating) fauna, with mosses and lichens on the old trees. The trees are predominantly native species, but there may also be non-native species, which have been planted, or which have regenerated naturally. The Gower parklands, like others in Britain, are nationally important because of their historic, cultural and landscape value and the scarcity of this habitat, but to date there have been no detailed surveys. One of the problems associated with maintaining parklands is the lack of younger generations of trees, which produces a skewed age structure, leading to breaks in the continuity of dead-wood habitat and therefore the loss of specialised and dependent species.

The most extensive and oldest of the Gower parklands is the Penrice Estate (Fig. 37). Its origins can be traced back to the twelfth century, when Henry de Beaumont, Earl of Warwick, conquered Gower and founded the Marcher Lordship. One of his knights took the name de Penrice, and was gifted the land that would in future form the Penrice Estate. The original wooden castle was succeeded in the thirteenth century by the stone structure that stands above the present house overlooking Oxwich Bay. This castle was in turn abandoned in the fifteenth century, with the Mansels building Oxwich Castle, a semi-fortified manor house nearer the sea. In the 1770s, the present Georgian villa at Penrice was built for Thomas Mansel Talbot who had inherited the estate through his grandfather's marriage to Mary Mansel. As the house was built, Thomas Talbot

FIG 37. The historic parkland of Penrice, showing the house with the earlier medieval castle behind. The tree in the foreground was once the site of a heronry. (Harold Grenfell)

commissioned William Eames, a student of 'Capability' Brown, to lay out the landscaped park at Penrice between 1776 and 1779. The present-day lakes, paths, trees and kitchen garden all date from that era. The pleasure gardens and orangery were added in the 1790s, as was the folly known as 'The Towers', which forms the main entrance to the park.

Penrice is one of the richest sites in Glamorgan for epiphytic lichens, those lichens that grow on other plants, and the only one in the county containing a significant concentration of old-forest species. A total of 93 different species were recorded here during the autumn meeting of the British Lichen Society held in September 1990. Some of the richest trees were a number of old planes *Platanus × hispanica* that occupy a sheltered position adjacent to a patch of carr woodland; they supported small growths of lichens such as *Catillaria sphaeroides*, *Parmeliella triptophylla*, *Sticta limbata* and *S. sylvatica*. Of these species only *S. limbata* showed signs of spreading onto younger trees. Large oaks in the higher parts of the park were found to support acid-loving communities dominated by *Evernia prunastri*, *Hypogymnia physodes* and common *Pertusaria* and *Parmelia* species, while a few of the mossier trunks held *Dimerella lutea* and *Normandia pulchella*. Ash trees *Fraxinus excelsior* in the lower parts of the estate carried *Arthopyrenia ranunculospora* and *Chromatochlamys muscorum*, whereas beech *Fagus sylvatica* was poorer, but supported *Opegrapha sorediifera*, *Pyrenula chlorospila* and *P. macrospora*. Caliciales, sometimes called 'pin lichens', are scarce at Penrice and represented only by *Calicium viride* and *Stenocybe pullulata*. They can be found most easily by 'sighting' along twigs against a contrasting background.

The late Georgian house at Stouthall was built for John Lucas the younger by the Swansea architect William Jernegan in 1787–90. Colonel Wood, the amateur archaeologist, who undertook excavations in some of the Gower caves, lived there from 1843 until his death in 1876. It is set in pleasure grounds and a very small park, which consists of a field to the north of the house, bounded on its outer sides by a thin line of beech. The park itself is probably contemporary with the house. The only features within it are an isolated oak and a stone circle, which were placed there by Colonel Wood. The circle was badly damaged a few years ago. The grounds also include a natural cave that was ornamented as a garden feature and an unusually well-preserved icehouse that is used by hibernating bats.

The early history of Fairyhill is unclear, but it is known that by the early eighteenth century it had become the property of the Lucas family, who also owned Stouthall at this time. Then known as Peartree, it was renamed Fairyhill when John Lucas took over the property in 1785. The miniature landscape park, in effect an ornamented field, lying to the south of the house and garden, was the work of John Lucas or his father Richard. Kilvrough Manor, now used by Oxfordshire County Council as a field studies centre, is situated in a small, but well-preserved, late eighteenth-century park and garden. The grounds are informally planted with ornamental deciduous and coniferous trees set in lawns. The park consists mainly of a large rectangular field with some fine deciduous and coniferous trees.

On the western edge of Swansea the park surrounding Clyne Castle, a two-storey castellated mansion originating in 1798 (but much added to and remodelled), is now a public park containing an outstanding collection of rare mature trees and shrubs, in particular rhododendrons, some of which are original introductions. The wilder Clyne Valley to the north retains most of its historic layout and some ornamental planting. The lower end contains the ruined remains of an arsenic and copper works, which was in operation between 1837 and 1860. Also in the valley are a number of 'bell pits', holes dug from the fourteenth century onwards to reach a coal seam close to the surface.

WHITEFORD LIGHTHOUSE

Dating back to 1865, the ornate Victorian lighthouse at Whiteford (Fig. 38) is the only surviving sea-washed cast-iron lighthouse in Britain. Almost 14 metres high and surrounded by over 6 metres of water at high tide, the lighthouse is a well-known feature on the north Gower coast. It is surrounded by common blue mussel *Mytilus edulis* beds and quicksand that still contains unexploded bombs from the Second World War, when the area was used as a practice range. It has not been in regular use since 1926, although it was used in both World Wars and to guide naval craft into Llanelli Dock in the 1960s. The structure was listed as an ancient monument by Cadw in 1979 and urgently needs restoration. Today it usually holds a large roost of cormorants *Phalacrocorax carbo* and as many as 158 birds have been recorded on the structure at a time.

Cormorants no longer breed in Gower, the last confirmed record being at Thurba in 1971. Colour-ringing has shown that the birds seen around the peninsula are associated with the colony on St Margaret's Island in Carmarthen Bay. The UK currently supports around 16,000 wintering individuals, representing over 20 per cent of the European winter population. Despite this the Government, in a move designed to appease anglers, is to allow up to 3,000 birds to be shot each year, ignoring the fact that its own research shows that cormorants have a negligible effect on fish stocks.

FIG 38. Whiteford Lighthouse, a major cormorant roost. (Harold Grenfell)

MARKET FORCES

The arrival of mechanised transport in 1922 changed the approach to farming in Gower virtually overnight, and from then on part of the summer production, mainly potatoes, swedes and green crops, was increasingly grown for direct sale off the farm. Not long after, about 1930, it was realised that as a comparatively frost-free area the peninsula was in a favourable position and this coincided with the introduction of new improved cropping varieties of early potatoes. Potatoes are still a core element on many farms, but the area of green crop vegetables has increased considerably. This maintained the area of arable land at a time when many arable areas were going over to grass. Milk production became a major feature once again in the late 1930s, when most of the farms had a milking herd of cows. They also kept pigs, sheep and store cattle, and grew hay, oats and mangles *Beta vulgaris* var. *esculenta* for their animals as well as wheat, barley and potatoes.

Today Gower is still traditionally farmed with small mixed arable, livestock and dairying enterprises, many of which also exercise ancient commons grazing rights, and this has significant benefits for the wildlife of the area. In contrast to the rest of Wales a large area of arable land remains and most farmers are still growing small amounts of cereal for their own use. Beef production, for so long a mainstay of the relatively small family farms, is now in decline, but in contrast sheep numbers have never been so high. It is currently a period of immense change in agriculture. The subsidies, which have been present for the last 40 years or so, are gradually being replaced by payments designed to improve the environment and farmers are no longer paid according to the number of animals they have. Traditional farming practices must be kept in place, but farming is no longer an attractive occupation for many young people and the average age of farmers is high. Very few people from outside Gower have come to farm, although whenever land has been sold, mainly due to people retiring, it has been bought by neighbours and amalgamated into larger holdings, but thankfully still retaining the family farm structure. In general the older farmers have kept their farmhouses and sold off their land to their neighbours.

THE DIVERSITY

These then are the factors that have moulded the Gower of today. Despite first appearances it is clear that virtually the entire peninsula has been affected by the activities of people over the millennia. Very few areas have remained pristine and unaffected and yet wildlife has adapted to the changes and, indeed, has often thrived on the diverse habitats produced as a result. The next section looks at this inheritance in more detail.

PART III

A Rich Variety

CHAPTER 5

South Gower Cliffs

The southern cliffs of Gower continue the Carboniferous Limestone and its delights.
William Condry, *The Natural History of Wales*

LIFFS ARE ONE of the most natural habitats on earth and contribute more to the variety of wildlife in an area than their surface coverage would indicate. Despite some areas being heavily quarried in the past, the south Gower coast is one of the classic British botanical localities, having many species that are nationally rare – and these are sometimes abundant. As with other areas of high plant diversity this richness results from a combination of geology, climate and history. Limestone cliffs typically support large numbers of scarce plants and, as described earlier, the Gower climate is characterised by mild winters, cool summers and a prolonged growing season. It is also one of the strengths of the southern coast that so much of it consists of a broad belt of semi-natural vegetation, unlike a great deal of Britain where coastal habitats have been ploughed and reseeded right up to the cliff edge. The south-facing cliffs, which at their highest are some 70 metres above sea level, rather than being vertical for the whole of their length, contain many areas that slope gently from the cliff top to the sea (Fig. 39). The slope is often quite gradual, with the cliff tops being cut by the slades and lying some way inland, but there are some remarkable features along the coastline such as the Knave, a conical rock that dominates the inlet to the west of Paviland (Fig. 40).

At the base of the main cliffs, which are for the most relict features, lie the present-day undercliffs. As described in Chapter 3, many of these are made of soft rock, formed by wave action on concreted material that has accumulated from the weathering Carboniferous Limestone above and blown sand from the sea. These

FIG 39. Looking east along the south Gower cliffs from Tears Point. (Harold Grenfell)

FIG 40. An aerial view of the remarkable conical rock known as the Knave. (Peter R. Douglas-Jones)

areas of soft rock are rich in invertebrates, and their insect communities, like the botany, are of national importance.

PLANT COMMUNITIES

The coastline is particularly noted for the range of habitats that occur, from intertidal rocks and the exposed maritime grasslands in the west, to blackthorn *Prunus spinosa* and hazel scrub within the more sheltered valleys in the east. In addition there is an interesting mosaic of habitats on the cliffs, the gentler slopes being covered by acidic soils while the limestone outcrops, containing crevice, ledge and scree communities, are surrounded by dry grassland which grades into neutral grassland and then into acid heath vegetation, often within a few metres of the outcrop. In comparison to other areas of coastal limestone, however, the maritime influence on the cliff vegetation is quite limited, due to the very high relict cliffs and the presence of extensive rocky beaches at the base of the cliffs that act as wave breaks. The large tidal range also reduces the amount of thrown spray reaching the cliffs, as the waves obviously break well away from the cliffs when the tide is out. The least maritime communities are the gorse and limestone heaths, acid grasslands, bracken and bramble, and the blackthorn scrub of the inland part of the cliffs.

Salt-tolerant plants on the lower part of the cliffs typically include spring squill *Scillia verna*, golden samphire *Inula crithmoides* (Fig. 41), rock sea lavender *Limonium procerum*, buck's horn plantain *Plantago coronopus*, thrift *Armeria maritima*, sea campion, scurvygrass *Cochlearia officinalis*, sea beet *Beta vulgaris* ssp. *maritima* and the only maritime fern, sea spleenwort *Asplenum marinum*. Sea spleenwort rarely grows far beyond the immediate spray zone and the most luxuriant plants only occur on the lower parts of the most exposed cliffs. In Gower it occurs in small numbers in crevices, overhangs and caves and is rather sparsely scattered along the coast. The saltwater spray it receives is important since it allows the fern to benefit from the winter warmth brought by wave-splash, the sea acting as a giant radiator that warms and cools very slowly, minimising the occurrence of frost to which sea spleenwort is extremely susceptible.

There have been few descriptions of the lichen flora of Carboniferous Limestone in Britain, so it is worth describing the situation on the Gower cliffs in some detail. The communities appear to be rather species-poor, with many western species absent. Well-illuminated limestone on the vertical faces of the cliffs is typically dominated by small crustose lichens that form small-scale mosaics, including *Xanthoria aureola*, *Ramalina siliquosa* and the orange crustose lichens of

FIG 41. Golden samphire, a plant of the spray zone. (David Painter)

the genus *Caloplaca* (Fig. 42). One species, *C. granulosa*, although frequently found in Gower, is extremely rare in the rest of Britain. On damp surfaces, with a slight to moderate degree of shading, these lichens are largely replaced by species such as *Acrocordia conoidea*, *Dermatocarpon miniatum* and in some areas the rarely recorded *Leptogium diffractum*. Despite the standard outcrops of rock having a relatively limited species diversity, a wider range of species exists in microhabitats, such as underhangs. Underhangs not receiving direct rain, for instance, are well colonised by a thick white form of *Direina massiliensis* f. *sorediata*, the thalus of which contains copious amounts of calcium oxalate. Associated species include *Caloplaca ochracea*, *Diploicia canescens* and the small dispersed thalli of *Placynthium garovaglii*.

Where soil has formed and filled the crevices in the rock, grasses and mosses such as tuberous pocket-moss *Fissidens taxifolius* and rock pocket-moss *F. dubius* are able to exist and begin to dominate the flora, together with a wide range of liverworts, such as *Riccia sorocarpa*. One species of lichen, however, *Squamarina cartilaginea*, is able to compete with these plants and grows out of the crevices and onto the adjacent surface, but in general this 'terricolous' lichen flora is poorly developed compared to sites elsewhere in Britain. The most diverse and interesting assemblages are associated with north-facing habitats.

On apparently bare areas of the rock are pinhole-sized pits, thin light-grey crusts and small black or yellow fruiting bodies which belong to a large number of endolithic (within stone) lichens that grow just beneath the rock surface. Not much is known about these specialised organisms and few of the current books on lichens even mention them. Studies into the process of rock penetration, however, involving isolation and growth of the organisms involved and the microscopic examination of rock surfaces, are slowly producing a better understanding of these fascinating communities. A proper survey of all the lichens on the cliffs is in fact long overdue, given that elsewhere many coastal lichen communities have been shown to be nationally important.

Although sea cliffs are a harsh environment for plants it seems that the species found on them, while not growing under ideal conditions, are able to tolerate a situation that is too severe for plants capable of growing on similar cliffs inland. Woody plants growing on the sloping sections of cliffs, such as juniper *Juniperus communis*, are often stunted and deformed, have slow growth rates and may be very old. Juniper is one of the most striking late-glacial relict species in Gower and is found mainly in sites that are protected from cliff fires, as it cannot regenerate

FIG 42. The lichens *Xanthoria aureola* and *Ramalina siliquosa* on the cliff face. (Margaret Hodge)

after being burnt. In contrast the competing gorse can regenerate and therefore tends to replace it, as happened at Seven Slades after a fire in 1965.

Other important plants to be found on the cliffs include nit-grass *Gastridium ventricosum*, purple gromwell *Lithospermum purpureocaeruleum*, white horehound *Marrubium vulgare* and wild asparagus *Asparagus prostratus*. Wild asparagus is confined to the coasts of western Europe and it is a rare and decreasing species with many colonies being of only one sex. There are probably less than 50 plants in Gower, although it can also be a very difficult species to see amongst other vegetation. The two best times to survey are in May–June before other vegetation grows up, and in autumn when the berries ripen and senescent plants appear yellow. Given its rarity, plants should not be collected. Since the population is so small it is thought that the species may be susceptible to genetic deterioration, through genetic drift and inbreeding. It has been suggested that the gene pool should be supplemented by introducing individual plants from other sites to counteract this. It is difficult to know, however, exactly how many individuals there are in a population as some clumps may be composed of more than one individual (as shown by some patches with plants of different sexes). Isolated fronds may be distinct plants or belong to an adjacent clump. The rhizomes of some large plants may also fragment, giving the appearance of more than one plant.

The first Gower record of wild asparagus was from Culver Hole in 1821 and this appears subsequently to have been the best-known site. It is likely that the population has been significantly reduced historically by collecting, and in 2001 only four plants remained. In 1904 H. J. Riddelsdell found a second group on cliffs in Oxwich Bay, but the exact location is unknown. There were no further records for Oxwich until plants were rediscovered in 1989. Two discrete populations are now recognised, the first on windblown sand on low cliffs and the second, found during a National Trust survey in 1996, on limestone cliffs. This second population may be Riddelsdell's original group. Dillwyn (1840) also reported wild asparagus 'on the Wormshead, and several other cliffs in Gower', and there was a record for 'sands of Broughton Bay near Whiteford Burrows' by H. J. Riddelsdell, but it no longer exists at these sites.

The absence of a number of the common species of limestone grassland is remarkable, with tor-grass *Brachypodium pinnatum*, dwarf thistle *Cirsium acaule*, upright brome *Bromopsis erecta* and meadow oat-grass *Helictotrichon pratense* all absent from the peninsula. Another common species thought to be absent, dropwort *Filipendula vulgaris*, has recently been discovered at an isolated location on Oxwich Point. Downy oat-grass *Helictotrichon pubescens* is abundant, while tree-mallow *Lavatera arborea* grows on the cliffs between Mewslade and Fall

Bay. This is a robust biennial up to a metre in height, with purplish flowers.

Several uncommon limestone species are relatively abundant in Gower, including hoary rock-rose, bloody crane's-bill *Geranium sanguineum* and spring cinquefoil *Potentilla neumanniana*. A number of species, such as basil thyme *Clinopodium acinos* and horseshoe vetch *Hippocrepis comosa*, approach the western limits of their range in the peninsula. The horseshoe vetch in Gower is the scarce late-glacial relic diploid, found only in scattered refuge sites in the west (like goldilocks aster and hoary rock-rose), not the later-arriving tetraploid of English chalkland. Other rare plant species in Gower that occur at a number of widely separated sites on the limestones of western Britain include the small restharrow, which also grows at one site on the Pembrokeshire limestone, in Devon on the Torbay limestone, and in the Channel Islands on Guernsey and Alderney. The hoary rock-rose (Fig. 43) is recorded from Gower, Pembrokeshire, North Wales, the west of Ireland and at two localities in northern England. Many of the species of open habitats which have distributions of this type, and which are in many cases limited to a few favourable naturally open refuge sites on basic soil, were more widely spread in the late and early postglacial periods when the climate was relatively warm and open base-rich habitats were common after the retreat of the glaciers and before the spread of the forests. Progressive acidification of the

FIG 43. Hoary rock-rose, a rare plant with a discontinuous distribution on the limestone of western Britain. (David Painter)

soil, the spread of woodland and the increasingly maritime climate in Britain after the formation of the English Channel have all contributed to the reduction in the range of the species to their present refuge sites, of which the Gower cliffs are an excellent example.

Areas of limestone heath are dominated by gorse, sometimes with bell heather *Erica cinerea* or bracken, and contain a large number of associated calcicole and calcifuge species in an intimate mixture. Gorse (Fig. 44) is one of the most highly structured plants, the tight cluster of rigid stems forming an ideal framework for web-spinning spiders such as *Theridion sisphium*. While gorse bushes usually occur as a more or less complete cover, the more open forms of heath in which it occurs as a mosaic with patches of grassland are probably a response to grazing. Anthills are common and support a different flora in which wild thyme *Thymus polytrichus* and common rock-rose *Helianthemum nummularium* are abundant. The most frequent species associated with gorse are ribwort plantain *Plantago lanceolata*, common dog-violet *Viola riviniana*, glaucous sedge *Carex flacca*, salad burnet *Sanguisorba officinalis* ssp. *minor*, cat's-ear *Hypochoeris radicata* and red fescue.

Away from the typical thin limestone soils, in places where glacial drift deposits have accumulated and there are thicker, more acid soils, the flora is dominated by bracken or purple moor-grass *Molinea caerulea*, with bramble and

FIG 44. Gorse and fox cub in Mewslade Valley. (Harold Grenfell)

FIG 45. Wall cotoneaster on Mumbles Hill Local Nature Reserve, a serious threat to flowers of the limestone. (Harold Grenfell)

sometimes common and western gorse *Ulex gallii*. Some of the most frequent associates are Yorkshire-fog *Holcus lanatus*, sweet vernal-grass *Anthoxanthum odoratum*, tormentil *Potentilla erecta* and wood sage *Teucrium scorodonia*. This community is often subject to fire.

Various species of non-native cotoneaster have become naturalised along the coast. It is likely to become an increasing problem in Gower as there are now some 80 species being cultivated for their ornamental fruits, all of which are very attractive to birds, which eat the fruits and then excrete the seeds, often some distance away from the original plant. Cotoneaster is also planted extensively as part of landscaping schemes in urban Swansea. On Pennard cliffs, a particularly species-rich area of cliffs where many rare native plants grow, entire-leaved cotoneaster *Cotoneaster integrifolius*, Diels' cotoneaster *C. dielsianus*, Himalayan cotoneaster *C. simonsii* and wall cotoneaster *C. horizontalis* have all established themselves and are spreading, having invaded the cliffs either from nearby gardens or from already-established populations elsewhere. The same species also occur on Mumbles Hill, a Local Nature Reserve, and at one time the reserve was covered with a deep cotoneaster scrub (Fig. 45). This was scraped off with a bulldozer and burnt in order to allow the limestone grassland to recover, but it will be a continuing task to keep it clear as it will grow back from the smallest remnant. The plants are also well established on the steep slopes of the hill, where management is impossible. As elsewhere in Gower, on Mumbles Hill there is an interesting distinction between the limestone grassland on the summit with autumn gentian *Gentianella amarella* and autumn ladies tresses *Spiranthes spiralis* and the maritime heathland growing on the lower slopes on pockets of windblown soil. Autumn ladies tresses also frequently occur on the short grassland that is cut regularly for amenity purposes on the more urban areas of the coast around Mumbles and Langland. Unfortunately this grass is often mown just as the plants are coming into flower.

YELLOW WHITLOWGRASS

The cliffs between Thurba and Deborah's Hole are a stronghold for yellow whitlowgrass, an attractive alpine flower which occurs nowhere else in Britain and which is now the 'county flower' of Glamorgan (Fig. 46). In 2002 Plantlife, the plant conservation charity, launched a campaign which it hoped would lead to each county in the United Kingdom adopting its own wildflower emblem. For Glamorgan the original voting list in 2002 included fen orchid *Liparis loeselii*, dandelion *Taraxacum* sect., yellow whitlowgrass, dune gentian *Gentianella uliginosa*, sea stock *Matthiola sinuata* and monk's-hood *Aconitum napellus*. The top two flowers from this round were yellow whitlowgrass and dandelion and the final vote, announced on 5 May 2004, confirmed whitlowgrass as the chosen species. The whitlowgrass family gets its name because the plants in question were alleged to cure 'whitlows', a painful inflammation of the finger or toe, especially near the nail.

Yellow whitlowgrass is locally common in narrow crevices on the upper cliffs between Pwlldu Head and Rhossili. The plant is, however, widely distributed in continental Europe, where it extends from the Pyrenees through the Alps to the Carpathians. It has been claimed that the Gower populations are very different from those in continental Europe and that it is therefore native to Britain. Molecular studies indeed show that the Gower population is genetically distant from any single European population and it seems most likely that it is again a late-glacial remnant, which passed through a bottleneck of small population size before subsequent diversification within the isolated relict area. Yellow whitlowgrass is a variable species, however, and most of the varieties appear to grade into one another geographically and morphologically.

The plant was not discovered in Gower until the late eighteenth century. Its comparatively late discovery is probably due to its extremely early flowering

FIG 46. Yellow whitlowgrass, the 'county flower' of Glamorgan, near Overton.
(Harold Grenfell)

season, inaccessible habitat and restriction to one small area in a little-visited part
of the country. It was first reported by William Turton in 1803 'growing wild
abundantly on walls and rocks around Pennard Castle', but was actually discovered
by John Lucas in 1795 'near Worm's Head'. Dillwyn's *Contributions Towards a
History of Swansea*, published in 1840, includes the following account of yellow
whitlowgrass in 'An alphabetical account of the rarer flowering plants and ferns
which have been found within twenty miles of Swansea':

> *Draba aizoides was first noticed on the walls of Pennard Castle, by the late Mr. Lucas,
> of Stouthall, who communicated his discovery to Dr. Coyte, of Ipswich, and it was the
> Doctor's fault, as he admitted to me, that the merit of this interesting discovery was
> withheld from Mr. Lucas. The plant was afterwards shown by Mr. Lucas to Dr. Turton,
> and the latter sent the specimen to Sowerby which has been figured in English Botany.
> It grows also on most of the higher cliffs, and in many inaccessible places along the coast
> from Pennard to Wormshead.*

While correct details of the distribution of yellow whitlowgrass in Gower were
given by Dillwyn and to a lesser extent by John Gutch the following year, later
botanists often knew only of the Pennard Castle locality (Fig. 47). Although the

FIG 47. Pennard Castle, the classic site for yellow whitlowgrass. (Harold Grenfell)

castle is constructed of Old Red Sandstone the whitlowgrass grows in crevices in the lime-rich mortar. For many years this was seen as the classic location and the early floras, following the descriptions of Turton and Gutch, gave its locality as 'Pennard Castle and rocks near' as though this was its sole location, which is simply not true. Such misinformation did protect the plant, however, as it resulted in collectors missing some of the best sites. Edwin Lees, for example, an astute amateur botanist from Worcester, wrote in *The Botanical Looker-Out* in 1842:

> The yellow Draba aizoides is now (March) in flower on its only known habitat in Britain, the deserted walls of the secluded fortalice of Pennard castle. Its singular aspect there will be noticed more in detail under the month of September at which time in 1839 I visited the spot. As it is an early flowerer it is an acquisition to any rockwork.

Yellow whitlowgrass belongs to the Cruciferae and the bright yellow flowers, which in some years may appear as early as the first week of March, have four free petals in the shape of a cross. It flowers freely in Gower, with about 90 per cent of plants flowering in any one year, and the potential for the population to expand is high. The fruits, however, which are set by the end of April, are often grazed heavily by snails, particularly brown-lipped snail *Cepaea nemoralis* and common snail *Helix aspersa*. In the more sheltered sites the snails can destroy the majority of the developing fruits before the seeds have matured, along with many flowers. When not damaged by snails the flowers can produce copious quantities of nectar and are open at a time of year when the only competing species for insect pollinators is gorse. Insects collected from whitlowgrass flowers near Overton in 1969 included the blowfly *Calliphora erythrocephala*, the hoverfly *Eristalis aeneus*, white-tailed bumblebee *Bombus lucorum*, red-shanked bumblebee *B. ruderarius* and early mining bee *Andrena haemorrhoa*.

Most of the plants grow in deep crevices in the limestone cliffs, forming cushions of compact leaf rosettes, although young specimens are often found in turf on thin soil around and below the primary cliff habitat. Their density is largely determined by the availability of suitable crevice sites and is commonly 1 to 5 plants per square metre. The species cannot regenerate from detached rosettes, because it cannot form adventitious roots and has no dormant buds. It also appears to be difficult for a seedling to survive for more than a few months near a well-established plant, but when an older plant dies it may be replaced by the growth of nearby seedlings surviving from the previous autumn. The light seeds are only spread a few metres from the parent plant and wider dispersal appears difficult. Yellow whitlowgrass is, for example, usually absent from apparently suitable habitats in former limestone quarries which have not been worked since the late nineteenth century, and the only walls it grows on are those of Pennard Castle.

Since 1987 whitlowgrass on the coast between Rhossili and Mewslade has been monitored on a regular basis. Its overall distribution has remained stable, but the counts have shown that there has been a slight decline, mainly of plants within easy reach of sheep, or of enthusiastic gardeners and collectors. On Pennard Castle there has been a 25 per cent decline since the early 1980s, with plants disappearing from the lower section of the walls. But there is no problem in growing it from seed, as it produces copious amounts and is self-fertile. Indeed it is better to grow native whitlowgrass than the imported continental material available from suppliers of alpine plants.

Yellow whitlowgrass is usually associated with a restricted plant community that includes three grasses, red fescue, sheep's-fescue *Festuca ovina* and cock's-foot

Dactylis glomerata, together with greater knapweed *Centaurea scabiosa,* salad burnet, Portland spurge *Euphorbia portlandica,* wild carrot *Daucus carota,* small scabious *Scabiosa columbaria* and wild thyme. This restriction to a narrow habitat and plant community is striking in view of the wide range of habitats that occur adjacent to the current populations.

VEGETATION MANAGEMENT

Despite the rich list of plants the first sight of the cliffs can be extremely disappointing. Grazing pressure from sheep along most of the south coast, especially the western end, is very high and as a consequence in places the turf is extremely short and many of the flowers eaten before they set seed (Fig. 48). In fact at the western end of the coast there is almost a total lack of flowers, despite the very high number of plant species present in the close-cropped grassland. The absence of flowers means that there are no pollen or nectar sources for the invertebrates. A reduction in grazing pressure would, in theory, help the conservation of the fauna enormously. Allowing higher vegetation to develop and more plants to flower would connect currently isolated sites, as more mobile species, such as bees and wasps, would forage more widely and have the opportunity to colonise new nesting areas. There is a clear gradient along the coast, ranging from cliffs dominated by long ungrazed scrub and bracken at the eastern end to severely overgrazed cliffs at the western end. Current sheep numbers are about three times higher than in 1866 if the data from parish returns are to be believed. Information drawn from the Rhossili Agricultural Returns suggests that sheep stocking levels dropped during the Second World War, but then increased rapidly to almost five times the number of grazing livestock units by 1984. This change reflects the improvement of grassland due to application of inorganic fertiliser.

In some areas the species composition resembles semi-improved grassland due to recreational pressure and proximity to improved pastures. This is particularly noticeable along the coast near Worms Head, where the effect is intensified by sheep lying up at night, which leads to localised heavy dunging in sheltered places. This issue of 'agricultural eutrophication' on the south Gower coast was the subject of a detailed study (Etherington and Clark, 1987) which focused on the stretch of cliff from Worms Head to Port-Eynon, part of which is common land. The conclusion was that since 1935 there had been a reduction in cover and abundance of prostrate species such as wild thyme, common bird's-foot-trefoil *Lotus corniculatus,* squinancywort *Asperula cynanchica,* common rock-rose and the rare hoary rock-rose, and an increase in agricultural weeds and

FIG 48. Sheep grazing on the Gower cliffs. Overgrazing of these slopes is a serious conservation issue. (David Painter)

perennial rye-grass. The increase in rye-grass is particularly dramatic as it was not present in 1935, but it is now a common component of the grassland. The deterioration of the botanical interest is due to an increase in the number of sheep grazing on the clifftop commons, coupled with the application of fertilisers to adjacent fields and certain areas of the grassland. These practices have led to an unparalleled increase in plant nutrients, both from inorganic fertilisers and from sheep urine and dung. The species that have declined cannot tolerate competition from tall, fast-growing species, which are favoured by the high nutrient levels.

Agricultural intensification east of Mewslade has long been of concern to conservation organisations, and several recent studies have been directed towards obtaining a clearer understanding of processes (Etherington and Clark, 1987; Dawson, 1989). Reseeding of clifftop grasslands and subsequent fertiliser applications have caused noticeable changes in semi-natural communities in many areas and there have been many negotiations with the graziers directed towards reducing these impacts. Such eutrophication is far less obvious within the National Nature Reserve and the places where it does occur are usually close to the areas used for stock feeding. Elsewhere, grazing continues to exert an impact by modifying the flora of the limestone grassland (bloody crane's-bill and greater knapweed are particularly sensitive to grazing) and by preventing a succession to gorse scrub in the more sheltered areas. In contrast Horton Cliffs and Slade Cliffs have valuable patches of limestone grassland, but parts of these are becoming scrubbed over, or are heavily grazed by horses and cattle, while at Slade Cliffs part of the common is regularly spread with manure. Cattle grazing is, however, a traditional form of management on the cliffs at Horton.

It is clear therefore that the cliffs are an unstable mixture of grassland, heathland and scrub that is maintained by a combination of grazing, burning and a harsh maritime climate. Relaxation of grazing is unlikely to lead to the succession proceeding beyond coastal scrub, but this would result in the loss of most of the grasslands except where these are located in an exposed position. It is likely that some communities of the lower cliff, such as the steeply sloping limestone grasslands, could be wholly maintained by existing physical and chemical factors due to their open and exposed character. Scrub communities on parts of the coast around Oxwich Point, for example, may have already reached a climax due to the effects of strong winds and salt spray, but there is likely to be scope for considerably more scrub development especially in areas such as Mewslade.

A recent survey of the area recommended that a comprehensive grazing plan should be developed in order to conserve the plants and insects of this very rich coastline. It has been difficult for the three conservation organisations that jointly own and manage the area, the National Trust, the Wildlife Trust and the Countryside Council for Wales, to tackle the issue because the situation is complicated by the land ownership. The most degraded areas are registered common land and are grazed by sheep owned by local commoners. There was an attempt in the early 1990s to address this issue through a trial reduction in grazing levels and it was hoped that lower overall stocking rates would provide sufficient herbage for the sheep, so that they would be less likely to graze the vegetation on the cliffs, but sadly the initiative did not get very far. In 1996, however, the Wildlife Trust bought back the agricultural rights associated with their property at Overton. Elsewhere in Gower the common rights must be strenuously protected, but given the seemingly insuperable problems here the removal of rights would, at least, restore the cliffs to their rightful glory. A reduction in overall livestock numbers, as a result of the reform of the Common Agricultural Policy since farmers are no longer being paid subsidies on the basis of the number of animals that they own, might, however, render this approach unnecessary.

Historically areas of gorse were burnt by the farmers who grazed sheep on the cliffs, as a means of promoting fresh, palatable growth and controlling scrub invasion. This burning still takes place during the winter months, but burns also occur in the dry summer months. Such events control the advance of scrub, and well-developed scrub communities are found only in situations that are well protected from fire such as old quarries or areas of scree. A severe burn can destroy the humus-rich topsoil together with all the microorganisms within it, leaving a sterile subsoil. The bare soil is susceptible to wind erosion, leading to the exposure of bulb and root systems and ultimately to the exposure of the limestone bedrock beneath.

Where areas of cliff vegetation burn the open exposed ground is colonised by a temporary but typical community of plants, scarlet pimpernel *Anagallis arvensis*, which often shows variable flower colours, cut-leaved crane's-bill *Geranium dissectum*, Yorkshire-fog, ox-eye daisy *Leucanthemum vulgare* and spring cinquefoil. The fire also activates the seeds of the gorse and these species then disappear as the gorse reinvades the area. A survey of nit-grass carried out in 1985 noted a positive association between the density of the species and previously burnt gorse stands (John, 1992). Effects on invertebrates are unknown, but such information as is currently available suggests that the size of the burn is an important factor regarding speed of recolonisation.

INVERTEBRATES

The mild climate and the wide variety of habitats combine to produce ideal conditions for invertebrates, and the peninsula's soft coastal cliffs have been known as a key location for bees, wasps and ants for many years. More than any other group of invertebrates they are under threat nationally due to the precise habitat requirements of many of the species, which make them very sensitive to environmental changes, and to the low population levels at which they normally occur. The ecological and economic importance of these insect communities cannot be overemphasised. The decline of bees, wasps and ants in the countryside is a reliable indicator of profound environmental poverty as they are a 'key piece in the environmental jigsaw and as they decline or become extinct at local or national levels so does a myriad of other organisms' (Fowles, 1996). It is therefore extremely important to conserve areas, such as Gower, that hold rich invertebrate faunas. Many nationally rare species occur in the peninsula, as well as many others that are extremely scarce in Wales. At the time of writing the Countryside Council for Wales and Liverpool Museum are about to complete a three-year study of the invertebrates of soft cliffs throughout Wales, ending with selected sites in Gower. More information may therefore be forthcoming in the near future.

The low cliffs of 'head' deposits from the last ice age are a noticeable feature of the coastline between Rhossili and Oxwich and occur less frequently from Pennard Burrows to Mumbles Head, where they tend to support more scrubby vegetation. The importance of the cliffs for insects relates to their capacity to provide a continuous supply of microhabitats rarely found elsewhere. The regular erosion of the crumbly soils creates areas of bare ground and maintains pioneer plant communities which can include large numbers of plants such as bird's-foot-trefoil, horseshoe vetch, kidney vetch *Anthyllis vulneraria* and hogweed *Heracleum sphondylium*. All these provide rich food sources for bees and wasps during the flight period and support large communities of plant-eating insects such as weevils. The bare areas supply nesting areas for bees and wasps and suitable hunting areas for ground beetles and spiders while seepages and pools provide the wet mud required by some species for nest building and refuges for insects with an aquatic stage in their life cycle such as craneflies. For instance the cranefly *Dicranomyia goritiensis* is known from coastal cliff seepages at Longhole Cliff. It has been agricultural policy in the past to bring as much land as possible into use and as a result the natural vegetation has in places been squashed into a narrow coastal belt. A small number of clifftop fields have therefore been included within a Tir Cymen agri-environment agreement and are managed as fallow or spring cereal and stubbles as an experiment to see if it is possible to increase the abundance and diversity of nectar sources in the vicinity of the soft cliffs.

Elsewhere in Gower there are few similar habitats, except for the west-facing solifluction terrace, 2 kilometres long, at the base of Rhossili Down. Despite its length it may be of less interest for insects, certainly in the southern part where the soft cliffs are mostly vegetated and stable and extremely heavily grazed by sheep. North of the Old Rectory, however, there is a rich leguminous sward, which is likely to support a varied invertebrate fauna, but this may be more similar to that of Llangennith Burrows than the typical Gower soft cliffs. The seepages and streams here provide a sharp contrast to the conditions on the south coast.

Some of the earliest invertebrate records are from Horton and concern the mining bees *Andrena rosae* and *Andrena marginata* noted in 1914 by Hallett, together with a nationally scarce 'nomad' cuckoo bee *Nomada flavopicta*. *Andrena rosae* nests in bare ground on light soils, including well-used paths, and possibly shares a communal nest entrance to its burrow with other females, as closely related species do. Its life history has not been studied in Britain and it is still unclear, for instance, which plant species are visited for pollen. The summer brood probably collects umbellifer pollen, but the spring brood might use a variety of early flowering plants. First-brood adults are on the wing between late March and the end of May, whilst the summer brood appears between mid-July and early

September. The bee was found again at Horton Cliff in March 2002, by P. M. Pavett from Cardiff Museum, but to date there have been no other records. Nomad bees, such as *Nomada flavopicta*, are wasp-like bees that are parasites of various mining bees; they do not actually feed on their hosts, but merely take the food that was intended for the host larvae. Like other cuckoo bees they have no pollen-collecting equipment.

More intensive surveys at Horton over recent years have shown that it continues to support a nationally important community of bees, including a nomad cuckoo bee *Nomada fucata* at one of its few locations in Glamorgan and long-horned eucera *Eucera longicornis*. There are also large colonies of long-horned eucera at the Sands and Fall Bay, with smaller populations scattered elsewhere. The south Gower coast may therefore be one of the most important British localities for this declining bee. The speciality of the Horton area, however, is a solitary mining bee, *Andrena hattorfiana*. Both males and females are the same size as worker honeybees, but are much darker. It was first reported in 1854 from Clyne Wood and there was evidently a colony established here as the associated cleptoparasite *Nomada armata* was also collected at the same time. It seems unlikely that the latter still occurs in Wales, but as the mining bee has recently been rediscovered here it would be worth surveying suitable localities along the coast. There were no further records of *Andrena hattorfiana* after 1854 until Hallett caught several females at Llangennith in 1921. After another long period without records P. M. Pavett collected two males on limestone grassland at Horton in 1993 and the species was also present there in 1995. The bee is dependent on the pollen of small scabious as the sole source of food for its overwintering larvae in their underground nests. Unfortunately the plant is extremely palatable to grazing animals and they often eat all the flowers.

The dotted bee-fly *Bombylius discolor* (Fig. 49) is mostly restricted in Wales to the short stretch of coast between Port-Eynon and Penmaen Burrows, with records from Horton Cliff, Overton Cliff and Overton Mere. This large species is easily distinguished by the spots on its wings and is on the wing from late March to mid-June, with numbers peaking in April. The bee-fly declined substantially in Britain during the 1960s and 1970s, mainly as a result of changing agricultural practices that destroyed its nesting sites and suitable flowers, although there was a limited revival in 1996 and 1997 in response to a sequence of hot summers. One of the best places to find the insect is on the cliff slopes a short distance to the east of Horton village. Little is currently known about this species, although it appears to be a parasite of some of the larger mining bees, probably *Andrena flavipes*, which are active in the spring. What is clear is that the bee-fly can only flourish in areas, such as the Gower coast, where large congregations of nesting bees are present.

FIG 49. Dotted bee-fly, a large species easily distinguished by the spots on its wings. (David Painter)

Other rare species found on the Horton cliffs include a mason cuckoo bee *Stelis punctulatissima*, which occurs only at only one other site in Wales (at Powys Castle Park) and a number of wasps including the spider-hunting or digger wasp *Priocnemis schioedtei*, a large red and black species that currently occurs nowhere else in Wales and whose prey includes sac or foliage spiders. In contrast solitary wasps such as *Cerceris arenaria* prey almost exclusively on weevils and the ground around their nesting holes is often littered with the bodies of the black vine weevil *Otiorhynchus sulcatus* and other related species. The weevil *Cathormiocerus maritimus* was found for the first time in Glamorgan in 2002 at Overton Cliff and Overton Mere.

Information on bees, wasps and ants from other parts of the south Gower coast is limited, but the low cliffs at Overton Cliff and Overton Mere support a number of bees including a brassy miner bee *Lasioglossum puncticolle* and *Hylaeus pictipes*, which, like the spider-hunting wasp, are found nowhere else in Wales, together with *Andrena hattorfiana* and *Nomada fucata*. The latter is a kleptoparasite of *Andrena flavipes*, which was incredibly abundant along the coast in June 2004 (Fig. 50). The ichneumon *Methocha ichneumoides* has been recorded from Common Cliff, Overton Mere and Overton Cliff, while the warmth-loving ant *Formica cunicularia* is often found along the coastal paths, with records from eight sites in

2002. Coastal footpaths can be important for burrowing insects as they provide patches of bare soil in sunny situations. The relief and aspect of the ground is also particularly important for ant species and the occurrence of the four common red ants of the genus *Myrmica* found on the Gower coast is related to this. *M. rubra* and *M. ruginodis* live in more thickly vegetated areas than *M. scabrinodis* and *M. sabuleti*, while *M. rubra* and *M. sabuleti* need warmer sites so they have more restricted distributions. If the cliff top is well vegetated *M. scabrinodis* may be absent.

The rare picture-winged fly *Myopites eximia* is associated with the splash-zone vegetation at the base of the cliff, developing in galls that it creates on the golden samphire. The gall is distinctive and the enlarged, hardened capitula, remaining above the basal leaves, are readily detected amongst the dead growth of the previous year. Galled capitula bear outgrowths that are the lignified walls of the attacked achenes standing out above the receptacle. Other insects characteristic of the area include the micro-moths *Epischnia banksiella*, whose larvae also feed on golden samphire, and *Coleophora ochrea*, the larvae of which feed on rock-rose.

Another moth whose larvae feed on rock-rose, in this case the withered and decaying leaves, is the silky wave *Idaea dilutaria* (Fig. 51). It is probably one of the most notable insects in the peninsula, being the only macro-moth present that

FIG 50. The mining bee *Andrena flavipes* that occurs in large, if compact, colonies and which was common on the south Gower coast in 2004, particularly on Horton Cliffs. (Jonathan Mullard)

FIG 51. The critically endangered silky wave moth, one of the most outstanding insects on the peninsula. (David Painter)

is listed in the *Red Data Book* and therefore recognised as critically endangered. The adult is quite plain in appearance, although as the common name suggests the wing surface has a silky sheen. Only three populations of this moth are known in Britain, one on the Great Orme in North Wales, another near Bristol and the one in Gower, which is by far the largest and most thriving. The silky wave occurs at six sites on the coast: the Knave, Overton Cliff, Overton Mere, Port-Eynon, the Sands and Oxwich Point. All of the sites are steep, south-facing areas of open calcareous grassland, and populations are confined to areas where grazing is light or absent. It used to be reported more widely in England and Wales, but some of the old records are misidentifications or the result of confusing changes of name in the past, so it may have always been a scarce species. Further research is needed on its ecology before there can be any confidence about its survival in this country, but the correct grassland management is obviously a key factor.

Additional species associated with rock-rose are the flea beetle *Aphthona herbigrada*, the seedbug *Macroplax preyssleri*, which is only known in Wales from Overton and Horton cliffs, and the nationally scare pollen beetle *Meligethes solidus*, recorded from Mumbles Head and Overton Mere.

The coastal juniper colonies support a characteristic fauna that includes juniper aphid *Cinara juniperi*, juniper shieldbug *Elasmostethus tristriatus* and two moths, juniper carpet *Thera juniperata* and juniper pug *Eupithecia pusillata*. In addition there are several species of micro-lepidoptera and flies that are known to be specific to juniper and which are internal feeders on the shoots, leaves, fruits and buds, but there have been no studies of these in the area so far.

Gower is also one of the twenty outstanding British localities for crickets and grasshoppers and related insects, with sixteen species having been recorded including grey bush cricket *Platycleis albopunctata*, Lesne's earwig *Forficula lesnei*, and tawny cockroach *Ectobius pallidus*. Species such as these, which are only found in the vicinity of the coast, still have a restricted distribution thought to result from the forest cover that was present when they arrived in Britain during the early postglacial period. For some reason they been unable to spread inland since the forest was cleared. Interestingly, on the continent they show no preference for coastal areas.

The grey bush cricket is a nationally scarce insect, but it can easily be found in Gower when active and calling in warm weather; it is harder to find when conditions are cooler. The colonies are at their peak between late July and September and in comparatively warm areas, such as the peninsula, a few individuals may persist into November. Lesne's earwig is also a rare and nationally scarce species that can be found in reasonable numbers in the area. It is particularly associated with old hedgerows or areas of scrub, especially where there is traveller's-joy or wild clematis *Clematis vitalba*, but this is by no means the only habitat and areas of tall herbage along the coast are also worth checking. Unlike the common earwigs it has much-reduced hind wings and so cannot fly. Areas of limestone scree along the coast support the mottled grasshopper *Myrmeleotettix maculatus*. This insect, whose song is said to resemble an old-fashioned watch being wound up, has a distinctive marbled appearance.

Cockroaches are a mainly tropical group of insects allied to the grasshoppers and crickets. While the most familiar species are those associated with human habitation, the three species of small native cockroaches are less well known. On the whole, these are secretive insects and much smaller than their larger, notorious cousins. Even the dusky cockroach *Ectobius lapponicus*, which is the largest, is only 11 millimetres in length. It is very difficult to distinguish adult females of this species from those of the tawny cockroach. The latter is found in a wide band across southern England, but only two colonies, the one in Gower and another recently discovered in Suffolk, are north of the Thames. Of the native species it is the least specific in its choice of habitat and can be found in woodland rides and clearings, in calcareous grassland, heathland and coastal dunes. More research is needed to determine the extent of the tawny cockroach in the peninsula and whether other species are also present.

Few butterflies are true species of coastal cliffs, but like the other insects they occupy a range of habitiats that provide an abundance of food and nectar plants and where the structural features of the vegetation provide suitable microclimates for larval growth, mating, egg laying and roosting. Species recorded from the coast include small blue *Cupido minimus*, there being a number of colonies where the larval foodplant kidney vetch is found, brown argus *Aricia agestis*, wall brown *Lasiommata megera*, grayling *Hipparchia semele*, small pearl-bordered fritillary *Boloria selene* and dark green fritillary *Argynnis aglaja*. Whereas the strongest populations of the small pearl-bordered fritillary are associated with the larger areas of common land the dark green fritillary is more of a coastal butterfly, although populations do occur inland in situations similar to those used by the former species. The adult dark green fritillaries have a preference for purple flowers as sources of nectar, such as knapweeds and thistles.

Notable beetles on the cliffs include three species in which the larvae feed and develop in the nests of bees and wasps, the rare *Metoecus paradoxus*, *Meloe prescarabaeus* and the oil beetle *Meloe violaceous*, which has been recorded from Slade. The oil beetle is so named because it can give off a strong-smelling liquid from a gland behind the head. In contrast to the other two species *M. prescarabaeus* is widespread on the Gower coast and larvae were abundant during 2003 and 2004. The Meloidae family are soft-bodied beetles with a narrow neck and often have short wing cases, which makes them relatively easy to identify in the field. They are of particular interest because of their complex life cycles, the early stages of the British species being parasites of solitary bees. In spring the female beetles lay several thousand eggs in the soil, in a number of different batches. The eggs soon hatch into tiny louse-like larvae, with strong claws, that crawl up onto dandelion heads and other spring flowers and await the arrival of the host insects. Only a small proportion find the right host and the unsuccessful larvae die. The success-ful ones are carried to the bee's nest, where they detach themselves and find an egg to eat. After this the larva feeds on the bee's food reserves of pollen and nectar, undergoing a series of moults before emerging as a mature adult. Other beetles found in the area include the bloody-nosed beetle *Timarcha tenebricosa*, which like the oil beetle also produces a fluid, the burying beetle *Necrophorus humator*, which buries carrion for its larvae to feed on, and the minotaur beetle *Typhaeus typhoeus*, which uses rabbit and sheep dung for its larvae.

Perhaps the most prominent beetle of the cliff grasslands, certainly during the late evening in June and July, is the glow-worm *Lampyris noctiluca*. Female glow-worms often appear a few days before the first male. The female usually begins to glow soon after dusk, which during the season is usually between 2200 and 2300 hrs. The display continues for two or three hours and if after that time the female has not been successful in attracting a mate she will stop glowing, retreat into the grass and return for another attempt the following night. The larvae feed almost exclusively on slugs and snails. Recent research has revealed that during the day the female tries to escape the light by using the abandoned burrow of a solitary bee, so it is important to conserve such bees if glow-worms are to survive in the peninsula. Dillwyn recorded in 1829 that glow-worms were 'not uncommon on dry hedgebanks; but the light is not so brilliant as it is on chalky soils, nor have I observed the small light in the males which is always sufficiently obvious about Dover [where he started his interest in natural history]. I placed some of these insects in oxygen, and could not detect any increase in their brilliancy.' There are only isolated reports of glow-worms on the Gower cliffs and elsewhere, and more work is needed to establish the size and location of populations. Indeed there is scope for further survey work on all the coastal invertebrates present in Gower, and in many cases more information on the life histories of species is also needed, in order that effective management strategies can be developed. Even now naturalists are only beginning to glimpse the intricate web that binds together invertebrates such as oil beetles, solitary mining bees, cuckoo bees and glow-worms, and there are undoubtedly more connections that need to be understood before the survival of these species can be assured.

REPTILES

The warm south-facing cliff slopes are also ideal for reptiles, and common lizard *Lacerta vivipara*, grass snake *Natrix natrix*, slow-worm *Anguis fragilis* and adder *Vipera berus* can all be found along the coast. Adders feed mostly on rodents and lizards, striking their prey to inject venom and then following the scent trail of the dying animal. They are most easily seen on dry cloudy days, when they need to bask to raise their body temperature. On a very hot and sunny day they might bask in the morning or evening sun, but they remain in the shade during the middle of the day. Elsewhere adders have declined in abundance since the 1960s, mainly because of habitat losses, but the populations in Gower have remained relatively strong. To date there have been no detailed studies of reptiles on coastal cliffs, but as they require dense ground cover, which in turn supports rich populations of insects and small mammals, the Gower cliffs are an ideal habitat. The Herpetological Conservation Trust is, however, coordinating a national adder census and if the project is a success it will become an annual count.

BIRDS

The Gower coast is an important area for scrub-nesting birds and these include linnet *Acanthis cannabina*, whitethroat *Sylvia communis*, stonechat *Saxicola rubetra* and yellowhammer *Emberiza citrinella*. The area is particularly noted for the extremely high density of breeding yellowhammers. The stonechat, which has its largest and most consistent populations in the maritime scrub land of the southwest of Britain, was listed in the *Swansea Guide* of 1802 and over 200 years later it is still a common sight on the cliffs, especially where there are gorse bushes. Feeding mainly on insects, worms and spiders, they are easy birds to see as they perch at the tops of bushes, where they give their distinctive call (Fig. 52). They breed densely on the coast and in some years there can be two or three pairs per kilometre. The cliffs near Worms Head and Common Cliff used to be of local importance for a small kittiwake *Rissa tridactyla* colony; this is no longer the main colony, however, as for some reason most of the birds disappeared from this location and took up residence on Mumbles Pier. Guillemots *Uria aalge* and razorbills *Alca torda* are also present. Other notable birds nesting on the cliffs are ravens *Corvus corax*, peregrine falcons *Falco peregrinus* and choughs *Pyrrhocorax pyrrhocorax*.

FIG 52. Stonechat, near Middleton, a common sight on the cliffs. (Harold Grenfell)

The chough was once a common breeding bird in Britain, but has declined steadily since the beginning of the eighteenth century and until recently was confined to Ireland, the west of Scotland, the Isle of Man and Wales. A few birds have, however, lately returned to their ancestral haunts in Cornwall. Up until the 1840s it bred regularly in Gower and Dillwyn considered it a fairly common bird. By the end of the nineteenth century, however, it had disappeared. The Reverend Davies noted in 1885 that 'The rocks which form part of this sandy cove [Three Chimneys in Broughton Bay] used to be frequented by a small colony of red-legged crows, the heraldic bird known as the chough but of late years they seem to have abandoned the place, as none have been seen here for some time.' One school of thought is that a succession of cold winters started the decline. The birds also suffered from indiscriminate shooting and trapping. Their feeding habits were unfortunate and as they searched in the clifftop grassland for invertebrates many were caught in rabbit traps, particularly after the introduction of the now illegal gin trap. A few of the trapped birds were kept as pets and Dillwyn records that 'My late friend, Mr Bowdler, of the Rhyddings, kept a tame one, which displayed the most extraordinary sagacity in pilfering and hiding whatever came in the way.' This is the man who 'bowdlerised' Shakespeare, by taking out all the 'rude' words and who stated, 'My object is to offer these plays to the public in such a state that they may be read with pleasure in all companies, and placed without danger in the hands of every person who is capable of understanding them.' Although criticised for tampering with Shakespeare's text, Bowdler deserves a certain amount of credit for making the plays well known to a wide audience. It is interesting to think that while he was editing the text he had to contend with an unruly chough. Many more choughs were sold for food. Sir John Llewelyn, Lord Swansea, recalled in 1900 that they had been sold in Swansea Market as 'Billy Cocks' and were 'much prized by French sailors as an article of diet'.

Following this decimation, from being a relatively common bird choughs became rare visitors to Gower. A family of four was seen in Caswell Bay in August 1944, and individuals were sighted in 1943, 1972 and 1974. It was not until 1990, however, that the first pair of choughs reappeared, and there was great excitement among local naturalists when the birds were seen prospecting for a nest site near Mewslade, but no nest was built. They usually begin breeding in late April, building a large cup-shaped nest of sticks, bound with grass stems and lined with wool or hair, in a cliff crevice or cave. Neither bird was ringed so their origin was unknown. Breeding was finally confirmed in 1991 (Fig. 53) when a pair produced three young, one of which was unfortunately taken by a peregrine immediately after leaving the nest hole. Following that date a pair, presumably the same birds,

FIG 53. Adult chough feeding the two surviving young in 1991, the first successful Gower brood since the late nineteenth century. (Harold Grenfell)

bred each year until 1994 and again in 1999. Unfortunately in 1995 a local farmer shot two birds near their breeding area, after which a number of conservation bodies set up the Gower Chough Group, to carry out annual surveys of the number of birds and their locations, in order to monitor the population.

Between 2000 and 2001 two pairs of choughs bred at Mewslade and Pennard and in 2002 a third pair nested at Pennard. Two different birds have attempted to breed at Bacon Hole, but although feeding at the nest site has been recorded no fledglings have been seen to leave the nest. The result of all this activity was seven birds fledged. At the last count there were fourteen choughs in Gower. They continue to nest in holes in the cliff and are therefore well protected from normal disturbance and predators. The Gower cliffs are a popular climbing area, however, and this activity could disturb the birds (Fig. 54). Climbing around Yellow Wall, and more recently the area around Bacon Hole, is therefore restricted. The restriction on Yellow Wall runs from 1 March to 15 August, and this long exclusion period is to allow time for a pair of birds to have a second attempt at breeding if the first fails. In the years when a successful brood is produced early the birds have usually left the nest by mid-June and climbing would not disturb them. The National Trust, who own the majority of the climbable Gower coastline, the Countryside Council for Wales and the British Mountaineering Council meet

FIG 54. Climber on the cliffs at Mewslade. (Harold Grenfell)

twice a year to discuss areas where climbing might disturb nesting birds or damage rare plants.

Only one set of fledglings has been ringed so not much is known about dispersal or survival, although one Gower-bred bird was reported at Stackpole on the Pembrokeshire coast. In addition a female ringed at Stackpole first bred in 2002 close to Bacon Hole and raised one chick. The female of the 1998 pair had been colour-ringed as a nestling at Castle Martin. There is obviously now some interchange of birds between Gower and Pembrokeshire, only a few miles apart across Carmarthen Bay. In fact there is generally a definite expansion of the chough's range in South Wales as birds are now also present at Dunraven Bay on the Glamorgan Heritage Coast to the east of the peninsula.

Food availability is one of the main factors influencing the breeding success of choughs in the peninsula and the maintenance of large areas of high-quality feeding habitat, rich in soil invertebrates, is extremely important for their survival. Choughs eat worms, caterpillars, ants and other insects such as beetles, particularly dung beetles. The birds like mainly short turf, less than 2 centimetres in height, together with open patches of bare ground. Microhabitats with large numbers of prey such as the yellow meadow ant *Lasius flavus* can be significant at certain times of the year. Populations of the ants occur at very high densities along much of the cliff line, being associated with undisturbed semi-natural grassland communities.

The peregrine falcon (Fig. 55) has continued to breed successfully on the cliffs since it returned to Gower in 1987, after a gap of 31 years, having been seriously affected at a national level by organochlorine pesticides eaten by its prey, usually pigeons. Prior to this populations in Gower had also been weakened by the Destruction of Peregrines Order of 1943. The peninsula was one of the areas identified where any person authorised by the Secretary of State for Air could take or destroy peregrines or their eggs. This was because 'it has been found that these birds are causing considerable losses among homing pigeons employed by the Royal Air Force and Army Pigeon Services.' In Gower, where there might have been two to four pairs before the decline, the bird returned later than elsewhere, but it is now once again securely established. Between 1987 and 1991 a pair bred annually, producing 13 young over the five years, including a brood of four in 1989. Recently there have been new sightings at Great Tor, with the possibility of a nest on the south face. Despite their extent, however, the cliffs have few potential nesting sites because most of them have a gentle slope; while on those that are vertical most of the ledges are too narrow. There is therefore limited scope for the creation of new territories and most of the young birds have left the peninsula. In north Gower the tors on the west coast supported breeding peregrines in the

FIG 55. Peregrine falcon at Mewslade, one of the classic areas for this species. (Harold Grenfell)

past, and offer the best prospects for the future, but to date the potential nest sites have not been occupied.

Peregrines generally choose the highest cliffs for nesting – that is those with the most commanding outlook and the best protection for eggs and young. Persecution of peregrine falcon chicks and eggs goes back at least 750 years and it has been suggested that the selection of nest sites has evolved as a response to human predation. Writing in his history of west Gower, published in 1894, the Reverend Davies says 'I should mention that Worms Head, and the Paviland Cliffs nearby, used to be a very noted place, as the haunt of the Peregrine Falcon; and some 20 or 30 years ago, a gentleman living in Gloucestershire, who followed the ancient sport of hawking, used to employ old Jeremiah Cox, one of Mr Talbot's Keepers, to procure him annually a pair of these young birds or their eggs.'

Ravens (Fig. 56) were once common throughout Britain, but like the peregrine a long history of persecution has restricted its range to the more remote and coastal regions. At one stage virtually all the gamekeepers and farmers in Glamorgan shot them as a matter of course. Thankfully a more enlightened approach developed and in 1907 the pioneer naturalist–photographer Richard Kearton took a picture of an adult raven on Pennard cliffs. The bird gradually

FIG 56. Raven calling and grasping turf with its bill. There are large young in the nest on the 'Patella beach' below, near Overton. (Harold Grenfell)

re-established itself during the early years of the twentieth century and in the 1950s about twelve pairs of ravens were breeding regularly in the Pennard area, mostly on the cliffs, but also on occasions in trees. They now breed at very high densities on the cliffs and occupy traditional territories, based on particular cliffs, or trees, that provide nest sites. Ravens have a varied diet; they will kill their own prey, usually small birds such as meadow pipits *Anthus pratensis*, but they also eat carrion and forage for eggs, reptiles, insects and seeds.

Green woodpeckers *Picus viridis*, the largest and most colourful of British woodpeckers, are a common sight on the Gower cliffs. They can often be seen feeding on the closely grazed turf, where they feed on ants and their larvae. The highest breeding numbers in Britain are in South Wales, as green woodpeckers are vulnerable to severe winter weather, which occurs relatively infrequently in this area, and they need high levels of sheep grazing to create the short turf they require for feeding.

A recent and exciting addition to the breeding birds on the coastal cliff slopes is the Dartford warbler *Sylvia undata*. The Dartford warbler is a relatively sedentary bird and is unusual among British warblers in not migrating for the winter. It is usually associated with dry heathland with mature heather and plenty of gorse, a habitat that is plentiful in the peninsula. In colder areas than Gower it runs the risk of starving to death in a severe frost when it cannot locate the insects on which it relies for food. The warbler is particularly associated with young gorse bushes as these have an abundant invertebrate fauna. In contrast mature bushes, which are hollow below the canopy and therefore contain fewer invertebrates, are not utilised by the birds. Gorse that is cut or burnt over a fifteen-year cycle, though, has been shown to provide an ideal habitat for Dartford warblers, and this is another factor that makes the Gower cliffs attractive to this species.

Dartford warblers were once found throughout southern England, but following a severe reduction in the bird's habitat it was rarely recorded outside Hampshire and Dorset until the mid-1990s. There is an interesting record, however, of an individual bird in Gower, at Langland in December 1969, and another individual was recorded in Singleton Park, Swansea, in April 1980. Two Dartford warblers were also seen during a survey of Llangennith Moors in 1991, but it was not until ten years later, in 2001, that the species was discovered breeding in the peninsula near Port-Eynon Point. More recently in 2003 there were sightings of birds at Rhossili. There has therefore been a clear westward expansion of its range in Wales. Growing numbers of native birds like the Dartford warbler, which used to stay close to the south coast, have now ventured northwards – and this is almost certainly due to global warming.

CHAPTER 6

The Surrounding Sea

You look out to sea, and even on the calmest days you can detect the sinister presence of the Helwick Sands by a line of darker blue. Once the wind blows they break white with foam.

Wynford Vaughan-Thomas, *Portrait of Gower*

I T IS IMPOSSIBLE to adequately describe the natural history of a peninsula without including the surrounding sea. The underwater environment, however, is an unfamiliar one to many naturalists due to the difficulties of access and the lack of research compared to terrestrial habitats. Marine ecosystems are also much simpler than terrestrial ones, not because they are less intricate, but because of the physical properties of sea water. These properties control the environment in ways for which there is no comparison in terrestrial communities. Waves, tides, currents, salinities, temperatures, pressures and light intensities for the most part determine the plants and animals that occur and these, in turn, have a major influence on the composition of sediments and the gases in solution.

The marine environment of Gower is greatly affected by the Severn Estuary. The Severn is one of our largest estuaries and because of its classic funnel shape, which is unique in Britain, it has the second highest tidal range in the world. Near Chepstow there is up to 14 metres between high and low tides. The vertical range around Gower is less, varying from about 4 metres on neap tides to over 9 metres on spring tides. To the east of Swansea the Bristol Channel is truly estuarine, the water has a very high silt content, and there is a limited range of plants and animals on the shore. Westwards though, around the peninsula, the water is highly saline and the intertidal fauna and flora is much more varied. Even so the shores still lack a proportion of the species that might be expected, partly because of occasional low surface salinities, but to a large extent because of the persistent high turbidity created by the large rise and fall of the tides. Such a high level of suspended sediment also reduces light penetration and the cloudy, silt-laden waters of the Bristol Channel therefore have a major influence on the types of communities present on the seabed.

There are many more species present in the waters around Gower than most people realise. Sharks, turtles, seals, porpoises, dolphins and even some of the larger whales have all been seen in the area and are an important part of this rich resource.

THE ROCKY SHORE

The features of Carboniferous Limestone shores are that they are very porous, eroded and pitted. The upper shore in Gower therefore tends to be very irregular, ridged, and fissured, becoming smoother lower down; extensive limestone platforms, once known as 'huvvers and scarras', are a characteristic of many sections of the coast (Fig. 57). Vaughan-Thomas (1983) mentions that 'This shelf is surprisingly wide in places – on Port-Eynon Point, for example, in Overton Mere

FIG 57. The extensive limestone platforms, known as 'huvvers and scarras', near Paviland. (Harold Grenfell)

and around Worms Head. I cannot think of any other section of the Welsh coast with quite the same type of feature.' The Intertidal Survey Unit of the former Nature Conservancy Council visited several stretches of the shore during the late 1970s and considered the area to be of primary biological importance, and more recently the Countryside Council for Wales has carried out a comprehensive study of the intertidal area.

The key species of rocky shores have a vertical zonation, which produces a distinctive banded appearance at low tide. A zone of lichens, a white barnacle zone and a zone of brown seaweeds dominate the upper, middle and lower shore levels respectively. The brown seaweeds are also separated, the channelled wrack *Pelvetia canaliculata* being highest on the shore, followed by the spiral wrack *Fucus spiralis*, and then the bladder wrack *Fucus vesiculosus*. The serrated wrack *Fucus serratus* is typical of the lower shore, while the lowest level of all is usually occupied by the oarweed *Laminaria digitata*. This pattern partly reflects the different degrees of tolerance to desiccation and submergence shown by the various species. The number of marine invertebrate species increases down the beach and barnacles and marine snails including periwinkles, top shells, dog-whelks and limpets are typical of the mid-shore. On the lower shore, these are joined by species less tolerant of desiccation such as sponges and sea firs. Various coastal birds feed on rocky shores at low tide and at high tide their place is taken by coastal fish.

The upper shore, which is only covered during high spring tides, is dominated by extensive bands of orange, grey and black lichens on the bedrock, with the orange lichen *Caloplaca marina* lying above a band of black tar lichen *Verrucaria maura* and associated species such as *V. amphibia* (Fig. 58). Marine animals characteristic of this zone, which hide in cracks and graze on the rocks, include the periwinkles *Melarhaphe neritoides* and *Littorina saxatilis*. A speciality of the Glamorgan coast is the small white woodlouse *Metatrichoniscoides celticus*, which lives beneath deeply embedded stones just above the high tide mark. Although naturally overlooked to some extent it does appear to be quite rare and most of the records are from the Gower cliffs. A few terrestrial insect species have also adapted to occupy air pockets in rock crevices in the intertidal zone and the Gower shores contain the very small (2.5 millimetres long) reddish-yellow ground beetle *Aepus robini*.

Below the lichen zone the majority of the shore is encrusted with the acorn barnacles *Chthamalus stellatus* and *C. montagui*, together with limpets. These grade into a lower zone dominated by the barnacle *Semibalanus balanoides*. In both of these zones there may be extensive common blue mussel beds within crevices and in areas between the bedrock. Lower down the shore mussels become even more dominant and can cover whole platforms. There are areas free of mussels,

FIG 58. Typically pitted and eroded limestone cliffs, with extensive areas of black tar lichen, at Mewslade. (Jonathan Mullard)

however, and in these serrated wrack occurs together with an understorey of red seaweeds. The species found in this understorey vary depending on the distance from low water and whether sand is present on the lower shore. High on the shore pepper dulse *Osmundea pinnatifida* occurs along with carragheen *Mastocarpus stellatus*, which has been used from about 1830 in herbal medicine as a treatment for lung complaints. Towards the lower shore more sand-tolerant red seaweeds can be found such as the red rose grass weed *Rhodothamniella floridula*, which forms distinct mats. Small hummocks of grass weed may also contain other smaller red and brown algae and species of worm and amphipod may burrow into the mat. Where sand scour is more severe, it may be rare or absent and ephemeral green seaweeds such as grasskelp *Enteromorpha* spp. and laver *Porphyra umbilicalis* dominate the substratum.

Laver, which is still collected locally to make laver bread, can be found throughout the intertidal area. Charles Frederick Cliffe in *The Book of South Wales* (1850) records in a footnote that 'seaweed bread or Laver cake if not one of the delicacies is one of the edible curiosities of the Gower Coast. In Gower and Swansea seaweed is rather a popular article of food, women attend Swansea market with baskets of laver cakes, which are sold at 1d. or 2d. each. It is got close to low-watermark, washed well in sea water to free it from sand, then boiled 12 hours and seasoned with salt.'

On the vertical sides of rock platforms there are communities of sponges, sea squirts, red algae and bryozoans (moss animals). In some locations the platforms can be almost completely covered by sponges such as breadcrumb sponge *Halichondria panicea* (Fig. 59), boring sponge *Cliona celata* and *Hymeniacidon perleve*. In the shaded areas of overhangs there tend to be more red algae such as *Ceramium virgatum*, a small red seaweed growing up to 30 centimetres tall, often on the stipes and fronds of larger seaweeds.

Particularly characteristic of the lower shore are the limestone boring species including the small anemone *Fagesia carnea* and the sponge *Cliona celata*, which appears above the rock surface as small yellow spots. The area also attracts large numbers of the common starfish *Asterias rubens* (Fig. 60), which often has the amphipod *Pariambus typicus* clinging to its upper surface; this was first recorded in Britain on the Gower coast. Under the rock overhangs at extreme low water a variety of sponges occur, including the purse sponge *Grantia compressa* and the syconoid sponge *Sycon ciliatum*. The latter prefers more sheltered conditions than the purse sponge, but both are seen in the greatest numbers during the autumn. Stunted white growths of deadman's fingers *Alcyonium digitatum* are quite frequent under these overhangs, together with various sea squirts upon which the spotted cowrie *Trivia monacha* feeds. Other species that occur on the lower shore include

FIG 59. Breadcrumb sponge, a common species in the intertidal zone. (Margaret Hodge)

the isopods *Dynamene bidentata* and *Gnathia maxillaris*. In drier crevices around the mid-tide level these are replaced by a sea slater *Sphaeroma serratum*, which is particularly abundant on the Worms Head causeway.

Often associated with the sea firs and bryozoans on rock surfaces and seaweeds are the sea spiders. Twelve of the eighteen or so British species have been recorded on the Gower shores. The most frequently found species are *Nymphon gracile*, *Nymphon rubrum*, *Endeis spinosus*, *Achelia echinata* and *Achelia longipes*, with the first two being the most abundant. *Nymphon gracile* occurs highest on the shore in the spring and summer, being found particularly on the hydroid *Dynamena pumila* that grows abundantly on serrated wrack, while *Achelia echinata* occurs in very sheltered, detritus-covered situations on the sea mat *Crisia eburnea*.

Although it grows on the lowest part of the shore, oarweed was cut traditionally on the south Gower coast and used as manure for the fields. 'A common of Oar growing in the sea' was recorded in 1673 at Bishopston, so it seems that its cutting and carting was carefully regulated. Similarly the Rector of Port-Eynon noted in 1801: 'Seaweed in great plenty, which is used for wheat and barley.' Oarweed was in fact cut almost to within living memory. At spring tides the shore bug *Aepophilus bonnairei* can also be found in this zone. It is a typical land-based bug with long antennae, but it actually lives below sea level, in little cracks in the rock where there are air pockets. This is the only time the bug is actually found on the land and it appears at the extreme low water mark and wanders around in the oarweed. It scavenges for animal material, such as dead or dying copepods.

FIG 60. Common starfish, which frequently has the amphipod *Pariambus typicus* on its upper surface. The first British record of this latter species was from Gower. (Margaret Hodge)

ROCK POOLS

On some sections of the coast, such as that between Port-Eynon and Oxwich Point, there are extensive rock pools. The smaller shallower pools support large areas of the common coralline seaweed *Corrallina officinalis* and other algae such as the brown seaweed *Dictyota dichotoma* and the red seaweed *Gelidium latifolium*. In contrast, large and deep pools are dominated by *Ceramium rubrum*, a very common red seaweed, on the middle shore, and by sea oak *Halidrys siliquosa* on the upper shore. These pools are also the home of amphipods such as *Gammarellus homari*, *Apherusa jurinei* and *Nototropis swammerdami*. Pools on the lower shore contain the prawns *Hippolyte varians*, *Thoralus cranchi* and the common prawn *Palaemon serratus*. In the middle shore pools the latter overlaps with the closely related *Palaemon elegans*, which is the only prawn found in the highest pools. Unlike *P. serratus*, which migrates offshore in winter, this species remains on the shore all year. At the top of the shore within the lichen zone pools may also support green algae such as *Enteromorpha* spp. and sea lettuce *Ulva lactuca*. All of the pools contain areas of sponges.

The shallow pools on the tidal causeway that links Worms Head with the mainland contain a variety of sea anemones, while in the deeper ones there is an astonishing range of unusual seaweeds and even seasonal specialities, such as octopus *Octopus vulgaris* and spider crabs. A particularly noteworthy resident is the tiny brooding cushion-starfish *Asterina phylactica*, only 1.5 centimetres across, that is otherwise only known from a very few localities in Pembrokeshire and north Cornwall. There is a star-like pattern of darker brown or green pigment along the centre of the arms and paler areas between the arms. As this species was only recognised recently, little is known about it.

The commonest fish in the pools are the blennies, particularly the shanny *Lipophrys pholis*, which emerges at high tide to forage over the shore. An adaptable species, it is also often found around artificial structures such as piers. The rare Montagu's blenny *Coryphoblenniuus galerita* can also be found on occasions. Common lobsters *Homarus gammarus* again occur in many of the pools, while sheltering under boulders low on the shore are most of the common British crabs. There is a great tradition of 'crabbing' in Gower, recorded eloquently by Vaughan-Thomas, but although some still goes on today it is not as it was. 'For the old crabbers respected skill and kept bright the names of the great men and women of the past, like Billy Hopkins of Port-Eynon, who had the reputation of going crabbing by moonlight, and Kitty "Crabs" of Oxwich ... They knew every hole, almost by name, some of them with strange histories.' The long spur of rocks beyond the Shipway, near Worms Head, for example, is known as the Crabart. Crabbers used a 'crabbing hook', a small hook at the end of a pole, to persuade the crabs and lobsters to leave their hiding places under the rocks and in the pools. The best hooks were known as 'penny-benders' because an old-fashioned penny coin could fit exactly inside the curving point of the hook.

OFFSHORE

The main underwater features of the Gower coast are a series of limestone ridges and gullies between Mumbles and Pwlldu Head with rich seaweed and animal turf, sand-inundated seaweed communities in the shallow water of Oxwich Bay, the wreck of the *Strombus* and other wrecks in Oxwich Bay, the mussel-dominated seabed between Port-Eynon and Worms Head, and the sandy sediments of Carmarthen Bay. Offshore the Helwick Bank, a long, shallow subtidal sandbank, is unusual in being very exposed to wave and tidal action. The only published studies relating to the subtidal area to date are those carried out by the Field Studies Council (Hiscock, 1979), when 21 sites were dived between Worms Head and Mumbles Head, and a 1995 survey carried out as part of the Seasearch Project, which involves volunteer divers recording information about the seabed and associated marine life (Bunker & Hart, 2002). There have been other limited studies of Carmarthen Bay and a fuller survey of the area was carried out in 1998 as part of a South West Wales Survey. This study will be published as part of the National Museum of Wales BIOMÔR reports series (Mackie, 2003). It did, however, confirm that areas of sediments in relatively shallow waters within Carmarthen Bay support a range of species including bivalves, amphipods and worms, many of which spend their time wholly or partly buried in the sediment. Both Carmarthen Bay and Helwick Bank provide a rich food source for birds and fish.

In the centre of the Bristol Channel south of Gower, extensive areas of the seabed are only covered with a thin layer of gravel, and to the east bedrock is exposed on the seabed. Subtidal bedrock does not extend more than a few hundred metres offshore except at East Helwick, where bedrock slopes away into deep water. The deeper-water rock communities off East Helwick have not been studied in any detail.

The coast to the west of Mumbles Head and around Pwlldu Head is exposed to both wave action and tidal streams. A shallow forest of northern kelp *Laminaria hyperborea* leads to low-lying bedrock with a rich mixed turf of red seaweeds and animals, including sponges. These red seaweeds include flat tentacle weed

Calliblepharis ciliata, iridescent ruffle weed *Cryptopleura ramosa*, cock's comb *Plocamium cartilagineum*, Irish moss *Chondrus crispus* and dulse *Palmaria palmata*. Due to the silty conditions seaweeds do not grow very deep. The northern kelp for instance extends only down to 1 metre below chart datum, compared with around 10 metres in west Pembrokeshire. Below this a turf of red seaweeds descends to 3 or 4 metres below chart datum and lower down animals dominate the communities. The water, however, is rich in food and some species, such as the common blue mussel and the subtidal reef sandworm *Sabellaria spinulosa*, thrive in these conditions.

The common names of sponges and sea squirts are usually fairly descriptive, being often named by divers rather than biologists, and animals present amongst the red seaweed turf include guarded flask sponge *Scypha ciliata*, golf ball sponge *Tethya aurantium*, white spiky sponge *Dysidea fragilis*, white hedgehog sponge *Polymastia mamillaris* and orange wisp sponge *Esperiopsis fucorum*. Sea squirts recorded from the area include the star sea squirt *Botryllus schlosseri*, light bulb sea squirt *Clavelina lepadiformis* (Fig. 61) and orange spot club sea squirt *Palladium punctum*.

There are a number of gullies, which provide a multiplicity of habitats for marine organisms. The gully sides are dominated by animals, including sponges, sea firs such as *Nemertesia antennina*, small colonies of deadman's fingers and

FIG 61. Tubeworms and light bulb sea squirts, one of many sea squirts recorded from the area. (Paul Kay)

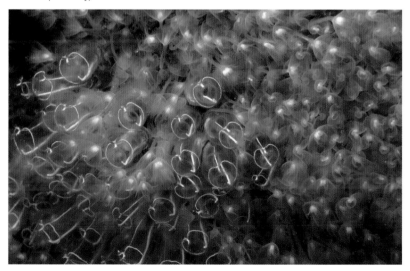

FIG 62. Dahlia anemone, one of the most colourful species found offshore. (Paul Kay)

dahlia anemones *Urticina felina* (Fig. 62). Sea squirts are again numerous and include the star sea squirt, light bulb sea squirt and the no spot sea squirt *Morchellium argus*. The bottoms of the gullies are colonised by species tolerant of the scouring effect of the tides such as jelly fingers *Alcyonium diaphanum* and horn wrack *Flustra foliacea*. The crevices and overhangs also provide shelter for the edible crab *Cancer pagurus*, velvet swimming crab *Liocarcinus puber*, common lobster and spiny spider crab *Maia squinado*. A common fish familiar to divers, the tompot blenny *Parablennius gattorugine*, also occurs in this area. It is a medium-sized fish that feeds on small invertebrates, including sea anemones.

In contrast to the rest of the coastline, Oxwich Bay provides a degree of shelter from wave action and tidal streams. The bay is only about 10 metres deep and the seabed is mainly sandy. Inshore, shallow bedrock is occupied by sand-tolerant seaweeds and mossy clumps of red rose grass weed occur together with larger species including little forked worm weed *Furcellaria lumbricalis*, slender red filament weed *Gracilaria gracilis* and red bottlebrush weed *Halurus equisetifolius*. Animals include common lobster and common shore crab *Carcinus maenas*. Conspicuous species in the shallow sandy areas include sand mason worms *Lanice conchilega*, razor shells and hermit crabs. Patches of mussels are widespread, as is the white horseshoe worm *Phoronis hippocrepia* and various sea squirts.

The *Strombus* and other wrecks in Oxwich Bay provide substrates raised above the generally low-lying and sediment-covered rock on the seabed and therefore support species that are not found elsewhere along the coast, or which are uncommon in other locations. These include the spiny antler sponge *Raspailia hispida*, white hedgehog sponge and plumose anemone *Metridium senile*. The *Strombus*, in particular, is the only known Gower locality for Devonshire cup coral *Caryophyllia smithii* and is also frequented by large conger eels *Conger conger* and by ocean triggerfish *Balistes balistes*. The ocean triggerfish was once a rare summer visitor to the area, but now breeds in the Bristol Channel, probably as a result of the warmer temperatures. The upper surfaces of this wreck, which lies in shallow water to the south of Oxwich Bay, are covered in foliose seaweed, including equally divided net weed *Dictyota dichotoma*. Conspicuous animals on the wreck include spike barnacle *Balanus crenatus*, rosy feather-star, candy-striped flatworm *Prostheceraeus vittatus* and bird's head coralline *Bugula turbinata*.

To the west of Oxwich Bay, between Port-Eynon and Worms Head, the coast is again more exposed. Much of the bedrock on this section has a dense covering of common blue mussels, which provide food for the common starfish. Large mussels tend to be found only in depths shallower than 3 metres; below this depth the beds are full of small individuals. Although mussels far outnumber any other species in terms of numbers and biomass the area is very species-rich, with many other organisms present in low numbers. The richness of the fauna associated with mussel beds in intertidal areas is well documented and the same seems to be true on the subtidal rock. Mussel beds are in fact among the most productive habitats on earth, often rivalling the productivity of tropical rainforests and kelp beds, due to their complex three-dimensional structure. They can often reach a considerable thickness and both the living and dead mussel shells increase the surface available for colonisation.

Mobile organisms move freely through the complex matrix of shells and interconnecting byssus threads, by which mussels attach themselves to hard surfaces. These species include common lobsters, bib *Trisopterus luscus*, ballan wrasse *Labrus bergylta*, pollack *Pollachius pollachius*, an anglerfish *Lophias piscatorius*, the uncommon ghost sea slug *Okenia adspersa* and the orange and black spotted sea slug *Thecacera pennigera*. There are large numbers of the latter at Mumbles and it is thought to be an introduced species that has developed a self-sustaining population.

At the time of the 1978 survey large populations of common starfish were present on the mussel beds, and at some sites there was a distinct line of densely packed animals working its way across the bed, leaving dead mussel shells behind. Where the mussels have been removed, by starfish or other agencies, blue-mouthed red sea squirts *Polycarpa scuba* occur along with a range of other species including *Taonia atomaria*, *Obelia dichotoma* and *Sertularia argentea*. Anemones include the cave-dwelling anemone *Sagartia troglodytes*. The anemone uses its tentacles to prey upon small shrimps and crabs. In turn it is preyed upon by the grey sea slug *Aeolidia papillosa* and the tompot blenny. Colour is not a good method of identifying sea anemones, and this is especially the case with *Sagartia*, which is more variable in colour than any other British sea anemone. There are two forms, a large form (*decorata*), which is typically up to 50 millimetres across the base and 100 millimetres tall, and a small variety (*ornata*) that is frequent amongst rocks or mussels; this form is usually green or brown and rarely exceeds 15 millimetres across its base.

OYSTERS

Like the common blue mussel, another bivalve mollusc, the native or flat oyster *Ostrea edulis*, also has a typical range of species associated with it. The polychaete worm *Polydora ciliata* burrows into the shell, weakening it and increasing the oyster's vulnerability to predation and physical damage, whereas the related *Polydora hoplura* causes shell blisters. Boring sponges *Cliona* spp. may also weaken oyster shells by boring into them, especially in older specimens

One of the earliest records of the oyster at Mumbles relates that Oystermouth villagers used to eat them on a regular basis and that children were fed oysters from a very early age as a cheap and easily obtainable supplement. The oyster beds were worked for their own needs until the early 1800s, when the skills of the villagers were improving and the size of the settlement was growing. More boats were being used and their catch was increasing as people had begun to recognise the potential demand for oysters. By 1830 the oysters were being sold along the South Wales coastline and were transported as far as Bristol. Transporting oysters over these distances required temporary storage and the oyster fishermen overcame the problem by building shallow holding pens called 'perches' in the intertidal shallows where they could hold a week's catch alive, in natural conditions, until an order could be met. Good examples of these can still be seen on the beach in front of the Salthouse at Port-Eynon. Each man's perch was safe from theft, protected by an unwritten agreement among the villagers. The fishing period ran from the beginning of September until the end of April. The oyster spawning months ran from May until August and the fishermen would rigidly adhere to this rest period. As in most fisheries, however, as trade increased larger boats were used, and the small rowing boats were replaced by larger sailing boats in the mid nineteenth century. The new boats increased the yield substantially and the industry appeared indestructible. In the 20 years between 1850 and 1870 Swansea and Gower experienced an oyster boom. The boats in Swansea alone were bringing in around 4,000 oysters per boat per day and the fishermen were making a lot of money. In 1871 when the trade peaked 10 million oysters were landed, fetching £50,000, and there were 600 men employed in the trade.

The quality of the oyster, the amount of money being made and the huge increase in demand as the fame of the shellfish spread began to cause problems. Boats arrived from London, Bristol and Liverpool and too many fishermen flooding what had been a very lucrative market began to cause a small, but steady, decline in the prices. By 1886 the trade had reached its lowest ebb with prices hitting rock bottom, to the point where the fishermen were struggling to make a living. By 1890 the few fishermen still operating were bringing in catches of only 200 oysters. The fishery continued at this level until, in 1920 and 1921, the flagellate protozoan *Heximata* spp. infected the oyster beds, causing mass deaths. Many populations did not recover and this effectively ended the industry, although one or two boats persevered until 1930, more as a pastime than for employment. Although the oyster beds still exist they remain depleted. Recovery of the populations is dependent on larval recruitment since the adults are permanently attached and incapable of migration. This is sporadic, depending on local environmental conditions and the presence of suitable substrates, especially adult shells or shell debris. At present it seems that the oyster beds will never improve significantly.

A recent survey of the two remaining oyster beds in Wales found oysters in many sites in the Milford Haven waterway in Pembrokeshire and none in Swansea Bay. Despite this result there are oysters present, but they are in low numbers, making them harder to find. Over-fishing, pollution and poor reproduction has brought about a devastating decline in the population.

MARINE CAVES

Marine, or littoral, caves form special environments within rocky shores and Britain has the most varied and extensive sea caves on the Atlantic coast of Europe. The communities present in caves vary considerably depending on the structure and extent of the cave system, the degree to which they are submerged and the exposure to scour, turbidity and surge, and their geology. Although the walls and roof are constructed of hard rock, the floor of the cave can either be soft or hard. Caves on the shore and in the shallow sublittoral zone are continually subject to wave action and therefore tend to have floors of coarse sediment and boulders that move and scour the inside of the cave. In Gower there is a high sand table and much of the inside of the marine caves, such as Bob's Cave under Mumbles Head (Fig. 63), tends to be worn by sand and therefore inhospitable to animals and plants. Where there is less sand, caves are typically colonised by encrusting animal species, and often support shade-tolerant seaweeds in the 'twilight zone' near their entrances. The caves themselves vary in size, from only a few metres in depth to more extensive systems, which may extend a considerable distance into the rock. While the Countryside Council for Wales has carried out several surveys of sea caves along the North Wales shoreline there has yet been no similar survey of the Gower coast and it is quite likely that a number of small, but species-rich, caves will be discovered by divers.

Caves in deeper water are subject to fewer disturbances and may have silt on the floor. The sponges *Dercitus bucklandi* and *Thymosia guernei*, solitary ascidians, bryozoans and the sessile larvae of jellyfish are characteristic of these deeper caves. Small deep caves also provide shelter for crabs and lobsters.

FIG 63. Bob's Cave under Mumbles Head, a large sea cave scoured by sand. (Margaret Hodge)

HELWICK BANK

The Helwick Bank, a linear sandbank aligned east–west, lies to the west of Port-Eynon Point, about 4 kilometres south of Worms Head. The Reverend J. D. Davies in his history of West Gower (1894) noted that 'At low water during extraordinary spring tides, I have been told that pilots have been known to jump from a boat on these sands and that these have been seen almost dry.' He goes on to record an ancient tradition with respect to the 'Helwicks', 'that there was once a road along these sands and that pieces of iron horse's shoes have been dredged up'. Davies also notes that 'Hele is an old Anglo Saxon word still in use and means to cover something up: to "hely potatoes" is a very common expression in Gower, also "to hely up the head", i.e. to cover it up with a whittle (a woollen shawl) or handkerchief.'

Subtidal sandbanks such as Helwick Bank are the result of relatively high energy conditions. As such they will be naturally disturbed by large changes in sea state, caused for example by storms. The animal communities found in and on Helwick Bank reflect the exposed conditions, being generally tolerant of high levels of disturbance. The first biological sampling of the Helwick Bank occurred during the late 1970s (Tyler & Shackley, 1980). This study was an investigation of the biology of the linear sandbanks on the north coast of the Bristol Channel and was not a specific study of the Bank, although samples were taken from it. It was not, however, a survey of an undisturbed environment, but represented a study of an area which at that stage had already been subjected to between 20 and 30 years of aggregate extraction. Unfortunately there are no biological data for the Helwick Bank and the adjacent seabed before dredging began. A very limited field survey was carried out in 2000, as part of the monitoring of dredging operations, to identify seabed habitats and the types and numbers of animals present. In 2001 a new joint survey involving the Countryside Council for Wales, the National Museum of Wales and the University of Wales at Bangor provided the first quantitative data on the invertebrate life associated with Welsh sandbanks, including Helwick Bank (Darbyshire et al., 2002). Although the 2001 survey found that the range of invertebrates in the sandbanks was generally lower than that of the coarser sediments nearby, the animals associated with the sandbanks often formed distinct groupings.

The seabed sediments of the Helwick Bank area are uniform, medium-grained sands with little or no fine or organic material. Sand-waves are present along its flanks, indicating that sand transport is occurring. To the south an area of megaripples (large ripples of sand on the seabed surface) merges to the west with an area of sand-waves and gravelly sand. Extensive research over the past 30 years has shown that the predominant sand transport pathway under the normal tidal regime south of the Gower coastline is towards the west. At the eastern end there is a link with the Port-Eynon subtidal area. Under particular weather conditions, for example during southwesterly storms, sediment will travel into the embayment, and into Port-Eynon Bay. Normally, however, sediment will tend to move out from the bay towards the south and west.

The shallow sandy sediments are colonised by a burrowing fauna of worms, crustaceans, bivalve molluscs and echinoderms. Mobile animals at the surface of the sandbank include shrimps, gastropod molluscs, crabs and fish. Sandbanks such as Helwick are also important nursery areas for fish such as sand eels *Ammodytes* spp., which are an important component of marine food webs. They prey on the eggs and larvae of other fish and crustaceans and themselves form a significant part of the diet of many of the commercially important fish species harvested in and around the Helwick Bank, including sea bass *Dicentrachus labrax*, and a number of species of flatfish. They also provide food for a number of seabirds and the Bank is therefore a key feeding ground for species such as puffins *Fratercula arctica* and razorbills and especially common scoter *Melanitta nigra*.

Studies have shown that large numbers of molluscs, echinoderms and crustaceans can be killed or damaged by dredging operations, together with extremely large numbers of the burrowing sand eel. The long-term impact of the dredging operations is difficult to determine, however. In 1996 a local dredging company applied for permission to extract 200,000 tonnes per year from the Helwick Bank for a ten-year period. This application represented both a continuation of existing practices and an increase in the sand that might be removed. A five-year licence was granted in 1998 to extract 150,000 tonnes per annum and in 2003 the company was granted a two-year extension to their licence. The extension permits the company to extract up to 214,000 tonnes of sand at no more than 107,000 tonnes in a year. There is intense local concern that the dredging might interrupt the movement and exchange of sediment between the shoreline and the seabed and that the dredging might reduce the protection given to the shore by the Helwick Bank.

Within Carmarthen Bay there are also several other smaller sandbanks in relatively shallow waters that support a range of species (including bivalves, amphipods and worms), many of which spend most of their time wholly or partly buried in the sediment. The Mixen Sands stretch westward from Mumbles Head and are marked by a bell buoy, but there are no records of the species that may be found there. In stormy weather, as with the Helwick, the sea can be seen breaking over the sandbank.

CARMARTHEN BAY

Carmarthen Bay contains a complex of unusually diverse marine habitats and associated species, including habitats important for migratory fish and migratory and wintering bird species. There is a wide range of seabed types, including mud, sand and rock, although fine sand characterises the majority of the seabed from Caldey Island in the west to Worms Head in the east. The bay, with its adjacent estuaries, sandbanks and extensive salt marshes, is one of the most varied stretches of coastline in the UK. It is designated as a Special Area of Conservation under the EC Habitats & Species Directive, and is a Special Protection Area under the EC Directive on the Conservation of Wild Birds, mainly because of the numbers of common scoter that occur here. In Britain this diving duck is considered a nationally threatened species because of its small and declining breeding population. Despite an estimated 20,000 individuals overwintering in Carmarthen Bay, by far the most significant British site for this species, there are only 200 pairs breeding in Britain and Ireland. The scoter is unusual among ducks in that the male is almost black, with only an orange-yellow patch on its bill. The female is dark brown with pale cheeks.

The bay encloses a wide range of rich and diverse marine habitats, species abundance and richness being strongly influenced by the prevailing wave and tidal regimes, with the eastern side of the bay, particularly Rhossili Bay, being open to the full force of the prevailing southwesterly swell. Two very similar animal communities have been identified in the bay, the first corresponding to areas where there are stronger tidal flows, increasing wave height and correspondingly coarser, cleaner sediments with a generally low species diversity, and a second community with a high species diversity which is dominated by deposit feeders. This second community can be divided again due to differences in abundance and diversity into two groups, one related to areas containing fine material and mud and one related to areas of clean fine sand.

The larger fauna of the seabed typically consists of the deposit-feeding polychaete worms *Spiophanes bombyx*, *Magelona* spp. and *Spio* spp., the amphipods *Perioculodes longimanus*, *Pontocrates arenarius* and *Bathyporeia* spp. and the bivalves *Mysella bidentata*, *Chamelea gallina* and *Fabulina fabula*. The latter species is an important food item for the common scoter. In areas of stronger tidal flows, increasing wave height and correspondingly coarser and cleaner sediments, such as off Rhossili, sedentary animals like the thin-shelled *Fabulina fabula* and the fragile tube-dwelling polychaete *Spiophanes bombyx* are much reduced and instead *Nereis cirrosa* and the cumacean *Pseudocuma longicornis* are present. The cumacean, a minute bottom-living, somewhat scorpion-like crustacean, is an active burrower in the upper few centimetres of sediment and is also highly mobile, making it well adapted to a constantly changing sand habitat. The burrowing crab or masked crab *Corystes cassivelaunus* is also a conspicuous species in this habitat, being adapted to the same conditions; it can also be found along the beaches (Fig. 64).

The brittlestars *Ophiura ophiura* and *Amphiura brachiata* occur in large numbers in the bay together with the large starfish *Asterias rubens* and *Astropecten irregularis*. Molluscs include the small opisthobranch *Philine aperta*, the common whelk *Buccinium undatum* and the dog-whelk. Cuttlefish *Sepia officinalis* are also present. Cuttlefish have an interior shell that is called a cuttlebone, and these are frequently washed ashore onto the Gower beaches. They are chambered and filled with gas that acts as a buoyancy control.

Despite the protected status of Carmarthen Bay, its seabed communities are currently under serious threat from the development of an unsustainable fishery. Local and international fishing-industry interests are eager to deploy hydraulic fishing gear to harvest razor shells for sale overseas. The hydraulic blade dredge is generally regarded by marine ecologists as one of the most destructive fishing methods, because of the harm it causes to soft-sediment areas. It operates by

FIG 64. The burrowing or masked crab, a common animal of the sandy seafloor and beaches. (Margaret Hodge)

directing water jets into the seabed in order to liquefy the sediment; suspending the shellfish in a slurry that is then sieved by the mesh of the dredge. Hydraulic dredges are an efficient method of harvesting shellfish, but have been found to seriously disturb benthic invertebrates and redistribute the sediment habitat. Unfortunately the area is not alone in being threatened by expanding shellfish fisheries; a similar situation exists in St Brides Bay, Pembrokeshire.

All these operations are licensed by the South Wales Sea Fisheries Committee, under whose jurisdiction these areas of seabed fall, but local naturalists are seriously concerned that the fishing interests are being given precedence over conservation issues, and legal action is currently being proposed at a European level to stop the dredging.

FISH AND FISHERIES

Fish species recorded from Carmarthen Bay include solenette *Buglossidium luteum*, sole *Solea solea*, plaice *Pleuronectes platessa* and dab *Limanda limanda*. Some of these were recorded by Isaac Hamon, who noted that 'along this coast there are these sort of fish taken or to be taken (viz) Salmon, hering, suen, cod, mackrell, plais, millet, sole, flooke, flawnders, Thornback, Skate, Whiting, Turbut, hawk, Conggereeles, bowman, bream.' Some 300 years later inshore fisheries are still well established in the area, with boats launching mainly from Burry Port, Swansea and Oxwich Bay. A number of angling boats also operate commercially under charter, catching species such as the tub gurnard *Trigla lucerna* (Fig. 65). This is the largest of the gurnards found around Gower, reaching a maximum length of 0.75 metres, although most individuals are between 0.5 and 0.6 metres. Like all gurnards it has a large head covered by protective bony plates, and the lower three rays of the pectoral fin are separate and fleshy. It is usually found on mud or sandy seabeds, feeding on small fish such as sand eels, gobies and dragonets *Callionymus lyra*, and on crabs and shrimps. They will also feed high in the water when there are plenty of small fish about and can sometimes be seen breaking the surface. The Welsh record rod-caught tub gurnard was caught from the shore at Langland Bay and weighed nearly 5 kilograms. Potting for lobsters, edible crabs and velvet swimming crabs takes place in the rocky areas inshore while offshore there is trawling for plaice, sole, whiting *Merlangius merlangus* and cod *Gadus morhua*. Tangle nets are used to catch rays and turbot *Psetta maxima*. Netting for bass takes place with both fixed and drift netting and there is bottom-set netting in winter using small-mesh nets to catch sole, whiting and cod.

In 2004 a sea sturgeon *Acipenser sturio* weighing 120 kilograms and nearly

FIG 65. Tub gurnard, the largest of the gurnards found around Gower. (Paul Kay)

3 metres long was caught in Swansea Bay. One of the largest European fish to breed in rivers, the sea sturgeon has been fished to the brink of extinction and is now a protected species. It should not have been killed and it seems that more information needs to be provided to fishermen about rare species. The elongated body tapers to a narrow pointed tip at the snout and lacks scales, apart from the five rows of whitish bony platelets, or scutes, that run the length of the fish. Sturgeons have no teeth, but feed opportunistically on bottom-dwelling creatures, feeling for prey amongst the mud with the sensitive barbels on the chin and then sucking them into the mouth. Their food consists mainly of invertebrates and small fish. Previously abundant along all European coasts, sturgeon are now restricted to a single population that breeds in the Gironde River in France and the species is consequently extremely vulnerable. These long-lived and slow-growing fish have been extensively fished both for their flesh and for the eggs, which are sold as caviar. A captive breeding programme is currently in progress with the long-term goal of reintroducing the fish to some of its former range. After some controversy about its sale by the fisherman who caught it, the sturgeon was sent to the Natural History Museum. The fish was probably more than 100 years old and it will eventually be held as part of the national fish collection.

Two years earlier, in July 2002, a fisherman caught a 3.6 metre thresher shark *Alopias vulpinus* off Gower. Thresher sharks are often present in British waters and can come very close to beaches, and have been seen swimming near Mumbles lighthouse. They will readily approach the shoreline following schools of fish, such as mackerel and herring, and can enter shallow bays or narrow passes between islands. Thresher sharks can often be seen swimming at the surface with their long caudal fin scything the water, whilst actively feeding upon small fish that seem to 'boil' ahead of the shark. The elongated tail is used as a specialised feeding tool, the shark first herding and then stunning fish with strong sweeping blows. Infrequently they will also eat crustaceans and even seabirds. Overfishing is threatening the thresher shark and populations are said to 'have collapsed' – in other words, they are close to commercial extinction. Even 'recreational' fishing of this species therefore needs to be discouraged.

Other sharks recorded from the area include mako shark *Isurus oxyrinchus*, porbeagle shark *Lamna nasus* and basking shark *Cetorhinus maximus*, which feeds on plankton. Basking sharks are migratory and occur near the coast during the summer. There were sightings off Gower during the late 1970s and a probable sighting by a water-skier off Oxwich in 1984. There is an interesting historical record by Dillwyn of a great hammerhead shark *Sphyrna mokarran* that was caught in Carmarthen Bay in 1839. Its stuffed skin was later sold for £28 as a sideshow curiosity. Dillwyn wrote to Henry de la Beche saying he had tried, but failed, to procure the fish. This species is a very rare vagrant from tropical waters and only five were recorded from British waters throughout the twentieth century. The strange shape of the head, from which the species gets its name, is thought to make the shark more sensitive to electrical signals, which they use to detect hidden prey; common stingray *Dasyatis pastinaca* being a favourite food.

Sharks, rays and the related skates are distinguished from bony fish by their cartilaginous skeletons. Species with long snouts are usually known as skates, while those with shorter snouts are called rays. A hundred years ago British waters were packed with both skates and rays, including the common or blue skate *Dipturus batis*, which can reach 3 metres in length. Today most species are in decline and the blue skate is now listed as endangered. Their current status around the Welsh coast is unclear, although there is evidence that the most common, the thornback ray *Raja clavata*, has declined in recent decades. The Welsh Skate and Ray Group and the Shark Trust are therefore collecting information on past and present catches to improve knowledge of the distribution and population trends of these important fish. Skates and rays have commercial, angling and conservation value and the South Wales Sea Fisheries Committee, like some other Sea Fisheries Committees, has set a minimum catch size under a bye-law. Although this is not the most popular method, it is hoped that the current bye-law will be replaced in due course, either by a new bye-law or by European legislation covering the twelve-mile (22-kilometre) inshore zone. The decline of most of these species is being used as a clear example of how the Common Fisheries Policy is failing, and to promote the urgent need for a change.

The common stingray is still, however, found inshore in reasonable numbers during the summer and must always be handled with great care, as there are venom sacs connected to spines along the slender whip-like tail, and a wound inflicted by these spines can be extremely painful. Electric rays *Torpedo nobiliana* have also been caught in Carmarthen Bay. These rays have rounded disc-like bodies and smooth skin and two dorsal fins located on a short, thick tail. The upper surface of the ray is dark greyish-blue to dark brown and the underside is white. The species can grow up to 2 metres long. The electric ray catches bottom-living fish in its pectoral fins and produces a powerful electric shock from specialised organs located in the pectoral fins, which stuns or kills the fish before it is eaten. As a result it was known locally as a 'numb fish', and Dillwyn records that:

> One of these men (fishermen), who called it a Numb Fish, told me he has known it to lie quite concealed in the mud, both in the weirs and in the sea, at low water, and that the shock creates a great surprise when it is accidentally trod on.

Ever the enquiring naturalist, he acquired a 'torpedo' that had been caught alive on the 17 July 1840 and kept it in a saltwater pool he had in his garden, but it soon died. Other rays common in the area include the thornback ray, the painted ray *R. microocellata* and the spotted ray *R. montagui*. The spotted ray has a flattened, diamond-shaped body with broad wing-like pectoral fins and a long tail. It is similar in size and shape to the thornback ray, but the latter has characteristic large spines with button-like bases scattered over its back.

PELAGIC SPECIES

As the Bristol Channel is funnel-shaped, faces southwest and has strong tidal currents it tends to act as a trap for species which may be brought to the south-western approaches by the Gulf Stream and the prevailing wind, such as the Portuguese man-o'-war *Physalia physalia* and the by-the-wind-sailor *Velella velella* (Fig. 66). Both are ocean-dwelling species that are often washed up around the Gower coast. In July 2003, for example, numerous specimens of by-the-wind-sailor were stranded along the southern end of Rhossili beach and there was a similar mass stranding, all along the South Wales coast, in September 2004. Like the Portuguese man-o'-war, by-the-wind-sailor is a pelagic colonial hydroid, a

FIG 66. By-the-wind-sailor, a common pelagic species often found stranded on the beaches. (Margaret Hodge)

complicated colony, some elements of which specialise in feeding, some in attack or defence, some in reproduction and some in movement. The float in this species, which is an oval disc, is deep blue in colour and can be up to 10 centimetres in length. Short tentacles hang down into the water from the float. A thin semicircular fin is set diagonally along the float acting as a sail, which gives the animal both its scientific name (from *velum*, a sail) and its common name. The colony feeds on pelagic organisms, including young fish, caught by stinging cells on its tentacles. In turn the sea slug *Fiona pinnata*, violet snail *Janthina janthina* and sunfish *Mola mola* prey upon the colony. Dillwyn records that in July 1824 there was a mass stranding of violet snail on Oxwich beach. Over 200 individuals were collected, including a related species, *J. exigua*. These 'purple sea snails' are pelagic molluscs that float on a 'bubble-raft'.

Several sightings of large sunfish have been made near Worms Head, and a specimen weighing 18 kilograms was caught in 1983; even larger specimens sometimes occur. One sunfish caught on the surface in Caswell Bay on 28 August 1851 was 1.8 metres long and said to weigh around 500 kilograms. The most recent sighting is from 2002. The fish's unusual rounded shape is reflected in its scientific name, as *Mola* is Latin for millstone. In 1843 the rare oblong sunfish *M. oblongus* was caught in Swansea Bay, but it has not been recorded since.

The large dustbin-lid jellyfish *Rhizostoma octopus* is sporadic in occurrence from year to year, but when present it occurs in large 'swarms' in the summer and autumn. Enormous numbers are often found in Rhossili Bay. Naturalists have struggled for more than half a century to record the distribution and abundance of dustbin-lid jellyfish in British and Irish waters. Today, low-flying aircraft are being used to survey wide areas and this method has revealed huge numbers of these jellyfish (roughly one per square metre) in Carmarthen Bay between April and November. What causes these jellyfish to aggregate in the bay is unknown, but they also occur in similar numbers in Tremadoc Bay, near Criccieth on the Lleyn peninsula. It is generally a species of coastal waters and can be found stranded on the shore, or in rock pools, by receding tides, but it is believed that some specimens probably live in deep water during winter. The animal has a solid appearance and varies in colour from whitish pale or yellow to shades of green, blue, pink or brown. Unlike some jellyfish there are no marginal tentacles and there are four pairs of very large oral arms on its under surface, hence the specific name *octopus*. The small amphipod crustacean *Hyperia galba* can be found throughout the body and more usually in its gastric or gonad pouches, where they are sought by some species of fish.

Another jellyfish, the blue jellyfish *Cyanea lamarckii*, which occurs in astonishing shades of blue and violet and can sting people, has also been found washed up on Gower beaches. It is a pelagic species that occurs in coastal waters all around the British Isles. The colour varies from translucent through pale yellow, pale brown, pale grey to light blue or purple. In faintly coloured specimens the blue tends to outline the pattern of the internal sculpting of the bell, which can grow up to 30 centimetres in diameter. The tentacles, arising from the underneath of the bell, are arranged in eight horseshoe or rectangular-shaped groups each with 40 to 60 tentacles.

Other species frequently recorded include the common jellyfish *Aurelia aurita*, which is almost certainly the most abundant of them all, and the compass jellyfish *Chrysaora hysoscella*.

TURTLES

While there is little information about jellyfish around Gower, it is known that they are the staple diet of the critically endangered leatherback turtle *Dermochelys coriacea*, which has been recorded from the area, together with loggerhead turtle *Caretta caretta* and Kemp's ridley turtle *Lepidochelys kempii*. The leatherback breeds in shallow tropical waters and it is clear that its extensive migrations are the result of following swarms of jellyfish. One of the mysteries of leatherbacks is how they can thrive almost entirely on jellyfish, which are composed for the most part of water. In British waters they occur seasonally and the majority of sightings, usually of adults, are between August and October.

A particularly large specimen was seen off Gower in September 1966 and was described in the newspapers as being 'the size of a small car with a head as big as a football'. Similarly in September 2003 a large turtle was seen in the Loughor Estuary, swimming at the surface in a westerly direction together with large blooms of dustbin-lid jellyfish. The leatherback is the world's largest sea turtle and the most widely distributed reptile; it has a shell normally up to 2 metres in length, and can weigh half a tonne. They are spectacular animals, and the largest specimen ever recorded was found stranded at Harlech in 1988. The turtle weighed 916 kilograms and was 2.91 metres long, and can now be seen in the National Museum in Cardiff. The same year a plastron, the underpart of a leatherback shell, was found in Three Cliff Bay, one of a number of occasions when dead animals have been washed up on the Gower beaches (Fig. 67). The leatherback's characteristic feature, as its name suggests, is a blackish leathery shell with seven longitudinal ridges along the back, three of which are clearly visible when the animal is swimming at the surface. The skin is also black and relatively smooth with pale spots. The black leathery skin, large size, and prominent ridges on the

FIG 67. Mark Winder, Head Warden for the National Trust, with the remains of a leatherback turtle found on the Worms Head causeway in 1996. (Paul Llewellyn)

back make them easy to identify. The leatherback is warm-blooded (endothermic), maintaining a body temperature of around 25°C, which is unusual as most reptiles are cold-blooded (ectotherms).

Populations of leatherbacks are in serious decline due to a number of factors, but the main threats have been a prolonged harvest of eggs and the incidental capture in oceanic fisheries. The international nature of this problem means that the survival of the species will depend on cross-border collaborations, focused not only on the tropical nesting beaches but also on the more temperate feeding grounds that lie thousands of kilometres away. Despite this, our knowledge of leatherbacks outside the breeding season remains almost nonexistent.

In April 2003 the Irish Sea Leatherback Project was established as a joint initiative between the University of Wales Swansea and University College Cork. Key elements of the project include aerial surveys of the Irish Sea, satellite-tracking leatherbacks from their tropical nesting grounds to identify the routes they follow to get to high latitudes, shoreline jellyfish surveys, schools workshops and public seminars. The project hopes to answer the issue of whether leather-backs are merely oceanic wanderers that find themselves in British waters or whether they form an important part of our natural heritage.

All other turtles seen off Gower are likely to be juvenile or subadult loggerhead and Kemp's ridley turtles. The loggerhead turtle is another large sea turtle, with a carapace up to a metre in length. It is a carnivorous species, feeding mainly on benthic invertebrates, especially molluscs and crustaceans, using its very bulky jaw muscles to crush their shells. Adult Kemp's ridleys are normally bottom-feeders, foraging in crab-rich shallow inshore waters. It is critically endangered and the total population of this species is thought to number no more than 900 adult females and an unknown number of males and subadults. The occurrence of these 'hard-shelled' species in the Bristol Channel is not a normal part of their life history; they have been blown from warmer waters by unusual weather conditions such as prevailing southwesterly storms. The animals are usually in very poor health, as hard-shelled turtles are not adapted to the cool seas around Britain, but prompt action can save a turtle's life and the Marine Conservation Society website provides guidance on this.

MARINE MAMMALS

Grey seals *Halichoerus grypus* frequently occur around the peninsula. On the Inner Head of the Worm up to 20 animals at a time haul-out on the dropping tide and can easily be seen from the former coastguard lookout station (Fig. 68). They

FIG 68. Grey seal on the shore of Worms Head. (David Painter)

also appear to breed on the Worm, although there are no specific records of this. Sometimes in the winter months one or two individuals can also be found on the shore near Sedgers Bank in Port-Eynon Bay. In contrast common seals *Phoca vitulina* are very rare in the region.

The harbour porpoise *Phocoena phocoena* is the most widespread and abundant cetacean in Welsh waters. Investigations of tooth ultrastructure and genetic studies indicate that there are possible subpopulations around the British Isles, one of which is based in the Irish Sea and around Wales. Porpoises are common both inshore and offshore although certain coastal features such as headlands and islands regularly attract high concentrations of animals. These habitats are characterised by strong tidal currents and the animals appear to forage in the tide races that form in their vicinity. Because of this the time of their appearance and location can be predicted to some extent by the tidal cycle. The two main areas of porpoise sightings off Gower are in the vicinity of Worms Head and Burry Holms, where strong tidal races occur on the rising tide between the islands and the peninsula. Because of the large tidal range in the Bristol Channel these races typically attain a velocity in the range of 2.8 to 5.5 kilometres per hour (1.5 to 3 knots) at the spring tides. Groups of up to 20 individual porpoises have been recorded at times, but they most often occur in small groups of one to three animals.

Although the porpoise has been identified as a locally important species, surprisingly little is known about this significant social predator and many basic questions, such as the size of the population around Gower and breeding success, remain to be answered. Although they are frequently seen, they are shy and secretive animals and, unlike dolphins, they rarely behave spectacularly or come to boats, and are therefore difficult to study. A practical scheme, the Gower Marine Mammals Project, which began in November 2002, aims to find answers to these questions. Volunteer cetacean watchers have been actively logging harbour porpoise activity in the area since the mid-1990s, but the new initiative involves permanently mooring hydrophones in Carmarthen Bay, off Burry Holms, off Port-Eynon and in Swansea Bay to continuously detect and record the porpoise echolocation calls. Results to date have been encouraging. A better understanding of the requirements of the species is essential if effective conservation measures are to be taken. Bottom-set gill nets cause the deaths of thousands of porpoises every year and in addition high levels of infectious diseases and parasites have been linked with exposure to pollutants such as polychlorinated biphenyls (PCBs) and heavy metals. Increased shipping in coastal waters and declining fishing stocks also threaten this slow-breeding species.

Common bottlenose dolphins *Tursiops truncatus* were recorded off the penin-sula in 2003 and commonly form groups of up to 25 individuals. Like porpoises, in coastal waters the animals often prefer estuaries, headlands or sandbanks, where there is an uneven sea floor and/or strong tidal currents. Locations such as Rhossili, Worms Head and Burry Holms are therefore key seawatching areas for small cetaceans.

At times larger cetaceans, such as sperm whales *Physeter catodon*, have been recorded. Gabriel Powell, the agent for the Duke of Beaufort, wrote on 12 March 1761 to the Duke's mother:

> I was last night informed that on Friday last a young whale came on shore near Whiteford Point in the Lordship of Lanmadock ... it measures 65 feet in length, 17 feet in heighth as it lay on the sands, and 7 feet from eye to eye, and seems to have had a bruise on the head. It is a male fish of the Sperma Ceti kind. The country perceived it sometime before it reached the shore and took it for the wreck of a vessel, so they were prepared to receive it. As soon as the tide left it they attacked it with hatchets, and in about five hours killed it. As it is a Royal Fish it belongs to my Lord Duke as Lord of the Seigniory.

Stranded cetaceans have been described as 'Fishes Royal' since 1324, when a statute was passed which gave the Crown qualified rights to cetaceans stranded or caught in the waters of England and Wales. In 1913 these rights were transferred to the Natural History Museum in London and ever since then the museum has been monitoring strandings. The National Stranded Whale Recording Scheme is now the centre of a coordinated investigation into the biology and ecology of cetacean populations around the British Isles, and can be accessed via the museum's website.

As Powell was engaged in a court case he could not go to the scene immediately, but on 26 March he wrote again:

> I returned home on Monday, and yesterday went down to see what I could make of the whale, but found about two-thirds of it had been plundered by the country, and the other third lies buried in the sands, and is now so nauseous that no one will work on it.

Powell also enquired at Bristol about the value of whale oil, but could find no one to buy it; meanwhile it seems local people had enjoyed a feast of whale meat. Sperm whales are usually only found in small numbers throughout the deep waters of the North Atlantic. Sightings in British waters are recorded mainly between July and December, but there is increasing evidence that small groups of males remain at high latitudes into the winter, and this is the period when strandings have taken place. The March stranding at Llanmadoc would therefore seem to fit this pattern. Whether it is due to the particular tidal flows in this area is not clear, but Llanmadoc seems to be a regular stranding place for cetaceans. The first volume of the *Glamorgan County History* (Tattersall, 1936) has a photograph of a school of false killer whales that were washed ashore in May 1934 (Fig. 69).

FIG 69. False killer whales washed ashore at Llanmadoc in 1934. (Colin Matheson)

There has been a surprising variety of species stranded on the Gower shores over the years, including a white-sided dolphin *Lagenorhynchus acutus* which was washed up on Rhossili beach in October 1967. Contemporary records reveal that 'Attempts were made to return it to the sea, but it finally had to be shot.' (In Britain the two options employed in the management of stranded cetaceans are euthanasia and reflotation, that is the release of animals after a variable period of treatment on the beach of origin, or close by.) Other species stranded at Rhossili include lesser rorqual *Balaenoptera acutorostrata* and common dolphin *Delphinus delphinus*. In addition Risso's dolphin *Grampus griseus* has been recorded from Port-Eynon, Sowerby's whale *Mesoplodon bidens* at Mumbles, and a bottle-nosed whale *Hyperoodon ampullatus* turned up in Broughton Bay in 1965.

THREATS

Located as it is, on the northern shore of the Bristol Channel and close to the main shipping lanes, Gower is constantly at risk from oil pollution. Half of the world's extracted crude oil is transported at sea by supertanker, and an important mainstay of tonnage at Avonmouth Docks, further up the Bristol Channel, is petroleum, with nearly two million tonnes of related products imported each year. A much greater quantity is transported to the Pembrokeshire refineries. Most of the oil released into the sea by shipping occurs from routine tank cleaning, during which oil is deliberately released. Much of this disperses naturally, and major oil pollution incidents are fortunately rare. To date there have only been two notable events that have seriously affected the marine environment around Gower.

On the afternoon of 12 October 1978 the oil tanker *Christos Betas*, fully laden with heavy crude oil, went aground to the west of the Pembrokeshire islands and about 111 tonnes of oil was released into the sea. For three weeks oil was washed up at each tide on the Gower beaches and there were a number of oiled birds. Between 21 October and 9 November 485 birds were recovered on the beaches (Fig. 70). Most were completely covered with oil and long dead. Guillemots and razorbills suffered the most, with over 300 birds of these two species recorded.

This incident was completely dwarfed by the events of 15 February 1996 when a supertanker full of oil (light crude this time), the *Sea Empress*, collided with rocks at the entrance to the Milford Haven waterway. During the next five days an estimated 72,000 tonnes of oil leaked from the ship, making it the third largest spill to have occurred in Britain and among the top 20 worldwide. Early fears that the oil would move north and affect the islands of Skomer, Skokholm and Ramsey were unfounded, but even so significant amounts of oil entered Carmarthen Bay.

FIG 70. The remains of an oiled gannet on the beach at Mewslade after the *Christos Betas* oil spill in 1978. (Harold Grenfell)

Extensive slicks were reported and an oil sheen spread rapidly over a wide area. Most of the oil was never recovered, neither from the surface of the water nor from the beaches, and it is thought to have sunk to the bottom of the bay. Over 7,000 seabirds of 29 different species were found dead or dying. Significant numbers of guillemots and razorbills were affected, but it was Carmarthen Bay's wintering flock of scoters that were most badly hit, with a minimum of 4,000 birds killed. Many corpses were washed ashore on Rhossili and Whiteford beaches. During the following weeks hundreds of thousands of dead and moribund molluscs, crustaceans and echinoderms were washed ashore around the bay, including areas such as Rhossili and the inlet and estuary, which had not been directly affected by heavy oiling. The long-term effects on marine life remain unclear. Bad as incidents such as these are, however, they account for less than 10 per cent of the total input of oil into the sea and there have been few studies on the continuous and low-level oil pollution that must affect the marine environment around the peninsula.

There are other pressures from commercial fisheries. The hydraulic dredging of razor shells in sensitive marine habitats so close to the peninsula must be questioned, as must the dredging for 'seed' mussels to feed the mussel beds of Swansea Bay, which has seen large vessels working the seabed close to the Knave and around Oxwich Point.

CHAPTER 7

Beach and Dune

The bay is the wildest, bleakest and barrenest I know – 4 or 5 miles of yellow coldness
going away into the distance of the sea.

Dylan Thomas, describing Rhossili Bay in a letter

PHOTOGRAPHS OF the beaches and dunes figure prominently in the holiday brochures and tourist guides and they are the focus of many people's visit to the peninsula. Few of the visitors, however, are aware of the wealth of wildlife that occurs in the beaches and dunes, much of which exists literally under their feet. These dynamic and constantly changing systems, sculpted by the winds and waves, and originating for the most part in the sands and gravels ground out by the glaciers of the last ice age, are some of the most natural habitats in the peninsula. They represent an internationally important resource for wildlife conservation, supporting many ecosystems and species of European importance. In particular the plant life of the Gower dunes is extremely rich; they are also nationally important for a wide variety of invertebrates.

The scale of the habitat is also surprising, with the vast sandy beaches giving way to extensive sand-dune systems, many of which grade into other habitats such as salt marshes or woodlands. Where the beach material is of larger size a number of shingle beaches have formed. It has been estimated that the sand-dune systems alone cover over 840 hectares, and with probably an equal area of beach at low tide it means that these habitats cover at least 1,600 hectares. Whiteford Burrows, a National Nature Reserve, includes one of the largest undisturbed calcareous dune systems in Britain, with the dunes covering nearly 400 hectares out of the total area of 827 hectares (Fig. 71). The remaining habitats consist of beach, salt marsh and former glacial moraine.

FIG 71. Whiteford Sands and Burrows, looking north from Cwm Ivy Tor. (David Painter)

SANDY BEACHES

The whole of the South Wales coast is exposed to Atlantic swell from the southwest which has crossed the Celtic Sea, and to waves from the south generated in the Bristol Channel or waves from the west and north generated in St Georges Channel. The Gower coast is therefore exposed to moderate wave action from the south, but there is locally some shelter from the southwest, notably at Oxwich. The west-facing beach at Rhossili is sheltered by Worms Head and offshore shallows in Carmarthen Bay, while Port-Eynon and Oxwich bays face southeast and receive additional protection from headlands to the west. In general the more sheltered the beach the more varied the fauna. The degree of exposure is reflected in the substrates found, with muddier, siltier sediments occurring in more sheltered areas. There are, for example, greater numbers of bristle worms in the silty beach at Oxwich Bay than there are at Rhossili, and the southern end of Rhossili beach has a larger number of species than the more exposed northern end. The fine sands in the sheltered southern corner contain dense populations of razor shells, tellins, surf clams and sand mason worms. There are also two striking predators, the bulky necklace shell *Polinices catenus* and the pink-banded shelled seaslug *Actaeon tornatilis*.

Hidden under the surface of the wide sandy beaches there are numerous animals, the most obvious of which, due to the visible casts and tubes on the surface of the sand, are the lugworm *Arenicola marina*, the sand mason and at extreme low water the tubeworm *Owenia fusiformis*. The latter is a thin, cylindrical, segmented worm, up to 10 centimetres long, that lives in a tough flexible tube buried in the sand with its anterior end just protruding from the surface. The tube is composed of sand grains or shell fragments glued together in an overlapping fashion.

Sandy beaches are the habitat that has been most successfully exploited by the bivalve molluscs. They burrow into the sand for protection by means of an extendable foot, maintaining contact with the water above with siphons that extend from the posterior of the animal. Some bivalves burrow only deep enough to cover the shell and have short siphons, others burrow very deeply and have long siphons, while the razor shells descend deep into the sand for protection and can move with ease up and down. There are three types of deep-burrowing bivalve molluscs, the tellenid bivalves, which have separate and very long siphons and a large foot, the razor shells, which have short fused siphons and a very large foot, and gaper bivalves, which have long fused siphons and a very small foot.

Tellenid bivalves found in the Gower sands include thin tellin *Tellina tenuis* and the similar *T. fabula*. Razor shells are widespread and include the razors *Ensis ensis* and *E. arcuatuis* and the pod razor shell *E. siliqua*. In slightly muddy areas the common razor shell *Solen marginatus* occurs instead. Unlike the other razor shells this slowly burrowing animal has a series of constrictions around its siphon, which allow it to break off small pieces, perhaps to distract a predatory bird or fish, as it gradually retreats into its burrow. The gaper bivalves include common otter shell *Lutraria lutraria*, which is one of the shells most frequently found on the Gower beaches, but due to its fragility and size by the time it is found it is often damaged. Other bivalve molluscs, such as common cockle *Cerastoderma edule*, banded wedge shell *Donax vittatus*, striped venus *Venus striatula*, thick trough shell *Spisula solida* and rayed trough shell *Mactra corallina*, are clearly not adapted for burrowing in sand and only create superficial burrows.

Where stones are mixed with the sand the burrowing anemones, the water anemone *Sagartiogeton undata* and daisy anemone *Cereus pedunculatus*, often occur attached to a fragment of shell or stone buried slightly below the surface. The common heart urchin or sea potato *Echinocardium cordatum* is also abundant, and the near-white fragile limy skeleton, or test, of this species can often be found along the strandline on Rhossili beach and Whiteford Sands. It is associated with the commensal bivalve *Tellimya ferruginosa*, which lives amongst its spines, and the amphipod *Urthoe marina*, which uses its burrows. As many as fourteen bivalves have been recorded with a single heart urchin, the adults living freely in the burrow while the young are attached to the urchin's spines by byssus threads. Other echinoderms found on the beaches include the brittlestars *Acrocnida brachiata, Ophiura albida* and *O. texturata*.

Sand-burrowing worms include sea worm *Glycera convoluta, Notomastis rubicundus, Phyllodoce maculata*, the bristle worm *Scoloplos armiger* (which can reach lengths of 12 centimetres with 200 or more body segments), the catworm *Nephtys hombergi* and occasionally the sea mouse *Aphrodite aculeata*, which is usually found near the extreme low water mark. Burrowing crustaceans on the Gower beaches include various species of sandhopper *Bathyporeia* spp., the isopods *Eurydice pulchra* and *Eurydice affinis* (relatives of the woodlice that hide in the sand at low water, emerging to feed on plankton as the tide comes in), the masked crab and the south-claw hermit crab *Diogenes pugilator* (Fig. 72).

This hermit crab is a small animal that is only found in a limited number of places in Britain and Ireland, as it is primarily a warm-water species. As such it may well be worth further study in relation to climate change. There are already signs that the crab is extending its range, as it was found for the first time on the west coast of Ireland in the 1990s. The species can easily be recognised in the field

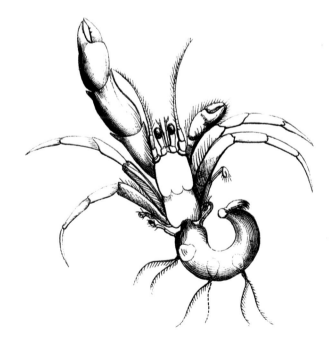

FIG 72. The south-claw hermit crab *Diogenes pugilator*, as illustrated in Bell's *British Stalk-eyed Crustacea*, published in 1853.

and during the summer is simple to find. It is distinguished from the common hermit crab *Pagurus bernhardus* in that the left claw is the largest one, not the right. The crab was first recorded in Britain at 'Worms Head' from specimens supplied by Dillwyn to Spence Bate around 1850 and described by him in the *Annals and Magazine of Natural History*. It was originally named *Pagurus dilwynii* after its discoverer by Thomas Bell, President of the Linnean Society, who had not actually seen it himself. By the time it was included in Bell's *British Stalk-eyed Crustacea* (1853) it had also been found in Cornwall. In his book Bell notes, 'The name applied to this species is one long-known to science, and honoured as the stimulator of natural history in this locality in the person of L. W. Dillwyn, Esq., Sketty Hall.'

The early descriptions mention the crab's ability to quickly bury itself in the sand. Because of such comments and subsequent studies on the ecology of this specialised species, the Gower location where Dillwyn collected it is more likely to have been Rhossili beach than the mainly rock habitats nearby at Worms Head. Some 150 years later it still occurs on this and other beaches facing onto Carmarthen Bay and in general needs gently shelving moderately exposed beaches facing southwest. The waves reaching these beaches spill when breaking rather than plunging and conditions are less turbulent than on steeper beaches. The sand also tends to be clean and well sorted and extends offshore rather than giving way soon to muddier sediments.

Most crabs generally feed by scavenging or by processing sediment with their mouthparts, and while the hermit crab can use both these methods it also has another technique. Like the mole crabs, which bury themselves in the sediment, it has pairs of extended bristles along its antennae and it uses these as a net to catch food. The crab digs itself into the sand so that just the rim of the shell shows and from this position sweeps its antennae alternately in circles about 30 to 40 degrees from the horizontal.

Another animal found in this habitat is the lesser weever fish *Echiichthys vipera*, which grows to around 10 to 15 centimetres. It spends most of its time in shallow water over sandy areas and can often be found during the summer months on the Gower beaches. This small burrowing fish, which lies partly buried on the lowest shore, should not be handled since it has venomous spines along its dorsal fin. People walking barefoot along the edge of the sea can be stung and there have been reports of incidents from areas such as Three Cliff Bay and Caswell. The sting can be painful and persistent, but is usually relieved by appropriate medical treatment. Death is extremely rare, although respiratory failure and gangrene have been reported. The venom glands provide the weever fish with protection against attacks by larger predatory fish.

THE STRANDLINE

Strandlines are an accumulation of debris at the high water level along the upper shore, which consists of natural flotsam – organic debris of marine and terrestrial origin – unfortunately supplemented today by artificial materials. Although strandlines are often short-lived, because of the way they are formed, they are of particular importance, especially on exposed shores, where they can act as precursors to sand dunes. The more permanent strandlines on the Gower beaches stabilise the foreshore, by enhancing the moisture and organic content of the sand, allowing pioneering plants such as sea sandwort *Honkenya peploides*, sea rocket *Cakile maritima* and saltwort *Salsola kali* to become established. These plants in turn aid the trapping of sand, assisting the formation of dune systems. Unfortunately Japanese knotweed *Fallopia japonica* has now begun a slow, but steady, colonisation of natural coastal habitats, appearing along the strandline of sand-dune systems. In rural areas, such as Gower, it is already an extremely aggressive competitor in open woodland and hedgerows as well as along the banks of watercourses, spreading by vegetative propagation from fragments of rhizome that are dispersed very effectively by water. The highest densities of knotweed in Britain are in South Wales and it may have spread from Maesteg, where it was first recorded in the wild around 1885 on a cinder tip.

Undisturbed strandlines are of importance because of their rich invertebrate communities, and the tangled driftwood and seaweed shelters a vast number of rove beetles, kelp flies and other species in addition to the ever-present sand-hoppers. Several of the beaches also have large populations of the rare strandline woodlouse *Armadillidium album*. This is a characteristic species, which occurs where the upper strandline contains abundant supplies of wood and other debris that remains undisturbed throughout the year. The animal is noticeably absent from beaches that are used by large numbers of people. The speciality of the Bristol Channel shores is, however, a particularly striking ground beetle, the cream and black *Nebria complanata* (Fig. 73). This sociable species shelters under driftwood during the day and emerges to prey mainly on sandhoppers at night. Attempts to tidy up beaches can be highly damaging to the beetle, and strandline disturbance needs to be kept to a minimum.

Beach litter is a major problem in Gower and plastic debris is present along the strandline of all beaches. Comparatively little of this is dropped by visitors to the area and most of the material is seaborne, some of it having travelled enormous distances. Seaborne litter is a continuing problem, particularly on Whiteford Sands and Rhossili beach, where bottles originating from South America are

FIG 73 A & B. The yellow and black strandline beetle *Nebria complanata*, which emerges at night to feed on amphipods. (David Painter / Harold Grenfell)

FIG 73 B.

regularly found. Much of this material is not biodegradable and can be unsightly.
As a consequence mechanical removal of the strandline has been adopted during
the summer months on some beaches, particularly in Port-Eynon Bay, as a cost-
effective way of cleaning the area. Unfortunately even this seasonal cleaning is
damaging to the wildlife of the strandline. Amphipods, such as the sandhopper
Talitrus saltator, are particularly vulnerable as only one generation reaches
maturity each year. The newly hatched juveniles are not strong enough to bury
themselves in the sand to avoid desiccation and rely instead on the freshly
deposited strandline seaweeds, which maintain a relative humidity of between
85 and 90 per cent over low tide. Studies have shown that the removal of
strandline seaweeds, even just during the summer months, effectively destroys
the populations. In addition the compaction of the sand by the machine effectively
kills any animals below the surface of the beach. If it is not possible to leave the
beach untouched, hazardous, unsightly or dangerous material such as glass,
plastics and sewage-related items should be removed by handpicking. Mechanical
beach cleaning has also been shown to have long-term effects on the stability of
dunes, especially in areas of high recreational pressure. This must be a concern
in Port-Eynon Bay, where the dunes are the only coastal defence for the villages
of Port-Eynon and Horton.

Various wading birds, gulls and crows feed along the strandline and roost on
the beach. Waders that occur include ringed plover *Charadrius hiaticula*, sanderling
Calidris alba, oystercatcher, curlew and dunlin. These species can be seen in varying

numbers throughout the year, but they are particularly abundant at migration time and in winter. The ringed plover is one of the few birds to nest on the Gower shore and one or two pairs attempt to breed each year at Oxwich just above the high tide line, although disturbance is a real issue. Gulls roosting on the beaches include herring gull *Larus argentatus*, black-headed gull *Larus ridibundus* and common gull *Larus canus* and quite large groups of several hundred birds can build up in the winter.

Blackpill is an important feeding station for migratory waders such as sanderling, ringed plovers and oystercatchers. These birds stop over to refuel on their global journeys, from Africa to Greenland and the Russian steppes, and back again. It is also an outstanding location for watching waders and gulls on a rising tide. The first Mediterranean gull *Larus melanocephalus* was recorded in 1970, and the adult ring-billed gull *Larus delawarensis* seen in 1973 was the first record for the UK. Both these species, which are non-breeding visitors to the area, are now regularly found amongst the other gulls and are also present at other locations around the coast. Other rare gulls recorded include Iceland *Larus glaucoides*, glaucous *Larus hyperboreus* and little gull *Larus minutus*. The yellow-legged gull *Larus cachinnans* is also occasionally spotted by regular bird-watchers. Bar-tailed godwit *Limosa lapponica* is present throughout the year, along with ringed and grey plover *Pluvialis squatarola*.

The fox is a frequent scavenger of the strandline, along with a number of other mammals including voles, mice and rats *Rattus norvegicus*. Even the brown hare will visit occasionally.

SHINGLE

The origin of the term 'shingle' is not clear, but it has been used for centuries to describe beaches composed predominantly of rounded pebbles. Shingle is defined as sediments coarser than sand, and smaller than a boulder, that is between 2 and 200 millimetres in diameter. Shingle beaches tend to form in high-energy environments where the sea can move and pile up pebbles on the shore above the tide line. Coastal systems dominated by shingle are an internationally important but diminishing resource as, like the sandy beaches, most are essentially relict features formed during the last glaciation. There are about sixty major shingle structures in Britain and two of these occur in Gower, at Pwlldu and Pennard. In addition there is a large relict shingle beach buried under the dunes at Oxwich (see Chapter 3), and smaller structures in Port-Eynon Bay at Horton, in Rhossili Bay and Oxwich Bay, and at Whiteford Point and Loughor. In the late 1920s there

was also a shingle beach at Salthouse Point, Crofty, the shingle resting on firm
sand that extended for a considerable depth below it, but this has now disappeared.

Together the remaining features provide a unique habitat for wildlife in the
peninsula. Many shingle beaches in Britain are now heavily managed for coastal
defence and increasingly for 'conservation'. In contrast the shingle beaches of
Gower, although comparatively small in extent, represent some of the most
unaltered examples of this habitat in Britain. Experience has shown that wherever
possible shingle structures should be left completely alone, and the urge to
preserve present features resisted, since in most cases physical change in the
structures favours ecological diversity.

Coastal shingle occurs in a number of settings and formations. Of the six
main types recognised worldwide, three are represented in Gower. The three-
ridge shingle beach at Pwlldu, which dams the Bishopston Pill and fills the former
bay, is an example of an 'embayment beach ridge plain' and consists of a series
of relict storm beach ridges and an active beach front (Fig. 74). The majority of
such structures are naturally dynamic and tend to move inland through a process
known as 'rollover'. During major storms, however, the crest of the ridge may be
overtopped or breached, creating shingle 'aprons' that spread over the rear area.

FIG 74. The largest shingle structure in Gower, the three-ridge shingle beach at Pwlldu.
(David Painter)

Pure shingle is uncommon in western Britain and Pwlldu is therefore important in this respect. But the shingle here is essentially anomalous in that the vast storm beach of limestone pebbles is a relic of the extensive limestone quarrying in the nineteenth century. In contrast the double ridge at Pennard is seemingly natural and an example of a 'barrier spit', partially blocking the entrance to Pennard Valley (and protecting a small salt marsh behind). The smaller shingle structures in Gower represent 'fringing beaches', formed from an accumulation of shingle on the upper shore.

Although shingle beaches may appear to be harsh environments, most formations of coastal shingle are partially vegetated; indeed this is the natural condition unless the shingle is regularly mobile. This vegetation can be abundant even if it is not species-rich. In particular shingle beaches provide an important habitat for lichens and, to a lesser extent, for bryophytes (mosses and liverworts). The pebbles themselves often support intricate mosaics of micro-lichens. There is an equivalent zonation of lichen to that found on rocky coasts, where the intertidal zone is black, followed by an orange zone and then above the highest tides a grey zone, although this zonation is less obvious on the shingle. In the intertidal zone pebbles are sometimes covered with the black thallus of black tar lichen and the nationally rare *Verrucaria ditmarsica*. Above this is a community of leafy yellow scales lichen and occasional *Caloplaca* spp., which generally occurs at the level of the highest spring tides. While on rocky shores the grey zone may be dominated by *Ramalina* species, on shingle there may be another black zone largely dominated by *Rhizocarpon richardii*. In some places this is succeeded by 'lichen heath', but for a variety of reasons it is rare to find a complete sequence, and the lichen communities of the Gower shingle are no exception to this. It is difficult to recognise a similar zonation pattern in the bryophytes, but there is clearly a transition from the unstable and saline foreshore where no bryophytes are present, through the heathy short turfs dominated by *Hypnum* spp., to the species-poor communities in the coarse grasslands on the landward side of shingle bars.

Shingle structures sufficiently stable to support perennial vegetation are a comparatively rare feature anywhere in Britain, and in this context the beach at Pwlldu is especially significant for the wide range of plants that occur, ranging from pioneer communities through to scrub. The classic pioneer species on the seaward edge include sea pea *Lathyrus japonicus*, Babington's orache *Atriplex glabriuscula*, sea beet and sea campion. There are no recent records of another pioneer, sea kale *Crambe maritima*, but it may still occur in Gower, where it grew in at least one locality in the 1950s. Heathland communities are particularly rare on shingle, but here heather *Calluna vulgaris* and lichen *Cladonia impexa* heath is present and wet heath with common reed *Phragmites australis* and water mint *Mentha aquatica* also occurs. It is interesting that the woody species at Pwlldu, such as blackthorn and common ivy *Hedera helix*, grow in isolation out of the bare shingle. The occurrence of these species and the general lack of soil at Pwlldu suggest that humus may be less important in vegetational development on shingle than previously thought, and that the level of moisture retention in the shingle is probably a more crucial factor. The amount of vegetation cover, which has a mulching effect, may therefore be more important than soil in the further development of plant communities on this site.

At Pennard the small sandy shingle spit supports a range of typical species including sea holly *Eryngium maritimum*, sea sandwort and common orache *Atriplex patula*. Unlike Pwlldu, Pennard Burrows are registered common land and grazed by cattle and ponies, and this produces a short sward with a poor range of plants. There are also high levels of recreational pressure, with fires of driftwood regularly being lit during the summer months. The shingle is often disturbed in this process to make 'fire-pits' and during the early 1990s a considerable amount of shingle was moved to the area of salt marsh behind to make a stone maze or labyrinth, but this has now been covered by the shingle moving inland. The shingle beach that once existed at Salthouse Point had a pioneer community of thrift, sea bindweed *Calystegia soldanella*, silverweed *Potentilla anserina*, small toadflax *Chaenorhinum minus*, common saltmarsh-grass and wild thyme, with red fescue and species of plantains *Plantago* spp., clovers *Trifolium* spp. and dock *Rumex* spp. nearer the shore. Finally at Whiteford there are some quite extensive well-vegetated and stable shingle 'recurves', with a good range of plants including lichens, extending southwards from the main dune and shingle spit into the salt marsh at Berges Island.

While the plant communities of shingle are quite well known there is little information on the animal communities, particularly the invertebrates. From what is known, however, the invertebrate fauna of shingle has some remarkable characteristics. While it consists of only a limited number of species, particularly in areas of open shingle, the community includes a high number of rarities. One of the key elements is the very distinctive structure of shingle, and while at first glance areas of pure unvegetated shingle may appear simple, at a small scale the habitat is highly complex, with large spaces between the pebbles. These spaces provide an unusual and secure habitat where spiders can construct webs and other species can hide from threats on the surface. They also provide protection from the weather, and deep in the shingle there are stable, humid conditions. The microclimate and structure of open shingle seems particularly to favour the hunting strategies of jumping spiders, and a rich group can be found. Species recorded elsewhere in Britain include *Phlegra fasciata*, which has been found on Pennard West Cliff and Horton Cliff, and the woodlouse spider *Dysdera crocata*, found on Llangennith Burrows. As yet, however, there are no records of these species from shingle sites in Wales.

In addition to creating the shingle habitat the sea provides a number of other features that are exploited by invertebrates. There is a detritus-based ecosystem along the decomposing strandline, including animals such as the common sandhopper *Orchestia gammarella*, which occurs in great numbers. Like those on sandy beaches the strandlines of shingle beaches are also of particular importance for woodlice. Woodlice have evolved from marine species (to which they are quite closely related) and are well suited to living on shingle beaches. Other common inhabitants of the high water mark and just above include springtails, mites, the common earwig *Forficula auricularia*, ground beetles, rove beetles, millipedes such as *Brachyiulus pusillus* and centipedes. Many of these strandline predators move out in favourable conditions to forage in the surrounding area. Strandlines on different shingle sediments and with different constituents contain different assemblages of invertebrates. There is still much to be discovered about the invertebrates of the Gower shingle and the sites would benefit from detailed surveying. Most groundwater associated with shingle structures is saline, but the presence of fresh water near the shingle surface, such as that supplied by the Bishopston Pill at Pwlldu, creates conditions required by a range of species. Variations and fluctuations in the height and chemistry of this water table have an enormous influence on which invertebrate species are present.

Several of the groups occurring on shingle, such ants and orb-weaving spiders, rely entirely on the structure provided by vegetation, while many invertebrates rely on vegetation as a direct food source. Many of the plant species also have their own particular groups of specialist invertebrates. Sea beet in particular supports a range of animals including the rare weevil *Lixus scabricollis* and the beet moth *Scrobipalpa ocellatella*. Sea campion forms small mats of vegetation on the surface of the shingle that provide shelter to a number of invertebrate species, including, elsewhere in Britain, the tortoise beetle *Cassida hemisphaerica* and the moth *Carocolum vicinella*, but there are no records of these species to date.

Shingle structures elsewhere in Britain can support large numbers of breeding birds, including gulls, waders and terns, but for most of the year there are too many people on the Gower beaches. As on the sandy beaches, the ringed plover is one of the few birds that attempts to nest in this habitat.

SAND DUNES

Like most of the dune systems in Wales, none of the Gower dune systems is entirely natural, although natural processes have obviously been responsible for their formation. The most unaltered parts of the dune are those immediately behind the beach, where the physical processes take place without being affected by human activities. Further inland, however, the vegetation of most of the dunes has been altered by a long history of grazing by sheep, cattle and rabbits, though information on this is sparse. This intervention has produced a complex mosaic of semi-fixed dunes, dune grassland and even sometimes dune heath, all of which are important semi-natural habitats. Dune heathland is very rare in Wales and there are only 41 hectares in the whole of the country, one of the main areas being Pennard Burrows. In the absence of grazing some areas of stable dune would probably have developed into scrub. There are no examples in Britain of primary dune woodland, although it would have been present before clearance by early people. In general it is the larger dune systems such as Llangennith and Broughton Burrows that are the most natural while the smaller dune systems, such as Penmaen and Pennard Burrows, tend to be heavily modified by heavy visitor pressure or grazing.

Sand dunes can be divided into four different types, depending on the circumstances under which they have formed: bay dunes, climbing dunes, spit dunes and hindshore dunes. All four types can be found in Gower (Table 7), and some dune systems are a combination of one or more, the prime example being Nicholaston Burrows, which has features of spit, bay and climbing dunes. Bay dunes, the commonest type in South Wales, develop from sand trapped within the shelter of rock headlands, the classic example in Gower being Port-Eynon and Horton dunes. In contrast the hindshore dunes, such as Oxwich, develop behind beaches that have a good sand supply and a prevailing wind which is onshore and which drives sand inland to form a series of dune ridges or mobile parabolic dunes. These dunes are often found on the most exposed areas of the coast. Spit dunes like Whiteford develop at the mouths of estuaries and depend mainly on river sediment for their supply of sand. Finally climbing dunes such as those at Pennard and Penmaen Burrows are the result of sand being blown up onto terrain inland of the main dune system and, in this case, covering large areas of steep cliff. The sand often only forms a thin veneer and the underlying rock exerts a strong influence on the plant communities that exist.

TABLE 7. Sand-dune systems in Gower. (Adapted from Barne *et al.*, 1995)

SITE	DUNE TYPE	AREA (HA)
Broughton Dunes	Bay and climbing	224
Pennard Burrows	Bay and climbing	87
Penmaen Burrows	Climbing	17
Nicholaston Burrows	Spit, bay and climbing	17
Oxwich Burrows	Hindshore and spit	76
Port-Eynon and Horton	Bay	19
Whiteford Burrows	Spit	400
	Total	**840**

DUNE ZONATION

At the beginning dune sand is rich in nutrients and calcium from crushed seashells, but these are soon washed out by rain, so dunes, in contrast to the sand on the beach, are relatively low in nutrients. The further from the shore, the fewer the nutrients in the sand, and this nutrient gradient is reflected in the zonation of dune plants. Plants growing on dunes are also faced with two problems, an almost constant shortage of water and the continual deposition of sand. Sand cannot store much moisture near the surface and plants need a well-developed root to bring water from deeper levels or a mechanism to reduce evaporation. Most naturalists are familiar with the general zonation of dune habitats from the embryo dunes to fixed dunes, but the processes of succession acting on the soils, plants and animals, geomorphological changes and the fluctuations in water levels are less understood. In reality there are few clear boundaries and one zone often blends into another across a gradient related to changes in one factor or another. In particular, on most of the Gower dune systems there is no clear division between the mobile, or yellow, dunes, and the fixed, or grey, dunes; instead there is a transition zone, which is often extensive. All of the sand-dune systems have a rich flora including many local, interesting and rare plants as well as the commoner dune species. Several hundred species of lichens, bryophytes, fungi and algae also occur. The dune system at Whiteford has a particularly fascinating flora and is home to several nationally important species of plant.

As described earlier, the embryo dunes, the first dunes above the high tide mark, are little more than small piles of sand which have accumulated around obstacles such as pebbles or driftwood in the strandline. These dunes are easily destroyed by erosion by wind and sea and by trampling, and are scarce on the heavily used beaches.

Behind the embryo dunes are the mobile or yellow dunes, which as their name suggests are loose sparsely vegetated dunes that grow and change shape as the wind deposits and erodes sand. The mobile-dune communities in Britain are dominated by marram grass *Ammophila arenaria*, which is specially adapted to live in these extremes of temperature and moisture and which grows up vigorously through the fresh sand deposited on it (Fig. 75).

Other plants of the mobile dunes are sea bindweed, sea spurge *Euphorbia paralias*, sea holly, a conspicuous plant which flowers in July and August (Fig. 76), and dune fescue *Vulpia fasciculata*. It was once thought that few other plants could survive in this hostile zone. A number of alien plants are, however, doing extremely well in this zone on the Gower dunes. Probably the most obvious of these is the large yellow flowered evening primrose *Oenothera glazioviana*, which now occurs in profusion on Port-Eynon and Horton dunes, along with fennel *Foeniculum vulgare*.

Next in the succession are the fixed or grey dunes, so named because they have been mainly stabilised by a covering of vegetation, do not move like the mobile dunes and lack large areas of bare sand. They include a number of habitats such as dune heath, dune grassland and dune scrub. Bloody crane's-bill, a scarce plant in Britain, but which is locally common in Gower, is a particularly striking and

FIG 75. Marram grass on Whiteford Burrows. (Harold Grenfell)

FIG 76. Sea holly, a widespread plant on the dunes. (David Painter)

FIG 77. Bloody crane's-bill, a nationally scarce plant, which is common on the fixed dunes. (Harold Grenfell)

attractive feature of the fixed dunes (Fig. 77) and is often associated with burnet rose *Rosa pimpinellifolia* and dewberry *Rubus caesius* in a distinctive plant community found in very few other places in Britain. Unfortunately Japanese rose *Rosa rugosa* has recently become established on a number of dune systems in South Wales and if it spreads widely could seriously affect the viability of this community.

Other notable plants found on the Gower dunes include ferns such as moonwort *Botrychium lunaria*, so called because its frond is fringed with half-moons, which is found in fixed dune grassland at Llangennith and Oxwich. The very small and rare annual hutchinsia *Hornungia petraea* is locally common at Pennard, Llangennith and Whiteford. Similarly lesser meadow-rue *Thalictrum minus* is locally common in grassland at Whiteford and is usually associated with large numbers of pyramidal orchids *Anacamptis pyramidalis*. The early sand grass *Mibora minima* is found at Whiteford (Fig. 78). The endemic British species Isle of Man cabbage *Coincya monensis* is still abundant on Pennard Burrows, which is its southernmost locality in Britain. This is some distance from its other stronghold on Formby Dunes in Lancashire.

On fixed dunes the increased stability of the surface and the increased nutrient and moisture regimes beneath the vegetation would normally allow scrub or woodland to develop. On dune systems such as Whiteford this process

FIG 78. Early sand grass at Whiteford Burrows. (David Painter)

is held in check by the grazing of ponies and rabbits, but where the grazing pressure is reduced, bedstraw, marram and false oat-grass *Arrhenatherum elatius* grassland swards grow rank, with grasses such as red fescue, Yorkshire-fog and cock's-foot taking on a more tussocky appearance and herbs such as hogweed, common knapweed *Centaurea nigra* and wild carrot growing profusely. Continued absence of grazing may allow the invasion of bramble into the grassland, producing patches of bramble and Yorkshire-fog with a rank growth of red fescue, smooth meadow-grass *Poa pratensis*, cock's-foot, false oat-grass and umbellifers around the bramble. Alternatively bracken may spread to form dense stands. Trees such as birch may also colonise areas of the dunes if the grazing is drastically reduced.

INSECTS

The Gower sand dunes are well known for their rich variety of insects, and in common with the other sand dunes in South Wales there is a tradition of record-ing that extends back to the nineteenth century, when few other areas of Wales received any attention from entomologists. The size of the dune systems is important, as the larger complexes contain a richer range of habitats. The compacted sand of the mature dunes is ideal for burrowing insects and the rich flora supports a wide range of invertebrate prey for sand-dune wasps, while the abundance of nectar sources ensures a plentiful food supply for bees. The brown-banded carder bee *Bombus humilis*, in particular, is common both in the dunes and on the south Gower coast. Despite its abundance here it is actually one of the most endangered species of bumblebee in Britain. The bee has a characteristic brown band on the upper surface of the abdomen, hence the common name. It nests on the surface of the ground, usually in grass tussocks, and forages for pollen and nectar throughout the summer months from May to September.

The real specialities of the dunes are the predatory insects, which include the robber fly *Pamponerus germanicus* (Fig. 79) and the stiletto fly *Dialinura anilis*. The robber flies typically frequent sand dunes just behind the marram grass belt and feed on other insects, some flying in search of food while others lie in wait and pounce on their prey. The proboscis of these flies is very hard and is used to pierce the prey and suck its juices. Their larvae are thought to develop in moist sand as predators of other invertebrates. At night the large black, smooth ground beetle *Broscus cephalotes* emerges from under stones and driftwood to feed in the sand dunes, preying particularly on amphipods and isopods. During the day it is replaced by the nationally scarce dune tiger beetle *Cicendela maritima*, whose

FIG 79. The robber fly *Pamponerus germanicus*, a common predator of the Gower dunes. (David Painter)

British stronghold is Wales, with records as far north as Morfa Harlech. In contrast, elsewhere in Europe it is a common and widespread species that is not always restricted to the coast. The tiger beetle has an annual life cycle, breeding in spring and summer and overwintering as pupae or adults in burrows situated in hard-packed sand.

Another striking insect is Britain's largest bush-cricket, the great green bush-cricket *Tettigonia viridissima* (Fig. 80). Despite its loud song this bright green insect, which grows up to 5 centimetres long, can be very difficult to see among the grass stems. Like the true crickets the bush crickets 'sing' by raising the wings and rubbing them together, but in these insects the left wing carries the teeth and lies on top of the right wing.

The common blue butterfly *Polyommatus icarus* is very numerous in some years, with a large number on the wing from June to August. Other butterflies found in the fixed dunes include the brown argus, grayling, dark green fritillary and marbled white *Melanargia galathea* (Figs 81 & 82). Whiteford is also one of the few Welsh localities for the grass eggar moth *Lasiocampa trifolii*, which is on the wing in August and early September.

Like the shingle beaches, the sand dunes are rich in spiders, although these invertebrates are often overlooked because their colour and markings blend so

FIG 80. The largest British bush-cricket, the great green bush-cricket. (David Painter)

well with the background. The most common spider found on the bare sand is the wolf spider *Arctosa perita*, a straw-coloured animal with diffuse black, brown and orange markings and two pairs of white oval patches on the abdomen. Wolf spiders are normally nomadic, active, ground-living spiders that actively hunt and pursue prey, without the help of a web. They usually attach their eggs to their spinnerets and carry them around with them. This species is an exception, however, and lives in a burrow in the sand, probably to protect itself from desiccation. It is itself preyed on by a small grey hunting wasp, the coastal spider-hunting wasp *Ceropales maculata*, which can often be seen flying backwards and forwards across the dunes in search of the spider or its burrow. The wasp stings the spider and buries it with an egg, as food for the larva that subsequently emerges. Another spider of the dunes that hunts without a web is the crab spider *Philodromus fallax*, named for the crab-like shape of the body and its habit of moving sideways like a crab. Instead of actively pursuing prey like the wolf spider

FIG 81. Marbled white butterfly at Whiteford Burrows. (Harold Grenfell)

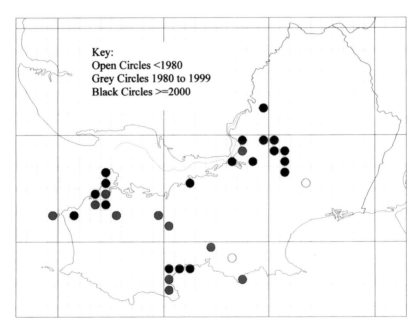

FIG 82. Distribution of marbled white on the peninsula. (Barry Stewart)

the crab spider waits quietly and ambushes passing prey. On the marram grass itself the most common spider is another crab spider, *Tibellus maritimus*, although this is not confined to dunes. A great variety of money spiders can also be found including *Ceratinopsis romana*, a small dark spider which is quite rare and confined to sand dunes in the southwest of Britain, but which is abundant in Gower.

Probably the most interesting of the dune spiders is the jumping spider *Synageles venator*, a very rare species only recorded from a few locations, of which Gower is one. Unlike most jumping spiders, which stalk their prey until they are near enough to pounce, this species does not actually jump. Instead it catches its prey by running fast along the stems of the marram grass. It is a particularly interesting spider in that it is an ant mimic. Spiders dislike ants since they are able to squirt formic acid as a defence and this jumping spider has taken advantage of this, copying the behaviour and appearance of certain species of ants that occur in the marram grass. To do this the spider runs around with its front legs held in the air like an ant's antennae, giving it the appearance of having six legs like an ant. Two white curved lines also run across the centre of the spider's abdomen like the two 'waists' of an ant. It carries out this deception so effectively that it is protected from attack by other spiders, which mistake it for an ant and either leave it alone or even retreat rapidly.

Other invertebrates found on the dunes include the common banded snail *Cepaea nemoralis* and the garden snail *Helix aspersa*. Vertebrates include the numerous common lizard, which in hot weather can be seen in exposed areas basking in the sun. There are also records of the rare sand lizard *Lacerta agilis*, but these need checking as the current distribution maps show that it is limited to southern England. Adder, grass snake and slow-worm can also be found.

FUNGI

Sand dunes are incredibly rich in fungi, and because of their role in decomposition and the mycorrhizal associations they form with higher plants they have a crucial role. In particular by producing phosphorus, nitrogen and other nutrients, such as calcium, potassium, sulphur and zinc, they help other plants to colonise the dunes. Around ten species of large fungi are restricted to dunes and most of these are specifically adapted to colonising the mobile dunes. As they are saprophytes, feeding on dead or decaying organic matter, they require dead marram grass or buried rabbit dung and a continuous supply of incoming sand. The commonest of these fungi is the marram brittle-cap *Psathyrella ammophila*, but the dune cup fungus *Peziza ammophila* and the dune stinkhorn *Phallus hadriani* also occur frequently in this habitat in Gower. At Whiteford the field bird's nest *Cyathus olla*, an ally of the puffballs, has also been found in the mobile dunes. This is a peculiar fungus that consists of a trumpet-shaped cup or 'nest', measuring about 10 millimetres in diameter, containing a number of small spherical spore masses or 'eggs'. The nests act as 'splash cups', and when hit by raindrops the spores, which are attached by very thin coiled cords to the outer wall of the cup, are splashed out to distances of more than a metre. In this process the cord becomes detached from the cup and helps the spore mass to stick to surrounding objects.

Other members of the Gasteromycetes, or stomach fungi, can be found in the mobile dunes alongside the field bird's nest. The more common species include brown bovist *Bovista nigrescens*, lead-grey bovist *B. plumbea*, grassland puffball *Lycoperdon lividum* and meadow puffball *Vascellum pratense*. Like the field bird's nest they all rely on some external agency to spread their spores, such as mammals or insects, or the physical effects of wind and rain. Rare species include the least bovist *B. limosa*, which was recently found at Whiteford Burrows in an area that had previously been burnt, and it seems to be a primary coloniser of such sites.

Further inland on the fixed dunes at Whiteford there is a surprisingly rich group of fungi. In fact in well-grazed dune grasslands such as this the number of fungi species can outnumber that of vascular plants. The most obvious fungi are the parasol mushrooms *Macrolepiota* spp., but these grasslands also support a great number of waxcaps *Hygrocybe* spp. In all about 24 waxcap species and varieties have been found in dune grassland in Britain, occurring only where the nitrate and phosphate levels in the soil are very low. As they cannot tolerate even small amounts of fertiliser they are excellent indicators of good-quality habitats and terms such as 'waxcap grasslands' and 'waxcap meadows' have begun to be used to describe such areas. The group contains some of our most spectacular and colourful fungi. Typical species which may be found at Whiteford include red species such as crimson waxcap *Hygrocybe punicea* and scarlet hood *H. coccinea*, yellow species such as *H. ceracea*, orange species such as blackening waxcap *H. conica* (Fig. 83) and green species like the parrot toadstool *H. psittacina*. The grazed areas also provide habitats for a variety of species dependent on dung, especially *Coprinus* spp. and *Panaelus* spp. Two giant puffballs, the mosaic puffball *Handkea utriformis* and the pestle-shaped puffball *H. excipuliformis*, which can reach heights of 15 or even 20 centimetres in the case of the latter species, are occasionally seen on the grassland areas at both Oxwich and Whiteford.

Despite the richness of the dune grassland it is perhaps surprisingly not the richest area for fungi on sand dunes, as more species of fungi have been recorded

FIG 83. Blackening waxcap *Hygrocybe conica* in the dune grassland at Whiteford Burrows. (David Painter)

in the wet depressions of the dunes than in all the other sand-dune zones put together. Species that can be found here include the true mushrooms *Agaricus* spp., the blewits *Lepista* spp. and the milk caps *Lactarius* spp.

DUNE SLACKS

The flat-bottomed dune slacks form a distinct type of wetland influenced by the freshwater table that underlies the larger dune systems in Gower. It is a common habitat on hindshore dunes and the larger spit dunes, but is absent from bay and climbing dunes. There are a few small dune slacks at Llangennith Burrows, while at Oxwich and Whiteford the dunes have been formed in low-lying areas and there are extensive systems of slacks. Indeed one of the main reasons for the designation of Whiteford Burrows as a National Nature Reserve is the quality and extent of the dune slacks. Some of the slacks are very dry and contain plant communities that resemble those found on fixed dunes, while others are damp and often flooded in late winter and early spring and have a wide variety of plants more commonly found in calcareous marshes and fens, including several rare species. A rare thalloid liverwort *Petalophyllum ralfsii*, which occurs in shallow calcareous dune slacks and habitats containing damp turf, is restricted to fewer than three dune slacks at Whiteford. The diverse vegetation of these damp areas also supports a wide variety of invertebrates including spiders, beetles and wasps. There are around 150 slacks at Whiteford, which vary greatly in size from around 70 square metres to 40,000 square metres, the latter slack being aptly known as the 'Great Plain'. Although they may appear to be scattered randomly across the area there are in fact three rows of slacks running parallel with each other down the long axis of the spit.

The slacks in the western row are medium-sized and elongated in the direction of the prevailing southwesterly winds. Located within the fixed dunes, they are deeply scoured and separated from adjacent slacks by tall dune ridges. In contrast the slacks in the eastern row are large and their orientation is not so pronounced. They are mainly surrounded by low fixed dunes or undulating dune grassland and grade into a transition zone with the salt marsh. The most southerly slacks of the western row and the most northerly slacks of the eastern row are quite different in character to the others because of their location on high dunes and they are small and often very dry. In contrast the central row of slacks is highly variable, reflecting the varied structure of the dunes along the centre of the spit.

The process of slack formation appears to have begun in the early medieval period when, as noted previously, the intensity of the onshore winds increased dramatically. The high winds scoured out deep hollows and piled the sand up in high ridges, aligned in parallel with the wind direction. Once formed, these ridges sheltered the eastern dunes from the worst effects of the wind and generally there would have been smaller quantities of sand deposited on the eastern side of the spit. These smaller dunes would have been shaped by the calmer inland winds. Such winds move the sand as a series of low waves perpendicular to the wind. This tendency of moderate winds to produce long, closely packed ridges can be seen at Whiteford today along the main accretion zone.

The dunes at Whiteford overlie an impermeable layer of glacial debris, but although considerable amounts of water seep out from the edges of the system it is not sufficient to prevent the water table from rising in most winters to flood many of the slacks. The slacks are therefore in effect temporary ponds, the wettest slack holding water up to half a metre or more in depth in some months of the year (Fig. 84). In contrast there are slacks where the water table never rises to more than a metre below the slack surface. In between these two extremes there is a complete range of water movement. It is this widely fluctuating water table that is largely responsible for the rich and diverse range of plants found in the slacks. The hydrology of coastal sand dunes is well understood and a typical cross-section from the sea to a drainage line at the landward edge shows the freshwater table

FIG 84. 'Slack 33' at the northern end of Whiteford Burrows. (David Painter)

rising in a dome shape, being highest above sea level along the mid-line. Fresh water constantly escapes to the sea, while sea water penetrates below the layer of fresh water on the seaward side.

The slacks differ in character in terms of their age, the level of the water table in summer, the duration of flooding, the calcium content of the sand, the degree of grazing by rabbits and so on. Each type of slack therefore contains its own distinctive flora and fauna. At Whiteford in the 1980s eight different plant communities were identified in the slacks, but the species composition of these has almost certainly changed since that date. Creeping willow *Salix repens*, a low-growing shrub with grey-green leaves, is a ubiquitous and important component of the vegetation of these areas. It is an extremely variable species and, at Whiteford at least, appears to have three distinct growth forms, 'red', 'downy' and 'brown', the different forms occurring in response to different environmental conditions. The brown form is the common form and probably represents the mature plant growing in optimum conditions. It is a large plant, over 40 centi-metres tall, erect with stout dark brown stems. The red form (Fig. 85) occurs in both the wettest and the driest slacks and may therefore represent a response to environmental stress. It is of medium height, some 15 to 30 centimetres high, is semi-erect or erect with thin brown stems covered with white hairs. Finally the downy form grows on the edges of the wettest and driest slacks and throughout a wide range of middle-moisture slacks. It is a small form, often under 10 centimetres tall, and is prostrate or semi-erect with thin red stems.

FIG 85. The 'red' form of creeping willow in a dune slack. (David Painter)

FIG 86. Southern marsh-orchid, a plant of the dune slacks. (Harold Grenfell)

The flora of the dune slacks at Oxwich and Whiteford is particularly rich and the southern marsh-orchid *Dactylorniza praetermissa* (Fig. 86), early marsh-orchid *D. incarnata* and marsh helleborine *Epipactis palustris*, the horsetail *Equisetum variegatum* and the sedge *Carex serotina* grow at both sites. The bee orchid *Ophrys apifera* (Fig. 87) and green-flowered helleborine *Epipactis phyllanthes* are also occasionally found in this habitat.

Many of the rarer plant species found at these sites are linked to specific phases in the early development of dune-slack communities, but the larger dune systems in Gower such as Whiteford and Oxwich are now highly stabilised with only a small proportion of bare sand, little wind-generated erosion and extensive areas of dune grassland and scrub. For instance the fen orchid (Fig. 88) is confined in Britain to damp calcareous dune slacks and fens, and the dune slacks of South Wales hold more than 90 per cent of the British population, the number of British sites having declined from over thirty to just eight. Evidence suggests that the major reason for the decline in fen orchid populations is the

FIG 87. The bee orchid, occasionally found in the dune slacks. (Harold Grenfell)

FIG 88. Fen orchid. The dune systems of South Wales hold more than 90 per cent of the British population. (David Painter)

loss of young dune-slack habitats due to undergrazing and stabilisation and lowering of water tables. It means that the populations at Whiteford and at Kenfig Dunes (to the east of Gower) are the largest and most important in Britain. While in the fens of eastern England the fen orchid consists of the typical comparatively narrow leaved form, the form found in the Gower dune is shorter and broader-leaved.

Also found at Whiteford, the petalwort *Petalophyllum ralfsii* is a rare and vulnerable species, widely but sparsely distributed in Britain. Due to weather conditions it varies greatly in abundance from year to year and may disappear from view completely in the summer, surviving as underground tubers. The main threats are loss of habitat due to dune stabilisation and natural succession and, due to its rarity in this country, the collection of specimens by naturalists. Other notable plants of the dune slacks include adder's tongue *Ophioglossum vulgatum*, a fern that also grows in woodlands and old pastures, round-leaved wintergreen, which is a nationally rare plant, and the dune gentian, which is confined to a small number of sites in South Wales.

The dune gentian (Fig. 89) has declined over much of Europe and is considered to be rare or declining throughout its range; at each known site it is currently limited to a small number of damp slacks. As it is an annual species population sizes vary from year to year. Some years there can be extremely large numbers of plants. In 1994, for example, a good year, it was estimated that there were more than 5,000 dune gentians at Oxwich. In habitats that have not been affected by deliberate changes in the vegetation it seems that the species has declined in response to stabilisation. Interestingly, a comparison of the genetic material of the dune gentian with the autumn gentian, alongside which it often grows, has shown that dune gentian falls within the normal range of variation of autumn gentian. There is the suspicion therefore that the dune gentian may not in fact be a separate species, but this does not reduce the importance of conserving these special populations and the habitat in which they occur.

FIG 89. Dune gentian, a species that is rare or declining throughout its range, but which occurs in large numbers at Whiteford and Oxwich. (Harold Grenfell)

In slacks dominated by creeping willow, as at Whiteford Burrows, the bright red leaf beetle *Chrysomela populi*, which looks like a large unspotted ladybird, is often common, while the flowers are visited by the mining bee *Colletes cunicularius* and the hoverfly *Eumerus sabulonum*. Plant-sucking bugs include the local species *Globiceps cruciatus*, *Monosynamma sabulicola* and *Macropsis impura*. Also common in some slacks is the crimson and black five-spot burnet moth *Zygaena trifolii*, a day-flying species of high summer. Open, wetter slacks contain important groups of wetland flies such as *Dolichopus notatus* and *Hercostomus nigriplantis*. In the wet slacks can also be found the aquatic larval stages of dragonflies, mayflies and caddis flies, together with water boatmen, the pond skater *Gerris lacustris* and whirligig beetles.

WHITEFORD TRANSITION ZONE

Along the eastern fringe of Whiteford Burrows, along a line of seepage from the dunes onto the upper salt marsh, light grazing by ponies has maintained an outstanding transitional habitat, which is highly regarded for both its plant and animal communities. Poaching of the soft peaty sediments keeps the lush vegetation open and creates pockets of damp mud which are ideal egg-laying sites for wetland flies with semi-aquatic larvae. The soldier flies, named on account of their bright coloration, which was thought to look like old-fashioned military uniforms, are a characteristic group of flies found at such seepages. Species at Whiteford include *Vanoyia tenuicornis*, *Oplodontha viridula*, *Oxycera trilineata* and *Nemotelus notatus*. The latter is common on the coasts of southern Britain and Ireland, the larvae being found in brackish pools.

Another speciality of this area is the very rare narrow-mouthed whorl snail *Vertigo angustior*, which also occurs in a similar brackish marsh habitat on Oxwich dunes and a few other British sites. The snail was first described by Jeffreys in 1833 following its discovery in flood debris at Marino, near Swansea. A hundred and fifty years later, in 1983, populations were found in the transition zone between the salt marsh and sand dune at both Whiteford and Oxwich Burrows and in Cwm Ivy Marsh. Like many non-marine molluscs the whorl snail has exacting habitat requirements which contribute to its localised distribution and vulnerability, the species preferring open habitats without shading in dune slacks and moist dunes. The continuation of grazing on the dune grassland and adjoining marsh is vital to sustain the structure of the habitat and the variety of species, and efforts are made to ensure that grazing levels do not change substantially. Once an abundant species in lowland Britain, it was suppressed by the growth of forests in the

postglacial period and is now considered to be in serious decline. The populations
in the seven remaining sites in East Anglia, Glamorgan and Cumbria are
particularly vulnerable to habitat disturbance and a change in the hydrological
conditions.

DUNE MANAGEMENT

For several centuries the stabilisation of dunes has been seen as a priority, but
in recent decades there has been a greater recognition of and respect for the
natural dynamics of these systems. While sand dunes are threatened habitats, it
is incorrect to regard them as 'fragile'; indeed they have the ability to regenerate
and repair themselves and naturally move towards a stable state. In areas where
for a variety of reasons it is impossible for real soils to develop, dunes can
also rework themselves, thus maintaining the early stages of succession. As
described in Chapter 3, external influences, particularly the stormy conditions of
the fourteenth to the nineteenth centuries, resulted in a long period of dune
destabilisation, sand drift and a general reworking of the dune landscape. During
this period techniques were developed for reducing sand drift by the planting
of marram grass, the use of thatch and sand-trapping windbreaks, and the
planting of introduced species of conifers such as those at Whiteford. There is
documentary evidence that in 1661 tenants of the manor were required to assist
in fixing and stabilising Whiteford Burrows.

Aerial photographs of the Gower dunes show considerable dune mobility in
the 1950s and 1960s resulting from disturbance caused by military training in the
1940s. Most of the damage was caused by the American army, who used some of
the dunes as a training ground for the Normandy landings. Oxwich dunes were
also used by the RAF. They set up a series of lights, mimicking those of a nearby
ordnance factory, in order to persuade enemy aircraft to waste their bombs on the
dunes. At the end of the war a local botanist described Oxwich dunes as 'a sandy
waste devoid of vegetation'. Many of the blowouts were actively eroding and one
ended in a tongue of mobile sand that spread out onto the road each winter.
Residents of Oxwich village often had to dig themselves out of sand drifts.
Similarly the dunes at Port-Eynon were also used for practice landings. Major
measures were also required at Port-Eynon and Horton dunes in 1978 when sand
movement resulted in the inundation of adjacent houses, and this was one of
the projects tackled by the Heritage Coast Project in the 1980s.

Today sand drift is generally less threatening than in the past and most dune
areas in the peninsula are, with some notable exceptions, more vegetated than they

have been for centuries. A more dynamic approach is taken to dune management, which takes into account the restoration and development of natural processes, rather than the protection of stable structures and patterns, bare sand being recognised as an essential element for dune species and communities. Dune stabilisation techniques are mainly used these days to counter erosion associated with recreation.

Residential and recreational development has encroached on many sites because of their high amenity value. Car parks, caravan and camp sites and golf courses are very common either on or adjacent to the sand-dune systems. Generally recreation on the Gower dunes is increasing, and many show the effects of heavy visitor pressure, perhaps none more so than Pennard Burrows. Much effort and money has been spent in the past by the local authorities and conservation organisations in managing public access at this site, with paths and wooden boardwalks constructed to reduce erosion. Unfortunately, in some respects, there is a strong 'beach culture' in the Swansea area and there are a considerable number of barbecues each year on the Gower beaches. Parts of the boardwalks and fences on the adjoining dunes end up being ripped up and burnt, despite being chemically treated timber. Information panels explaining the background to management have also been destroyed. Efforts to restore eroded areas of dune by 'secret' planting of marram grass, without using fences or signs, have also failed, as the continuing erosion destroys the new planting before it has a chance to establish. Under such pressure there is an increasing tendency to scale back conservation activity on the eroded areas of dunes, with the result that significant areas of the more heavily visited dunes are now in poor or declining condition.

A number of British dune sites, such as Whiteford, were planted with conifers in the nineteenth and twentieth centuries. The idea of planting conifers was introduced from mainland Europe, where the planting of the wastelands of dune and heath was much more systematic than here. The ecological problems associated with such plantings are now recognised, and the conifers are being slowly cleared from Whiteford and dune vegetation is being allowed to re-establish, though a plantation at the southern end of the dune system has been retained as a landscape feature. The planting of conifers has destroyed a large area of dune grassland and slacks at Whiteford, causing a change in the soils, lowering the water table and resulting in pines seeding into the surrounding dunes. Experience elsewhere has shown that the organic litter layer must be removed in order to reduce the initial levels of nutrients and remove the non-native seed bank; this not only allows any original buried seeds to germinate, but also stimulates some sand movement.

Scrub is a natural component of dune vegetation, and in the absence of a relatively high level of grazing scrub will gradually invade the area. In particular species such as the introduced shrub sea buckthorn *Hippophae rhamnoides,* which is not a native plant on the west coast of Britain, have threatened the remaining slacks at Whiteford. The ability of sea buckthorn to fix atmospheric nitrogen enriches the nutrient-poor dune soil, and since it can propagate by vegetative reproduction the removal of the shoots above ground is not always a totally effective means of control. Removal of the few bushes that escaped a successful clearance campaign during the 1970s and 1980s, or those that regrow or recolonise, is still needed.

THE FUTURE

The area of naturally dynamic coastal shingle remaining in Britain is very small. With a continuing rise in sea level and a limited supply of new shingle the gradual erosion and retreat of shingle features such as Pwlldu seems inevitable. The sand-dune systems are also being squeezed between rising sea levels and other habitats inland, and with little new sand coming into the system it seems that in future the effects of storms will be to reduce the area of dune, not necessarily to bring more offshore sand into the system. The storms during the winter of 1989/90 for example had a dramatic effect on the exposed western side of Whiteford Dunes: the three lines of dune ridges which had built up between Prissen's Tor and Hill's Tor since the 1930s were severely eroded, leaving only half of the final ridge in place, a retreat of over 50 metres. The frontal dune scarp running from Hill's Tor to Whiteford Point also retreated by 10 metres at the southern end, reducing to 5 metres at the northern end. A considerable amount of sand was also lost from the beach in front of Prissen's Tor. The vulnerability and dynamic nature of beaches and dunes means that the dredging of offshore sandbanks can only add to this problem.

CHAPTER 8

The Worm, the Holms and the Mumbles

There was monstrous thick grass that made us spring-heeled, and we laughed and
bounced on it, scaring the sheep who ran up and down the battered sides like goats.
Even on this calmest day a wind blew along the Worm. At the end of the humped and
serpentine body, more gulls than I had ever seen before cried over their new dead and the
droppings of ages.

Dylan Thomas, *Who Do You Wish Was With Us?*

GOWER HAS THREE corners, at Mumbles, Rhossili and Llanmadoc, all of them defined by the limestone cliffs. Where you would expect to find a fourth corner to complete the compass of this roughly rectangular peninsula, at Gowerton perhaps, the hard geology is hidden by the broad sweep of the estuary. At each of the three corners there is a tidal island, or in the case of the Mumbles, two tidal islands, Middle Head and Mumbles Head. Rhossili has the famous Worms Head; known locally as 'the Worm', itself divided into an Inner Head, Middle Head and Outer Head, but here they are joined by a bridge of rock, the Devil's Bridge, and by Low Neck. Llanmadoc has the island of Burry Holms. Because of their relatively small size and the fact that they are not offshore these areas have been generally ignored in any of the surveys of Welsh islands. Although they are tiny in comparison to some of the other islands, they add an extra dimension to the peninsula and its natural history. There is also a small tidal island at Sedgers Bank on the western side of Port-Eynon Bay, but the only area above the high tide line is a minute storm beach covered with a relict sand dune on which sea spurge, sea bindweed and common restharrow *Ononis repens* grow. Berges Island, now forming part of Whiteford Burrows, has not been an island for a very long time. Grove Island, a low-lying island which was said to have existed 'not far from the Mumbles rocks', is reputed to have been destroyed by a tidal wave that struck the South Wales coast on the morning of 20 January 1607 – but there are no reliable records of its existence, only a mixture of personal reminiscences, speculation and legends.

Worms Head, Burry Holms, Mumbles Head and Inner Head are all remnants of the core of an anticline separated from the mainland by a fault, the pounding of the sea having eroded the limestone along the weakness. Burry Holms, for example, is separated by a 'sound' that formed along the Broughton fault. It is not entirely clear when the islands become separated from the peninsula and more research is needed, but the best estimates are between 3,000 and 4,000 years ago.

WORMS HEAD

The western extremity of the Gower limestone forms the long promontory of Worms Head, a name derived from the Old English *wurm*, meaning a dragon, and at certain times and in certain conditions the serpent-like shape of the island is clear (Fig. 90). As Wynford Vaughan Thomas noted, 'It really does look like a vast serpent, coiling its way out to sea and rearing its head as it makes its final plunge westward.' It is one of the most photographed landmarks in Wales. The Worm is cut off from the rest of the peninsula at high tide and the natural tidal causeway, between the Inner Head and the mainland, is exposed by the ebb tide about two-and-a-half to three hours after high water. It takes at least 15 minutes of rough scrambling to cross the causeway, but as it is only clear for a short time it is always necessary to check the tide times before attempting to reach the island. Even Dylan Thomas, who was a frequent visitor to the Worm, made the mistake of falling asleep on the Inner Head and had to wait for low tide:

> I stayed on that Worm from dusk to midnight, sitting on that top grass, frightened to go further in because of the rats and because of things I am ashamed to be frightened of. Then the tips of the reef began to poke out of the water and, perilously, I climbed along them to the shore.

On the south side of the Outer Head is the Blow Hole, an inconspicuous opening surrounded by an area of bare rock (Fig. 91). The hole marks the end of a long fissure that passes right through the island to a submarine cave on the north side. Some of the earlier accounts state that the entrance to the cave is uncovered at very low tides, but this has not been confirmed recently. As the water in the fissure rises and falls with the swell the air is drawn in, or forced out, through the

FIG 90. Worms Head, in winter, from Rhossili Bay. (Harold Grenfell)

FIG 91. David Painter, CCW Reserve Warden, at the Blow Hole in 2004. (Jonathan Mullard)

opening. When the wind is in the west the Blow Hole was said to produce a strange hollow booming sound and a spray of water that could been seen from some distance. The conspicuous but intermittent spout-like spray of sea water that can be seen rising impressively up the north side of the Worm today, when the tide is right and there is a reasonable swell, is produced by a different rock formation at the outer end of the Middle Head, rather than by the hole itself. It occasionally rises higher than the Outer Head and can be seen from Cwm Ivy Tor, several kilometres away. The phenomenon of the Blow Hole was known to William Camden, who visited the Worm twice in the sixteenth century, noting that:

> Toward the head itself, or that part which is farthest out in the sea, there is a small cleft or crevice in the ground, into which if you throw a handful of dust or sand, it will be blown back again into the air. But if you kneel or lie down, and lay your ears to it, you will then hear distinctly the deep noise of a prodigious large bellows. The reason is obvious; for the reciprocal motion of the sea, under the arch'd and rocky hollow of this headland, or promontory, makes an inspiration and expiration of the air, through the cleft, and that alternately; and consequently the noise, as of a pair of bellows in motion. I have been twice there to observe it, and both times in the Summer season, and in very calm weather. But I do believe a stormy sea would give not only the forementioned sound, but all the variety of other noises.

On the exposed south side of the Inner Head there is a large expanse of broken and eroded rock, which tends to form flat platforms near the low water mark. The upper shore in this area is steeper and there are some rock pools, while the lower shore has ridges and gullies, often running parallel to the shoreline.

The island is known to have been used by people since the Upper Palaeolithic. The Inner Head has an incomplete promontory fort and together with Lewes Castle was used as a strategic position. The fort on Inner Head has not been excavated, but by analogy with the excavated Knave Fort, they are presumed to be Iron Age structures. From the contents of two middens found on the Outer Head, where a fragment of Romano-British pot and an ironworker's mould have been recovered, it seems that the occupants collected shellfish from the seashore and kept pigs, cattle, goats and primitive sheep, comparable to present-day Soay sheep. Shells in the middens include limpets, periwinkles and mussels. Both middens are unfortunately subject to severe erosion from the sea.

On Inner Head is a small rectangular structure shown on maps as a sheepfold, which seems too elaborate for this purpose, particularly as it is associated with field banks that surround at least two fields. Further west are two rectangular hollows cut into the slope below the footpath. They appear to be hut bases and could be anything from medieval to Iron Age in origin. The rectangular structure may be a crude cottage, a *bwthyn* (Welsh for bothy). The existence of this cottage, the discovery of an iron ploughshare in 1984 on the northern side of the island and the field boundaries all point to the cultivation of this area during the nineteenth century.

Agricultural activities are still taking place on the island today. In contrast to the Middle and Outer Heads, the Inner Head (Fig. 92) is grazed by sheep under a National Trust licence. Stocking levels are agreed with the grazier by the Trust and the Countryside Council for Wales and around 35 sheep are present from 1 October until 12 April, this being equivalent to about 5 sheep per hectare. The grass has a reputation for producing extremely tender mutton, and the Talbot family of Penrice used to graze a flock on the Worm between September and March. They considered that there was nothing to equal 'Worms Head mutton' as the animals had been fed on grass salted by the sea winds. One animal was killed every week for the Talbot table and a local farmer went across between the tides every Tuesday to bring it onto the mainland. If they were at Margam or London it was sent to them live, in a specially made travelling box. Sheep are so fond of the isolation and the grass growing on the Worm that they are unwilling to return to the mainland. One Rhossili farmer, Wilfred Beynon, reported that a whole flock of his sheep escaped from their mainland field in the summer of 1932 and attempted to cross the treacherous causeway leading to the Worm. They were caught by the rising tide and all seventy animals were drowned. In *Yesterday's Gower* (Thomas, 1982) he noted that:

> I don't know what it is, but once you put a sheep out on Worm's Head, it can't be kept away from there ... Once they've had a taste of the grass out there, they'll never be safe again – that's a bit of family wisdom, now.

As might be expected the Inner Head is botanically very similar to the main-land cliffs, with squinancywort, bloody crane's-bill, hoary rock-rose, common rock-rose and small scabious growing on the thin soil of the upper south-facing slopes above mixed red fescue grassland and thickets of gorse. If the sheep were removed, or the grazing pressure was reduced, it is possible that a more natural scrub and perhaps even woodland vegetation would eventually develop over part of the Head. It is quite likely that the larger islands, Worms Head and Burry Holms, were covered in some woodland when they became separated from the rest of the peninsula. (The onset of grazing probably coincided with the removal of the remaining woodland.) Even now oak woodland and scrub still persists on some

FIG 92. The Worm, looking seawards from the Inner Head. (Harold Grenfell)

quite small and isolated stacks off the Pembrokeshire coast. So although today the vegetation of the Gower islands consists mainly of maritime grassland, it is probably not the climax vegetation in all areas. In the 1950s, when most of the larger offshore islands around Wales were designated as Sites of Special Scientific Interest, they often had extensive areas of rich maritime grasslands and heath-lands. It was assumed that these plant communities were self-sustaining and the only management they needed was protection from people. Too late it was discovered that many of these plant communities did not represent the natural vegetation at all, but that they were in fact the product of many centuries of agricultural management, which included the harvesting of rabbits, bracken and gorse.

In 1977 two fenced enclosures were erected on the south side of the Inner Head to exclude grazing animals, including rabbits, and over the past 27 years a thick layer of red fescue has developed, in stark contrast to the shorter and more species-rich turf on the other side of the fence. Rabbits are present on all of the islands, and by selectively feeding on certain plants they can completely alter their ecology. Moderate grazing by rabbits prevents any particular species dominating, especially vigorous and tall-growing species, thus allowing the smaller species, which would normally be shaded out, to grow.

The dense turf of red fescue that has developed in the enclosed areas, the springy 'monstrous thick grass' noted by Dylan Thomas, also covers the more sheltered parts of the Middle and Outer Heads. Turf 'mattresses' are a particular feature of ungrazed islands in southwest Britain and they may represent the climax vegetation of some exposed and ungrazed sea cliffs. Amongst the red fescue can be found sea beet, sea mayweed *Tripleurospermum maritimum*, and abnormally large spring squill, with rock sea-spurrey *Spergularia rupicola*, thrift and white clover where the grass is not so thick. A number of changes have taken place since Professor McLean studied the area in 1935 and recorded that the turf was over half a metre deep. Following the destruction by fire of a large area of ungrazed grassland on the Middle Head in 1957, the Nature Conservancy reseeded the eroded soils with unimproved Danish red fescue in 1958. The plants established sufficiently to prevent serious soil erosion during the following winter, but by the summer of 1959 they were dying and as they did so the native species re-established itself. Perhaps as a result of the fire red fescue no longer forms a 'largely pure' turf on the Middle and Outer Head, and it is now associated with abundant creeping thistle *Cirsium arvense* and smooth meadow-grass, neither of which was observed by McLean, together with many other species – a similar plant community, in fact, to that found on parts of the Inner Head, despite the presence of sheep. High up on the slope of the southern side of the Inner Head, the red fescue mattresses gradually give way to limestone heath and grassland.

The aspect and shelter from the prevailing southwesterly winds also contributes to the character of the grassland on the north side of the Inner Head. Here salt deposition is reduced, with the result that there are fewer maritime species than would normally be expected in such an exposed location. There is an area of bracken and bramble at the eastern end of the Inner Head, which is monitored to ensure that the more valuable grassland communities are not reduced. Although bracken is an extremely invasive plant there are a few areas where it cannot colonise, including places exposed to large amounts of salt spray, but as areas are sheltered it is a problem and able to advance into what would seem to be very exposed locations. This is because salt damage is dependent on summer storms; winter storms have little or no impact on the buried rhizomes. Bracken was unrecorded in a botanical survey of the Worm carried out by the Reverend Riddelsdell in 1910, but by the end of the 1960s it covered an area of 1,000 square metres on the southeastern side of the Inner Head.

During his botanical survey the Reverend Riddelsdell found that the Outer Head was almost entirely covered by thrift and sea campion. Also present were sea storksbill *Erodium maritimum*, bluebell *Hyanthoides non-scripta* and cowslip. The latter, described as common and abundant by Riddelsdell, is still present, along with the gorse on the eastern end of the Inner Head. The eastern end of Middle Head was stated to be 'bright red to the distant observer with masses of sorrel'. Gulls started to nest on the Worm towards the end of the nineteenth century and it seems that the dense sheep's sorrel *Rumex acetosa* was a result of this.

Gulls and other colonial seabirds, such as puffins, can have major effects on the vegetation of islands. This is due mainly to the deposition of guano and the physical damage caused by trampling and extracting nest material. Although guano is very rich in nutrients and may initially stimulate plant growth, as the nutrient levels increase the soil eventually becomes toxic and unable to support plant life. However, buck's horn plantain, sea campion, spear-leaved orache *Atriplex prostrata*, sea mayweed, sea beet, common scurvygrass and sheep's sorrel may grow abundantly in moderate concentrations of guano. Mary Gillham noted in an article on the vegetation of coastal gull colonies (1964) that 'Patches of sorrel, dock, chickweed and hogweed on Worms Head, indicate more precisely than any map where gulls once nested' (Table 8).

The unusual character of the grasslands on the steep strike slopes of the north-facing side of the Inner Head is due to the area once being the site of a herring gull colony, which was abandoned as a result of increasing visitor pressure in the 1960s. The colony had already decreased substantially as a result of egg collecting during the Second World War, from a recorded peak of around 1,000

TABLE 8. Plants recorded from Worms Head gull colonies in June 1963. (Adapted from Gillham, 1964; names updated)

COMMON NAME	SCIENTIFIC NAME
Sea campion	*Silene uniflora*
Sea mouse-ear	*Cerastium diffusum*
Common chickweed	*Stellaria media*
Knotgrass	*Polygonum aviculare*
Sheep's sorrel	*Rumex acetosa*
Curled dock	*Rumex crispus*
Sea beet	*Beta vulgaris* ssp. *maritima*
Spear-leaved orache	*Atriplex prostrata*
Common mallow	*Malva sylvestris*
Common bird's-foot-trefoil	*Lotus corniculatus*
Hogweed	*Heracleum sphondylium*
Common nettle	*Urtica dioica*
Thrift	*Armeria maritima*
Field bindweed	*Convolvulus arvensis*
Ribwort plantain	*Plantago lanceolata*
Sea mayweed	*Tripleurospermum maritimum*
Groundsel	*Senecio vulgaris*
Lesser burdock	*Arctium minus*
Spear thistle	*Cirsium vulgare*
Creeping thistle	*Cirsium arvense*
Golden samphire	*Inula crithmoides*
Perennial sow-thistle	*Sonchus arvensis*
Prickly sow-thistle	*Sonchus asper*
Dandelion	*Taraxacum* sect.
Spring squill	*Scilla verna*
Red fescue	*Festuca rubra*
Perennial rye-grass	*Lolium perenne*
Fern-grass	*Catapodium rigidum*
Cock's-foot	*Dactylis glomerata*
Soft-brome	*Bromus hordeaceus* ssp. *hordeaceus*
Yorkshire-fog	*Holcus lanatus*

pairs in 1941 to only 460 pairs by 1945. In addition to the above species hogweed, creeping thistle, sheep's sorrel and curled dock *Rumex crispus* are also typical colonists of the nitrogen-enriched soils of seabird colonies and they persist here long after the colony was deserted.

Worms Head, and to a lesser extent the mainland cliffs incorporating Lewes Castle, Thurba and Paviland, is the largest seabird colony in Glamorgan with kittiwake, guillemot, razorbill, fulmar *Fulmarus glacialis* and shag *Phalacrocorax aristotelis* present. The auk and kittiwake breeding populations are regionally important, the only other colonies in the Bristol Channel occurring on the island of Lundy, although far more significant numbers of birds occur along the coast of south Pembrokeshire. For centuries local people, who collected the eggs, exploited the colonies for food. Following the area's designation as a National Nature Reserve, however, access to the top of the Outer Head was prohibited between 1 March and 31 August. At one time volunteers patrolled the area to turn away casual visitors in case they affected the nesting birds, but this practice was abandoned in the 1980s. In 2004 it was decided that the small number of visitors who make the journey to the Head are not a problem and the warning sign has since been removed. No amount of disturbance can compete, however, with the amazing mass picnic of Bethel Sunday School, Llanelli, which took place on the island at the height of the breeding season in 1854. All 400 members of the school marched to Llanelli docks to the singing of the chapel choir and set sail on two ships captained by members of the Sunday school. The sea was calm and they landed safely on the island, where they said prayers and opened the huge hampers they had brought ashore. By the time their picnic was over the tide had retreated so all the people crossed the causeway and marched singing along the cliffs to Rhossili village. The Rector saw this invasion coming and ordered the church bells to be rung in welcome. It was long remembered in Rhossili village that the unexpected guests drank the village well dry.

The remains of puffins, dating back at least 10,000 years, were found in Port-Eynon cave in the early 1930s, but the first contemporary account of puffins breeding in Gower was in 1848, when the species was reported to nest in rabbit burrows on the Worm. Predation by rats caused a decline towards the end of the nineteenth century; it seems that a few puffins continued to breed at this site until comparatively recently, but there are no birds nesting today (Fig. 93). Rats are omnivorous opportunists that will readily feed on the eggs and chicks of ground-nesting seabirds, and they will also kill adult birds. The *Glamorgan County History* published in 1936 noted that 'rats are a serious menace to the species that nest in accessible sites; they have thinned out the Puffins to such an extent that only some half-dozen pairs survive and these have been forced to take refuge in the cracks in

FIG 93. There are still a small number of puffins in the area, but breeding has not been recorded for many years, due to predation by rats. (Harold Grenfell)

the sheer north face of the Head.' The total number of birds was small, the highest count in the period from 1980 to 1992 being five individuals. There have been no studies of the number of birds taken by rats, or indeed the number of rats on the Worm, but their presence is well known, as indicated by the quote from Dylan Thomas. Predation by rats may well still be the main factor in limiting the number of puffins, which dig shallow burrows in the soft turf, or occupy old rabbit burrows. Control measures may need to be introduced if the birds are to return.

The *County History* also records other factors that have affected seabirds on the Worm in the past. 'Fortunately the promontory is now, and has been for some years, a nominally protected area, but in spite of this, its small colony of Cormorants is frequently raided and the nests destroyed by human agency.' The destruction had been going on for some time. In 1862 Kit Morgan, a resident of Parkmill, writing in his book *Wanderings in Gower*, enthusiastically related the 'sport' that could be had on the Worm:

> There are thousands of birds to be found here – gulls, cormorants, lundibirds (guillemots) and puffins. They fly in crowds over your head. If you take a boat and sail round the Head you can shoot away until you are tired.

There was still a serious problem in 1949 when Arthur Webb noted that 'of late years even such a common bird as the herring gull has had a hard struggle for survival, even on the supposedly protected Worm's Head'. Worms Head was at the time a statutory Bird Sanctuary protected under the Wild Birds Protection (Glamorganshire) Order of 1948. This was the last in a series of Protection Orders renewed virtually every five years following the Wild Birds Protection Act of 1880. The Act was, however, suspended for a short period from February 1918 to June 1919, following a request by Glamorgan County Council, in order to allow the eggs of guillemots, puffins and razorbills to be taken for food. In 1948 John Beynon, then tenant of the Worm, had contacted Glamorgan County Council:

> As tenant of Worms Head I am writing to you to see if anything can be done to protect the wild birds on the Head. I understand there is a bye-law passed for that purpose but not put in force. At present people from town come down and rob the nests by the hundreds and I want to see it stopped. If I can be any assistance to you, I shall only be too glad.

Only in the 1950s was the pressure reduced and the conservation value of the area generally recognised.

It is difficult to establish when kittiwakes first nested on the island, but they were often seen on the cliffs of the Outer Head during the early twentieth century. Up to 60 birds were recorded in July 1928, although there was no sign of breeding activity and no nests were seen. Nesting was not confirmed on the Head until July 1943, when two pairs bred. Numbers appeared to increase after this date, but the inaccessible location made surveys difficult. In 1952, however, surveys from a boat confirmed that kittiwakes were still breeding and a subsequent count in 1955 found 17 nests. By the mid-1960s the colony had expanded to about 150 pairs, with nearly 70 nests visible from the Head itself in 1966, and in 1984 the total Gower population was believed to consist of over 500 pairs. Counts in 1986, however, found that the colony had declined to 153 nests and a further count from the sea in 1996 found that it consisted of only 128 nests. This decline appears to have been related to increased predation by peregrines and greater levels of human disturbance, but in the meantime colonies had been established elsewhere on the Gower cliffs. In 1992 kittiwakes expanded their breeding range still further east, nesting on Mumbles Pier for the first time.

Guillemots have been known to breed on the Worm since at least 1802. Photographs of the main breeding ledge taken in 1907 suggested that there were around 300 pairs there, a similar number to that present in 1925. There was a decline in numbers from 1925 until 1966 when only 50 breeding pairs were seen.

Numbers recovered after this date and a count from the sea in 1996 found 177 birds on the north-facing ledges of the Outer Head. Razorbill populations have followed a similar pattern, with 250 pairs reported in 1925 and only 10 pairs by 1974, while in 1991 around 35 pairs were present (Fig. 94). Fulmars were first recorded in Glamorgan on the Head in 1946, but breeding was not confirmed until 1956 at Lewes Castle on the mainland.

Great black-backed gull *Larus marinus* was listed as 'Black and White Gull' in the *Swansea Guide* of 1802 and in 1848 Dillwyn considered the species to be 'not uncommon' on the coast. Although described as a very common resident in Glamorgan in the late 1890s the species bred only in small numbers, principally on the Worm. The colony apparently reached its greatest size in 1941, when there were 25 pairs, before declining to one pair in 1955, probably as a result of increasing disturbance by visitors. From 1967 until 1979 one or two pairs always bred on the island, but surveys in the early 1990s found that it had ceased to breed in Gower. A colony of about 30 pairs of lesser black-backed gulls *Larus fuscus* existed in the 1920s, but now only isolated pairs occasionally breed on the island. Today the majority of the nesting birds can be found on the flat roofs of industrial buildings to the east of Swansea.

FIG 94. Populations of razorbills are recovering after a decline in numbers. (Harold Grenfell)

BURRY HOLMS

Burry Holms, the name derived from the Old Scandinavian word for an island, *holm*, is also rich in wild flowers and seabirds (Fig. 95). Like Worms Head the island is cut off by the sea at around half-flood. On the Llangennith Tithe Map, dating from the 1840s, it is marked as 'Holmes Island', and it was also mentioned as an island in a charter of 1195. At their highest point on the western side the cliffs reach a height of some 30 metres.

There is an important early Mesolithic site on the island, which has been excavated over a number of years as part of a research project by the National Museum. The excavations are producing a rich variety of flints, and a later prehistoric roundhouse has also been found. An investigation of a small Bronze Age barrow on the summit many years ago produced a bronze pin. There are also ruins of a monastic settlement and an Iron Age promontory fort, consisting of a single bank and ditch, bisects the island (Fig. 96). Excavations have shown that the earliest structure below the medieval ruins was a timber church situated within a small stone-walled enclosure resembling an Irish 'cashel'. Two similar structures exist nearby, but have not been excavated. The sixth-century saint, St Cenydd, has strong associations with this area and there are several fourteenth- and

FIG 95. Burry Holms, the name being derived from the old Scandinavian *holm*, which means island. (Harold Grenfell)

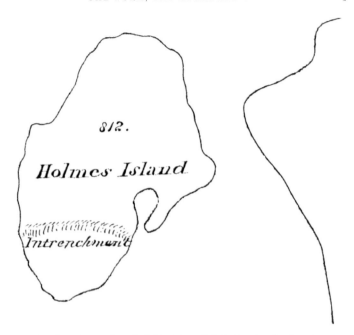

FIG 96. 'Holmes Island', as depicted on the Tithe Map of 1848, showing the Iron Age earthwork that bisects the site. (West Glamorgan Archive Service)

fifteenth-century references to hermits using the chapel of 'Kenyth at Holmes'. The medieval ruins may represent a centre of pilgrimage connected with his memory (Fig. 97). Once there was an automatic lighthouse on the island, but this was decommissioned and removed in 1966.

On the exposed rock surface around deep rock pools in the lower portion of the cliff there is an algal zone consisting of various brown seaweeds, including a variety of wracks *Fucus* spp., knotted wrack *Ascopyllum nodosum* and channelled wrack. Higher up in the spray zone are two lichens, leafy yellow scales and *Lecanora atra*. Above the lichens, where soil forms in the clefts in the rock, the dominant plants are thrift, rock samphire *Crithmum maritimum* and common scurvygrass, the presence of scurvygrass being affected by gulls, whose droppings and food remains add nitrogenous material to the soil. Twenty pairs of herring gulls were recorded nesting on the island during a census in 1959, although only a few pairs remain today. The rock crevices also contain sea campion and golden samphire together with orpine *Sedum telephium* and rock sea-spurrey.

Around sixty plant species have been recorded from the island as a whole. Windblown sand from Llangennith Burrows to the east covers the landward slopes and is dominated by marram grass. In contrast the cliff tops to the west support Yorkshire-fog, curled dock, lady's bedstraw *Galium verum*, common bird's-foot-trefoil, spear thistle *Cirsium vulgare* and carline thistle *Carlina vulgaris*. In spring the northwest of the island is covered in spring squill. The ditches of the earthwork contain a rich community of plants including cock's-foot and germander speedwell *Veronica chamaedrys*, together with salad burnet, common centaury *Centaurium erythraea* and cleavers *Galium aparine*. The well-used paths across the island are marked by sea storksbill, buck's horn plantain, sheep's sorrel and the very variable autumn hawkbit *Leontodon autumnalis*.

The few invertebrate records include green tiger beetle *Cicindela campestris*, an active, ground-dwelling beetle of sandy places (Fig. 98) and white-tailed bumble-bee, one of the commonest and most widespread bumblebees. A monarch butterfly *Danaus plexippus* was seen in October 1995 and marbled white and clouded yellow *Colias croceus* have also been recorded. Mammals are restricted to rabbit and short-tailed vole *Microtus agrestis*, while birds recorded on the island, in addition to herring gulls, include skylark *Alauda arvensis*, meadow pipit, jackdaw *Corvus monedula*, wheatear *Oenanthe oenanthe* and stock dove *Columba oenas*.

FIG 97. The author's children at the ruins of the medieval monastic settlement on Burry Holms. (Jonathan Mullard)

FIG 98. Green tiger beetle, an active predator of sandy places. (David Painter)

THE MUMBLES

Isaac Hamon noted that:

> In this parish (Oystermouth) is a safe harbour as well on the sands or flats, as alsoe in ye roade, commonly called Mumbles roade, here is two banks or Islands near the roade, commonly called ye outer mumble & the middle mumble there is another bank or small cliffe almost an island wch they call the inner mumble, in Welsh the 3 mumbles are called ye tair twarchen.

As with the other islands, the name of the Mumbles is thought to be derived from another language, in this case from the French *mamelles*, meaning breasts, but there may be a Welsh derivation from *mammoel*, which means a bare place or spot. The prominent twin limestone islands mark the western boundary of Swansea Bay (Fig. 99). Middle Head is accessible at mid-tide and Mumbles Head on most low tides, but as with the other islands the rising tide quickly isolates both of the Mumbles and great care is needed to avoid becoming stranded. During spring tides people have been stranded for many hours.

On Mumbles Head itself is the lighthouse, built in 1793, which is now Gower's only working light, and a coastal defence fort of 1861. Underneath the Head the

FIG 99. The Mumbles, viewed from Bracelet Bay. (Jonathan Mullard)

huge cavern of Bob's Cave penetrates deep into the south side of the island. In 1844 the island was the scene of some very early experiments in 'overwater telegraphy' conducted by John Dillwyn-Llewelyn and Sir Charles Wheatstone, which anticipated by many years Marconi's experiments with radio further up the Bristol Channel.

As on the Worm, red fescue forms a deep sward on Mumbles Head itself, while other plants present include sea stock, rock samphire and thrift. Hoary stock *Matthiola incana* grows on the cliffs below the old lighthouse site and as it is a garden escape the plant may have been introduced by past lighthouse-keepers (it also grows on the cliffs below the lighthouse at Nash Point on the Glamorgan Heritage Coast). The habitat appears to suit it, probably because the ancestral plant seems to be a rare native of the southern chalk cliffs that was modified by plant breeders in the eighteenth century. It is now confined to Sussex and the Isle of Wight. The cultivated version forms silvery bushes, covered in flowers from late spring to mid-summer, and is highly scented and very attractive to insects, being pollinated by bees, moths and butterflies.

In contrast to Mumbles Head, Middle Head is separated from the mainland for only two or three hours each side of the high tide. Plants occurring here in addition to the usual species include sea plantain *Plantago maritima*, ploughman's-spikenard *Inula conyzae*, perforate St John's-wort *Hypericum perforatum*, Portland spurge and hemp agrimony *Eupatorium cannabinum*. On the deeper soils of the lower slopes bracken, ragwort *Senecio jacobaea* and ivy occur. Inner Head, which is the elevated part of the adjacent mainland, has more species, mainly other garden escapes such as red valerian *Centranthus ruber*.

During the autumn migration the Mumbles, together with the adjacent Mumbles Hill, form part of the route across the Bristol Channel for small birds, such as swallow *Hirundo rustica*, martins, wheatear, redstart *Phoenicurus phoenicurus*, pipits and various warblers. At peak periods over a thousand birds per hour have been recorded passing over the islands.

MANAGEMENT

Worms Head is owned by the National Trust and managed as a National Nature Reserve by the Countryside Council for Wales, while the Mumbles are owned by the local authority and Burry Holms by a private landowner. The Worm was notified primarily because of its important seabird populations, but the maritime vegetation was also considered an important factor and it would qualify as a Site of Special Scientific Interest on botanical grounds alone. The present conservation management strategy for the island is about maintaining all habitats at their optimum condition and distribution for maximum species diversity, and there is little intervention. There is comparatively less interest in the other, admittedly much smaller, islands. More needs to be done to improve our understanding of these special corners of Gower.

CHAPTER 9

Inlet and Estuary

By scummed, starfish sands
With their fishwife cross
Gulls, pipers, cockles and sails
Out there, crow black, men
Tackled with clouds, who kneel
To the sunset nets
       Dylan Thomas,
    Prologue from *The Poems*

D AUNTING, DRAMATIC and lonely are just a few of the words that have been used to describe the Burry Inlet and Loughor Estuary. It is an untamed place and one of the last refuges of real wilderness in this part of South Wales. From its seaward end, bounded by the long sandy finger of Whiteford Burrows National Nature Reserve in the south and Pembrey Burrows in the north, to the tidal limit close to Pontardulais and the M4 motorway it covers more than 9,500 hectares. It is the largest estuarine complex wholly within Wales and dominates the north side of the peninsula, forming a real divide between Gower and Llanelli to the northwest. At low water, due to the wide tidal fluctuations (about 8 metres on average) over 70 per cent of this vast area is exposed on a regular basis, revealing a shifting landscape of sandbars, mud and glistening water channels. During spring tides 1,400 million cubic metres of sea water enter and leave the estuary twice daily. The inlet and estuary is a complex region where salt water meets fresh water, sea meets land and the seasons and tide bring constant, but cyclical, change.

Estuaries are defined as the downstream part of a river valley, subject to the tide and extending from the limit of brackish water, while marine inlets are defined as areas where sea water is not significantly diluted by fresh water. Using these definitions most of the area under consideration is an inlet, but to many people, locals and visitors, it is simply 'the Burry' or 'the estuary' or 'the Burry Estuary' (Fig. 100). Together with the nearby estuaries of the Taf, the Tywi and the Gwendraeth ('the three rivers') the River Loughor forms a single functional unit around the inlet, and research has shown that there are important interchanges of sediment and species between the four areas. A substantial area of South Wales drains, from the source of the Loughor on the Black Mountain, through the estuary and inlet to the Bristol Channel.

The national and international importance of the area is reflected in a multitude of often overlapping designations. There are five Sites of Special Scientific Interest (SSSI) within and around the estuary and one National Nature Reserve (NNR); it is a Ramsar site under the 1971 International Wetlands Convention, a Special Protection Area (SPA) for wild birds, a Special Area of Conservation (SAC) under the European Habitats Directive, a Geological Conservation Review (GCR) site, and of course most of the inlet falls within the AONB. In addition there are extensive National Trust properties and six Wildlife Trust reserves along the southern shore. But the area is much more than the sum of its constituent parts.

FIG 100. Aerial view of the Burry Inlet and Loughor Estuary. (Royal Commission on the Ancient and Historical Monuments of Wales)

THE GREAT MARSH

In the more sheltered areas, where plants have been able to colonise the intertidal mud flats, the fourth largest area of salt marsh in Britain has developed. It currently covers 2,121 hectares (Fig. 101). When the salt marsh first began to grow is not known, but the now wooded limestone cliffs along the Gower shore were active sea cliffs 5,000 years ago so any marsh must have originated later. The marsh on the southern side has accumulated in the shelter of Whiteford Point, a shingle ridge, which seems to have originated as a glacial moraine later covered by sand dunes. Sediments forming the marsh derive mainly from the redistribution of glacial deposits, together with sand and shell fragments from the seabed. The area is of national significance due to the variety of features, which include erosion cliffs, creeks and saltpans. The current marsh has grown from east to west along the southern shore and this sequence has provided important insights into saltmarsh dynamics, sediment transport and sea-level changes around the British coast. At the eastern end the mature marshes at Berthlwyd have well-developed terraces and there is an eroding marsh cliff, while to the west at Landimore the marsh is cut by numerous creeks and pans (Fig. 102). Research has shown that the upper parts of the marsh are very stable, with the creek patterns changing very little over hundreds of years, while the lower reaches vary considerably due to the channels being blocked by fresh sediment and new courses developing.

The sediments of the marsh are unconsolidated and easily eroded, so at any point in time the marsh represents a delicate balance between sedimentation and erosion. Although apparently level it has a gradient of 1:240 towards the sea, interrupted by the presence of small breaks of slope, which indicate that it has built up and subsequently eroded, the secondary marsh developing at a lower level. The development of these terraces or 'micro-cliffs' is caused by scour associated with the main estuary channel.

On the Gower shore there has been very little land claim in comparison to sites elsewhere in Britain, where saltmarsh succession is often truncated by embankments and other coastal defences. On the north shore, in contrast, the urban development of Llanelli has led to a significant loss of habitat except near Penclacwydd where the Wildfowl and Wetlands Trust have their only Welsh centre. As early as 1850 over 730 hectares had been destroyed ('reclaimed') by industrial development. The only substantial area to be enclosed on the south side is Cwm Ivy Marsh, an area adjacent to Whiteford Burrows, which was separated from the tidal marshes in 1638 by the building of an earthen sea wall,

FIG 101. The marsh at Llanrhidian, looking west towards Landimore along the ditch at the edge of the field system. (Harold Grenfell)

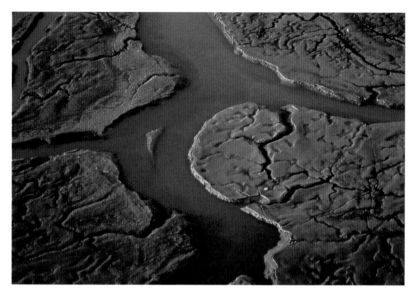

FIG 102. Creek patterns on Landimore Marsh. (Peter R. Douglas-Jones)

subsequently given additional protection by a drystone facing. The salt gradually leached away and the resulting freshwater marsh was divided up and fenced. Cwm Ivy is now considerably lower than the salt marsh outside the enclosing sea wall. In 1974 the sea overtopped the wall and to prevent a repeat the boundaries were subsequently increased in height.

Development of the marshes took place naturally until the mid eighteenth century when a breakwater, or 'training wall' of slag blocks was built diagonally across the low-water channel of the river to aid navigation to the port of Llanelli. The aim of the training wall was to use the natural power of the tide to scour a channel to the port. The wall succeeded in its objective, but it also produced changes to the overall regime in the inlet and estuary and as a consequence areas of sediment deposition and erosion were drastically altered. Once there were many different channels in the estuary, today there is only one. In July 1764 John Wesley, travelling to Gower on one of his preaching tours, was able to ride across the estuary from Kidwelly with a local guide. Once the wall was completed this became impossible.

Marsh on the southern side of the estuary extended at the expense of the sand flats, and the moorings at Pen-clawdd, formerly served by a channel deep enough for seagoing vessels, rapidly became too shallow for use. Old maps and documents show that between 1790 and 1900 the marshes increased in area by 307 hectares and by 1960 had covered a further 252 hectares. The end of Llanelli as a port in the early part of the last century meant that the training wall fell into disrepair and it was finally breached in the 1950s. The estuary is still in the process of reverting to the natural pattern of water movement, with the main channel gradually moving south again. As the wall continues to collapse this process will continue until a situation close to the original sediment distribution is reached.

The vegetation of salt marshes is usually confined to the region between the mean high water of neap tides and extreme high water of spring tides, and like other intertidal communities it shows a marked zonation at different levels. One of the features of the area often remarked upon by visiting naturalists is the undisturbed and complete succession from open sand and mud flats through pioneer saltmarsh communities to upper salt marsh and dunes, marshy fields, or even woodland. The greatest diversity of plant species is found on these upper fringes of the marsh, especially in the transition zones where it merges with sand dunes, water meadows or freshwater marsh. Particularly interesting plant communities are found at Whiteford Point, Llanrhidian and near Loughor.

The major part of the saltmarsh vegetation consists of a relatively small number of salt-tolerant plants adapted to regular immersion by the tides, and there is a clear zonation according to the frequency of inundation. At the lowest level, where pioneer communities are dominated by glasswort *Salicornia* spp., annual sea-blite *Suaeda maritima* and common cord-grass *Spartina anglica*, the plants can stand regular immersion, while the species in the upper marsh can only withstand being occasionally covered by the tide. The muddy sediments in this area also support extensive beds of the nationally scarce dwarf eelgrass *Zostera noltii*.

Common cord-grass is a new species, which originated at the end of the nineteenth century as a result of hybridisation between the native small cord-grass *Spartina maritima* and the smooth cord-grass *Spartina alterniflora*, a naturalised alien introduced from America in the 1820s. Since its introduction on a small area of marsh west of the Burry Pill in 1935, to aid its 'reclamation' as grazing land, common cord-grass has colonised substantial areas of the estuary. It now dominates a broad belt of the lower salt marsh and has also invaded the creeks to the upper salt marsh. Eastwards it extends a considerable way up the estuary. The vast area of cord-grass below the sea wall at Pen-clawdd did not exist before 1955, but by 1975 it had spread over the whole area. These extensive swards are of little value to wildlife and are considered to be a threat to bird feeding areas. In Swansea Bay efforts were made to control its spread as it was thought to be a threat to the tourist industry, but on this side of Gower it was left unchecked. In the 1960s there were calls for the marsh to be sprayed from the air with herbicides, a potentially disastrous procedure for the other vegetation and intertidal life; thankfully this did not happen.

At the present time nearly 18 per cent of the saltmarsh area is covered by the cord-grass, although some long-standing areas are contracting for reasons not fully understood. There are similar reports from other parts of Britain. A number of causes for the decline have been suggested, including a lack of sediment accretion, water-logging, wave damage, oxygen deficiency, pathogenic fungi and a loss of vigour within the species due its lack of genetic variation. Whatever the future status of the plant in the estuary there is no doubt that the spread of common cord-grass has dramatically influenced the flora of the lower salt marsh. Unfortunately there are no published accounts of the vegetation of the inlet prior to its introduction, although there are several tantalisingly brief or introductory descriptions in the literature.

The low- or mid-marsh communities are, in contrast, dominated by a closely grazed sward of the common saltmarsh-grass with sea-purslane *Atriplex portulacoides* frequent along the creek sides and wherever there is reduced grazing pressure. Grazing has a noticeable effect on the structure and composition of saltmarsh vegetation, most obviously by reducing the height and diversity of plants. The common sea lavender *Limonium vulgare*, for instance, appears to be confined to relatively less-grazed sites such as south of Loughor and the western side of the Burry Pill. Several other species also occur, usually at low densities, notably greater sea-spurrey *Spergularia media*, sea aster *Aster tripolium*, sea arrowgrass *Triglochin maritimum*, English scurvygrass *Cochlearia anglica* and sea plantain.

In the mid to upper zones of the marsh there is an extensive sward of common saltmarsh-grass mixed with red fescue and other species such as thrift and sea milkwort *Glaux maritima*. The upper edge of the grazed salt marsh is marked by a belt of the tall unpalatable sea rush in which most of the species of the red fescue community occur, with the addition of parsley water-dropwort *Oenanthe lachenalii*, autumn hawkbit and sedge *Carex* spp. North of Llanrhidian the sea rush belt is several hundred metres wide and traditionally it was cut in late summer to provide rushes for bedding and to improve the grazing. This practice was revived briefly by local farmers during 1975 when bedding straw become prohibitively expensive. A few of the graziers still cut the rush for bedding, and for young store cattle there is nothing better, even though it breaks down more slowly than straw. Two striking and rather uncommon saltmarsh plants are locally abundant in the highest grazed marsh, marsh mallow *Althaea officianalis*, which has attractive pink flowers in July (Fig. 103), and sea wormwood *Serphidium maritima* with its aromatic pinnately divided leaves. This plant community, avoided by grazing animals, is a

FIG 103. Marsh mallow, an uncommon saltmarsh plant, which is abundant on the marshes. (David Painter)

distinctive feature of the area. Much of this upper salt marsh is now managed as part of the Tir Cymen agri-environment scheme run by the Countryside Council for Wales, the local farmers having entered into 10-year agreements based on continuing current farming practices.

Further upstream the limit of salt water is characterised by extensive areas of brackish swamp dominated by common reed and sea club-rush *Bolboschoenus maritimus*, and at Llangennech this merges into reedmarsh and invading willow scrub, with abundant common club-rush *Schoenoplectus lacustris*. Diverse upper marsh swamps with tall stands of yellow iris *Iris pseudacorus* are present especially at the western end of the inlet in and around Cwm Ivy Marsh, which is of particular interest as a lowland fen meadow.

MARINE AND TERRESTRIAL INVERTEBRATES

The marine invertebrate community appears to be typical of saline, muddy sand environments. In areas of fine sand cockles are abundant along with lugworm, amphipods and worms. In muddier sediments the sand-gaper *Mya arenaria*, peppery furrow-snail *Scrobicularia plana* and mud-snail *Hydrobia ulvae* are found in extremely large numbers alongside the polychaete worms *Spio filicornis* and *Spiophanes bombyx* and the common ragworm *Nereis diversicolor*. Predators in the community include the snail *Retusa obtuse*, which feeds on mud-snails, the polychaete *Eteone longa*, which eats other polychaete worms, and general crustacean scavengers such as the common shore crab and the brown shrimp *Crangon crangon*. The lower part of the estuary is one of the few places in Britain where the polychaete worm *Ophelia bicornis* is found. On the whole, however, there is a lack of knowledge about the marine invertebrate communities, which will have to be addressed if serious decisions about the conservation of the area need to be taken. We probably know, to the nearest 10 individuals, how many oystercatchers there are in and around the Burry at any one time, but almost nothing is known about the vast majority of the invertebrate species the birds depend on, or their abundance. Nearly all the research to date has been a by-product of studies concerned with cockles.

Lugworm are used by sea anglers as bait, and as angling has increased in popularity so has the demand for lugworm. In addition anglers are now much more prepared to purchase supplies of bait from tackle dealers where prices can be very high when demand outstrips supply, especially in the autumn and winter when cod and whiting are in season. This has led to large numbers of bait diggers visiting the inlet and estuary, some of whom are employed on a commercial basis. Commercial lug diggers and experienced anglers dig a large trench with a standard garden fork, turning the sediment over and returning the spoil to the trench, but some bait diggers dig a trench two or three forks wide and place the spoil in mounds either side of the trench. The latter approach obviously affects a wider area. Due to a concern about the effects on the cockle beds bye-laws were initially introduced by the Sea Fisheries Committee in 1987. Subsequently studies by Cardiff University showed that both methods killed substantial numbers of cockles, and additional bye-laws were introduced in 1992. These prohibited bait digging in the lower three-quarters of the inlet, to protect the cockles, and there-fore indirectly created a conservation area for lugworm. There is no mechanism, however, for a Sea Fisheries Committee to directly restrict the harvesting of a marine organism unless it is classified as a 'sea fish'.

Although no detailed account of the vegetation of the salt marshes in the inlet and estuary has ever been published, salt marshes in general have been classic areas for the study of plant ecology. Researchers have been attracted by the extreme nature of the habitat, the relatively small number of species involved, the clear zonation and the effects of easily measured environmental factors. In contrast to the great quantity of published work on saltmarsh vegetation, the ecology of the associated terrestrial invertebrates has been little studied, although excellent studies of particular groups have been made. Locally work was carried out in the 1960s and 1970s on the ecology of spiders and saltmarsh mites, and on the influence of ant colonies on saltmarsh vegetation, but more research is needed to properly understand the community as a whole.

An interest in the spider fauna of the Gower salt marshes began in July 1964 when, during the course of an ecological survey of the spiders and other arthropods of the sand dunes at Whiteford National Nature Reserve, a single female of an unknown but distinctive money spider was found by G. H. Locket. This was subsequently described as a species new to science under the name of *Lasiargus gowerensis*. At the time there was considerable discussion as to whether the new species should be included in the genus *Lasiargus* or that of *Baryphyma*, as it had characters similar to both. It was eventually concluded, however, that it was a member of the second genus and it is now known as *Baryphyma gowerense*, the only species to be named after the peninsula (Fig. 104). The original animal is now preserved in the Natural History Museum as the species holotype. A holotype is the particular specimen which is first described and which carries the name of the species. Holotypes are used because concepts of a species may change over time and biologists must have criteria for assigning the original name. Having the original specimen to go back to is essential.

The female animal varies in length from 2.7 to 3.3 millimetres, while the male is slightly smaller at 2.6 to 3.1 millimetres. The head is elevated into a distinctive lobe with long curved hairs at the front. The abdomen is black, rather elongate and tapering, covered with widely spaced hairs, and has four impressed dots. The legs are a uniform light yellow-brown and covered in long hairs, with two rows of long conspicuous hairs on the underside. The double row of hairs is particularly conspicuous in the female.

The original specimen was found in a deep accumulation of drift material on the sandy foreshore of Berges Island, a small extension of sand dunes from Whiteford Burrows, but further searching failed to locate specimens in the drift material. Only in 1967 was it realised that the searching was being undertaken in the wrong area. Instead it was decided to look at some of the adjoining habitats, and large numbers of immature specimens were found in the vegetation on the higher parts of the salt marsh, occurring only in a narrow band dominated by sea rush and red fescue. Later the spider was also found in a small estuarine marsh on the north side of Oxwich National Nature Reserve. In the mid-1990s surveys revealed that the spider was actually quite widely distributed, although extremely local in its occurrence, on purple moor-grass dominated fens in lowland Wales and Norfolk. Its ecological requirements are not understood, however, and its full distribution in Britain is not yet clear.

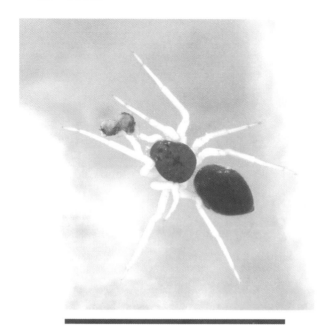

5mm

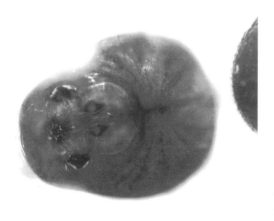

1mm

FIG 104. The Gower money spider *Baryphyma gowerense*, the only species named after the peninsula. A close-up of the male, showing the characteristic head of this species. (Natural History Museum)

In general the spider fauna of salt marshes is not rich and most species are found elsewhere, particularly in freshwater marshes, but a few, like *Baryphyma gowerense*, are characteristic of salt marshes or even confined to this habitat. Another money spider, *Erigone longipalpis*, is also fairly common on the Gower salt marshes.

THE COCKLE FISHERY

The Burry Inlet and Estuary is better known for its edible cockles than for any other fishery. There are significant mussel beds, particularly at Pen-clawdd and Whiteford Point, but it is the cockle fishery that dominates the area. Although it is a fishery steeped in history, there are no written records or photographs until the 1880s, when the cockle gathering came to be regarded as picturesque and worthy of recording. Iron Age middens (refuse heaps) found in the dunes at Whiteford show that the resource has been utilised for thousands of years, but gathering on a larger scale did not take place until the cockles began to be gathered as a supplement to income as well as diet.

In the early 1900s it was estimated that there were as many as 250 gatherers in the Burry, mainly women as the men were at work in local manufacturing industries. Some authors stated that as many as 500 families supplemented their income from the beds, but it seems that this figure is somewhat exaggerated. In contrast the modern fishery supports less than 100 people, gatherers and processors, and few women are involved. Each person collected about 130 kilograms per day, the cockles being simply raked out of the sand when the beds were exposed at low water. They were then washed and sieved to remove excess sand and to reject any undersized animals. It was, and is, backbreaking work and the tides can be dangerous. Despite the gatherers knowing the area intimately there have been many tragedies in the past, not only due to the speed at which the tide comes in, but also because of the patches of quicksand which at times are almost impossible to identify. But even with the danger of the tides and the hard work it can be very tranquil out on the sands. The cockle gatherers say that they can hear the cockles 'singing'. 'They come to the surface of the sand and all open their shells for water at the same time. It sounds like a melody. When we tread on them, the singing takes on different tones' (Roberts, 2001).

The collected cockles were placed in panniers across the backs of donkeys and taken to the shore (Fig. 105). So many donkeys were involved that the hillsides around the villages were said to echo with their braying all night. Cockles were either sold 'shell on' or more usually as boiled meat, the cooking being carried

FIG 105. Cockle gatherer at Pen-clawdd around 1948. (Estate of Evan Evans)

out in small processing plants close to the gatherers' houses. The cockles are now cooked in modern processing factories to meet current hygiene standards, but in the past they were simply boiled up on crude stoves, constructed from a few stones and metal bars. The meat was sold to nearby markets at Llanelli, Swansea and Neath. Until a few years ago the resulting empty cockleshells were regarded as a waste product and simply dumped in large spoil heaps. They were often used, in the same way that gravel might be, to make cockleshell paths for the cottages, and such paths used to be a characteristic feature of the area. They were previously free to anyone who wanted them, but increasing interest in garden design now means that the shells for the first time have a value.

The cockle women were well-known figures and had almost a regulation dress for going to market, with red and black stripes, black and white aprons, grey plaid shawls and flat straw hats with raised brims on which they carried a wooden pail of cockles. At the same time they carried two large baskets on their arms. Before the train ran to Pen-clawdd the women used to walk the seven miles into Swansea, balancing the wooden pails on their heads. They walked barefoot to save their shoes and on the outskirts of town would wash their feet and put on their boots to go into town. To this day this area of Swansea is still called Olchfa, which means in Welsh 'the washing place'. The arrival of the railway meant that fresh cockles could be sent greater distances, and women went to lodge in towns to the east of Swansea where they could receive deliveries by rail and then market them. At its height the cockle industry was both extensive and complex and contributed significantly to the local economy.

In the 1920s major developments took place in the fishery. Firstly the horse-drawn cart was introduced in place of the donkey and panniers. This enabled an individual to gather over 520 kilograms per day, four times as much as previously. Secondly as manufacturing declined in the area men were drawn into the gathering to collect these enhanced loads and the harvesting of stocks intensified. Together these changes had such an effect on the cockle beds that in 1921 a minimum landing size was introduced by the South Wales Sea Fisheries Committee to protect the breeding stock. The main commercial beds cover little more than 2.5 square kilometres, a small area compared with the other main cockle fisheries in Britain, so they cannot support intensive activity. By 1952 so many cockles were being taken that the Committee was forced to consider setting a limit to control the amount taken in any one day, but it took until 1965 before the fishery was licensed, to limit the quantity of cockles removed.

Despite the constraints on exploitation, attempts have been made to improve the efficiency of the hand gathering. At one stage a hand dredge was designed which consisted simply of a toothed blade fixed in front of a rectangular mesh box to hold the catch. The gatherer moved backwards, pulling the handle of the dredge towards him with sharp sideways movements. There were many complaints that the dredge damaged the young cockles and permission for its use was withdrawn in 1969.

The fishery may cover a comparatively small area, but its production is nationally important. In the mid-1960s catches almost equalled that from the rest of the UK, although due to natural variability in the amount of cockle 'spat', which settles each year from the plankton, the size of the stock and the catch vary as well. Moderately good settlements of spat in 1965 and 1967 ensured that catches remained high until the early 1970s when physical changes in the substrate caused by the southward movement of the main river channel, probably due to further collapse of the training wall, resulted in a rapid decline in the number of cockles in the traditional beds. There was some erosion of the beds, but the main problem was a substantial reduction in the amount of fine sediment and an increase in coarse sediment, which is less suited to cockle settlement and survival. This period of particularly poor catches coincided with an increase in the number of oystercatchers. Despite there being no evidence of a link between the two facts the wrong conclusions were drawn and there was a demand from the gatherers that the birds be culled to protect the cockle stocks. The oystercatchers were claimed to be eating up to 250 grams of cockles per day and to be taking up to ten times as many cockles on an annual basis as the gatherers. This figure was based on studies on the Conwy Estuary in North Wales and took no account of the fact that many of the birds fed well away from the commercial cockle beds.

After a preliminary research programme consisting of cannon-netting and colour-ringing, which produced few results, over 9,238 birds were shot during the winter of 1973/4. There was a bounty of 25 pence on each bird. Peak counts of birds at that time were 20,000 per year. An international outcry followed the culling, which was halted prematurely, and no further culls have ever taken place. By the winter of 1975 the species had recovered to pre-cull levels and in the winter of 1986 these levels were exceeded. Since then there has been a reduction in numbers, suggesting that changes are determined by breeding success elsewhere. An analysis of the issue in 1977 concluded that the oystercatcher's impact on the cockle population was much exaggerated and that cockle stocks would recover naturally. This has proved to be the case.

The cockle industry today is precisely as it was in the 1700s except that the horses and carts, which replaced the donkey and panniers, have themselves been replaced by tractors and trailers. This last change only happened in 1987. Whereas in the other major cockle fisheries in the Dee Estuary and Morecambe Bay vessel suction-dredging and mechanical harvesting using tractors has been allowed, the rake and the sieve still prevail in the Burry. The Sea Fisheries Committee approach, through the licensing regime, of providing maximum stability for a locally based industry has led to arguably the most sustainable cockle fishery in Britain. A limited number of licences, about 55, are issued each year for the hand-raking of cockles only. Gathering takes place all week except on Sundays to a quota of 300–600 kilograms per person per day. No night collection is allowed. The minimum cockle sizes are set via riddle size (a handheld measurement device) to allow the survival of sufficient spawning stock.

An approach was made to the Committee in 1991 to license the use of harvesters adapted from agricultural machinery, but a decision was deferred until a scientific study had been carried out. Trials of a tractor-towed cockle harvester subsequently took place in the Burry Inlet on one day in October 1992 (Fig. 106) and the effects on cockle populations, other invertebrates and birds were intensively monitored by a range of organisations. The tractor dredger was very efficient at removing adult cockles from shallow depths and the cockle gatherers were surprised at the large number of cockles gathered from areas they considered uneconomic to harvest by hand. The conclusions were that tractor dredgers could

FIG 106. Trial of a mechanical cockle harvester in October 1992. (Jonathan Mullard)

work out adult cockle beds very quickly and that their numbers would need to be strictly controlled. In the end the proposal was not pursued, although markets for seafood are increasing and extra demand is fuelling higher prices. It is not inconceivable that one day tractor dredgers will be at work in the estuary, but it would be a mistake. The current hand-raking fishery, locally based and with an enforceable daily quota system, removes 20 to 30 per cent of the cockle biomass annually in a non-destructive way.

This sustainable harvest was stopped abruptly in July 2001, however, when a sample of cockles indicated the possibility of diarrhetic shellfish poisoning, which could cause a serious health risk to anyone eating them. It is caused by the presence of marine dinoflagellates *Dinophysis* spp. These dinoflagellates are widely distributed and sometimes form 'red tides', but not all species produce toxins. The result from eating infected products is vomiting and diarrhoea. Although the effectiveness of the test was disputed by the gatherers a temporary prohibition order on collecting was immediately placed by the local authorities. This ban was on and off from July 2001 until August 2002 with the longest break in this period being for 10 months, the greatest gap in gathering ever recorded. Although there was a previous break in 1996, as a result of the oil spill from the *Sea Empress* disaster, the positive DSP tests created a very difficult time for the gatherers, their families and the processors who make a living from the estuary.

New European directives on pollution, quality control and health have led to requirements for inward investment and the 'picturesque' processing sheds previously used have been replaced by new facilities. In 1994 a group of cockle gatherers created a joint company to process the shellfish, investing in a state-of-the-art cooking facility capable of producing many tonnes daily; there are now three such plants in the area and they take most of the cockles gathered. The benefits, however, have been top prices for quality produce and increased markets. The industry is no longer purely local and most of the cockles collected in the estuary are sent abroad to countries such as France and Spain, which have over-fished their own cockle beds. The high demand has considerably increased the price of cockles, which have risen from around £200 per tonne in the mid-1990s to around £600 per tonne in 2004. The trade in Britain is now worth over £20 million a year. Unlike elsewhere in Britain, where migrant workers have been used, with results such as the tragic drowning of 20 cockle gatherers in Morecambe Bay in February 2004, the licensing system has so far meant that the licence holders are still the same people and families that have worked in the fishery for decades.

FISH AND FISHERIES

Specimens of almost all British marine fish species have been recorded from the area, but sea bass, mullet Chelon labrosus and flounder Platichthys flesus are regarded as typical of the estuary and surrounding coastal waters. Other species such as plaice, sole, cod and whiting are regarded as regular visitors. In the past herring Clupea harengus was also plentiful. The principal methods of fishing for these species are by fixed net or rod and line (Fig. 107). Boat netting is not allowed and no regular trawling takes place. Fishing takes place on a seasonal basis according to the availability of species, with bass and mullet in summer and autumn, flounder in autumn and winter and cod in winter.

Total commercial landings of these species from within the estuary are minimal, with only a few people now setting nets on an irregular basis, often 'for the pot'. At low tide lines of abandoned metal stakes, formerly used to support fixed nets, can be seen at the tip of Whiteford Point, clear evidence of the much greater fishing activity in the past. Many of the fishermen were miners seeking to supplement their income, fishing the inlet and estuary with 'field nets' in between working shifts at the colliery. Much of the work was done at night, alone or in small groups. It was dangerous work, but the men knew every part of the shore and could operate in almost complete darkness if necessary. Most of the nets were fixed to the base of the poles, although the herring fishermen strung their nets three-quarters of the way up the pole, as the herring came into the inlet much

FIG 107. Father and son hold a locally caught sea bass, weighing around 1.5 pounds (0.7 kilograms), before returning it to the sea, as it is underweight. (Harold Grenfell)

nearer the surface than other fish. The catch, often 18 to 20 kilograms of fish, would, as with the cockles, be transported back to the shore by donkey.

Bass are exploited all around the coastal area, through the use of rod and line, net, and to a lesser extent trawl. Due to the pressure on the stocks the inlet has been designated as a bass nursery area. For this reason, boat fishing for bass is seasonally restricted. Catches of bass and other species dependent on the estuary from Carmarthen Bay are significant, however, with the Sea Fisheries Committee estimating that over 25 tonnes of bass are landed annually.

As the season progresses, the anglers tend to concentrate upon sea trout *Salmo trutta* and, to a lesser extent, Atlantic salmon *S. salar*. The sea trout run starts in April and usually reaches a peak in late May and early June. The first fish to enter tend to be the larger, multiple-spawning ones, with the main run of maiden fish in late May and June. During July and August the smaller shoal sea trout, known as whitling, enter the rivers. The salmon that do enter the rivers tend to do so during the summer and autumn. The best months for sea trout fishing are therefore usually June, July and August, while salmon fishing tends to be restricted to September and October. Although these are the principal months, sea trout and salmon can be caught throughout the season from March to October. The Loughor has an average recorded annual catch of only 9 salmon and 195 sea trout.

Non-commercial species include both the sea lamprey *Petromyzon marinus* and the river lamprey *Lampetra fluviatillis*, primitive jawless fishes resembling an eel. Both fish need clean gravel for spawning and marginal silt or sand for the burrowing juveniles. The larva feeds by filtering fine particles during the five years of its freshwater life, while the marine stage develops a sucker-like mouth to feed on marine fish such as the shad *Clupea alosa* and salmon before eventually returning to fresh water to spawn and die.

Other species which occur in the area include two members of the herring family, twaite shad *Alosa fallax* and allis shad *A. alosa*. The estuaries feeding into Carmarthen Bay contain the only viable populations of shad in the UK and for this reason the area is of national importance. While twaite shad is found along most of the western coastline of Europe allis shad is rare and declining. Like the herring, shad feed on zooplankton, filtering it from the water through comb-like gill rakers. Both fish have streamlined bodies, distinct circular scales with a toothed edge on the lower margin, and a membrane partially covering each eye. The only reliable way of separating the two species is by counting the gill rakers; twaite shad have only 40 to 60 while allis shad have 90 to 130.

Sand eels, particularly the lesser sand eel *Ammodytes tobicnus*, are common in the estuary and provide an important food resource for many other fish and for seabirds. They are also the basis of a small bait industry.

BIRD POPULATIONS

If there is one feature of the inlet and estuary that attracts the interest of naturalists it is the importance of the area for birds. The sand, the alluvial mud with its wealth of invertebrate fauna, the salt marshes and sea-washed turf offer a wide range of habitats. The estuary is the most important wholly Welsh estuary for waterfowl, being valuable both as a wintering area and as a resting area during the spring and autumn passage for many artic-breeding species. The area lies on a major migratory flyway and many birds moving to and from other wintering areas on the Mediterranean and European coasts stop for a while on their journey. The area increases in importance when there are periods of severe cold weather in eastern England and birds move to the comparative warmth of the west.

The Burry Inlet qualifies as a wetland of international importance due to the sheer number of birds present during the winter. It regularly holds more than 20,000 birds, with a total average count in the late 1980s of nearly 47,000 (Table 9). The inlet is also of international importance for the wintering populations of pintail *Anas acuta* and oystercatcher, with 1.7 per cent and 3 per cent respectively of

TABLE 9. Waders and wildfowl on the Burry Inlet. Average peak winter counts 1983/4–1987/8. (Data abstracted from Prys-Jones, 1989)

COMMON NAME	SCIENTIFIC NAME	AVERAGE COUNT	QUALIFYING LEVEL FOR NATIONAL IMPORTANCE	QUALIFYING LEVEL FOR INTERNATIONAL IMPORTANCE
Shelduck	*Tadorna tadorna*	1,385	750	1,250
Wigeon	*Anas penelope*	5,353	2,000	5,000
Teal	*Anas crecca*	2,083	1,000	2,000
Pintail	*Anas acuta*	1,889	250	750
Oystercatcher	*Haematopus ostralegus*	17,812	2,800	7,500
Knot	*Calidris canutus*	5,488	2,200	3,500
Sanderling	*Calidris alba*	167	140	150
Turnstone	*Arenaria interpres*	579	450	500
Shoveler	*Anas clypeata*	217	90	1,000
Golden plover	*Pluvialis apicarius*	2,020	2,000	10,000
Grey plover	*Pluvialis squatarola*	705	210	800
Curlew	*Numenius arquata*	1,312	910	3,000
Other species		7,836		
			qualifying level	qualifying level
Total		**46,846**	**10,000**	**20,000**

the European population (Fig. 108). Oystercatchers wintering on the inlet originate mainly from mainland Scotland, the Faeroes and Iceland, as well as more local birds from the Pembrokeshire islands, and these patterns have remained unchanged since monitoring started in the 1960s. Once settled in the estuary birds probably winter there for life, and some initially ringed during the 1960s were still present in the 1990s.

The area is also of national importance for three species of wildfowl, brent goose *Branta bernicla*, shelduck *Tadorna tadorna* (Fig. 109) and shoveler *Anas clypeata*. Five species of waders also meet the same criteria: curlew, bar-tailed godwit, grey plover, dunlin and knot *Calidris canutus*. Vast densely packed flocks of thousands of knot are often a distinctive feature of the south shore. There are a small number of resident eider duck *Somateria mollissima*, which was adopted as the symbol of the Glamorgan Wildlife Trust. The eider duck is one of the enigmas of Gower ornithology. Although both males and females are present all year round and some prebreeding behaviour has been observed there is no evidence that successful

FIG 108. Around 3 per cent of the European population of oystercatchers overwinter in the inlet and estuary. (Harold Grenfell)

FIG 109. Male shelduck in the estuary. The area is nationally important because of the numbers of wildfowl using the area in winter. (Harold Grenfell)

breeding has occurred in the whole period from about 1900, when they were first recorded, until today. The population has fluctuated in number, rising from 30 birds in the 1950s to over 200 in December 1988, followed by a rapid decline to the 15 to 25 individuals present during the early 1990s. Numbers have now risen again to over 115 birds in 2001.

Dylan Thomas's 'fishwife cross gulls' are present throughout the year in varying numbers. The highest numbers occur in August and September, when regular flocking after the summer breeding season occurs. Of the five gull species recorded three species show a considerable increase: black-headed gull, lesser black-backed gull and great black-backed gull, while common gull numbers have remained static and herring gull has significantly decreased in numbers. This decline is almost certainly linked to the closure of nearby refuse tips.

The extensive reedbeds at Llangennech support breeding reed warblers *Acrocephalus scirpaceus* and sedge warblers *A. schoenobaenus* as well as reed buntings *Emberiza schoeniclus*.

A significant addition to the bird list is the little egret *Egretta garzetta*, first recorded in 1984 (Fig. 110). Until comparatively recently the little egret had been a rare visitor, with only single birds seen, but now counts of 130 birds or more are common during the winter. Severe cold weather can prove difficult for the egrets, but the relatively mild winters on the estuary mean that it can overwinter here.

FIG 110. Little egret, first recorded in the area in 1984. Over 130 are now present during the winter months. (Harold Grenfell)

It bred for the first time in Britain in 1996 and there were more than 30 pairs nesting at nine sites in 1999. It is probably only a matter of time before it breeds in the inlet and estuary. The little egret has been joined recently by another 'exotic' bird, the Eurasian spoonbill *Platalea leucorodia*. Between 50 and 100 individuals are recorded in Britain each year, mostly on passage or as wandering juveniles. To date only single birds have been seen here, but it did breed in Britain in 1998, for the first time in many centuries.

Systematic work on the wildfowl, wader and gull populations by dedicated local researchers, especially Robert Howells, started in 1949, and over more than half a century of continuous recording an incredibly detailed knowledge of the area and its value for birds has been built up. In 1969 the British Trust for Ornithology and the RSPB started the Birds of Estuaries Enquiry. From this date until 1984 weekly counts were made of the whole inlet, and after 1984 the weekly counts were replaced by counts on at least eight days per month. In total 56 species of birds have been recorded in this way. Such an intensity of observation is probably unequalled anywhere else in Britain and certainly was a major factor contributing to the recognition of the area's national and international importance.

The distribution of birds in the inlet and estuary varies according to the season and the state of the tide, but there are some constants that make it easier for the bird-watcher to locate various species. Ducks and waders in particular have different requirements for their roosts. Waders need exposed ground, the smaller species preferring short grass, sand or shingle while the larger species, especially curlew and redshank *Tringa totanus* (Fig. 111), are able to roost in fairly long vegetation. Ducks usually roost on the water in a belt near the edge of the marsh. On high spring tides, however, virtually all birds move to Whiteford. The majority of birds feed on the marsh from Whiteford to Salthouse Point, although oystercatchers, knot and pintail feed on the sandbanks in the centre of the estuary. A separate group of oystercatchers and turnstones *Arenaria interpres* feed on the mussel scars to the north of Whiteford Point.

Despite the wealth of bird life the south side of the inlet is not a popular place for bird-watching. Whiteford Point is the area most visited by bird-watchers, although it is a long walk out to the hide at the end of the spit and good views of the birds are only possible at certain states of the tide. There are few large concentrations of birds conveniently near roads north or south of the inlet where they can easily be seen. In this respect the National Wetlands Centre at Penclacwydd on the north side, run by the Wildfowl and Wetlands Trust, is fulfilling a demand and is very popular, especially with family groups.

Wildfowling, a traditional coastal activity formerly pursued for food, is now

FIG 111. Redshank at Pen-clawdd . (Harold Grenfell)

continued as a sport. Until the early 1950s foreshore and marsh shooting was more or less unregulated, but with the passing of the Protection of Birds Act in 1954 some of the wildfowlers shooting in the inlet worked to create organised clubs to obtain definite legal rights to shoot in certain areas and to exercise some control over the activities of their members. Two Wildfowlers' Associations were eventually established, covering the north side and the south side respectively. Both administer their shooting responsibly and have a good conservation record. Today the activity is governed by the Wildlife and Countryside Act 1981, which allows the shooting of ducks and geese on the foreshore between 1 September and 20 February inclusive. In the inlet and estuary it is mainly wigeon *Anas penelope* that are targeted, together with some teal *A. crecca* and mallard *A. platyrhynchos.* The total estimated annual 'bag' is around 200 birds, an insignificant figure in conservation terms considering the number of birds that overwinter in the area. The West Glamorgan Wildfowlers' Association leases shooting on some 2,000 hectares of Llanrhidian Marsh from the National Trust and the area is wardened by members of the clubs in conjunction with the National Trust and the Countryside Council for Wales. In 1964 the Association voluntarily gave up shooting rights over parts of the marsh adjacent to Whiteford National Nature Reserve. This gesture by the wildfowlers meant sacrificing the most important 'flight line' used by wigeon, and as a result numbers have increased.

The short-eared owl *Asio flammeus*, a scarce winter visitor, can often be seen in the late afternoon, in autumn and winter, hunting over Llanrhidian Marsh. It bred near Pen-clawdd during the nineteenth century and there is evidence to suggest that breeding occurred in some of the dunes during the early 1920s, but there have been no recent records. There have, however, been a few sightings of birds during the summer, such as the two individuals seen on Fairwood Common in June 1986, which suggest that it has bred in the area comparatively recently.

COMMON-LAND GRAZING

The salt marshes have been used as common-land grazing for hundreds of years. A survey of Gower Anglicana in 1583 stated 'The lord and tenants of this Lordship may enter all commons as Llanrhidian Marsh and any other and have done tyme out of minde, without contradiction as farre as we know without lett or interruption.' All the grazing marshes are now registered common land and the sea-washed turf sustains large numbers of sheep as well as ponies and cattle. Currently about 300 Welsh mountain ponies, 6,000 ewes and their lambs and 30 cattle graze the area (Fig. 112). This intensive grazing creates a sward that is attractive to overwintering wildfowl and waders, while less intensive grazing produces a tussock structure that is used by breeding waders.

FIG 112. Ponies and sheep grazing on the marsh at Wernffrwd. (Harold Grenfell)

In total the marshes on the southern side of the estuary cover an area of 1,098 hectares, approximately half of the salt marsh in the estuary. All this salt marsh is grazed, in contrast to the salt marsh on the north side, which is one of the best national examples of ungrazed salt marsh. The ownership of the area is divided between the Crown Estate, the Duke of Beaufort's Somerset Trust, the National Trust and a private landowner. Many of the commoners are farmers who have lands within the Manors of Landimore, Weobley or Llanrhidian with rights over the manorial wastes including the marshes.

From time immemorial the commoners have moved their sheep according to tide and season, and as there is a substantial tidal range in the Burry the farmers need to consult their tide tables when managing their stock. A 7.0 metre tide causes no problems and will not cover any of the grass, while a 7.5 metre tide covers about half the marsh and an 8.0 metre tide covers the whole marsh. Wind speed also has an effect on the height and speed of the tide, while the tide tends to fill the many pills and reans first, cutting off the exit from the marshes. As a result some sheep have to be moved on a 7.5 metre tide and all sheep on an 8.0 metre tide. Each farmer knows the area where his sheep may be grazing and therefore the time available before high tide to move animals.

In contrast to the sheep, which will drown if left out unattended, the ponies know the marsh well and will walk in with the tide. Sometimes they will remain standing on the higher ground, even up to their stomachs in the water, knowing that the tide will eventually go out. Occasionally ponies standing in this way are forced off by the depth of water and then swim in single file to the shore led by the dominant mare. Unfortunately well-meaning but uninformed members of the public who do not know the ways of the marsh see ponies standing deep in the water, assume that they are going to drown and ring the police, the RSPCA and other organisations. Despite regular publicity about the issue the perception continues.

The grazing is good and the animals thrive on it. Being covered by the tide twice a day in the course of the tidal cycle brings nutrients and silts which feed the sward throughout the seasons. There is a problem for the sheep, however, in constantly eating salt-washed, silt-laden turf in that they lose their teeth early. The lambing cycle of a ewe on the marsh is only about three crops whereas a hill farmer would expect five or six crops. False teeth were tried and fitted to the sheep some years ago, but they did not appear to be successful. But salt-washed mutton is a local delicacy and some butchers place special orders for marsh sheep and lambs. Until about 1904 the fleeces from the sheep were spun into yarn and woven into quilts and blankets in the mills at Llanrhidian; today they are virtually worthless.

Nearer the enclosed fields bounding the upper shore, the 'inbye' land, there are large areas of sea rush where there is always some well-sheltered grass for the harder winter weather. Little is known, however, about the grazing behaviour of animals in salt marshes. Selective grazing, trampling, dunging, nutrient redistribution and the interactions of different grazing species are all likely to be important factors in determining the nature of the saltmarsh vegetation. Some initial studies of pony grazing on the salt marsh were undertaken by the University of Swansea in 1975 and 1976, but these have never been followed up. These preliminary studies showed that a wide range of saltmarsh plants was grazed and that the preferred plants varied widely between different individuals and at different times of year. Analysis of dung showed that in general saltmarsh-grass and red fescue form the major part of the diet. Some groups of ponies do graze and trample common cord-grass, maintaining short, open swards in places, while other areas remain ungrazed. Similar work undertaken in the early 1970s in Bridgwater Bay, Somerset, found that areas of cord-grass could be converted into saltmarsh-grass pasture in five to ten years by sheep grazing, but there does not seem to be enough grazing pressure on the Gower marshes for this approach to be effective.

THE FUTURE

At the height of concern about the invasion of common cord-grass and shortly after the oystercatcher cull, it was noted that the inlet and estuary had 'a history of thoughtless interference' (Nelson-Smith & Bridges, 1977), with proposals intended to favour only one interest conflicting with the needs of others. Also in the writer's mind at the time was the proposal by the Loughor Boating Club for a tidal barrage across the Loughor. The Club had contracted Swansea University's Engineering Department in 1969 to carry out a feasibility study for a barrage 'to contain a freshwater lake of 400–600 acres [162–243 hectares] with a new Swansea to Llanelli link road across the top'. The intention was to use the area for water sports. Although no further progress was made the issue is still raised in the local newspapers every few years. Today, with the international importance of the estuary well understood and better liaison and consultation between the various local and regional interests, the barrage is unlikely to be built. There is, however, growing concern about an issue that was scarcely recognised in the 1970s, and that is a rise in sea level. Changes in sea level due to global warming are likely to cause great changes to the inlet and estuary over the next hundred years.

Sea level is currently rising at a rate of about 2 millimetres per year and the forecast is that the level will rise approximately 40 centimetres by 2100. The rate of the rise depends on three different factors, some of which researchers are more confident in than others. The first definite factor is that increasing global temperatures are causing sea water to expand as it warms. Secondly there is a moderate certainty that melting glaciers will add to the volume of the sea, and finally there is a concern that the instability of ice sheets could contribute to large-scale and sudden sea-level rise.

Salt marshes and intertidal areas are obviously sensitive to a rise in sea levels, but they are not passive elements of the landscape and as the sea level rises the surface of the marsh and sands will also rise due to inputs of sediment and organic material. If this input keeps pace with sea level then the marsh and sands will grow upwards. If it does not, then they will be steadily submerged. In this situation vegetation will be covered by the tide for progressively longer periods and it may die, giving way to bare intertidal areas or even open water. Direct losses of habitat due to sea-level rise can be offset by higher areas converting to marsh, but there is comparatively little room for this on the south side of the estuary. If current predictions are correct, in a hundred years or so the sea will once more wash against the limestone cliffs of north Gower and the inlet and estuary, as we know it today, will have disappeared.

CHAPTER 10

A Common Resource

*Then there is the Gower peninsula, a world on its own, and one where commons play a
large and somewhat unusual part.*
    W. G. Hoskins & L. Dudley Stamp, *The Common Lands of England and Wales*

COMMONS HAVE been part of the Gower landscape for centuries and
throughout that time, perhaps even for a thousand years, they have
been almost untouched. As previously mentioned, the original limits
of the commons are amongst the oldest, if not the oldest, surviving boundaries
in the peninsula. As a result they are havens for a wide variety of wildlife, as well as
representing a remarkable historical and cultural legacy. Inland the large areas
of common, dominated by sandstone heath ridges, including the soaring sweep
of Cefn Bryn, 'the backbone of Gower', are the most prominent features of the
peninsula. Covering more than a third of the total area, they form, for most people,
a backcloth to the more popular coastline. Visitors seek the high points to park
their cars and go for a short walk to see the 'wild ponies', but, on the whole, the
inland commons are left to themselves even on the busiest summer days. Elsewhere in lowland Britain there has been a widespread decline in grazing animals
on commons, village greens and sand dunes, with a subsequent loss of wildlife
interest, but in Gower the commons are still an important part of the farm
economy. The siting of farmsteads emphasises this, situated as they are on the
edge of commons, such as on Cefn Bryn and Hardings Down, where farm gates
open directly onto the grazing land. Nearly three-quarters of the area covered by
the Gower commons is lowland heathland, and the peninsula is one of the most
important areas in Britain, and indeed Europe, for this habitat.
    There are three main areas of common land, the sea-cliff commons, the

saltmarsh commons and the 'inland' commons. The wildlife and history of the
sea cliffs and salt marshes has been covered in previous chapters; this chapter will
therefore, for the most part, be concerned with the latter.

LAW AND PRACTICE

It is a popular misconception that commons are public land, but although the
local authority owns Fairwood Common most of the Gower commons are still
owned by the 'Lord of the Manor' or his successor in title. There used to be two
main hereditary owners, the Duke of Beaufort and the Penrice Estate, until the
latter sold their common land and manorial waste to the National Trust in 1964.
The other major owner is Llangennith Manors, a Company set up by a group of
commoners who bought 500 acres (202 hectares) of common land in 1974 from
the Lord of the Manor of Llangennith East and Llangennith West. The local
authority, which was then the County Borough of Swansea, was given Fairwood
Common by the Lord of Kilvrough Manor, Arthur Owen Thomas, in 1935.

The law of common land is notoriously complex and much of the legislation
dates back to the nineteenth century. While the aim of the earliest legislation was
in fact to facilitate the enclosure of commons, by 1876 perceptions had changed
and the Commons Act of that year put the emphasis on regulation rather than
enclosure. In terms of the conservation of common land one of the most
important pieces of legislation is Section 194 of the Law of Property Act 1925.
This applies to all the Gower commons and prohibits a number of actions unless
the prior consent of the Welsh Assembly Government has been obtained. The Act
has helped protect commons across Britain from the erection of buildings, the
construction of car parks and other similar proposals. Fencing is often permitted
to contain animals so long as adequate public access is allowed. The National
Trust Act of 1907 set out that the Trust should keep all the commons it owns
'unenclosed and unbuilt on as open spaces for the recreation and enjoyment of
the public', and the commons that it owns are therefore accessible in their entirety.

Another key piece of legislation is the Commons Registration Act 1965, which
required that all common land or manorial waste should be registered with the
County Councils, which were designated as Registration Authorities. People
claiming ownership of land and those who grazed it or claimed other rights had
to register their claims. A number of small areas of common land have been lost
as a result of this: for example, Gabriel Powell's survey of 1764 refers to 16 acres of
common land on Worms Head, which is not on the current register. To qualify
for grazing rights on the Gower commons a farmer had to own land adjoining or

adjacent to the common and for every 1.5 acres (0.6 hectares) of farmland they were entitled to claim grazing on the common for one cow, or one horse, or five sheep. The total fixed number and type of animals that each commoner is entitled to graze is known as their 'stint'. No one could have anticipated how complex the registration process would be. Hearings to decide claims on the Gower commons have still not been completed, 34 years after the passing of the Regulations in 1971, and they are probably the last areas of common land in Britain to be registered. There is a great difference, however, between legal and actual grazing levels, with the number of animals present at any one time being much lower than the legal number (Fig. 113). Commons do, however, accumulate astonishing numbers of rights.

As described in Chapter 4, from the Norman period onwards all land was presumed to be manorial, that is situated in a manor, this being the principal social, agricultural and economic unit. Some land was cultivated solely for the benefit of the lord and was known as his 'demesne' land. All of the common land of Gower was included in either a demesne manor or a mesne manor, the latter being manors held by vassals of the lord. Land not suitable, or needed, for cultivation was considered as 'manorial waste', and people gradually acquired by custom certain rights in relation to this waste. Even as late as the mid nineteenth century, when the tithe commissioners surveyed Llangennith parish, the large hill and dune commons were still described in the tithe award as 'Lord's Waste'. The prevention and control of encroachments on common or manorial land was an important matter for the steward of the Lordship of Gower. From the early medieval period onwards the commons provided a valuable resource for the

FIG 113. Cattle on Pengwern Common. Note the gradual transition from the common to woodland. (Harold Grenfell)

Lord's tenants, providing additional grazing, as well as economic benefits such as the right to cut gorse for feed and bracken for bedding, to remove turf and to quarry stone. The manorial tenants themselves fiercely guarded the area over which their common rights could be exercised, and their successors continue to do so today.

All these rights involved the ability to take advantage of the natural products of the land in question and 'were the residue of rights that were much more extensive, rights that in all probability are older than the modern conception of private property. They probably antedate the idea of private property in land, and are therefore of vast antiquity' (Hoskins & Stamp, 1963). These rights were not simply charming local customs: in many cases people depended on their rights for their survival in that they allowed them to obtain fuel and feed their animals, and even provided some of their own food. This is the origin of the common land system that remains very much an essential part of the local economy. The rights, which are attached to properties adjoining the common and not available to the public at large, have been handed down through the generations for nearly a thousand years and are held by individuals known as commoners. Today there are about 500 commoners with rights over the common land.

Writing in the New Naturalist volume on *The Common Lands of England and Wales* (1963), Hoskins and Stamp noted:

> *No changes could be effected in the management or use of the common without the consent of the whole body of commoners. This has been a powerful safeguard in preserving our commons from hasty and ill-considered change, usually under some temporary and passing pressure. We probably owe some of our most unaltered commons to a few awkward old men here and there, who refused to agree to what seemed a desirable change in the eyes of the majority.*

Even as late as 1981 the local authority, in the *Swansea District Plan*, proposed 'single and multi-use zones on Cefn Bryn to accommodate a country park, a small site for touring caravans, some forestry and a substantial amount of agricultural land', and almost as an afterthought 'a remote wild zone with some grazing and limited public access'. The document goes on to say, with considerable understatement, 'The problem is one of preparing management schemes which will be implemented and respected by all concerned.' Despite the number of such ill-considered proposals over the last hundred years the protective approach of the commoners and landowners has ensured that nearly 7,000 hectares of common land has survived in Gower (Table 10), probably a greater proportion than in any other similar area of lowland Britain.

TABLE 10. The Gower commons. (Adapted from Penford *et al.*, 1990)

CL UNIT	NAME OF COMMON	AREA (HA)
1	Rhossili Downs and Cliffs	1354.4
2 (S)	Newton Cliffs and Summerland Cliff	34.8
2	Hardings Down	112.1
3 (S)	Bracelet Common	31.5
3	Ryers Down	87.0
4	Llanmadoc Hill / Tankey Lane Moor	209.7
5	Landimore and Llanrhidian Marsh	2300.0
6	Llanrhidian Hill and the Common	6.5
8	Cefn Bryn with Manorial Waste	826.3
9	Pengwern Common	157.9
10	Welsh Moor and Forest Common	101.4
11	Mynydd Bach y Cocs	65.1
12	Pen-clawdd, Gowerton Marshes	320.0
13	Pennard Cliffs and Burrows	224.4
13 (S)	Middle Head	1.4
14 (S)	Langland Cliffs	20.6
14	Bishwell Common	13.4
15	Fairwood and Clyne Commons	754
16	Bishopston Valley	40.6
17	Barlands	14.6
69	Penmaen and Nicholaston Burrows	39.7
107	Oxwich Point and Slade Cliff	15.0
108	Overton Cliff and Cliff Common	6.3
110	Hillend Burrows Llangennith	243.3
	Total	**6,980**

Numbers refer to Common Land Units as recorded in the Common Land Register. There are duplicate numbers (S) for commons situated or registered separately in the old County Borough of Swansea and CL 110 has been deregistered following hearings.

In Wales, even though encroachment on and enclosure of common land had been a noticeable feature from the late sixteenth century onwards, at the beginning of the nineteenth century around 25 per cent of the land area was still common and waste. Although in 1672, for example, the Mansels, owners of the Margam and Penrice estate, stipulated in a lease to one of their tenant farmers that he could 'enclose the waste land, if he thinks it fit', much of the Gower commons remained unenclosed. By granting such 'liberty to enclose and manure' the Mansels did, however, achieve the enclosure of Port-Eynon Moor in the late seventeenth century. The enclosure of the 282 acres (114 hectares) began in 1684 and was completed within a decade, creating several new farms and extending others. Mead Moor and Brynsil Top, a short distance to the east and now part of the extensive woodland known as Mill Wood, were probably enclosed at the same time. Only after the Inclosure Act of 1801, which was designed to extinguish common rights through a legal process, easing the procedure and reducing the costs of enclosure, did the formal or large-scale enclosure of grazing commons gather pace. Most of the common land in Gower, however, escaped enclosure and the essential character of many of these areas has remained unchanged over hundreds of years. Between 1900 and 1945, however, Clyne and Pennard Commons were partially converted to improved grassland for golf courses and an airfield was created on Fairwood Common.

The earliest surviving general survey of Gower, which mentions most of the common land, only dates from 1650. There are other later surveys, which provide many details of the Gower commons, such as that prepared in 1764 by Gabriel Powell, Steward to the Duke of Beaufort (Morris, 2000). Probably the most comprehensive survey, however, is that undertaken for the Duke of Beaufort in 1826 by Rees Jones, a surveyor from Loughor, and presented in his *Book of Plans of Commons and Wastes*. Twelve commons were covered in this survey, including Fairwood, Pengwern and 'Cefn Brin'. Only small encroachments are shown on these maps and the boundaries of the commons are virtually the same as they are today, indicating that little change has taken place since these surveys.

While variations in the ownership of commons can influence their conservation value and management, it is the exercise of common rights that, within environmental constraints, has shaped the commons, producing the range of habitats that make them so important for wildlife. The wide range of activities covered under these rights, such as the grazing of stock, collecting of timber, or taking of fish, have their origin in local custom. In each community the local economy, geography and balance of power have all played their part in shaping the use of the common. There are a number of legally defined rights of common, including grazing or pasture, estover (the right to gather litter, firewood, bedding etc) turbary (peat or turf cutting), piscary (fishing rights), pannage (the right to turn pigs out to eat beech mast or acorns) and common in the soil (the right to dig gravel, sand, etc for use on the commoner's holding). The existence of piscary rights on some of the Gower commons is curious as many of them, Cefn Bryn being a notable exception, have no fishable water. Similarly pannage strictly means allowing pigs to forage in woodlands on acorns and beech mast, but it is registered on Llanmadoc Hill, a common with no woodland. Although turbary rights are no longer exercised, peat cutting, in the past, is likely to have influenced the topography and vegetation on commons such as Clyne and Fairwood. Turbary rights have also been registered on several commons unlikely to support peat such as Barlands Common, but turbary can also include the right to take grass turf.

Apart from that of grazing the majority of these rights are no longer used. On Cefn Bryn, for example, the rights include 128 registered grazing or pasture rights, 94 estover rights and other rights for common in herbage, coire (the right to take stone from the soil) and piscary. The pasture rights are for sheep, cattle, horses, ponies, donkeys and poultry. While there is still some bracken cut on Cefn Bryn for animal bedding, as opposed to being cut for conservation reasons, of these numerous rights only the right to graze is really exercised these days, and for ponies, cattle and sheep only. It is a long time since donkeys and poultry grazed the slopes of the common.

GRAZING ANIMALS

The evolution of the landscape of lowland Britain since the end of the last ice age has been shaped by the activities of grazing animals, in particular sheep, cattle and horses. Eighteen breeds of sheep, three breeds of cattle, one breed of pig and one breed of horse have been identified as having close associations with Wales. Once every valley had its own type of sheep and nearly every village its particular shape of pig. Occasional references to heifers or oxen of certain colours can be found in the wills of Gower farmers in the Tudor and Stuart periods. Two breeds are mentioned most often. Firstly the reds, belonging to a constant strain noted by Walter Davies (1814–15): 'a very pretty breed of red cattle, in shape like the Glamorgan browns, but not so large, like the Devon breed, if not the same'. There were also the blacks, the native Gower breed often referred to as 'our old blacks' by farmers in the early nineteenth century.

The animals developed from these by the early livestock improvers of the eighteenth century have resulted in the breeds we know today, such as the Glamorgan Brown. Crossbreeding certainly went on, and the wills refer to brown, brindled or 'bragged', spotted and yellow cows. On David ap Richard's farm in 1602, for example, there was a herd of eleven dairy cows and heifers, three of which were red, two black, and two brown; two others were white-faced reds, another a white-faced black, the last animal having a speckled head, white belly and black back. The surviving breeds, though reduced in numbers, are an important component of the Welsh landscape and their preservation contributes to wildlife conservation in areas such as Gower. Studies have shown, for example, that the grazing patterns of Welsh ponies are very good in creating habitats that are suitable for birds and that they create an excellent vegetation structure and a mosaic of different plants that benefits many other animals. Cattle such as the Hereford cross, which despite their name have a long association with Wales, are also good at maintaining vegetation structure, while the Hereford beef short-horn cross is considered to be very good at controlling invasive grass. Much of this evidence is anecdotal, and very little is known about the precise effects that the grazing of individual breeds has on plant communities and the associated animals. It is recognised, however, that wet heath is best managed by being grazed by horses and cattle rather than sheep, which graze too uniformly. On the Gower commons today the main grazing animals include several varieties of Welsh mountain sheep, together with continental breeds of cattle and the Welsh mountain pony (Fig. 114).

Although there have been a number of estimates over the years there are still no accurate figures for the number of animals grazing the commons. Different commoners, for example, put sheep on at different times of the year and although there are animals grazing every week of the year there are considerable variations

FIG 114. Ponies grazing Cefn Bryn Common on a March morning after a rare snowfall. (Harold Grenfell)

in the total number of sheep present. Some commoners will take their sheep off the common for tupping and lambing in February and not put them back again until June. Many of these animals are hefted, a heft being an area habitually grazed by an individual flock that has been bred to stay in a particular area, even though there is no physical boundary. Cattle are normally taken off the commons during the winter months of December, January and February, but again this varies depending on the commoner and the common. The main strongholds of the Welsh pony, apart from Llanrhidian Marsh, are Cefn Bryn, Fairwood, Pengwern and Pennard commons. On Cefn Bryn the area is large enough for there to be two herds, one on the Reynoldston side of the common and one on the Cilibion side. Altogether there are approximately 80 ponies with two stallions, one for either side of the hill.

THE WILDLIFE OF DUNG

Cattle have been continuously present in Britain for at least 8,000 years and there is consequently a rich and intricate web of insect species associated with the presence of grazing animals and particularly their dung, which is rich in organic matter and minerals. Many of these insects are regarded as being rare or scarce in Britain and they depend on the continuation of traditional agricultural practices. A fully grown cow can produce between 30 and 40 kilograms of dung in a dozen pats and 25 litres of urine per day. A fresh cowpat attracts numerous insects, which gather around the dung for a variety of purposes including mating and egg laying, drinking the moisture from its surface and preying on other insects. In Gower, especially during hot weather, one of the first arrivals is the horn fly *Haematobia irritans*, an aptly named blood-sucking fly that only rarely leaves the animals on which it congregates to feed. The female horn flies quickly move down to the fresh dung to lay their eggs and then rapidly return to the animal's coat. They have even been seen to lay eggs on dung before it has reached the ground. It seems therefore that the eggs need to be laid in excreta that is close to body heat to ensure their successful development. The number of invertebrates in each cowpat increases rapidly and after a few days individual deposits may contain up to a thousand developing insects, mainly fly larvae. The common dungfly *Scatophaga stercoraria* is one of the most noticeable species and at times it is very abundant. It has been estimated that in a year the dung produced by one cow supplies enough food to support an insect population equivalent to between 20 and 25 per cent of the animal's body weight, and in consequence it may increase the population of dung-related insects in its immediate area by more than three million.

Over time the insect communities associated with the dung change, mould growth within the mass attracting a new range of animals including fungus midges and numerous beetles such as the common dor beetle *Geotrupes stercorarius*. Known as the 'lousy watchman' because it is often infested with mites, this beetle is a key component of the dung community. The male and female beetles work together to excavate shafts under the dung and then pull it down these shafts and lay their eggs in it. The adults also feed on the dung themselves and they usually bury far more than they ever use. The dor beetles therefore have an essential role in removing dung and speeding the return of nitrates to the soil. A related species, the minotaur beetle, is associated with the dung of rabbits and sheep, though in this case it is only the female that does the digging. Even in areas where earthworms dominate the breakdown of organic debris, these beetles are important in modifying material and making it usable for earthworms. Dor beetles also accelerate bacterial growth and, unlike earthworms, incorporate manure and carrion as well as plant material into the soil.

An extremely large number of fungi grow and fruit on the dung of sheep, cattle and horses. Many of these species are confined to this habitat and have evolved various specialisations. One of the peculiarities of the dung community is a group of mosses whose spores are spread to day-old dung by dung flies. None of these dung mosses are common and all show declines in their recorded distributions. To entice the flies the mosses have evolved a swelling at the top of the capsule stem which produces volatile compounds that smell similar to fresh dung, and some moss species have brightly coloured stems for the same reason. Only two species, cruet collar moss *Splachnum ampullaceum* and narrow cruet-moss *Tetraplodon mniodes*, are found in lowland Britain and both have been recorded from the northern end of Rhossili Down, but they are likely to occur on other commons as well. Cruet collar moss in particular has demanding habitat requirements and mainly attracts flies using dung in very wet conditions. Only in certain habitats does dung survive long enough for it to be utilised by these mosses, and this factor alone probably accounts for their restriction to nutrient-poor or semi-natural vegetation such as that found on the commons.

Dung excludes light for several months as it is decomposing and therefore kills the plants underneath; although recolonisation soon takes place, the effects on the vegetation may last up to 18 months. A fringe of taller vegetation also develops around the fresh dung, and prominent in this plant community are nutrient-loving species such as perennial rye-grass and white clover.

Along with the ever-present earthworms, which actively feed on the interior and draw dung down into their burrows, these organisms more or less complete the breakdown of the dung, returning the nutrients to the soil, and eventually only fragments of the crust remain. These provide an attractive resting place used by a variety of insects for basking in sunny weather. One rare fly found on the Gower commons, the hornet robber fly *Asilus crabroniformis*, actively chooses these desiccated fragments of dung to lay its eggs. This is our largest robber fly and an impressive insect, being a convincing mimic of the hornet when seen in flight (Fig. 115). It is therefore unlikely to be overlooked by the observant naturalist, but the precise reason for this odd behaviour is still not fully understood. It may be that the dung is a much safer environment at this stage as many of the predators have departed. There is no evidence, however, that the newly hatched larvae of the robber fly remain in the dung. It has been suggested that they prey upon the larvae of the common dor beetle; their flight periods are indeed closely synchronised, and the robber fly usually appears around dung that has been used by these beetles. Repeated searches of dor beetle burrows elsewhere in Britain, however, and examination of their larvae and pupae, have so far failed to find any robber fly larvae. On maturity the larva pupates in the free-draining soils of the commons and then emerges in midsummer as an adult to hunt for grasshoppers and other prey. The robber flies are powerful animals with sharp piercing mouthparts that penetrate the exoskeleton of other insects, allowing them to suck their prey dry. The adult tends to fly in an arc to take flying prey from behind, although

FIG 115. Mating hornet robber flies. The robber fly is a conspicuous element of the dung community. (David Painter)

it will also strike at grasshoppers on the ground. 'The name robberfly aptly conjures up the image of the highway robber, ready to pounce on the unsuspecting victim' (Stubbs & Drake, 2001). As the cowpats in which the hornet robber fly lays its eggs have to be exactly the right age, the removal of cattle from an area for even one season can lead to its extinction. Climate change may also be having an effect on its survival, because the behaviour of adults is affected by temperature.

Another rare member of the dung community that definitely has an association with dor beetle larvae, being a parasite in their burrows, is the beetle *Aphodius porcus*, which has been recorded from Fairwood Common. Though most dung beetles are very active in collecting dung, a few such as *Aphodius* are known as 'cuckoo parasites' because they eat and lay their eggs on dung another beetle has collected, often eating that beetle's eggs as well as appropriating their dung.

The increasing use of persistent parasite treatments for cattle, such as avermectins, is thought to be having an effect on species such as the robber fly as they kill its hosts in the cowpat, although more research is needed. These treatments, first developed in the 1980s, are given to grazing animals to remove gastrointestinal parasites, mainly nematodes, but unfortunately they have other side effects. It has been found for example that insects feeding on dung containing avermectins are either rendered infertile or produce malformed larvae incapable of development. As a result the droppings of treated animals degrade much more slowly than would otherwise be the case. There are also suggestions that traces of avermectins in dung may make it more attractive to dung beetles. If this is the case then there are serious long-term problems both for this vital insect community and for many other species that feed upon them. There are currently no restrictions on the use of avermectins by farmers in the Tir Cymen or Tir Gofal agri-environment schemes; there is a presumption against their use on SSSIs and Wildlife Trust reserves where the robber fly occurs, but these areas are in practice not always free of avermectins.

The insects and especially beetles associated with dung form an important part of the diet of the larger bats, such as the horseshoe bats for which Gower is a stronghold, mainly during the late summer and autumn when the young are laying down fat reserves prior to hibernation. Greater horseshoe *Rhinolophus ferrumequinum*, lesser horseshoe *R. hipposideros* and serotine bats *Eptesicus serotinus* rely heavily on beetles in the autumn and possibly the winter. It is a common misconception that bats hibernate continuously throughout the winter months. All species wake up at fairly frequent intervals. The temperatures they require change through the winter and the bats will move to new overwintering sites if necessary. They often travel many miles, and if the weather is mild enough they will also feed. Horseshoe bats in particular wake up very frequently and may feed throughout the winter – and even in February they feed on dor beetles. Nearly half of the diet of lesser horseshoe bats during the winter consists of dung flies. If this winter source of food was denied them through the widespread use of avermectins, the bat populations of Gower could be seriously affected. The extraordinary adaptation of the dung mosses to use dung flies to disperse their spores also makes them potentially vulnerable to the use of these chemicals. Alternative methods of treating intestinal parasites need to be developed. Recent studies on the effects of avermectins suggest that this is an issue that needs to be urgently addressed.

PLANT AND ANIMAL COMMUNITIES

Despite potential problems with parasite treatments this constant grazing is vital in maintaining both the open character of the commons and the rich variety of wildlife. The abundant oak seedlings found on many of the commons indicate that, despite centuries of grazing, these areas would rapidly revert to woodland if the use of common rights ceased. Lightly grazed areas such as Barlands and Clyne commons, for example, are now becoming overgrown. Not only does the removal of vegetation by grazing animals influence the succession of vegetation, but the physical effects of trampling and grazing also play an important role in creating important microhabitats for many species. Grazing also creates a varied vegetation structure, increases the diversity of plant species and reduces competition from dominant species. In particular it keeps the streams and runnels across the commons open, and this provides ideal conditions for many insect populations, particularly dragonflies and damselflies.

The natural vegetation of the commons was probably a mixed woodland of sessile oak *Quercus petraea* and downy birch *Betula pubescens*, with alder in wetter sites and broad buckler-fern *Dryopteris dilatata*, bluebell and creeping soft-grass *Holcus mollis* abundant in the field layer. A few bog-moss *Sphagnum* spp. mires probably existed in the wettest sites, but open heathland and moorland would have been restricted to the exposed slopes of Rhossili Down and Cefn Bryn. Today the commons occupy the more infertile, stony and ill-drained areas of acid soil, and they have mixed open heath vegetation interspersed with areas of marsh and bog, with a few surviving oak–birch and alder woods around the edges. The abundance of common cottongrass *Eriophorum angustifolium*, heath rush *Juncus squarrosus*, purple moor-grass, mat-grass *Nardus stricta* and deergrass gives the commons an upland character despite their lowland position (Fig. 116). Rocky outcrops and scree on the commons form a valuable habitat for lower plants and there is a

FIG 116. Common cottongrass on Cefn Bryn Common. The presence of cottongrass and other species, such as heath rush and purple moor-grass, gives the commons an upland character. (Jonathan Mullard)

particularly notable bryophyte and lichen flora on and around the boulder field on Rhossili Down, with mosses including drooping thread-moss *Bryum alpinum*, arctic fork-moss *Campylopus atrovirens*, squirrel-tail moss *Pterogonium gracile* and fringed hoar-moss *Hedwigia ciliata*, the latter at its only site in Glamorgan.

Although at first sight the vegetation of the Gower commons may appear to be uniform there is in fact a complex pattern of vegetation types, including wet heath, dry heath and acidic grassland and scrub, and the proportions of these habitats vary markedly from common to common. The Biological Survey of Common Land, for example, recorded ten different habitats on Cefn Bryn alone (Table 11). Although this is the largest and one of the most complex commons in the peninsula the mosaic of habitats is typical of many of the Gower commons. Nearly half of Cefn Bryn is covered in continuous bracken, which is dominant on the summit and upper slopes of the sandstone ridge, where it is interspersed with areas of heathland dominated by bristle bent *Agrostis curtisii*. Much of the bracken-covered area also has an understorey of bristle bent rather than deep bracken litter (and sometimes bluebells, which flower before the bracken canopy develops) and could be returned to grass heath by management. This has been one of the main themes of the Tir Cymen agri-environment scheme, which was

TABLE 11. Habitats on Cefn Bryn Common. (Adapted from Penford *et al.*, 1990)

HABITAT	AREA (HA)	% COVER
Continuous bracken	395.7	47.8
Wet heath/acidic grassland	236.2	28.6
Dry heath/acidic grassland	101.8	12.3
Species-rich grassland	28.1	3.4
Acid flush	24.5	3.0
Scattered bracken	20.8	2.5
Acid grassland	15	1.8
Standing water	2.2	0.4
Streams	1.0	0.1
Scattered scrub	1.0	0.1
Total	**826.3**	**100**

taken up by the commoners in the early 1990s. In areas where the bracken community is more open other species present include Yorkshire-fog, harebell *Campanula rotundifolia*, common dog-violet, field wood-rush *Luzula campestris* and foxglove *Digitalis purpurea*.

Bracken is an extremely aggressive and vigorous plant in the open conditions of the commons. The plant colonises an area initially by spores and thrives in conditions where there is a reasonable depth of soil. Once established, bracken spreads principally by vegetative means through its horizontal rhizomes, which can grow up to one metre in length each year. The shade produced by the fronds reduces the ability of other plants to grow and when combined with a thick layer of litter can completely obliterate other plants. This extreme condition is not often reached in Gower, and other plants can survive beneath the fronds as well as grasses. Bracken cannot grow where the soil is compacted or where trampling occurs, and this explains why many paths across the commons are free from the plant. The large areas of bracken on many commons restrict the area available for grazing and may force sheep onto vulnerable vegetation such as heathland.

The management of the bracken and gorse on the commons has been a matter of debate for many centuries, as this extract from a survey of 'Oxwych Manor' undertaken around 1632 shows. In referring to the new enclosed 'Porteinons moore' the surveyor notes that:

And the Lords tenants paying justments did alwaies use to cut furres and fearnes upon ye said moore, and none to our knowledge did ever seek the Lords licence soe to doe, and we conceaiue yt they may doe soe still. But the said tenants did use by consent to leave some standing bushes of furres for shadowe and shelter unto theire sheepe and cattle depasturing upon the said justmt land. And when such standing bushes in convenient places for being preserved and left, weare suddenly cutt and destroyed, they did use to threattne punishmt upon the offenders in that kinde.

Many naturalists consider that bracken is an integral part of the vegetation of common land. It supports a characteristic insect fauna and provides breeding sites for birds such as whinchat *Saxicola rubetra* (particularly where there is gorse – 'whin' is another name for gorse) and formerly nightjar *Caprimulgus europaeus*. Indeed the nightjar used to be known locally as the fernowl, as it emerges at dusk, after lying motionless on the ground amongst the bracken during the day, to feed on flying insects. 'The burbling churr of the fernowl in the July dusk' (Tucker, 1951) was a common sound at the beginning of the twentieth century, but they seem to have disappeared from the peninsula. It is a summer migrant that has been declining in numbers and range since the 1930s and the last Gower records date back to the late 1970s. Many reasons have been put forward to account for this decline, including a decline in the numbers of large insects caused by changes in agricultural practices and climate change. It is extremely likely that the nightjar will return to Gower, as a 1992 survey estimated that the population in Wales had increased by 230 per cent since 1981. To date, however, its distinctive call has not been heard.

HEATHLAND

Due to a combination of location, topography, geology and soils the Gower heaths can be neatly divided into two areas. To the west of Cefn Bryn dry lowland heath grades into humid heath with small pockets of wet heath, while to the east there are much larger areas of wet heath. Cefn Bryn, located centrally, provides a link between the two types and has features of both. Despite this clear division the dry heath often occurs as a mosaic with wet heath, acidic mire, bracken, acid grassland and purple moor-grass pasture.

The three large commons of Rhossili Down, Llanmadoc Hill and Cefn Bryn contain the majority of the dry heathland and are notable for the presence of substantial areas of western gorse and bristle bent, a plant community which here is at the northern limit of its range in Britain, being more usually characteristic of lowland heaths in Devon and Cornwall (Fig. 117). In addition to these two indicator species heather, bell heather, cross-leaved heath *Erica tetralix* and purple

FIG 117. Western gorse on the Bulwark, an Iron Age hillfort on Llanmadoc Hill, with Hills Tor and the Burry Inlet in the background. (Harold Grenfell)

moor-grass also occur. Tormentil occurs as scattered individual plants amongst the other vegetation. The heathland supports a typical invertebrate fauna including the heather beetle *Lochmaea suturalis*, various springtails and spiders. The gorse spider mite *Tetranychus lintearius* can be found occasionally on the gorse. These tiny red mites live in large colonies and spin webs which completely cover the gorse. They feed by sucking the sap and cells from the foliage until it becomes a bleached yellowish-white colour, and growth is reduced.

In contrast the wet heaths, mainly Pengwern, Fairwood, Clyne and Welsh Moor and the northern parts of Cefn Bryn Common, are defined by vegetation communities dominated by deergrass and cross-leaved heath, along with purple moor-grass and heather, and it is the mixture of these four species that gives the vegetation of these areas its particular character. The Gower commons are considered to be one of the best areas in Britain for wet heath communities, and their importance will increase as this habitat continues to decline elsewhere in Britain. Particular species of note include the marsh fritillary butterfly *Euphydryas aurinia* and whorled caraway *Carum verticillatum*. Whorled caraway is a medium-height perennial with white, dome-shaped flower heads. Its oblong leaves are finely divided with segments arranged in rings around the main leaf midrib.

Within the wet heathland there are many flushed areas with a richer flora, including stalked spike-rush *Eleocharis multicaulis*, marsh violet *Viola palustris*, round-leaved sundew *Drosera rotundifolia*, lesser skullcap *Scutellaria minor*, heath spotted orchid *Dactylorhiza maculata* and bog asphodel *Narthecium ossifragum*. Scarcer and more local plants include saw-wort *Serratula tinctoria*, bitter-vetch *Lathyrus linifolius*, royal fern *Osmunda regalis* and bog-myrtle *Myrica gale*. In the dampest areas bog-bean *Menyanthes trifoliata*, bog pondweed *Potamogeton polygonifolius* and marsh cinquefoil *Potentilla palustris* occur. Rarer species of flushed heathland, such as hare's-tail cottongrass *Eriophorum vaginatum*, oblong-leaved sundew *Drosera intermedia* and white beak-sedge *Rhynchospora alba*, are known from only a few sites in Gower.

The brightly patterned marsh fritillary (Fig. 118) is without doubt the best-known invertebrate found on the commons, and the importance of the Gower colonies has long been recognised. The species is declining in almost every European country and Britain is now one of the major strongholds, but even here its numbers have been substantially reduced over the past 150 years. Changes in grazing stock and practices, afforestation and agricultural 'improvements' are all factors that have contributed towards this decline. The species, like many others, often occurs in well-separated colonies that form part of a 'metapopulation', within which there is an interchange of individuals. All the colonies are therefore interdependent and have to be protected, rather than just one or two sites. They

FIG 118. Marsh fritillary butterfly, the best-known invertebrate found on the commons. The Gower colonies are nationally important. (Harold Grenfell)

are often small, however, and susceptible to extinction, so extensive mosaics of habitats such as those provided by the Gower commons are essential for the species' long-term survival (Fig. 119).

The main larval host plant is devil's-bit scabious *Succisa pratensis*. The females lay their eggs on the larger scabious plants, typically those growing where the height of the vegetation is between 8 and 20 centimetres. The fritillary is therefore very susceptible to grazing pressure and most colonies occur where there is light grazing by cattle or horses. Very few occur in areas of the commons grazed by sheep, since sheep are highly selective feeders and graze the food plant preferentially, rendering it small and unsuitable for egg laying. In contrast Welsh ponies are less selective feeders and avoid devil's-bit scabious flower heads. Populations fluctuate greatly in size from year to year, with larvae occasionally reaching enormous densities. The fluctuations appear to be dependent upon weather, food supply and the proportion of caterpillars killed by two parasitic braconid wasps, *Cotesia melitaearum* and *C. bignellii*, the latter apparently being more common in Wales than the former. In some years parasitic wasps can kill 75 per cent of the larval population. It is thought that the wasps control the size of marsh fritillary colonies, preventing them from outstripping the supply of food plant. They are thus an integral element in the butterfly's population dynamics and are themselves of significant conservation value.

The nationally scarce double-line moth *Mythimna turca* has been recorded from Cefn Bryn, Pengwern and Clyne commons. In Britain the species is now confined to South Wales and southwest England (Somerset, Devon and Cornwall), where it is chiefly associated with wet grassland. The adult, which flies in June and July, is reddish-brown in colour with black cross-lines on the forewings. It occurs in wet grasslands, and in woodland clearings and rides. Little is known about its requirements, although the pale brown larvae feed at night on grasses, such as cock's-foot, wood meadow-grass *Poa nemoralis* and field wood-rush.

Along with the marsh fritillary and double-line can be found some scarce beetles such as the flea beetle *Longitarsus holsaticus*, which feeds on louseworts *Pedicularis* spp., and the metallic-blue jewel beetle *Trachys troglodytes*, which also feeds on devil's-bit scabious. The jewel beetle has been recorded from Fairwood Common and Oxwich Point and seems to be more common in coastal areas such as Gower. The tussocks and leaf litter of purple moor-grass provide shelter for a wide variety of grassland invertebrates during bad weather. The money spider

FIG 119. Map showing the distribution of marsh fritillary in West Glamorgan. Note the reliance on the wet and marshy grassland in the northeast of the peninsula. (Barry Stewart)

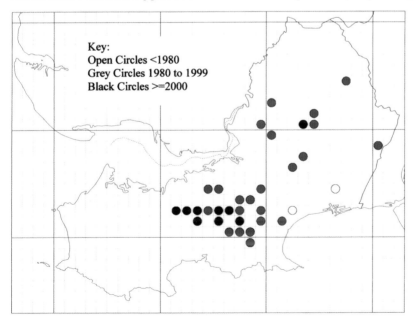

Glyphesis servulus, which appears to need rank moor-grass, has been recorded from this habitat on Fairwood Common.

The narrow-bordered bee hawk moth *Hemaris tityus,* a fast day-flying bumble-bee mimic, has been recorded from a number of commons (Fig. 120). Its larvae feed on devil's-bit scabious, but the adult moth visits a variety of flower species for nectar. Once widespread in Britain, it appears to have retreated to western areas of the country and it is classified as nationally scarce. The lowland area to the north of the main ridge of Cefn Bryn is an important site for dragonflies and damselflies. The gravel-bottomed streams support small populations of the nationally rare southern damselfly *Coenagrion mercuriale* (Fig. 121) and the scarce blue-tailed damselfly *Ischnura pumilio* (Fig. 122). They breed only in clear weedy boggy streams and runnels in lowland heathland.

Other important insects found on the wetter parts of the commons include the black bog ant *Formica candida,* which is found only on Rhossili Down, the valley bogs of the New Forest and the Dorset heaths and is listed as an endangered species. A number of factors have been identified as causing its decline, including excessive grazing pressure and trampling of nests, natural succession leading to an increase in scrub, and genetic isolation, inbreeding and loss of genetic 'fitness'. Further research is needed to identify the precise habitat requirements and suitable management. The first Welsh record, reported as *Formica fusca* ssp. *picea,*

FIG 120. Narrow-bordered bee hawk moth at Fairwood Common in August 1991, on the hand of Brian Pawson, CCW District Officer. (Jonathan Mullard)

FIG 121. The nationally rare southern damselfly, which breeds in the boggy streams on Cefn Bryn Common. (Harold Grenfell)

FIG 122. Mating blue-tailed damselflies on Fairwood Common. (Harold Grenfell)

is of a worker collected by J. W. Allen 'in a marshy spot' at Rhossili in 1913. This record was subsequently questioned and considered to be probably a misidentification of *Formica lemani*. A brief search of suitable habitat on Rhossili Down in 1992 by members of the Bees, Wasps & Ants Recording Scheme was unsuccessful, but a more extensive search in 1996 resulted in the species being found again, at White Moor in the northeast of the Down. Certainly there is no reason now to doubt the first Rhossili record. Subsequently, in 1997, transects across the site found 74 active nests, with an estimate of between 84 and 4,790 nests across the entire area, a mean of 2,420 nests. This is the largest colony in Britain. The nests are made from fragments of purple moor-grass, bog-moss and pellucid plait-moss *Hypnum jutlandicum* formed into a small mound around tussocks.

The wet heaths also support a wide range of bird species and whitethroat, skylark, linnet, swallow and goldfinch *Carduelis carduelis* are frequently recorded. Anthills are also numerous due to the lack of ploughing and agricultural improvement and the ants in turn provide food for green woodpeckers. Curlew can often be seen on Fairwood Common, where the heathland provides ideal locations for breeding. Overwintering snipe *Gallinago gallinago* are not uncommon and barn owls *Tyto alba* hunt over some of the commons.

The barn owl was recorded under the name of the 'white owl' in the *Swansea Guide* of 1802 and in the late 1890s it was considered to be a regular breeding resident. Persecution in the following decades and severe winters in the 1940s reduced its numbers, and thereafter populations fluctuated until the late 1970s, when there was a noticeable increase in sightings. Surveys have shown that there are around 10 breeding pairs in Gower. Gower is considered to be a stronghold for the bird because, although agricultural change has been associated with its decline elsewhere, the traditional farming practices in the peninsula have allowed it to survive. It is clear, however, that many traditional nesting sites have been lost through buildings falling into advanced decay, while others have been lost because of development for housing, or through 'maintenance'. At Oxwich church and castle, for example, renovation work led to the desertion of the site, while at Penmaen they have not been seen since a barn was converted into housing. What is noticeable is that where a nest site has been lost, barn owls appear to have deserted the locality completely. This suggests that there is shortage of traditional nesting sites, as studies elsewhere have shown that if one site becomes unsuitable the birds revert to another location within their home range. The existing local populations need to be linked through the erection of nest boxes at abandoned traditional sites and where there are suitable habitats. The remaining nest sites include Cheriton church and Stouthall. A study of the bird's pellets has revealed that they feed mainly on short-tailed vole, with common shrew *Sorex araneus* and wood mouse *Apodemus sylvaticus* featuring as the most common secondary food sources. Interestingly, as the animal is a localised species that occurs sporadically, the remains of water shrew *Neomys fodiens* have been found in pellets at some sites. There are no other records of the shrew in Gower, but little mammal recording has been undertaken.

In the past one of the most common and conspicuous animals on the commons was the brown hare, but it is now much scarcer. Foxes are important predators of young hares and where foxes are common there are likely to be few hares. Adult hares normally live to 3 or 4 years, but very rarely do they survive much longer.

ACID GRASSLAND

Lowland acid grassland is typically found on nutrient-poor, generally free-draining soils overlying acid rocks and, as in Gower, often forms a mosaic with lowland heathland. As with other lowland habitats, there has been a substantial decline in acid grassland during the twentieth century, mainly due to agricultural intensification, and it is estimated that less than 30,000 hectares now remain in Britain. It is characterised by a range of plant species, especially grasses such as common bent *Agrostis capillaris* and sheep's-fescue, and is maintained by regular grazing, especially by sheep. If the grazing is reduced the grasses are replaced by heather, cross-leaved heath and bell heather. Two of the commonest plants associated with this bent–fescue grassland are tormentil and heath bedstraw *Galium saxatile*, which occur along with harebell, bird's-foot-trefoil, milkwort *Polygala serpyllifolia*, common dog-violet and often wood sage. The presence and abundance of these species depends on the community type and the specific locality, acid grassland being very variable in terms of species richness. The habitat can range from relatively species-poor (with fewer than 5 species per 4 square metres) to species-rich (having in excess of 25 species per 4 square metres). It can support a high density of bryophytes, while parched acid grassland can be rich in lichens. The coarse grassland also provides a suitable habitat for butterflies and moths, including the small heath *Coenonympha pamphilus* and green hairstreak *Callophyrys rubi*.

COMMONS MANAGEMENT

The Gower Commoners Association was formed in 1957 with a view to protecting the rights and interests of all the commons in Gower. Prior to this time individual informal associations existed for each common, but the commoners felt that they could protect their interests better if they united under one organisation. The Association's principal objective is to ensure that there is effective management of the commons.

One of the key concerns of commoners, especially on the larger commons, is the number of animals killed in traffic accidents. Due to the increasing numbers of deaths many animals have been withdrawn from the commons and a consequent reduction in the amount of grazing is changing the structure of the vegetation. It is not generally realised by motorists that the road is legally part of the common and the animals therefore have as much of a right to be there as their vehicle (Fig. 123). In general visitors to the area drive slowly because they are unfamiliar with the roads and the commons and do not kill many animals; unfortunately it is local people commuting to and from Swansea who cause most of the accidents. The Gower Commoners Association, in conjunction with the local authority, has erected fencing and cattle grids on some commons at the

FIG 123. Ponies and vehicles on the 'Red Road' near Broad Pool on Cefn Bryn Common. Traffic accidents are a major cause of death. (Jonathan Mullard)

eastern end of the peninsula, close to the urban area. Clyne Common, for example, was fenced and gridded in the late 1970s. While fencing and gridding can be beneficial to the vegetation and wildlife by reducing the number of animals killed, the visual impact of the fencing is an issue and it is also unpopular with access organisations.

The commons are frequently burnt with the intention of improving the grazing. Most are burnt on a two- or three-year rotation to provide an 'early bite' for the animals. This produces a patchwork of acidic grasslands and heather-dominated communities. It seems that burning was not an important element of commons management before the nineteenth century, traditional practices and the scale of grazing up to that date effectively maintaining the low-nutrient status of the common and its open plant communities. Heather was particularly valued as winter fodder for sheep in severe weather, and gorse was used both as fuel, especially for bread ovens, and as cattle feed. In Wales crushed gorse was also used as 'chaff' for horses, and care was taken to ensure that a useable amount was retained on the commons. The custom of feeding animals, especially horses and calves, with gorse remained fashionable in fact until the beginning of the twentieth century and gorse mixed with straw, hay, or bran was considered to be very nourishing. There was therefore deliberate management and conservation of the available resources. Only when activities such as the cutting of bracken for bedding and gorse for fodder ceased, and the grazing levels declined, did increased burning become necessary to keep the grazing open. Much of the management for conservation is about replacing burning by mechanical cutting and removal of the cut material to keep the nutrient levels low.

The burning comes under the control of the Heather and Grass Burning Regulations and is generally allowed only between 1 November and 31 March in lowland areas such as Gower. In the past there has been a large amount of burning, and just before the cutoff date of 31 March, assuming the weather was suitably dry, many of the Gower commons were set on fire (Fig. 124). Palls of smoke visible from the centre of Swansea and hectares of blackened common were the result. Although burning is now less prevalent, it continues to this day and still causes problems. Part of the reason is the large area of the commons characterised by purple moor-grass and gorse, habitats that are traditionally burnt to improve the grazing. While some burning can be beneficial to heathland, on most of the commons it is still carried out too frequently and when it is combined with heavy grazing it results in a loss of heather. In Gower it especially encourages the spread of bracken, particularly when it temporarily reduces competition from heather. Burning is particularly damaging to invertebrates and lower plants, which often only survive on rocky outcrops where they are protected from the flames. The

FIG 124. Burning on Cefn Bryn Common. (Harold Grenfell)

damage caused depends partly on how dry the underlying soil is. If the ground is wet the fire tends to be superficial, but if the ground is dry a severe 'deep burn' can result, which destroys both the seed bank and the roots of plants. The fact that many of the commons contain wet heath means that the fires are not as damaging as they otherwise might be. In many cases, however, the frequency of burning is such that it is still damaging and in general the activity is having considerable effects on the wet heath communities, despite the efforts of conservation organisations.

On some of the commons, particularly Cefn Bryn, rhododendron, an invasive non-native plant, is encroaching rapidly adjacent to woodlands where it was originally planted for game cover. Rhododendron was first introduced in the late eighteenth century, probably from Spain or Portugal. It became especially popular on country estates in Victorian times, providing ornamental value as well as cover for game birds. Rhododendron thrives in milder, wet climatic conditions, where there are poor, acidic soils, and is therefore unfortunately well suited to the Gower commons. Unless established stands are constantly kept in check they expand into adjacent areas, rapidly eliminating the majority of native plant species.

Rhododendron seeds are tiny and dispersed by wind, and a large bush can produce several million seeds per year. Seedlings have difficulty becoming established in areas where there is already continuous ground cover from native plants. Establishment is best in disturbed areas where the native vegetation has been in some way disrupted, providing an opening in the plant cover. The seedlings also germinate well in areas covered in moss, perhaps because of the water-holding capacity of the mosses. Mycorrhizal associations specific to ericaceous plants, including heathers, provide a competitive advantage and allow rhododendron to flourish in nutrient-poor soils. It therefore has an advantage over other non-ericaceous plants, which may not have their own mycorrhizal network. This explains why the plant is so successful at colonising heathland, as the heathers which grow there have already established suitable networks. It is not possible to control rhododendron by grazing as it contains potentially toxic chemicals.

THE FUTURE

In July 2002 the Government published its intentions for future legislation relating to common land and town and village greens. This legislation is intended to enable the agricultural management of common land by statutory commons associations, to set up regional representative advisory bodies to advise the Welsh Assembly, to create new powers of last resort in relation to common land that is not being managed sustainably and introduce controls on the lending, leasing or selling of rights of common and the unilateral surrender of common rights. Of these the most contentious in relation to the Gower commons is the lending of rights of common, which breaks the centuries-old link between the common and adjacent farms. It is not, however, a completely new issue. An increasing problem on English commons in the late eighteenth century was 'surcharging': that is people outside a manor or parish, often from a distant township, buying a single field to which common rights were attached and then abusing their entitlement.

Until recently, there was considerable difficulty in establishing the extent to which common rights might be licensed to another person. Following a judgment in the House of Lords in 2002, however, it became clear that all rights of common registered under the Commons Registration Act 1965 may be licensed, sold or leased, and on some commons this has taken place. This can break the essential link with the local community and make management of the common much more difficult. The new Commons Bill (2005) will prohibit the severance of common rights, preventing commoners from selling, leasing or letting their rights away from the property to which those rights are attached.

Until recently the public had a right of access to only around 20 per cent of common land in Britain. Although in practice both the public and the landowner generally ignored the law, access to this privately owned land, in line with the situation elsewhere, was legally confined to public rights of way. Away from such routes the public never had any right even to simply walk across common land, except on National Trust land or where a special access deed had been agreed. The implementation of the Countryside and Rights of Way Act 2000, however, resulted in access to all registered common land in England and Wales. All common land which was registered under the Commons Registration Act 1965 is now legally available for public use, and detailed maps are available on the Countryside Council for Wales website. At present it is uncertain whether people's awareness of their new rights will have a great impact on the wildlife and the traditional management of these areas. Only time will tell if the unique character of the Gower commons will remain for future generations to enjoy.

CHAPTER 11

Pills, Pools and Marshes

*The old water mills are now derelict and only in a very few cases are the mill-wheels
intact. The floodgates no longer pen the waters, which hitherto loitered in the pounds and
gurgled through the penstrocks. The streams once again murmur unleashed along their
ancient waterways.*

Horatio Tucker, *Gower Gleanings*

GOWER IS A DISTINCT hydrological region, separate from the rest
of Glamorgan. In particular, rainfall over most of the peninsula is
much less and the hydrology is much more lowland in character
than in the rest of the county. Open freshwater areas are scarce in South Wales
and consequently much of the wildlife associated with freshwater marshes, ponds,
streams and rivers is of particular interest to the naturalist.

There are no large rivers in Gower, although there are numerous streams such
as the Morlais, known as the Morlais River, and the Burry Pill, which drain into
the inlet and estuary, while others such as the Bishopston Stream and Pennard
Pill drain directly into the sea. Together the Morlais River and the Clyne River
to the south form a convenient boundary to the peninsula. Most of the lower
sections of the watercourses are known as 'pills'; the English word *pill* has been
interpreted as a loan from the Welsh *pyl*, 'a tidal creek, a pool in a river'. The word
'lake' is also sometimes used, in this case meaning stream, as at Moor Lake near
Lagadranta and Diles Lake at Hillend. The particular names of these pills can
also be interesting. Caswell, for example, is derived from *carswell*, meaning 'cress
stream', and water-cress *Rorippa nasturtium-aquaticum* can still be found along
its course.

Other freshwater habitats include pools, ponds and springs. Of the numerous pools that occur on the commons the largest and best known is Broad Pool on Cefn Bryn Common. There are also a large number of farm ponds, mainly in the west of the peninsula. For geographical reasons freshwater marshes are relatively uncommon in the west of Britain and large unpolluted, undisturbed examples such as Oxwich are rarer still. The marsh is therefore one of the most interesting and valuable freshwater habitats in the peninsula, especially as the reedswamp it contains, which covers about 40 hectares, is one of the largest in Britain.

THE DRAINAGE PATTERN

The dominant influence in terms of the drainage pattern is the limestone that outcrops to the north and south of the central ridge of Cefn Bryn. The result is that there is subsurface drainage over quite large areas (Fig. 125). The flow regimes of the small streams, many of which arise from the sixty or so springs which exist, are very even, low flows, maintained by an extensive groundwater store in many areas. Depressions in the ground, disappearing streams, underground drainage, dry valleys and other similar characteristics are typical of limestone areas such as Gower. Such terrain is generally known by the German term *karst*. Karst landscapes are primarily the result of limestone being selectively chemically

FIG 125. Drainage patterns in north Gower, showing the typical distribution on limestone. (Joint Nature Conservation Committee)

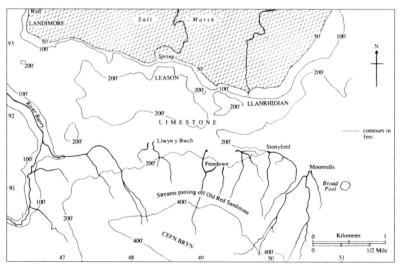

FIG 126. Green Cwm, a good example of a dry valley system, with the Llethrid Stream flowing underground and emerging at the Parkmill resurgence. (Harold Grenfell)

dissolved by acidic natural waters. The best example of the Gower karst is the dry valley known as Green Cwm, which has well-preserved features both on the surface and underground, the underground features extending across the entire width of the narrow limestone outcrop (Fig. 126).

In north Gower a small section of limestone, which receives water draining from Cefn Bryn, collects it in a number of sinks, or swallets, which have their resurgences (the locations where the streams reappear at ground level) at Leason and Llanrhidian. This is the form associated with classical limestone drainage patterns. Water passes off an impermeable rock, sinks into the limestone and re-emerges at a scarp-like slope, in this case represented by the old cliff line of the estuary. Similarly on the south side of Cefn Bryn there are more sinks in the Nicholaston area, adjacent to the south Gower road. All are visible from the road, but are situated on farmland. The Nicholaston sinks occur almost immediately the streams leave the Old Red Sandstone of Cefn Bryn and reach the soluble limestone, and take the form of circular or oblong depressions, with a hole which takes the water into the ground. Downstream of the sinks shallow dry valleys are visible and these were probably the courses of the streams before the development of the more recent sinks. They meet the old cliff line in deep gullies, which go down the steep cliff face to the sand dunes and shoreline at Nicholaston Pill. The systems at Nicholaston have, however, been affected by agricultural improvement and many of them are piped where the stream crosses arable land.

A good example of a disappearing stream is the Llethrid Stream, the valley itself being a fine example of a complete dry valley system extending across the limestone outcrop, between a stream sink and a resurgence, each close to the boundary of the limestone. The stream, which rises on Forest Common, passes beneath the north Gower road and enters a swallow-hole about 200 metres to the south at the base of a wooded slope. This main sink is the entrance to Llethrid Swallet, while in the left bank below the sink lies Tooth Cave. The underground route of the watercourse is inaccessible, but Llethrid Swallet and Tooth Cave have passages that act as a flood overflow route. For a distance of about 2 kilometres from this hole the stream passes underground, along Green Cwm, to emerge at the Parkmill, or Wellhead, resurgence. This resurgence is impenetrable as it now lies under a pool impounded to allow the pumped abstraction of the water. Llethrid Swallet provides about 20 per cent of the water at the resurgence, the rest coming from percolation input and other smaller sinks. The flow time through from Llethrid Swallet is about 20 hours. On the opposite side of the valley to the resurgence is a smaller spring, Kitchen Well, which is fed entirely by percolation water. Below the resurgences the stream flows over the surface to reach the sea at Three Cliff Bay via the Pennard Pill (Figs 127 & 128).

FIG 127. Pennard Pill as it reaches the sea. (Harold Grenfell)

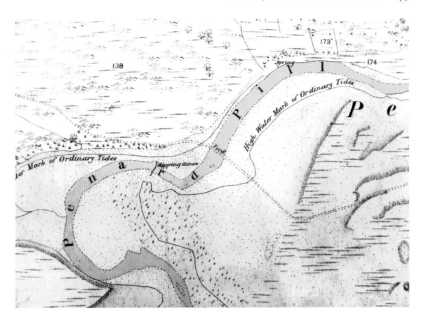

FIG 128. Pennard Pill as shown on the Ordnance Survey map of 1877. (West Glamorgan Archive Service)

Similarly, the source of the watercourse draining into Bishopston Valley is a broad area of indistinguishable drainage on Fairwood Common, and Bishopston Pill goes underground at the Barland Quarry sink, flowing through caves along joints and bedding planes in the limestone before reappearing above ground as a surface stream in the lower part of the Bishopston Valley, meeting the sea at the shingle beach in Pwlldu Bay.

FLORA AND FAUNA

There is a varied flora in and alongside the various streams, brooklime *Veronica beccabunga* being particularly common, while pink water-speedwell *Veronica catenata* is locally frequent on western Gower in shallow streams on calcareous soils. In watercourses near the sea amphibious bistort *Polygonum amphibium* is often found.

On the banks hemlock water-dropwort *Oenanthe crocata* and yellow loosestrife *Lysimachia vulgaris* occur along with a wide variety of plants including blinks *Montia fontana*, marsh-marigold *Caltha palustris* (Fig. 129), winter-cress *Barbarea*

FIG 129. Marsh marigold, a common plant of the Gower streams and marshes. (Harold Grenfell)

vulgaris, lesser spearwort *Ranunculus flammula*, lesser water-parsnip *Berula erecta* and great willow herb *Epilobium hirsutum*. Where streams cross acid soils hard fern *Blechnum spicant* is common. Most of the invasive, non-native streamside plants such as monkeyflower *Mimulus guttatus*, although widely naturalised elsewhere in Glamorgan, are still scarce and local in Gower. The exception is Japanese knotweed, which is spreading rapidly along the streams, as described in Chapter 7.

There is little information available on the species of fish in the Gower streams and their distribution, mainly because there is very little angling interest in the freshwater habitats. More research is needed, but species known to occur, apart from the ubiquitous three-spined stickleback *Gasterosteus aculeatus*, include ten-spined stickleback *Pungitius pungitius*, roach *Rutilus rutilus*, perch *Perca fluviatilis* and brown trout *Salmo trutta*. Some fish of inshore waters, such as thick-lipped grey mullet *Mugil labrosus*, flounder and common goby *Pomatoschistus microps* can be found in the lower reaches of the Gower streams, together with a variety of estuarine animals.

Rivers and streams can also support rich and varied wildlife communities well away from the aquatic zone. Riparian areas in the peninsula, that is margins, banks and adjacent land next to the watercourse, are very important for many plants and animals, including otter *Lutra lutra*, water shrew and water vole *Arvicola amphibius*. Many more species of terrestrial invertebrates also live beside rivers and streams than in them. The banks of streams passing through woodland are especially rich and have their own particular faunas, with giant lacewings *Osmylus fulvicephalus*, or moss-breeding craneflies such as *Dactylolabis transversata* and *Tipula yerburyi*.

The otter was very common in Gower until the early 1960s when, along with other species such as peregrine, they were affected by pesticides entering the food chain. These pesticides, used in seed dressings and sheep dips, caused the otter to become extinct over most of its range in Britain. Due to this otters were absent from the area for over twenty years. There was a slow recovery following the prohibition of the chemicals concerned and by the time the third Welsh otter survey was carried out in 1991 signs of otters were found once again on the Loughor and Tawe rivers and one spraint (dung sample) was found in Oxwich Marsh close to the coast. Since that date otters have become abundant again and are almost certainly now making use of every stream, river and wetland. As they are at the top of the food chain the presence of otters indicates the high quality of these habitats. The animals also make extensive use of the coast and have been observed hunting in the sea close to Oxwich Point.

Although the streams are relatively small the habitats on the bank sides and adjacent areas are good and there are many potential breeding sites available in the extensive reedbeds, scrub thickets and rush pasture. A number of tree-root holts have also been found, mostly in ash and oak trees. Despite initial impressions, all the signs are that Gower is able to support quite a large and thriving otter population, and the animals are certainly breeding. Typical signs of breeding activity have been recorded at suitable sites and small otter prints, obviously made by young animals, have been found on the lower reaches of the Burry Pill. Additions to the population also come from animals travelling into Gower along the estuary. Otters from the Tawe river system may also be able to reach the peninsula via the Afon Llan, which shares a watershed with some of its tributaries.

Mink *Mustela vison* are occasionally seen in and around Oxwich Marsh and its main feeder stream. One took up residence in a hole in the main sluice wall in 1982 and another adopted the cabin of a floating reedcutter in 2000. Both were shot by reserve staff, as was another in 2001. The expansion of mink populations has been mirrored in many parts of Britain by a reduction in the range of water voles, though they have always been comparatively scarce in South Wales. Researchers at Oxford University have, however, found evidence that as otters increase along rivers and streams mink decline, so the increased number of otters may be having a beneficial effect in other ways. There have also been instances in which otters have killed mink.

Possible water vole signs, such as holes in the bank, are often seen along Gower watercourses, though the animal itself is more elusive. In Britain as a whole, it has been calculated that 94 per cent of formerly occupied sites may be lost, with an even greater reduction in actual numbers, making this the most dramatic population decline of any British mammal in the twentieth century. On the other hand there is good evidence that the population decline had begun well before mink became widespread, probably due to pollution and habitat degradation, and so a number of factors, probably interacting, have played a role in the decline. Gower with its generally high-quality habitats has therefore, by default, become a stronghold for water vole.

Birds recorded along the rivers and streams include grey wagtail *Motacilla cinerea*, grey heron *Ardea cinerea* and kingfisher *Alcedo atthis*, although the latter is a scarce bird in Gower. Dippers *Cinclus cinclus* have also been recorded on the Clyne River and Pennard Pill.

OXWICH MARSH

The origin of the marsh goes back some 2,500 years, to when the sea deposited a shingle ridge across the western end of Oxwich Bay. Dunes gradually formed on the ridge as the onshore winds blew in the drying sand from the beach at low tide, a process that is still occurring today, though at a much reduced rate. The lagoon trapped behind the dunes eventually silted up with sand blown inland, and this led to the creation of freshwater and salt marshes. By the twelfth century the salt marsh and dune meadows had sufficient grazing value to be shared by the manors of Oxwich, Penrice, Nicholaston and, even though it lay some distance away, Horton. This grazing was important because of the shortage of meadow land for fattening stock and providing winter hay, and the hayward, who supervised the grazing, ensured that the dunes remained stable. The fact that the marsh was originally salt marsh is confirmed by a warrant issued in 1694 by Sir Edward Mansel of Margam to Thomas Vosse, which appointed Vosse as his water-bailiff 'within the Port of Oxwich and creeks within the Bay of Oxwich'.

The common reed was frequently used for thatching cottages, and a number of such cottages still existed in the early 1900s, though all these have now been reroofed, mostly with slate. Only a few cottages with straw thatch survive today, one of them, Margaret's Cottage in Oxwich village, situated close to the reedbed that may have supplied its first roof. Although the reedbed in its current form is only 70 or 80 years old, and even though there were small reedbeds in places before this date, the reeds might not have been of roofing quality (Fig. 130).

Two hundred years ago the current freshwater marsh was mainly salt marsh, and the sea was able to flow around the end of the dunes to flood the low-lying

FIG 130. Oxwich Marsh in winter from the lookout tower. (Harold Grenfell)

land almost as far as the village. Most of the salt marsh was reclaimed from the
sea by Thomas Mansel Talbot, then owner of Penrice Estate, at the end of the
eighteenth century. As early as 1769 he was contemplating 'erecting a Sea Wall or
Bank across Nicholaston Pill to prevent the flowing of the Sea on high Spring
Tides over Oxwich Marsh so as to make it of greater Value by the Acre than what it
is at present' (Davies, 1814). In earlier periods drifting sand had blocked some of
the creeks and the return of stormy conditions in the seventeenth century led to
the rate of siltation increasing, which prompted Talbot to take action. Around
1794 he instigated a series of works that included digging a ditch around the
perimeter of the marsh to contain spring and stream water, together with a series
of internal drainage ditches. He then excavated a meandering ornamental lake
running the length of the marsh, two smaller ponds in Penrice Park and an
extensive ditch system to drain away the fresh water flowing into the marsh from
the numerous small streams and springs along the old cliff line. The land was
gradually converted to rough pasture, dissected by drainage channels, which was
mostly used for cattle grazing. Walter Davies was highly enthusiastic about the
success of the operation from an agricultural viewpoint: 'Before the tides were
excluded, the marsh afforded healthy pasturage for sheep but it is now quite the
reverse ... it has now become excellent pasturage for cattle and horses.' The system
worked very well, the vegetation changing from salt marsh to pasture, and for

about the next hundred years provided rich grazing for cattle, though not without cost. Three men had to be employed throughout the summer to keep the ditches clear, and the sea wall and sluice needed regular attention. The channel below the sluice also had to be dredged out each winter using a horse-drawn wooden plough.

It is not known exactly when the system created by Mansel Talbot began to deteriorate, but the decline probably started in the 1920s when Glamorgan County Council raised the level of the main road across the marsh; though culverts were installed the road had the effect of damming most of the water on the landward side. Another factor was the break in maintenance due to the shortage of men and materials during and immediately after the First World War. Whatever the initial reasons, during the early years of the twentieth century the maintenance of the area was reduced. The internal ditches were still being cleaned by a small team of men in the summer of 1939, but examination of the course of the outfall channel on aerial photographs taken in 1941 suggests that this had been neglected some time earlier. Other aerial photographs reveal that the marsh vegetation was already well developed by 1945, with the marsh to the west of the road being dominated by beds of yellow iris and bulrush *Typha latifolia*, although cattle were still grazing the back of the marsh by Abrahams Wood and potatoes were grown on drier ground near Oxwich village until 1946. The east marsh, which was influenced by salt water, consisted of reedbed with open muddy flats and tussocks of rushes supporting a colony of black-headed gulls. It is likely that local memories of large numbers of wildfowl and snipe date from this period, when the marsh was more open, with larger areas of shallow water and low fen, than at present. Further changes occurred in 1948, when there were several major breaches in the sea wall. These were not properly repaired until 1963, and during the intervening period sea water was able to wash freely in and out of the system during spring high tides.

As a result of the drainage system becoming neglected the ditches became partly or completely choked, the sluice fell into disrepair and water started to spread out over the surrounding land, turning the pasture into freshwater marsh. The grazing animals finally had to be removed and this allowed aquatic plants to spread from the drainage channels. Within twenty years the character of the area had totally changed, and it had become an immensely rich area for wildlife. The sluice was renovated in 1983 and, together with the weirs above it, helps to keep a suitable water level. Today the freshwater marsh comprises four main habitats, open water, reedswamp, floating fen and damp woodland, each with its characteristic communities of plants and animals (Fig. 131).

Of the forty or so species of dragonflies and damselflies which have been recorded in Britain about fifteen are known from Oxwich Marsh, being closely associated with the areas of open water, as their larval stages are fully aquatic,

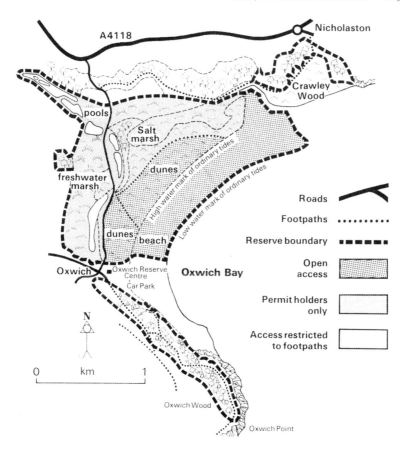

FIG 131. Map of Oxwich Marsh showing the main habitats. (Countryside Council for Wales)

feeding on invertebrates on the pond bottom. Nine species have been recorded breeding at Oxwich, including the azure damselfly *Coenagrion puella*, large red damselfly *Pyrrhosoma nymphula*, blue-tailed damselfly *Ischnura elegans*, hairy dragonfly *Brachytron pratense* and the largest of the 'hawker' dragonflies, the emperor dragonfly *Anax imperator*.

Many species of fish occur, such as eel *Anguilla anguilla*, rudd *Scardinius erythrophthalmus*, roach, brown trout and the two stickleback species. Grass snakes occur in the damper areas around the marsh and can be seen swimming across open water in search of prey. They feed on tadpoles, frogs and toads, as well as fish, newts, and occasionally mice and small birds. Most hunting is done underwater, and prey is typically swallowed alive. It is both Britain's biggest snake, growing well over a metre in length, and our only egg-laying snake. Females lay eggs in June or July, normally in rotting vegetation, which acts as an incubator. The eggs hatch into miniature versions of the adults in September.

Wildfowl are not particularly numerous at Oxwich, compared to the inlet and estuary. In the 1980s there were rarely more than 200 birds present, even in the depths of winter, and numbers are now reduced further as the area of open water has diminished. The presence of freshwater species, such as shoveler *Anas clypeata*, pochard *Aythya ferina* and tufted duck *Aythya fuligula*, on the other hand, is important as their numbers are limited in South Wales due to the scarcity of the habitat. Mallard, teal and coot *Fulica atra* can also be seen on the open water, and breed in the marsh.

The reedswamp is not a particularly rich area botanically as it is dominated by common reed to such an extent that in most places little else has a chance to grow. The bird life, however, is outstanding, and in some years there are up to 400 pairs of reed warblers, 80 pairs of sedge warblers and 40 pairs of reed buntings. The reed warblers form one of the largest colonies in Wales and they breed at a high density with a correspondingly high number of fledglings. Water rails *Rallus aquaticus* are present all year round and are known to breed. Their numbers are difficult to measure, due to their secretive habits, but their strange grunts and squeals are heard throughout the year. The song of the grasshopper warbler *Locustella naevia*, a continuous call said to be like the rewinding of a fishing reel, can be heard in the summer from the margins of the reedswamp where these birds nest. After occurring as a winter visitor for several years bearded reedling *Panurus biarmicus* nested for the first time at Oxwich in 1974 and up to six pairs bred each year until 1989.

Bitterns *Botaurus stellaris* have probably been associated with Oxwich Marsh for several centuries. The bittern's call is a deep resonant 'boom' that can be heard several kilometres away and its generic name *Botaurus* is said to be derived from the Latin *boatum tauri*, 'the bellowing of a bull'. In spring the call is said to resemble the lowing of a calf. In the past the bird's eerie cry in the night doubtless terrified people who were unaware of its origin and the sound may have been attributed to supernatural agencies. In the Gower dialect the bittern was known as the *bumbagus*. Horatio Tucker noted that 'Whether the early Wessex colonists brought the word with them ... or whether they coined it after their introduction to the bird at Oxwich, is not known, for no trace of this word can be found in the South Country dialects. Possibly the word was originally *boom bogey*.' Up until 1998 the marsh was a key wintering site and birds were present each year, but no individuals have been recorded since that date. While people have sometimes stated that the species has bred at Oxwich these claims, based on evidence such as sightings of two birds at the same time, or a juvenile bird in late summer, have never been substantiated. In 1999 there were only 19 breeding males in Britain (the majority in the south and east of England) and the present trend for the British population is one of falling numbers – but the long-term prospects for the species are thought to be good, unless there are cold winters, if habitats like the marsh remain in their present condition.

Herons are often seen in the marsh, although the numbers of birds in the area are not what they once were. The once thriving heronry nearby, on the island in the middle of Penrice Lake, peaked at 34 nests in 1978, but steadily decreased through the 1980s, as a result of trees dying of old age and nest branches breaking off after heavy snowfall. In 1993 it was down to a single nest and there have been no nests since. Instead birds dispersed to another site at Oxwich, by the Middle Pond, but there were still only three nests there in 2004. Most of the Penrice colony seems to have moved to north Gower, with heronries developing at Landimore, Llanrhidian and Weobley.

The reedswamp also once contained a starling *Sturnus vulgaris* roost, which in late summer consisted of anything up to 30,000 birds. Sadly this magnificent spectacle of massed birds in flight is now rarely seen. In most years one or two rare vagrant birds occur in the reedswamp, and in the past these have included marsh harrier *Circus aeruginosus*, purple heron *Ardea purpurea*, little bittern *Ixobrychus minutus*, Savi's warbler *Locustella luscinioides* and aquatic warbler *Acrocephalus paludicola*. Cetti's warbler *Cettia cetti* was first recorded in 1977 and rapidly established a breeding population of up to 20 singing males each year, making Oxwich the Welsh stronghold for this species.

Marshes such as Oxwich are superb, but often overlooked, habitats for small mammals and support a rich variety of species, with shrews being particularly abundant. The open habitats dominated by reed have been shown elsewhere to be especially good for water shrews and even harvest mice, both these species being unaffected by the presence of standing water. Harvest mice in fact are often the most abundant small mammal in wetlands. They have even been found in the emergent vegetation in open water and have been considered as the mammalian equivalent of the reed warbler. The distribution of harvest mice in Wales is very patchy, and they seem to be most frequently recorded in purple moor-grass grassland on bogs, but as a species it is easily missed. The first Gower record for harvest mice, in 1980, confirmed this liking for purple moor-grass, when harvest mice nests were found in tussocks of the plant on dune grassland adjacent to the reedbeds at Oxwich. The same year nests were also found in purple moor-grass on Cefn Bryn. There are estimated to be about 10,000 animals in Wales along the coastal strip, but while water shrews and water voles can often be seen amongst the reeds or swimming across the dykes at Oxwich, there are no records of harvest mice. Sadly the nesting site at Oxwich was burnt by vandals in the mid-1980s and this may have destroyed the local population before the animals had a chance to colonise the marsh. As harvest mice are clearly present in the peninsula it would be worth carrying out some surveys of the marsh to establish if they are using this habitat. If they are found there may be a conflict for naturalists, however, as recent research has shown that bitterns, once thought to feed only on fish and amphibians, often eat small mammals, and that both water shrew and harvest mouse are a frequent food item.

The floating fen developed as a result of plants colonising the mat of iris and bulrush, which grew out across the surface of the flooded grazing land. This makes it delicate, easily damaged and in places very treacherous, as the thin mat can easily be broken. Although the areas of floating fen at Oxwich are small, they are rich and fascinating places for wildlife, especially plants. In spring the area is carpeted by marsh-marigold, followed by numerous other species, including southern marsh-orchid, skullcap *Scutellaria galericulata*, gipsywort *Lycopus europaeus*, marsh lousewort *Pedicularis palustris*, yellow iris and the poisonous hemlock water-dropwort. Bog-bean and marsh cinquefoil grow in the wettest parts on the edge of open water and there are scattered clumps of the rather local lesser bulrush *Typha angustifolia*. The animals of the fen have been little studied, but it is probable that there is a rich variety of invertebrates. Snipe use the fen extensively in the winter, although few other birds appear to feed, roost or breed there.

Where the ground is drier, for at least part of the year, due to the water table dropping or because plant litter has raised the ground surface, bushes and saplings have colonised the marsh. These damp winter-flooded woodlands, known as carr woodland, are dominated by alder and willows *Salix* spp. As they are a transitional habitat they are characterised by a mixture of plants from both wet and dry areas, including water mint, common marsh bedstraw *Galium palustre*, meadowsweet *Filipendula ulmaria*, bracken and herb Robert *Geranium robertianum*. Flocks of small finches, mainly chaffinch *Fringilla coelebs*, goldfinch, siskin *Carduelis spinus* and lesser redpoll *Carduelis cabaret*, feed in the tops of the alders in winter, extracting seeds from the small cones. In summer the bird community of the woodland is dominated by willow warblers *Phylloscopus trochilus* and wrens *Troglodytes troglodytes*, which nest low in the undergrowth. The scattered bushes are also important sources of insect food for reed warblers and provide song posts for reed buntings and willow warblers.

MARSH MANAGEMENT

Marshes are immensely dynamic, complex and productive systems, but are quite short-lived. Although Oxwich Marsh, in its current form, is only about eighty years old, the habitats change quite rapidly as plant succession takes place. At present reed, iris and bulrush are invading open water, scrub is invading reedswamp and fen and reed is invading fen. At the same time the whole area is gradually silting up due to material being washed down by the inflowing streams. The marsh would inevitably develop into damp deciduous woodland if left unmanaged and there would be a serious decline in the wildlife value of the area, with the loss of various habitats. Over the last twenty years or so therefore control of scrub in the reedswamp and fen has taken place and reed has been cut back in the channels and ponds.

The plant succession is also influenced by the type and behaviour of the water because the different stages require different regimes. Common reed for example grows best in nutrient-enriched water at high fluctuating levels, whereas fen vegetation does best if the water is at a lower level and is stable and low in nutrients. The solution to these issues depends on being able to control the quality, flow and level of the water in the marsh and therefore a lot of marsh management is about engineering, building weirs and bunds, cleaning ditches, and repairing culverts, the sea wall and the sluice.

In 1963, when Oxwich became a National Nature Reserve, extensive reedbeds had developed in the west marsh, though mixed and poor fen, open water and carr woodland were still present. At the time this was considered to represent a good balance of habitats, especially as the area was valued mainly for its rich bird life, particularly the various warblers. The marsh was also felt to have potential for becoming a breeding area for a number of species rare in western Britain, including bittern, marsh harrier, bearded reedling and purple heron, all of which, as described previously, were regular visitors. In addition the water quality was excellent and there was little invasion by scrub. Management of the area was therefore low-key and there was little direct intervention. By the middle of the 1970s, however, there was concern about the rate at which scrub and emergent vegetation in the ditches and ponds was spreading. Scrub control by cutting and chemically treating the stumps was introduced and common reed in the main ditches was cut using a small purpose-built raft with a motorised scythe mounted at the front (Fig. 132). Attempts to use this raft to control water-lilies *Nymphaea* spp. failed, as did using a suction pump to remove silt.

In the early 1980s another concern emerged, that of water quality. Some

FIG 132. Cutting water lilies at Oxwich in the 1970s using a purpose-built raft. (Countryside Council for Wales)

deterioration had been noted earlier, thought to be associated with the increasing sediment in the ditches and open water and the high silt content of winter floodwater. Then a series of isolated events, involving accidental releases of sewage and farm slurry, together with fertiliser runoff, compounded the problem and there were algal blooms and a rapid spread of dense carpets of greater water-moss *Fontinalis antipyretica*. This nutrient enrichment and its impact on the various plant communities became the main influence on the management of the area. A detailed survey of the marsh in 1981 showed that the fen vegetation was rapidly being overtaken by common reed as a result of the nutrient-rich waters spreading throughout the marsh. A programme of works was therefore designed to provide control over water levels and the flow of water through the marsh. Towards the end of the decade, when budgets for management were reduced, the emphasis moved towards developing ways of ensuring that future maintenance was viable and cost-effective. For the last ten years or so the marsh has been managed on a 'care and maintenance' basis, with the sluices and weirs kept in good working order and an annual programme of scrub control. The scrub, mainly alder and willow, is invasive, particularly around the fringes of the marsh and alongside recently re-excavated ditches. Small stands and lines of scrub are left and this benefits both reed and Cetti's warbler by providing a spread of feeding opportunities throughout the marsh.

SLUXTON MARSH

In dramatic contrast to the vast area of Oxwich Marsh, Sluxton Marsh at
Whitemoor consists of a single field to the east of Rhossili Down. It is of special
interest because of the variety of habitats associated with the marshy grassland;
these include reedbeds, swamp and an area of acidic flush, together with scattered
blocks of willow scrub. The majority of the marshy grassland is dominated by
purple moor-grass along with sharp-flowered rush *Juncus acutiflorus*, sweet vernal-
grass, sheep's-fescue, Yorkshire-fog, carnation sedge *Carex panicea* and tormentil.
The stands of fen meadow are particularly interesting as the vegetation is
generally richer in species than the purple moor-grass pasture, with plants such
as tawny sedge *C. hostiana* and flea sedge *C. pulicaris* present. Other areas consist
of rush pasture, dominated by sharp-flowered rush and including common
marsh bedstraw and greater bird's-foot-trefoil *Lotus uliginosus*. The acid flush is
dominated by the sharp-flowered rush, purple moor-grass and various species
of bog-moss.

The small areas of reedbed are dominated by common reed, together with
smooth-stalked sedge *Carex laevigata*, bog-bean and broad buckler-fern, while
the swamp is dominated by greater tussock-sedge *C. paniculata*. There are
few records of invertebrates, but the shallow, warm and permanently flowing
watercourses that cross the site hold a population of southern damselfly.

POOLS AND PONDS

While pools and ponds have been a feature of the British landscape for thousands
of years it is only fairly recently that their importance as a habitat has been recognised. Nationally they support at least two-thirds of Britain's freshwater plant and
animal species, including many that are uncommon. Despite their importance to
wildlife these water bodies are consistently undervalued, probably because of their
small size, familiarity and perceived abundance. In Gower, because of the other
attractions of the area, they are for the most part simply overlooked.

There are two main types of standing water bodies, eutrophic waters and
mesotrophic waters, and both occur in Gower. Of the six largest bodies two are
eutrophic and four mesotrophic. Eutrophic waters are highly productive because
plant nutrients are plentiful, either naturally or as a result of artificial enrichment.
Planktonic algae and zooplankton are abundant in the water column and the
submerged vegetation is diverse, with numerous species of invertebrates and fish.

There is often a marginal fringe of reeds, which is an important component of the aquatic ecosystem. Bottom-dwelling invertebrates such as snails, dragonflies and water beetles are also abundant. In contrast mesotrophic water bodies have a narrow range of nutrients, but contain a higher proportion of nationally scarce and rare aquatic plants. Invertebrates are particularly common, with important groups such as dragonflies, water beetles, stoneflies and mayflies present.

According to the current Ordnance Survey map of Gower there are, or were, some seventy-five farmyard and field ponds, many near to or adjoining field boundaries, or tucked away in field corners. As about one-third of these are shown as being very small, it is likely that many of these have been filled in or naturally silted up since the map was surveyed, probably in the 1970s. Although ponds gradually fill in with silt and debris and vegetation through natural succession it is best to maintain them in all stages of succession, so that there are both new ponds and well-vegetated ones in the same area. Moreover, a number of medium-sized ponds seem to have almost completely disappeared. As a rough estimate therefore about half of the ponds, fewer than forty, may survive. In addition to this total there are forty waterbodies on common land and five ponds in woodlands.

BROAD POOL

Broad Pool is the largest natural water body in the peninsula and one of the best-known features in central Gower (Fig. 133). It was given to the Glamorgan Naturalists' Trust, as it was then, in May 1962 by the Duke of Beaufort as the Trust's first nature reserve. Covering over a hectare, it is a very shallow pool, less than 1.3 metres deep even at peak midwinter water level. The pool is situated on a flattish area of limestone overlain with boulder clay and is surrounded by heath with bog-mosses in the wetter areas.

The earliest mention of Broad Pool is in an affidavit by John Long of 1 October 1705, showing that it was a clear landmark at that date and suggesting that it had been so since the 1640s. The earliest map of the area, an estate map of Walterston and Cilibion of 1785, shows Broad Pool clearly labelled as 'Cevan y Brynn Pool', with the tenth milestone from Swansea beside it. This and all later maps show the pool almost exactly the same size and shape it is today. It has been suggested that the name 'Broad Pool' comes from the name of the surrounding area, Broad Moor, and is not a reference to the size of the feature. Whatever the origin of the name it is clear that the pool has been an important area of open water that has existed for at least 400 years and has been maintained as such throughout this time.

FIG 133. Broad Pool, the largest pool on the commons, from the southwest. (Jonathan Mullard)

Although the pool appears to be natural in origin, being a clay-plugged depression, it has been modified by the removal of sediment and vegetation from the late eighteenth century onwards. Licences to dig mud were issued in both the eighteenth and nineteenth centuries, and this was probably mixed with lime for use as a fertiliser. Without this type of intervention there is little doubt that it would have filled up with vegetation long ago. It is possible that the pool has been enlarged by these activities. Its position, immediately beside the main road across the common (the so-called Red Road owing to the underlying red sandstone) makes it a convenient site for watering stock, and it is possible that material was dug out to make the road. More recently it is known that no material was extracted from the pool between 1936 and 1984. During the prolonged drought in the summer of 1984 Broad Pool dried up completely, the first time this had happened since the 1970s, when even in the exceptionally hot year of 1976 a small amount of water remained. Since the pool had begun to silt up the Trust decided to take a risk and take heavy machinery into the pool, hoping that the clay lining would not be broken. In all nearly 2,000 tonnes of plant material and silt was extracted, and luckily the restoration work was successful. Approximately one-eighth of the area was left untouched to allow recolonisation by plants and animals.

The pool is notable for the presence of fringed water-lily *Nymphoides peltata* (Fig. 134). This attractive species is a native of eastern England and was a rare

FIG 134. Fringed water lily, a native of eastern England and a rare alien in Wales. Introduced to Broad Pool during the late 1940s or early 1950s. (Harold Grenfell)

alien in Wales, although it now occurs in many other pools in Gower and Swansea. It was introduced to the pool during the late 1940s or early 1950s by persons unknown. The plant grew well, but in 1960 there was still a lot of open water and the fringed water-lily occupied only a small area near the road. The location of this species on the roadside edge of the pool is significant as the first Glamorgan record in 1984 of another alien species, New Zealand pigmyweed *Crassula helmsii*, was also from Broad Pool and it is likely that the pool's convenient situation, adjacent to one of the main Gower roads, is the reason for the occurrence of alien plants at this site. The pigmyweed is sold in garden centres as an oxygenating plant for aquaria and garden ponds.

By 1970 the fringed water-lily had almost completely covered the pool and the Trust was considering ways to halt its spread. At the same time other vegetation was encroaching, mainly soft-rush *Juncus effusus* and sharp-flowered rush together with marsh pennywort *Hydrocotlyle vulgaris*, bog-bean and in places common spike-rush *Eleocharis palustris* and bulrush. During the late 1970s the bog-moss *Sphagnum auriculatum* started to increase, together with *S. squarrosom, S. fimbriatum, S. recurvum* and *S. subnitens*. By 1982 the mats of *Sphagnum auriculatum* were so extensive that they were visible over a large part of the water surface, even during the winter, and it seemed as though the pool might turn into a bog. Following the work in 1984 clumps of pondweed *Potamogeton* spp. appeared together with one small clump of the white water-lily *Nymphaea alba*, which had been previously recorded from the site but not seen for a number of years, and floating club-rush *Eleogiton fluitans*. Other plants recorded from the site include lesser bladderwort, lesser marshwort *Apium inundatum* and alternate water-milfoil *Myriophyllum alterniflorum*.

Broad Pool is an important breeding site for amphibians and supports a rich aquatic invertebrate fauna, including fourteen species of dragonflies. The black darter *Sympetrum danae*, the male of which as its name implies has a completely black body and legs, seems to be increasing in numbers near Broad Pool. The pool also supports five species of water boatman and four species of water beetle. Particularly obvious invertebrates include the large black horse leeches *Haemopsis*

FIG 135. Wood sandpiper, a rare migrant, near Broad Pool in August 2004. (Harold Grenfell)

sanguisunga, which can often be seen swimming in clear water. The only fish in Broad Pool seem to be three-spined sticklebacks, although rudd occur in pools elsewhere in Gower and were reported some years before the drought.

The pool is also a very attractive site for visiting birds and a wide range of species have been recorded including migrants such as ruff *Philomachus pugnax*, spotted redshank *Tringa erythropus*, wood sandpiper *Tringa glareola* (Fig. 135), whooper swan *Cygnus cygnus*, Bewick's swan *C. bewickii*, goldeneye *Bucephala clangula*, common sandpiper *Actitis hypoleucos* and Jack snipe *Lymnocryptes minimus*, together with common species such as water rail, grey heron and little grebe *Tachybaptus ruficollis*.

OTHER WATER BODIES

Broad Pool lies at the centre of a scattering of smaller pools on the north side of Cefn Bryn Common, which because of the hydrology must be regarded as part of the same complex. Near the pool itself are several small depressions, up to 5 metres across, which contain standing water during the winter but dry out completely in most summers. About 10 metres northeast is a much larger depression, which is considerably deeper than the pool. It appears that this depression has no boulder-clay plug and that water can drain freely, since it is always dry with bracken growing in it. The large-scale Ordnance Survey map of 1877/8 shows two smaller pools, one about 200 metres north and one 200 metres northwest of Broad Pool. The smaller one is still full of water during the winter, but is very shallow and usually dries out during the summer. The larger pool to the northwest seems to have become a sinkhole and now only contains a small area of shallow water during the wettest periods. A further much larger sinkhole, where the largest stream from Cefn Bryn Common disappears underground, lies some 400 metres to the northwest of Broad Pool. On the Duke of Beaufort's commons map of 1826 this sinkhole is shown coloured blue, suggesting it was filled with water, although it is labelled as a sink. The depression now never holds any standing water except in exceptionally wet conditions, and is covered with grass and bracken. From this evidence it appears that sinkholes can form from areas that begin life as pools, and it is possible that this could happen to Broad Pool at some stage.

There are also a number of pools, including Red Pool, along the ridgeline to the south of Arthur's Stone (Fig. 136). These features, including those that are ephemeral, are important not only for watering stock but also for a wide range of insects and other invertebrates. They contain many of the common aquatic

FIG 136. Red Pool, an ephemeral pool on the ridge of Cefn Bryn Common. The stock-trampled margins are an important, and under-recorded, habitat for invertebrates. (Jonathan Mullard)

invertebrates such as water bugs, water beetles, mayfly nymphs, stoneflies and caddis flies, together with a number of dragonflies. These pools are especially significant for the invertebrates that occur in the stock-trampled margins, as the damp peaty soils at the edges are generally a valuable habitat for invertebrates. In the 1950s and 1960s Fonseca (1973) recorded numerous rare flies from the Gower commons, including representatives from families such as the Tabanidae, Dolichopodidae and Muscidae, which have larvae that live in damp soil. These records are difficult to relate to specific sites, however, and it would be useful to have a modern study.

Ephemeral pools are a severely threatened habitat, associated mainly with heathland. They are usually thought to be restricted to heathland in southern England, but this is obviously not the case. Nationally, like pools of all types, they have been lost due to destruction by agricultural activities, although this is not an issue on the Gower commons. Ironically most of the threats to ephemeral pools come from inappropriate habitat management, particularly the deepening of these temporary pools to create permanent ponds. This has certainly happened on Cefn Bryn, as part of the otherwise pioneering Tir Cymen agri-environment scheme, and before this in the early 1990s the former Gower Countryside

Service used volunteers to deepen some of the water bodies near the summit of the common.

Plants recorded elsewhere as associated with ephemeral pools include pennyroyal *Mentha pulegium* and the rare and threatened three-lobed water crow-foot *Ranunculus tripartitus*. There are no recent records of pennyroyal, but it has been recorded in the past from several heathland areas in the peninsula and it may still grow at some of the sites. Whether these historic records were associated with temporary pools is not clear. Three-lobed crowfoot, on the other hand, which is at the limit of its British range in Gower, certainly occurs in ditches and ponds near Rhossili and is disappearing as a result of changes in agriculture and the loss of the habitats in which it grows.

Temporary pools on heathland in southern England often hold two of Britain's rarest crustaceans, the fairy shrimp *Cheirocephalus diaphanus* and the triops *Triops cancriformis*. Both of these remarkable crustaceans have highly specialised ecological requirements. The fairy shrimp, in particular, is an enigmatic creature found in seasonal and temporary pools, puddles and wheel-ruts. The eggs persist in dry mud after breeding pools dry up in summer and hatch after autumn rains replace the water. It is an extremely local species, but often abundant where it does occur. Given the similarity of habitats and climate to the English sites, investigation of the Gower pools would be worthwhile.

On Ryers Down there are four small pools, the largest of which contains three locally important plants – lesser marshwort, floating club-rush and marsh St John's-wort *Hypericum eolodes* – as well as a number of other aquatic plants. Spiked water-milfoil *Myriophyllum spicatum* is common in ponds and ditches over much of the peninsula, but is replaced in western Gower by alternate water-milfoil, which prefers acid water. Mare's-tail *Hippuris vulgaris* is a very local plant occurring in ponds and marshes. The pools on Ryers Down are also important for invertebrates, particularly flies such as the rare predatory fly *Dolichopus phaeopus*, together with the equally rare beechafer, or bee beetle *Trichius fasciatus*, for which this, together with Pengwern Common, is one of the few sites in southern Britain (Fig. 137). It is an extremely hairy beetle, about 14 millimetres long, with wasp- or bee-like black and orange-yellow markings on its elytra; the thorax and abdomen are a light brown. The adults are seen from June to September and visit flowers including thistles and thyme.

A farm pond at Horton is the only recorded breeding site in the Swansea area for great crested newt *Triturus cristatus*, but it is likely that it occurs elsewhere in the peninsula. In contrast the palmate newt *T. helveticus*, the smallest of the three newt species found in Britain, is abundant, being frequently found on the commons, where it breeds in the small pools in the spring. The common newt

FIG 137. The rare beechafer, or bee beetle, on common knapweed at Pengwern Common. (Harold Grenfell)

T. vulgata also spends much of its time on land, but between early spring and midsummer they can be found in shallow water at the margins of ponds, pools and streams.

DECOY WOOD POND

A short distance to the east of Broad Pool, on the edge of Cefn Bryn Common, lies Decoy Wood, named after the decoy pond it contained, which was used to catch wild ducks (Fig. 138). The pool, clearly visible on the first edition of the Ordnance Survey map of 1884, was roughly square in shape with curving and tapering ditches leading off from each corner. In this it followed the regular pattern of decoys constructed in the nineteenth century, although the device itself was perfected in Holland in the late sixteenth century. It was a large enough feature to require a dedicated boat and its associated boathouse. As it is not shown on the map of 1848, but is on the 1877 map, it seems to have been constructed between these two dates. A search of the relevant record books for the Penrice Estate has not revealed further details. More than two hundred decoys were built in Britain, but only a few now remain and these are used for ringing and research, rather than catching

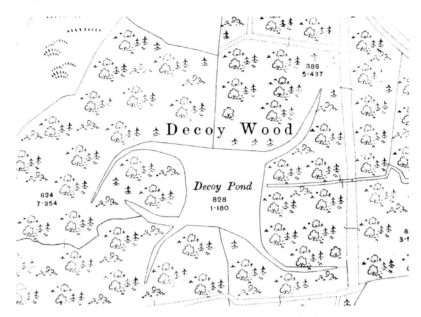

FIG 138. Decoy Wood Pond, as shown on the first edition of the Ordnance Survey map of 1884. (West Glamorgan Archive Service)

ducks for food. As well as the feature at Decoy Wood it seems that there was also a decoy, or decoys, at Stouthall, since there is a reference to spoonbill *Platalea leucorodia* in the *Swansea Guide* of 1802, which was said to be 'sometimes caught in the decoys at Stouthall'. The exact location of this other decoy pond is not known and even the Decoy Wood pond has today almost disappeared, although the courses of the ditches are just still visible on the ground despite its being planted with conifers. They are shown as curving watercourses on large-scale maps of the area. Although the pond itself is now very overgrown, and there is no open water remaining, the area is very boggy and open and with some effort it would be possible to restore this feature. The conifer plantation is in need of thinning, with many windblown trees, and when this work is carried out it would present an excellent opportunity to clear the immediate area of the decoy.

Duck decoys were typically set in woodland and consist of a pond, usually 0.5 to 1.5 hectares, shelving at the sides and surrounded by trees and shrubs. The ditches, called 'pipes', were usually 50 to 70 metres long, 5 to 8 metres wide at their mouth and tapering off at the far end. The water was around 0.5 metres deep at the mouth and a few centimetres at the ends. The pipes were screened in and covered with netting on iron hoops and had small channels or feeders to keep the water moving.

The success of the system depended on the mobbing behaviour of ducks when they are confronted by a predator. On even small decoy ponds there could be several thousand ducks resting during the day, and by using a trained dog, which the ducks will follow, the 'decoyman' was able to entice them into a pipe and catch them by driving them into a net at the end. The system allowed several catches a day to be made. In the close season the ponds were used by the birds to breed and collect on.

Plants on the boggy site of the pond include yellow iris (Fig. 139), common marsh bedstraw, marsh thistle *Cirsium palustre,* water mint, purple loosestrife *Lythrum salicaria,* water forget-me-not *Myosotis scorpioides* and mullein *Verbascum* spp. The area is important for dragonflies and damselflies and seventeen different species have been recorded including emperor dragonfly, golden-ringed dragonfly

FIG 139. Yellow iris on the boggy site of the Decoy Pond. (Harold Grenfell)

FIG 140. Golden-ringed dragonfly, one of 17 species recorded from the area of Decoy Wood. (Harold Grenfell)

Cordulegaster boltonii (Fig. 140), southern hawker *Aeshna cynea* and yellow-winged darter *Sympetrum flaveolum,* an infrequent immigrant to Britain. Damselflies include emerald damselfly *Lestes sponsa,* large red damselfly and azure damselfly.

LLANGENNITH MOORS

At first glance the large-scale Ordnance Survey map of Gower looks as though the colour printing is inaccurate to the west of Llangennith village. Instead of the normal black lines for field boundaries they have been printed in blue. There is no mistake, however, for here water-filled ditches and not hedges, banks or walls act as field boundaries. Llangennith Moors, covering some 50 hectares, is one of only three grazing marsh systems still in existence in this part of South Wales (Fig. 141), the other two being Cwm Ivy Marsh and Margam Moors to the east of Swansea. Margam Moors is all that remains of the extensive coastal grazing marsh that once stretched from the River Kenfig to the River Neath, the remainder having been destroyed by industrial development.

Llangennith Moors was included in the strip field system and although by 1844, when the tithe commissioners surveyed the parish of Llangennith, they had been enclosed, the meadows and withy bed on its eastern side were described as 'in landshares' and were partly unfenced. The Moors owe their origin to the sand dunes of Hillend and Llangennith, which have impeded the drainage. As a young man in the early 1880s Phil Tanner was employed on farm work by local farmers and by the squire at Hillend. He had to work for twelve or thirteen hours a day, beginning at 7.00 am. His main occupation was 'laking' on the Moors. This involved the cutting and clearing of the ditches that marked the boundaries of the fields (Fig. 142).

The management of the area has clearly changed over the past 160 years. The tithe map for 1844 reveals that the central part of the system was cropped for hay, with corn, pasture and a small withy bed restricted to the slightly higher land in the vicinity of Hillend and Llangennith village. During the Second World War parts of the central area were ploughed for both potatoes and spring cereals.

FIG 141. Llangennith Moors, with Rhossili Bay and Worms Head in the background. (Harold Grenfell)

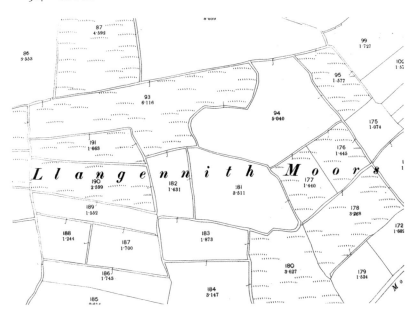

FIG 142. Map of Llangennith Moors showing the pattern of ditches. (West Glamorgan Archive Service)

Small-scale arable cropping continued until the early 1950s, but the current use consists of summer grazing for beef cattle, together with a few horses and sheep. One field on the southern edge has been drained to form a campsite.

Owing to its varied agricultural past the present vegetation of the Moors is quite diverse. In the southern part of the system there are agriculturally unimproved enclosures dominated by sedges *Carex* spp., creeping bent *Agrostis stolonifera* and lesser spearwort *Ranunculus flammula*, together with marsh-marigold and southern marsh-orchid. Elsewhere the former arable enclosures contain soft-rush and plants such as yellow iris and lady's smock *Cardamine pratensis* are abundant. Several enclosures have reverted to marsh and these contain dense stands of soft-rush, meadowsweet and common reed.

The flora of the ditches which divide the enclosures was surveyed in detail by the Countryside Council for Wales in 1991. A wide variety of locally uncommon plants were found, including greater tussock-sedge, spiked water-milfoil, mare's tail and unbranched bur-reed *Sparganium emersum*. In general the ditches can be divided into two types, marshy ditches, which have very limited or no open water and represent the final stages of the colonisation of the ditch by plants, and ditches where there is a significant amount of open water. Periodic cleaning of the ditches takes place to maintain their function as field boundaries and this creates a range of plant communities across the marsh as a whole. While the initial impression of the Moors is of a series of level fields separated by a network of narrow drainage ditches, closer inspection reveals a substantial main drain which runs westward through the system before it exits through the sand dunes at Diles Lake on Rhossili beach. The upper section of this drain has a diverse vegetation more typical of riversides, including meadowsweet and Indian, or Himalayan, balsam *Impatiens glandulifera*, which was introduced to British gardens in 1839 and has since become widely naturalised.

The marshy ditches have a similar flora to some of the less improved enclosures, being dominated by tall emergent species such as soft-rush, yellow iris, branched bur-reed *Sparganium erectum*, together with Yorkshire-fog and creeping bent, but prickly lettuce *Lactuca serriola*, common centaury and yellow loosestrife are also found. Ditches with large amounts of open water contain aquatic species such as water-plantain *Alisma plantago-aquatica*, fool's water-cress *Apium nodiflorum*, lesser water-parsnip, water-starworts *Callitriche* spp., water mint, water-cress, water forget-me-not, broad-leaved pondweed *Potamogeton natans*, lesser pondweed *Potamogeton pusillus* (a regional rarity) and water-pepper *Polygonum hydropiper*.

The drainage ditches of coastal levels are an important habitat for dragonflies and damselflies. An invertebrate survey in 1991 also recorded a number of scarce and local fly species such as the danceflies *Hilara fulvibarba* and *H. lundbecki*, the latter being a predatory coastal fly often seen visiting flowers near the shore. Other species found along the ditches include the stiletto fly *Thereva nobilitata*, whose larvae feed on decaying material in soil, *Syntormon pumilus*, a small metallic blue fly with long legs which is often found in damp, well-vegetated places, and *Oplodontha viridula*, a widespread, but local, bright green and black soldierfly usually found in marshes and pond margins. Adults of the soldierfly are commonly found on flowers, especially those of low-growing species. It is most active in warm sunny conditions and on a cool day, or in windy weather, they seek shelter.

There has been no detailed survey of the birds of Llangennith Moors and many of the records are rather old, although species recorded breeding in the area include mallard, moorhen *Gallinula chloropus*, reed bunting, stonechat, sedge warbler, linnet, yellowhammer, grasshopper warbler, skylark and meadow pipit. Large populations of breeding lapwing used to occur within living memory, but there has been a considerable decline in numbers, which may be linked with the change from mixed farming to summer grazing only. Among the most interesting winter records are those of a pair of water rail in 1964 and 45 golden plover

Pluvialis apricaria in 1966. As mentioned in Chapter 5, two Dartford warblers were also seen in 1991.

Diles Lake was originally the point at which the outflow from the Moors emerged as a seepage through the dunes and out onto the beach. An outflow pipe was installed during the early 1970s to improve drainage, but as the pipe frequently became blocked with plant material an exit for the main drain was cut through the dunes in early 1985. The creation of this new exit channel had serious effects on the moors and they became much drier. By 1995 it was clear that action needed to be taken if the flora and fauna of the area were to be conserved, and a management plan to control the water level was prepared by the Countryside Council for Wales in conjunction with the then National Rivers Authority. This was not implemented until 2000, however, due to the complicated land ownership in the area, the Moors being owned by seven different farmers, with the landholdings scattered across a number of separate enclosures.

CWM IVY MARSH

Along with the yellow iris, characteristic of the upper part of the estuary, the smaller grazing marsh at Cwm Ivy contains meadowsweet, common spike-rush, blunt-flowered rush *Juncus subnodulosus*, greater bird's-foot-trefoil and water horsetail *Equisetum fluviatile*. The drainage ditches on the lowland fen meadow form most of the field boundaries and have their own characteristic species including fool's water-cress and lesser water-parsnip. Other notable plant species include brackish water-crowfoot *Ranunculus baudotii*, thread-leaved water-crowfoot *Ranunculus trichophyllus*, sharp rush *Juncus acutus* and fine-leaved water dropwort *Oenanthe aquatica*. The damp neutral grassland is dominated by grasses such as Yorkshire-fog, with soft-rush and common sedge *Carex nigra*. The rare flat sedge *Blysmus rufus* has also been found here in the past.

THE FUTURE

Recent research has shown that acid rain is still affecting large parts of the British landscape and in other parts of Wales lakes and streams are still comparatively species-poor. Aquatic insects, such as dragonfly and damselfly larvae, and the fish and birds that feed on them, are particularly affected. Despite significant improvements in the east of Britain, including an 80 per cent reduction in acid rain from land-based sources, in the west there has been no change because of the

influence of marine shipping. Clouds of sulphur and nitrogen dioxide generated
by ships sailing across the north Atlantic are drifting over Gower and falling as
acid rain. Unless international action is taken there will be a steady rise in marine
pollution and it is predicted that by the end of this decade shipping will account
for 45 per cent of acid rain in Europe. The effects of this acidification have not
been noticeable in the peninsula to date, but the outlook seems less assured.

Many wetland habitats are essentially ephemeral features, natural succession
converting them rapidly to dry land if they are not managed. In itself natural
succession should not be of concern, particularly if new freshwater habitats were
being created, but they are not. The maintenance and enhancement of the
freshwater habitats, from the smallest ephemeral pool to the largest marsh, must
therefore be given a higher priority. If, for example, the conservation interest of
Oxwich Marsh is to be maintained more work is needed on reprofiling ditches,
scraping away accumulated peat and building more sophisticated bunds.
Unfortunately this work is likely to be extremely expensive, and in addition work
on National Nature Reserves is now focused, after meeting the basic commitments,
on maintaining those features that are important on a European scale as part of
Special Areas of Conservation. The freshwater marsh does not fall into this
category and there are therefore no resources for this essential work. At the time
of writing there is the possibility of external funding and it is to be hoped that this
is secured. While the marsh and its management has changed over the centuries,
and although it is clearly for the most part an artificial feature, now that we know
so much about the richness of its wildlife it would be an incalculable loss, both
to Gower and to the wider environment, if it was allowed to disappear.

CHAPTER 12

Woods, Hedges and Fields

The natural vegetation of the Gower plateau is stunted oak–ash forest and scrub. Where exposed to the westerly winds, heathland develops, but in the deep combes and along the old cliffs a thicker forest is to be expected.

J. G. Rutter, *Prehistoric Gower*

ONLY A SMALL AREA of the peninsula, some 7 per cent, is woodland. As always in Gower, however, there is a great variety of habitats and they range from ancient woodlands through secondary woodlands to modern conifer plantations. In particular Gower contains one of the most extensive areas of ash woodland in Wales and is near the western extreme of the habitat's range in Britain. These woodlands, which are of European importance, have developed along the series of largely interlinked valleys and ravines cut into the limestone and also on coastal slopes and cliffs, where there are unique transitions through scrub to sand dunes, freshwater marsh and salt marsh. Elsewhere they give way to fields and, particularly in the northeast of the peninsula, the intermixed fields and woodlands are a characteristic feature of the area, the *subboscus*, the lower part of the Welshry wood. The hedges that define the fields are themselves a significant wildlife habitat and are also important for historical and cultural reasons. They provide an essential refuge for many woodland and farmland plants and animals and are thought to act as wildlife corridors allowing movement and dispersal between other habitats. Gower is also an area of drystone walls and stonefaced banks and in some areas of the peninsula these are an important component of the landscape, with their own characteristic flora and fauna.

The hedges and walls enclose a considerable number of arable fields that have important populations of rare plants, dating back to the Neolithic period, growing alongside the crop. These plants, once denigrated as agricultural weeds, are now known as archaeophytes and have an immense cultural significance. It is becoming increasingly clear that Gower is one of the British strongholds of this ancient flora, but until recently little effort has been made to conserve these rare and interesting species. Other fields are pasture and some contain the remains of traditional orchards, once a characteristic feature of the area and now more or less ignored.

WOODS

The woods, such as Ilston Cwm, Cwm Ivy and Kilvrough Manor Woods, contain a great diversity of trees and shrubs and a variety of vegetation communities and sub-communities are recognised, but generally they are dominated by ash and pedunculate oak in varying proportions. In some, such as Kilvrough Wood, hybrids between the pedunculate and sessile oak are common. At the top of the woodlands and on the steep slopes, where the soils are often thin, dry and calcareous, ash dominates (Fig. 143). Where the soils are moderate or deep, heavier and more acidic than those higher up, the oak tends to dominate the ash. Until recently wych elm *Ulmus glabra* was also present in large numbers, but its

FIG 143. Ash woodland on the north Gower cliffs. Looking north along the escarpment from Cilifor Top in winter. (Harold Grenfell)

occurrence has been reduced dramatically by Dutch elm disease. Sometimes the woods also contain considerable amounts of small-leaved lime *Tilia cordata*, field maple *Acer campestre* and sycamore. Where there is sufficient light reaching the ground the invasive sycamore is often abundant in the shrub layer, along with large numbers of ash seedlings, but it only occurs occasionally as a canopy species. Although present almost everywhere it is generally more abundant on the deeper, heavier soils, which it appears to prefer. Spindle *Euonymus europaeus* and wild privet *Ligustrum vulgare* are frequent as well, although other plants which might generally be expected to occur in such conditions, especially buckthorn *Rhamnus catharticus* and spurge-laurel *Daphne laureola*, are rare in the shrub layer.

The ground flora of the ash woods is again rich and is usually dominated by ramsons and dog's mercury *Mercurialis perennis*, together with hart's-tongue fern *Phyllitis scolopendrium* and soft shield-fern *Polystichum setiferum*, which is very abundant on shaded slopes. Ferns such as male-fern *Dryopteris filix-mas*, lady-fern *Athyrium filix-femina* and broad buckler-fern are also locally frequent and in places dominant. In Parkmill Woods and Llethrid Valley there are populations of the locally uncommon royal fern, a dramatic plant that sometimes grows up to 3 metres high, hence its name (Fig. 144). This fern of wet woods was one of the species most heavily affected by the Victorian collectors. Several woods have dramatic spring displays of bluebells. Other notable species include wood spurge *Euphorbia amygdaloides*, toothwort *Lathraea squamaria*, herb Paris *Paris quadrifolia*, butcher's broom *Ruscus aculeatus* and stinking hellebore, all of which are most abundant in eastern or southern Britain and, like the trees themselves, are nearly at the western or northwestern limits of their ranges in Gower.

Stinking hellebore, a perennial of woods and scrub on calcium-rich soils, was first recorded in Glamorgan around 1803 by Dr Turton, who discovered it between Parkmill and Pennard Castle. It was still there in abundance in 1840, when it was noted by Gutch, but it is now very rare in the Parkmill area even though the woodland appears to have changed little since Turton's day. Although individual plants are long-lived, seedlings are rare and since it was formerly used as a medicinal plant, being given powdered as a remedy for worms, it may have been affected by over-collecting.

Areas of scrub woodland, dominated by ash, hazel and blackthorn, and in some places with buckthorn and dogwood *Cornus sanguinea*, survive in various locations on the south Gower cliffs. These woodlands were probably more extensive in the past, but repeated fires and intensive grazing by sheep have resulted in their replacement by gorse and heathland. Good examples of this type of woodland can be seen on the south side of Oxwich Point, where purple gromwell and pale St John's-wort *Hypericum montanum* grow at the margins of the scrub, and in

FIG 144. Royal fern, a spectacular plant that sometimes grows up to 3 metres high. (David Painter)

Ramsgrove Valley, where a variety of common whitebeam *Sorbus porrigentiformis* grows in the scrub. Three unusual trees, the small-leaved lime mentioned earlier, rock whitebeam *Sorbus rupicola* and wild service tree *Sorbus torminalis*, and two scarce shrubs, juniper and butcher's broom, can be found in the rockier parts of Crawley Wood. There are also significant stands of butcher's broom around Oxwich Point, which is its westernmost location in the peninsula.

The surviving fragments of oak–birch woodland have, where they are least disturbed, a varied flora that includes a number of upland species. The upper part of Penrice Wood, for example, has a luxuriant moss community including fuzzy fork-moss *Dicranum majus*, feather moss *Hylocomium splendens*, juicy silk-moss *Plagiothecium undulatum* and rose-moss *Rhytidiadelphus loreus* under an open canopy of birch and oak. Rose-moss can be particularly abundant on the floor of Gower woodlands, and is distinguished by a reddish stem, with the leaves having the appearance of being swept to one side of the stem and branches. In the upper part of Clyne Wood there is an open wood of oak and birch with hazel, alder buckthorn *Frangula alnus* and crab apple *Malus sylvestris* occurring alongside wood horsetail *Equisetum sylvaticum* and lemon-scented fern *Oreopteris limbosperma*.

Berry Wood, near Knelston, is an example of ancient oak woodland with coppice standards, which is situated on poorly drained glacial drift over the Millstone Grit (Fig. 145). Both pedunculate and sessile oaks are present, together with ash, hazel, grey willow *Salix cinerea*, rowan and aspen *Populus tremula*. The oldest oaks are estimated to be around 200 years old and are located on the western side of the wood. The remainder of the wood is much more recent and is made up of even-aged stands of oak, birch and ash. This suggests that much of the wood was felled at some time and allowed to regenerate naturally. A number of other Gower woods, such as Prior's Wood, are examples of secondary woodland. Here the woodland canopy is made up of a considerable number of species including sweet chestnut, beech, ash, alder, birch, sessile oak, elm and small-leaved lime. This variety, together with evidence from old maps, which show that the site was originally called Priors Meadow, suggests that the wood has developed as a result of natural regeneration, probably aided by planting in the Victorian period. Parts of many other Gower woodland blocks are also secondary woodland, including Oxwich Wood, where large areas were affected by extensive limestone quarrying in the past.

Several areas, particularly at Kilvrough and the southwestern end of Park Woods, have in the past been planted with beech. Although the beech dominates, ash is often also frequent along with other elements of semi-natural woodland including a field layer dominated by bluebells, ramsons, wood anemone *Anemone nemorosa*, lords-and-ladies *Arum maculatum* and enchanter's nightshade *Circaea*

FIG 145. Berry Wood, near Knelston, a nature reserve managed by the Wildlife Trust. (Harold Grenfell)

lutetiana. The Forestry Commission started planting in Glamorgan in 1921. Regarding Gower, the Commission's guide to the *Glamorgan Forests*, published in 1961, noted, 'Its woodlands of oak, beech and other broadleaved trees, stand on southward-facing slopes and are very much in the public eye. Therefore their management is closely concerned with retaining the scenic amenities, though at the same time it is believed that valuable timber can be grown and harvested without ever causing harm to the peninsula's marvellous views.' The main blocks of forest in Gower are Park Woods, Mill Wood and Mead Moor. Conifers planted in Park Woods and Mill Wood by the Forestry Commission included European larch *Larix decidua*, Corsican pine *Pinus nigra* var. *maritima* and Sitka spruce *Picea sitchensis*. Mill Wood is an ancient woodland that was later an estate wood and as a result it has a large number of tree species including oak, ash, beech and small-leaved lime. The flora underneath these trees is interesting and varied with plants such as wild daffodil *Narcissus pseudonarcissus* ssp. *pseudonarcissus*. Scattered throughout the wood are large, old, veteran trees which themselves support a number of animal and plant species. There are also the remains of a sixteenth-century corn mill that gives the wood its name and which still retains three large millstones.

INVERTEBRATES

The most important wooded common is Bishopston Valley, which is owned by the National Trust, although woodland has also developed on other commons where grazing has ceased, such as Newton Cliffs and Summerland Cliffs. Bishopston Valley, however, contains both ancient and recent secondary woodland and the underlying limestone has produced a rich flora that includes both small-leaved lime and wild service tree. The damp and shady woodland floor with its carpet of rich leaf litter and rotting wood provides a variety of habitats, which have a rich invertebrate fauna, including snails, millipedes, woodlice and ground beetles. The land winkle *Pomatias elegans*, the only winkle found on dry land, common or two-toothed door snail *Cochlodina laminata* and tree snail *Balea perversa* are locally characteristic of calcareous woodland such as this. The land winkle is easily recognised as it carries a shell lid (operculum) on the rear of its foot, while the frontal part of the head is prolonged into a snout. It moves by lifting one side of its foot after the other, appearing to move forward on two feet. The tree snail is also unusual (perverse) because the whorls on its shell are coiled anticlockwise with the aperture on the left, rather than the more usual clockwise direction. The shell has a distinctive turret shape and is up to 1 centimetre tall.

Centipedes and millipedes, otherwise known as myriapods (literally many feet) are also common in this habitat, and Gower is a particularly interesting area for these animals. At the northern end of Park Woods near Llethrid, for example, there is an exceptional mean overwintering density of nearly 800 individual millipedes per square metre, 16 different species being present including a flat-back millipede *Brachydesmus superus*, a snake millipede *Ophyiulus pilosus* and a spotted snake millipede *Blaniulus guttulatus*. Five species of centipede have also been recorded from the site, a stone centipede *Lithobius variegatus*, *Geophilus insculptus*, *Strigamia acuminata*, *Brachygeophilus truncorum* and *Haplophilus subterraneus*. This latter species is one of the longest and broadest of the British 'geophilid' or ground-loving centipedes. It is up to 70 millimetres long, and it may be 1.5 millimetres at its broadest point. Bishop's Wood was one of the three sites from which *Geophilus osquidatum* was first recorded in Britain and the site of the second British find of *Chordeuma proximum*.

The harvestman *Sabacon viscayanum* ssp. *ramblaianum* was also first discovered in Britain, in 1980, in the woods at Parkmill. It has now been found in 22 localities in South Wales. Because the early finds were close to industrial workings it was suggested that the harvestman had been introduced to Britain, but since these sites invariably include old, damp woodland, which is the usual habitat of the species, it is considered instead to be a 'relict' species whose range was once more extensive, but which has since become fragmented.

Little is known about the flies of the Gower woods and many records date back to the 1950s and 1960s when Fonseca (1973) extensively surveyed Nicholaston Wood and Oxwich Wood. He recorded a large number of scarce flies associated with old woodlands including *Coenosia stigmatica*, *Hydrotaea velutina*, *Helina abdominalis*, *Fannia gotlandica*, *Fannia carbonaria*, *Eustalomyia vittipes*, *Delia tarsifimbria* and *Aulacigaster leucopeza*. It is thought that many of these flies disappeared when dead trees were removed around 1960, although at least one of the flies recorded by him, the hoverfly *Brachypalpus laphriformis*, was still present in the mid-1990s.

Other insects, however, are known to be numerous in the woodlands, especially in the open sunny glades. A varied shrub layer on the glade edges will support a variety of woodland moths and the rich flora of grassy rides can support a large and important fauna of plant-feeding beetles, bugs and leafhoppers. The waved carpet moth *Hydrelia sylvata* is a highly localised species that occurs in woods in Gower that have a long history of coppicing and where there are open sunny areas with young specimens of the larval food plants, which are alder, birch, sallow and blackthorn (Fig. 146). The adult moths are on the wing in June and July, resting by day among the bushes, but they can also be occasionally found on tree trunks. The larvae feed between July and August, pupating in September to

FIG 146. Waved carpet moth, a highly localised species which occurs in woods that have a long history of coppicing. (Barry Stewart)

overwinter in an earthen cell until they emerge the following July. Because of this limited period on the wing and the fact that it occurs at a low density over much of its range it is likely that the species is under-recorded.

Two small tree-dwelling species also often overlooked by the casual observer are the purple hairstreak *Quercusia quercus* and whiteletter hairstreak *Satyrium w-album* butterflies. The purple hairstreak (Fig. 147) is a true woodland butterfly and the caterpillars, which are extremely well concealed, feed mainly on oak buds and leaves. This close association is reflected in its scientific name, which uses the Latin word *quercus*, meaning 'oak', twice. The numbers of adult butterflies vary greatly from year to year, but it has been recorded from Oxwich, Nicholaston, Llethrid, Crawley and Park woods. The adults typically fly high around the tree canopy and only rarely descend to paths and clearings, the females tending to be more visible than the males. Purple hairstreaks are aggressive butterflies and will attack other insects which fly into their territory, even wasps. They feed on the sugar-rich honeydew deposited by aphids on ash and aspen leaves. The whiteletter hairstreak is a very local species and its caterpillars feed exclusively on elms, which are fast disappearing due to Dutch elm disease. There are only a few records from well-monitored sites such as Bishop's Wood and Oxwich. The adults spend a lot of time visiting bramble and privet blossom for the nectar and the honeydew left by aphids. Elsewhere the species may be seen wherever wych elm, or other

FIG 147. Purple hairstreak butterfly in Llethrid Cwm. (Harold Grenfell)

regenerating elms, are found, but it is unlikely that more than one or two individuals will be present. In contrast speckled wood *Pararge aegeria* is a common and widespread species found in a variety of locations, not confined to woodland.

BIRDS

The Gower woodlands support a wide diversity of breeding birds, as well as providing shelter and food for migrants in spring and autumn. In particular Bishopston Valley is recognised as being especially important for the variety and quality of the breeding bird community and the number of wintering species. The great spotted woodpecker *Dendrocopos major* is common in both coniferous and deciduous woodland and the characteristic 'drumming' of its bill against a resonant piece of wood, which is a means of declaring ownership of territory, is a frequent sound in early spring (Fig. 148). In contrast the lesser spotted woodpecker *Dendrocopos minor* is a much rarer bird in the peninsula, but it may be under-recorded, as unlike the great spotted woodpecker it is a difficult bird to find. It has been regularly sighted in the Oxwich Bay area over the last forty years, and also occurs in Clyne Woods.

Another breeding bird in the woods is the buzzard *Buteo buteo*. This is the commonest bird of prey in Wales and the wooded valleys and mixed agriculture in Gower combine to create an ideal habitat. Other birds include summer migrants such as blackcap *Sylvia atricapilla* and chiffchaff *Phylloscopus collybita*, which normally breed in deciduous woodlands where there are mature trees and a good understorey. The tiny insectivorous goldcrest *Regulus regulus* and the nuthatch *Sitta europaea* are also present along with the treecreeper *Certhia familiaris*, which occurs in most of the deciduous woodlands. Little owl *Athene noctua* and tawny owl *Strix aluco* are widespread and common breeding residents in the Gower woodlands. There are recent signs, however, of a decrease in numbers, the reasons for which are not clear. Of the two species the little owl is the less abundant, but it can still be seen fairly easily, particularly in the west of the peninsula. Regarding the long-eared owl *Asio otus* Dillwyn recorded that 'In December 1825, Mr Talbot shot one at Penrice, where the specimen is preserved; and three or four have since been killed in Gower, but it is far from common in this neighbourhood.' Perhaps not surprisingly, long-eared owls are now scarce throughout Britain and nest almost exclusively in conifers. The last confirmed breeding record in Gower was in 1919, although a single bird was found dead in Mill Wood in 1987. As it is the most nocturnal owl it is easily overlooked and may still be present.

Finally, there used to be a sizable colony of rooks *Corvus frugilegus* in Oxwich

Wood behind the church. In 1975 this was one of the largest rookeries in Gower, but the last record, of only 25 nests, was in 1992; the birds seemed to have moved to the nearby Pittsog's Wood, where there were 22 nests in 1993. The bird's optimum habitat is a mixture of arable and grazing land, which ensures a constant food supply throughout the year, and Gower would therefore appear to be an important area (Fig. 149). There is indeed a concentration of rookeries on the better land in the south and west of the peninsula. Some of these sites may be of considerable antiquity. Intensive surveys during the 1980s and early 1990s found that 811 nests at 16 rookeries in 1983 had declined to 658 nests at 17 rookeries in 1992. Stouthall was consistently the largest rookery in the area throughout this period, with 278 nests in 1984, making it one of the largest rookeries in Wales at the time, but it

FIG 148. Great spotted woodpecker in Cheriton Wood. A common species in both deciduous and coniferous woodland. (Harold Grenfell)

FIG 149. Rook foraging in winter near Reynoldston. (Harold Grenfell)

declined when many of the beech trees had to be felled as they were considered to be unsafe. Although the overall number of nests varied from year to year, sometimes quite noticeably, the general trend from the mid-1980s onwards has been one of a gradual reduction in numbers. Cereals are an important food source for rooks and a clear correlation can be drawn between the decline in the area of cereals grown in Wales and the numbers of rooks. The crucial months for young birds are July and August, when they are dependent on a source of grain.

MAMMALS

British bats can be divided into two groups, depending on their roosting requirements, cave and woodland bats. Both groups are well represented in Gower, although the cave-roosting species are the most obvious and thought by many people to be the only bats present. In contrast, the woodland bats are secretive and choose roosting places where they are difficult to see, and as a result are seldom encountered except when they form nursery roosts in buildings. They include the common, or 45kHz, pipistrelle *Pipistrellus pipistrellus* and the soprano, or 55kHz, pipistrelle *P. pygmaeus*.

Almost all studies of pipistrelle bats until a few years ago assumed that there was only one species in Britain, but, as the alternative names suggest, the use of the ultrasonic bat detector has identified two clearly different species. The other predominantly woodland bat is the noctule *Nyctalus noctula*, which is found in the woodlands in Parkmill and Oxwich and in parts of Mumbles. This is the bat often seen flying high in the clear air. The brown long-eared bat *Plecotus auritus* is also a relatively common woodland bat that roosts and hibernates mainly in trees and buildings. It is known as the 'whispering bat' and picks food off the leaves of trees, listening and watching for the insects and spiders as they move about on the foliage. Natterer's bat *Myotis nattereri*, Brandt's bat *M. brandtii* and whiskered bat *M. mystacinus* are also associated with woodland and forage along hedgerows and the woodland edge for flies and other insects. In addition they catch a considerable number of spiders. Another bat of parklands, pasture and woodlands, the serotine, has been found in the roof of a house in Swansea and a good visual identification has been made of large bats seen flying near Llanrhidian.

It would be premature to say that all the species of bats in Gower are known. More survey work needs to be done, with the bat detector, for species such as barbastelle *Barbastella barbastellus* that are associated with areas of old woodland. Most of the Gower woods are probably managed too well to leave the kinds of splits, areas of flaking bark and crevices this species favours as roost sites, but it might be worth searching woodland near Ilston. Bechstein's bat *Myotis bechsteinii* is another species that would be worth looking for. It roosts in holes in trees and prefers old trees with dead branches. The areas of mature woodland in Parkmill, Oxwich and Bishopston Valley all have features that could suit this species.

Once the fauna of the Gower woods was more exotic than it is today. Dillwyn (1848) says that the wild cat was still occasionally seen in Clyne Woods and to the north in the Neath Valley. It was regarded as 'vermin' and heavily persecuted, as he noted in relation to activities at Margam, to the east of the peninsula:

> During an active extermination of the vermin in Margam Park, which commenced in 1824, twelve of these animals were killed within two years; and my friend Mr Talbot says that one of these, which is now preserved at Penrice Castle, weighed twelve pounds; and he was told by his keepers that some of the others were considerably larger.

Persecution of vermin was a continuing theme in Gower, as elsewhere, during this period and the Reverend Davies (1894) mentions in his survey of the parishes of Llanmadoc and Cheriton (and referring to Cheriton church) that:

> I was informed by several old people that it was the invariable custom when anyone killed vermin, such as weasles, stoates, polecats, &., to bring them to the churchyard, and

nail them up in a certain ash tree. At the annual vestry meeting, held on Easter Monday,
these animals were counted and those who killed them were paid so much a-piece out of
the church rate; a guinea was allowed for a fox.

Dillwyn also recorded that the pine marten *Martes martes* occurred in the
peninsula and it is true that until the nineteenth century pine martens were found
throughout much of mainland Britain. However, fragmentation of habitats,
persecution by gamekeepers and martens being killed for their fur drastically
reduced this distribution. Today the total population for England and Wales is
estimated to be only 150 individuals, although it may be as low as 40. The species
is therefore unlikely to return to Gower.

A polecat *Mustela putorius* was recorded in November 1969 by Pip Hatton,
the Nature Conservancy Warden, at the side of the road near Cilibion. He noted,
'It was caught in the headlights on the grass verge and instead of moving, curled
its body round and snarled at the lights.' Polecats are medium-sized animals with
distinctive black and white facial markings. As indicated by the above sighting
they are predominantly nocturnal, and tend to hunt on the ground, avoiding
swimming or climbing, with rabbits being the main prey. The preferred habitats
are woodland edges, farm buildings and field boundaries, and polecat territories
are closely related to the presence of rabbit warrens. The animal is now widespread in Wales and is expanding rapidly into England.

Badgers are again widespread and there are about 400 setts recorded in Gower,
but it is difficult to assess the size of the population (Fig. 150). Many of the setts
are in 'textbook' positions at the edge of woodland adjacent to pasture, although
they are also found near the tops of the Old Red Sandstone hills which form the
spine of the peninsula. Setts are also located in sand dunes, close to the seashore.
A badger has even been found asleep on the rocks at Mewslade.

A national population study conducted in the mid-1990s by Bristol University
suggested that badger numbers are generally stable in the UK, but unfortunately
illegal persecution continues. About one-third of the Gower setts have evidently
been interfered with and the Glamorgan Badger Group patrols the most
vulnerable setts at irregular intervals. Many badgers are also killed or injured as a
result of road traffic accidents. This is especially so in the tourist season, when the
amount of traffic on the peninsula's roads increases dramatically. Hot summers
can also increase the number of road deaths, because in dry weather, when
earthworms do not come above ground, badgers forage further than normal from
their setts and can be at greater risk from road traffic. Other issues affecting the
conservation of badgers include the dramatic rise in the number of cattle with
bovine tuberculosis, an infectious and contagious disease of cattle caused by the

FIG 150. Badger in Nicholaston Wood. (Harold Grenfell)

bacterium *Mycobacterium bovis*. Since the mid-1970s thousands of badgers in Britain have been culled in response to outbreaks of tuberculosis, because of circumstantial evidence that badgers spread the disease. Thankfully there has been no culling in Gower to date and this crude approach is now becoming discredited.

The native common or hazel dormouse *Muscardinus avellanarius* was recorded from Berry Wood in 1969, but has not been detected there since. Apart from bats, the dormouse is the only British mammal to hibernate (in the true sense of the word) and their name is thought to originate from the French word *dormir*, meaning 'to sleep'. The animal is no longer as widespread or abundant as its name suggests and its distribution is now limited to the south and west of England, parts of Wales and a few outlying populations in the north of England. Dormice are mainly confined to those habitats that provide a rich variety of edible fruit and seeds within a complex physical structure, such as woodlands and areas of species-rich shrubs such as hedgerows. They very rarely come down to the ground, spending most of their time climbing among branches in the hunt for food. In particular they require a sequence of suitable foods to be available in the tree and shrub canopy through the summer. While they are often thought of as woodland species, the earlier literature mentions a much wider range of habitats including hedges, thickets and commons. Nests have also been found low down in coastal scrub, less than 1 metre above the ground, close to the grass that is used to construct them.

The current status of the dormouse is not clear, although a recent survey found signs of its presence in a number of locations. In 1965 a dormouse nest was found in Cilibion Plantation, a conifer plantation with a broadleaved edge consisting of coppice with standards, and in 1998 there was a record of a distinctively gnawed hazel nut at the same site. The other stronghold for dormice appears to be Gelli Hir Wood, where there was a sighting in 1999 of an adult in a bird box and a gnawed nut was found in 2001. Dormice are easily overlooked, however, being very elusive animals that are rarely seen even in parts of the country where they are relatively common. In addition they occur in very small numbers, at a level of only six to ten per hectare, even in prime habitats. They are also small and strictly nocturnal and during daylight hours are fast asleep in their nests. Dormice are regarded as poor colonisers and are therefore prone to die out in isolated habitats, a viable population needing access to at least 20 hectares of suitable territory. Much more research is needed before the distribution and strength of the Gower populations can be properly understood.

HEDGES

There are two generally recognised hedgerow types, assart hedgerows and enclosure hedgerows, which correspond to the ancient and planned countryside described by Oliver Rackham (1986). Both types occur in Gower and intimately reflect past land use in the peninsula. Assart is the informal and often pre-medieval practice of creating farmland from previously untouched woodland, heathland and fenland, whereas enclosure is the deliberate planting of hedges to enclose formerly open ground, which was usually the medieval field system. Assart hedgerows normally therefore have a much richer flora and fauna than enclosure hedges as they have been derived from the original woodland or from rough wood pasture, unfarmed heathland etc. Some enclosures have been dated as far back as the fifteenth century, but most date from the seventeenth and eighteenth centuries when the popular hedging plants were hawthorn and blackthorn.

The areas of assart and enclosure hedges can be easily identified by looking at a modern large-scale map. The assart areas have an intimate pattern of small fields, the boundaries of which are often curved or very irregular and are sometimes massive structures full of mature trees. Some roads can be clearly seen to cut through this pattern and the fields thus pre-date the road. This is the classic ancient countryside as described by Rackham and is formed as a result of medieval or pre-medieval assarts. In areas of planned countryside, on the other hand, the field system generally derives from post-medieval enclosures and the boundaries are usually straight and enclose larger fields. The enclosure hedges are often treeless. This clear division often breaks down around settlements where small parcels of land are directly associated with houses or are used as allotments or paddocks.

The classic example of assart hedgerows in Gower is the community or parish of Llanrhidian Higher, which stretches inland from Wernffrwd and Llanmorlais and is bounded by the commons to the south (Fig. 151). Llanrhidian has the largest area of assart hedgerows in the peninsula and undoubtedly the best hedges in terms of geographical extent, general antiquity and total hedgerow length. The fields here in the subboscus are mainly very small, with herb-rich grassland, and there is a large amount of ancient woodland, which complements the value of the hedgerows (Table 12). The hedges are well stocked with trees, mostly pedunculate oak, with some ash and frequently with shrubs that have grown to maturity. Often the trees have grown from coppice or an old laid hedge. They are usually very high and wide and have a substantial bank. Dense bases surrounded by bramble are a frequent feature and this both protects the herb layer from grazing and provides a good habitat for invertebrates and birds. As in all areas of Gower, hawthorn and blackthorn are frequent, but here they are complemented by hazel, holly *Ilex*

FIG 151. Hedgerows in winter near Wernffrwd. (Harold Grenfell)

TABLE 12. Trees and shrubs of Gower hedgerows. (Adapted from Lawrence & Higgins, 1998)

COMMON NAME	SCIENTIFIC NAME	% OF ASSART HEDGES CONTAINING THE SPECIES	% OF ENCLOSURE HEDGES CONTAINING THE SPECIES
Blackthorn	Prunus spinosa	96.6	97.1
Hawthorn	Crataegus monogyna	91.4	100.0
Hazel	Corylus avellana	89.7	44.1
Pedunculate oak	Quercus robur	82.8	26.5
Holly	Ilex aquifolium	77.6	26.5
Grey sallow	Salix cinerea	65.5	44.1
Dog rose	Rosa canina	62.1	41.2
Ash	Fraxinus excelsior	55.2	17.6
Honeysuckle	Lonicera periclymenum	31.0	32.4
Elder	Sambucus nigra	27.6	76.5
Field rose	Rosa arvensis	25.9	2.9
Sycamore	Acer pseudoplatanus	24.1	5.9
Goat willow	Salix caprea	22.4	5.9
Gorse	Ulex europaeus	15.5	17.6
Alder	Alnus glutinosa	10.3	0
Silver birch	Betula pendula	8.6	0
English elm	Ulmus procera	6.9	0
Rowan	Sorbus aucuparia	6.9	2.9
Wych elm	Ulmus glabra	6.9	0
Downy birch	Betula pubescens	5.2	0
Field maple	Acer campestre	5.2	0
Crab apple	Malus sylvestris	3.4	0
Guelder-rose	Viburnum opulus	3.4	0
Wild cherry	Prunus avium	3.4	0
Alder buckthorn	Frangula alnus	1.7	0
Crack-willow	Salix fragilis	1.7	0
Gooseberry	Ribes uva-crispa	1.7	0
Dogwood	Cornus sanguinea	1.7	2.9
Beech	Fagus sylvatica	0	2.9

aquifolium, grey sallow *Salix cinerea* and dog rose *Rosa canina.* Other trees and shrubs include crab apple and field maple. There is a diverse herb layer that includes species such as tutsan *Hypericum androsaemum,* scaly male-fern *Dryopteris affinis,* betony *Stachys officinalis* and devil's-bit scabious. The latter two species demonstrate that hedges can be a reservoir for grassland species as well as woodland species.

In contrast the entire western end of the peninsula, west of a line from Landimore to Port-Eynon, is a landscape dominated by enclosure hedgerows. The wildlife value of these hedges may be less than that of the assart areas, but it is still important. The areas of enclosure are still very much as they appear on the estate and parish maps of the late eighteenth century and the hedges are thus at least 200 years old. The fields are not over-large, the hedgerow network is still relatively dense and the hedges are often very substantial, providing a good habitat for breeding birds, and species such as yellowhammer and song thrush *Turdus philomelos* are frequently recorded.

WALLS

Like many areas of Britain, Gower has its own style of drystone walling. Here, given the large areas of common land, the walls are built with an overhang on the outside to help keep animals out of the field they enclose. Walls provide a variety of different habitats and microclimates in a comparatively small space and there is always an exposed, wet side and a drier, warmer side. Even a well-maintained wall contains numerous holes providing habitats for a variety of invertebrates including spiders, woodlice, millipedes, bees and wasps. Wood mice and bank voles *Clethrionomys glareolus,* toads and slow-worms also find the cavities in walls attractive. A semi-derelict wall is more attractive than a well-maintained one since there are more sheltered spaces and more is covered in soil. However, such a condition is relatively short-lived, and once it is reduced to less than half its height the value of a wall for wildlife decreases considerably. They therefore need to be sympathetically maintained if they are to continue to be of interest (Fig. 152).

Probably the earliest survey of the flora of Gower walls was undertaken by the Caradoc and Severn Valley Field Club, who had their first 'Long Meeting' in Gower during July 1893 and recorded 'walls richly covered with moss and ferns, among which were noticed the wall-rue *Asplenium ruta-muraria,* maidenhair spleenwort, black stalked spleenwort, scaley fern, hart's tongue, &c., &c.' (Anon, 1896). In crevices ivy-leaved speedwell *Veronica hederifolia* and white stonecrop *Sedum album* can be found. The latter is probably introduced, but some authors think it may be

FIG 152. Drystone wall above Devil's Truck, near Rhossili. (Harold Grenfell)

a native plant of southwest Britain. Lichens also grow well on the stones. A variety of snails can be found including common snail, which uses walls as hibernation sites, rock snail *Pyramidula rupestris*, strawberry snail *Hygromia striolata* and hairy snail *H. hispida*. Great black slug *Arion ater*, large red slug *A. rufus* and hedgehog slug *A. intermedium* are also present in many walls.

FIELDS

In the peninsula there are compact nucleated villages with a subsidiary pattern of single farms. The fields tend to be large and regular in shape and have descriptive names in English such as Green Field, Limekiln Close and Longfurlong, the latter name arising because the field had previously been managed as part of an open common field. This is in clear contrast to upland Gower, where single farms and hamlets dominate and the names of the small irregularly shaped fields are Welsh. In the early 1970s Michael Williams (1972) used the field-name data from tithe redemption surveys completed between 1838 and 1848 to plot the precise boundary of the Welsh and English cultural frontier in Gower. Allowing for the greater stability of field names compared with the spoken languages he claimed that they represented the linguistic situation of the late 1700s and early 1800s. His work confirmed, as expected, that peninsular Gower was the core of the

English-speaking area and that upland Gower was Welsh-speaking. The neck of the peninsula between Pen-clawdd and Swansea was the transition zone between the two areas, where a belt of woodland, the *coed* or *boscus*, began and continued northwards. Similar work around the same time by Emery using farm names taken from the first edition of the Ordnance Survey one-inch map published in 1830 suggests a boundary between English and Welsh Gower running from northwest to southeast along a line of common land from Welsh Moor to Clyne Common.

ARABLE PLANTS

The plants that grow in the arable fields include not only the crop plant itself, but also other species. There has been debate for some time over the status of arable plants in Britain, and whether they are native or introductions, but it is now almost certain that the vast majority of British arable plants are not strictly native. Instead they were probably brought here by Neolithic farmers as agriculture spread to Britain around 3,500 years ago. As seed corn was exchanged between neighbouring farms the plants were transferred with them. With no effective methods of control, distinct communities of plants developed over the centuries alongside the intended crop plant. These communities, which show slight variations in species composition depending on the climate and soil type, appear now to be completely natural and their ancient ancestry is not appreciated. With the assistance of new genetic analysis these plants might reveal their origins and provide a record of the movement of agriculture into Britain. Different plants probably arrived in various areas of Britain, as farming spread from separate parts of Europe and the present patterns could be 'fossils' of former distributions. Financial support and advice is now available to farmers in Gower who sign up to the arable options within Tir Gofal, the Wales agri-environment scheme, and they are encouraged to leave the field margins unsprayed and unfertilised. Without the help and support of farmers the outlook for arable plants is very depressing.

As much of the recent history of farming in Wales has been involved with grazing animals it is easy to forget how important arable cultivation was in the past. From the Neolithic period onwards cereals were extensively cultivated, especially in lowland coastal areas such as Gower. The arable plants found today represent just a fragment of this rich past, much of which has been destroyed in the last fifty years or so by the intensification of arable farming, which has involved massive advances in technology and huge increases in efficiency, crop quality and crop yields. Many species of plants which once grew in the fields alongside the crop have declined, some to the point of extinction, since they cannot compete with dense highly fertilised crops. As a result arable fields now contain a large proportion of Britain's most endangered plants and arable field margins are identified as one of the highest-priority habitats. In the *New Atlas of the British and Irish Flora* (Preston *et al.*, 2002) arable plants are identified as the group that has undergone the most remarkable decline in distribution during the last thirty years.

In the older literature many of these species are referred to as 'arable weeds', being definitely, as the dictionary defines it, 'a plant growing where it is not wanted' as far as the farmer was concerned. New descriptions use the term 'arable plants' in recognition of their conservation importance. Probably the most well-known arable plant is the poppy *Papaver rhoeas*, but it is interesting that, compared to England, poppies are relatively uncommon in Wales and fumitories, a close relative, occur in abundance instead. Nationally scarce species found include tall ramping-fumitory *Fumaria bastardii* and common ramping-fumitory *F. muralis.*

In contrast to many other parts of Britain, the continuous history of mixed farming in Gower has preserved the habitat of what was once a plentiful and diverse arable flora. A study by Quentin Kay (1997a) showed that the arable plant communities in Gower are still very much richer in species than the increasingly impoverished arable floras that are now the normal situation for lowland Britain. The arable plants also often extend right across the field, rather than being mainly confined to the margins, as so often is the case in England. This has an additional advantage in that wintering flocks of birds prefer to forage in the centre of the fields away from the hedges where there may be predators.

Although many of the plants are still present, they are considerably reduced in abundance. While it is still not too difficult to find Gower fields with scattered specimens of increasingly rare plants like corn marigold *Chrysanthemum segetum* (Fig. 153), sharp-leaved fluellen *Kickxia elatine* or wild radish *Raphanus raphanistrum* these species are no longer as common as they were twenty years ago. Unfortunately there are no recent records for some arable plants that used to occur extremely locally or as rarities, such as corn chamomile *Anthemis arvensis* and lesser snapdragon *Misopates orontium*, but it seems highly likely that they will be found again, along with other species not previously recorded from the area. Until 2002 broad-fruited cornsalad *Valerianella rimosa* was thought to have been extinct in Wales until it was found in a Gower field, the first record for fifty years. Similarly, small-flowered catchfly *Silene gallica*, once thought to be lost from Gower, was recorded again in 2003.

Arable plants vary in their adaptation to the specialised habitat of cultivated

FIG 153. Corn marigold, an increasingly rare plant, in a field near Middleton. (Harold Grenfell)

land, and three broad classes are recognised. First are *obligate* plants, which only grow in cultivated land. Wild radish is a good example since it appears to grow only in cultivated land throughout its world range. Some semi-obligate plants grow mainly in arable land in Britain, but also occur in some isolated natural habitats where they seem to be native. It seems likely, therefore, that they have originated from weed populations in the past. The nit-grass found on the Gower cliffs probably originated in this way, first arriving in the peninsula as an annual weed of cultivated land. Like the nit-grass, arable plants of this class are often ecologically restricted, declining on arable land and rare or scarce in their natural habitats. The second class is *facultative* plants. These grow both as plants in arable crops and also in other habitats in the same geographic area. A familiar example is annual meadow-grass *Poa annua*, which is now the most widespread and abundant non-crop plant in the arable fields. Annual meadow-grass is, as its name suggests, an annual, but facultative plants are often perennials, such as creeping buttercup *Ranunculus repens*. Many facultative plants show considerable variation within the species, with clear genetic differences between arable and non-arable populations. The third class is *casual* plants. These are species which occasionally appear as arable plants, originating either as a result of natural dispersal from other habitats in the same area or as introductions with seeds or fertilising material such as slurry. They are normally non-persistent and usually grow as isolated individuals.

TABLE 13. The 20 most abundant arable plants in Gower. (Adapted from Kay, 1997a)

RANK	COMMON NAME	SCIENTIFIC NAME
1	Annual meadow-grass	*Poa annua*
2	Fat hen	*Chenopodium album*
3	Chickweed	*Stellaria media*
4	Pineappleweed	*Matricaria discoidea*
5	Common orache	*Atriplex patula*
6	Prickly sow-thistle	*Sonchus asper*
7	Perennial rye-grass	*Lolium perenne*
8	Creeping buttercup	*Ranunculus repens*
9	Redleg	*Persicaria maculosa*
10	Shepherd's purse	*Capsella bursa-pastoris*
11	Pale persicaria	*Persicaria lapathifolia*
12	Groundsel	*Senecio vulgaris*
13	Knotgrass	*Polygonium aviculare*
14	White clover	*Trifolium repens*
=15	Black bent	*Agrostis gigantea*
=15	Scentless mayweed	*Tripleurospermum inodorum*
=17	Scarlet pimpernel	*Anagallis arvensis*
=17	Spear thistle	*Cirsium vulgare*
19	Cut-leaved dead-nettle	*Lamium hybridum*
20	Field woundwort	*Stachys arvensis*

Examples from Gower include rosebay willow-herb *Chamerion angustifolium* and common gorse.

Some of the long-established arable plants are distributed very locally in Gower, even though they occur in some abundance, at least in some fields, in the areas where they occur. A notable example is annual nettle *Urtica urens*, which is a locally abundant and problematic plant in many fields in the Rhossili and Pitton area, but has not been seen elsewhere. Field pennycress *Thlaspi arvense* and henbit dead-nettle *Lamium amplexicaule* are also only noted from the Rhossili area.

Bryophytes (mosses, liverworts and hornworts) are a characteristic component of cultivated land in Britain, but knowledge of their status, distribution and ecology lags well behind that of arable vascular plants. A number of species are considered members of a typical arable bryophyte community, including the liverworts *Riccia glauca* and *R. sorocarpa*, and around fifteen mosses. A fairly large proportion of the known arable-land bryophyte flora occurs in Gower, but very little research on this subject has been carried out. Survey work is needed to understand the distribution, status and occurrence of bryophytes in different crop types and under various management regimes. The hornworts in particular appear to be declining in arable fields. Not much is known about them and only two species have been recorded in Gower to date, the very rare *Anthoceros agrestis*, found on a muddy track at Burry Pill in 1963, and the uncommon *Phaeoceros laevis*. Once again more research is needed. In Britain hornworts generally behave as annuals, germinating in early summer and producing spores in early winter.

PASTURE LAND

A large proportion of Gower fields are improved grassland, but a significant number, especially in the northeast of the peninsula, are examples of rhos pasture. Rhos pasture (from the Welsh *rhos*, moor) has been a feature of the South Wales landscape for centuries. It is the species-rich marshy grassland of western Britain and is a habitat that only occurs on the Atlantic seaboard of Europe. The pasture is found on unproductive, damp soils along valley bottoms and streamsides, on common land and wet hillsides, where traditional low-intensity cattle grazing or occasional summer hay cuts maintain the flower-rich turf. Wales contains half the rhos pasture in Britain, with Glamorgan accounting for around 10 per cent of the Welsh resource. Although the habitat is recognised as being of international importance and a small number of sites in Wales are specially protected as Sites of Special Scientific Interest, at the current rate of loss few sites will remain.

The Gower pastures support a characteristic flora with purple moor-grass and rushes, heath spotted orchid, tormentil, devil's-bit scabious, cross-leaved heath, whorled caraway, bog asphodel, carnation sedge, marsh violet and meadow thistle *Cirsium dissectum*. Together with the Gower commons such pastures are a stronghold for the marsh fritillary butterfly, whose food plant is devil's-bit scabious, and are important for breeding birds such as skylark, meadow pipit and reed bunting. They also support a wide diversity of invertebrates, reptiles and amphibians, which attract otters.

ORCHARDS

Although the fact is not well known today, historically Gower was always associated with fruit production and there were once a large number of orchards. The majority of these were in the area around the villages of Llanrhidian and Llangennith, the remainder being spread evenly across the peninsula. Walter

Davies, in 1815, mentions Gower and notes that small orchards were 'still pretty frequent there and produce an abundance of apples'. Many of the orchards are indeed small, but sadly some have disappeared completely and many are in a derelict state. As the trees finally die they are not being replaced. A total of eighty traditional orchard sites have been identified, but a survey in 1994 showed that just six orchards were still more or less intact. Only one of these six showed little or no tree loss, the remaining five being used for grazing, or for the storage of farm machinery. The residual sites are indicated by odd trees scattered around the area of the former orchard. A number of orchards have also been lost due to housing developments on the edge of Swansea, such as the development at Dunvant known as 'Y Berllan', the word *berllan* always signifying orchards in the Welsh language. A house built in 1894, beside the road from Caswell to Bishopston, was also originally called Berllan because it stood on the site of an old orchard.

Traditional orchards have many features that make them of value to wildlife and even in their present derelict state the Gower examples are important (Fig. 154). Fruit trees are relatively short-lived and as a consequence produce decaying wood more quickly than most native hardwoods, making them important refuges for invertebrates, and for hole-nesting and insectivorous birds. Old fruit trees are also an important habitat for mosses, liverworts and lichens, though

FIG 154. Apple orchard at Frogmore Farm, the best remaining orchard in Gower. (Harold Grenfell)

there has not been a comprehensive survey of the remnant orchards. The tree blossom itself provides an early source of nectar for bees, moths and other insects that in turn attract a variety of birds. In the summer the canopy provides nesting sites and food for insect-eating summer migrants while in the autumn the fallen fruit provides a source of food for a wide range of animals, including insects, mammals and birds, particularly song thrushes, fieldfares *Turdus pilaris* and redwings *T. iliacus*. Orchards can also have a herb-rich grassland sward, which may be managed as a meadow or pasture, while shadier sites can give rise to plant communities that are more typical of the flora of hedgebanks. Yellow meadow ant mounds are often found in old undisturbed grasslands such as orchards.

There has been almost no research on the Gower orchards, and information is needed both on the wildlife of these areas and on the particular varieties of fruit tree that occur. The *Glamorgan County History* (Tattersall, 1936) describes the varieties grown in the county as mostly culinary, such as Bramley Seedling, Newton Wonder, Lord Derby and Lane's Prince Albert, with some dessert apples including Beauty of Bath, James Grieve, Allington Pippin and Worcester Pearmain, but there are no site-specific records. An immense number of local fruit varieties exist in Britain, and these cultivars are an important wildlife element in their own right. It is possible therefore that varieties of apple particular to Gower once existed, and indeed they may still do so, remaining unrecognised perhaps on a single dying tree. Even now it is not too late, if there is the support of the farmers and landowners, to rescue the orchard heritage of the peninsula.

THE FUTURE

Despite the potential loss of the orchard heritage, the conservation of the woods and hedges seems assured. The larger areas of woodland are now protected by statutory designations, and through the efforts of the Coed Cymru initiative many of the small farm woodlands are under better management than they have been for decades. More still needs to be done, however, especially in relation to those woodlands on farms that are being managed under the Tir Cymen or Tir Gofal agri-environment schemes. Hedges too are being revitalised and managed more sympathetically for wildlife as part of these schemes. In contrast, the survival of arable plants depends very much on the continuation of relatively low-intensity arable farming, and the prospect for this is by no means assured.

CHAPTER 13

Caves and Swallets

[There is a] hole at the Poynt of Worme heade, but few dare enter it, and Men fable there
that a Dore within the spatius Hole hathe be sene with great Nayles on it; but that that is
spoken of Waters there rennynge undar the Ground is more lykely.

John Leyland

GOWER IS ONE OF the main cave areas in Britain and the 'holes', as the Gower caves are traditionally called, have been well known for centuries. Leyland, the antiquary appointed by Henry VIII to record his kingdom, had not only heard of the hole at Worms Head, but also records a tradition that an underground passage linked Worms Head with a cave at the head of the Gwendraeth Fach in Carmarthenshire (Fig. 155). Unfortunately for Leyland the cave systems are not as extensive as that or even as large as those in the Peak District or the Mendips. There are a surprising number of caves, however, and many of these are of international importance. The majority are located in the limestone cliffs on the south coast, the key areas being the stretch from Rhossili to Port-Eynon Point, that from Three Cliff Bay to Pwlldu Head and the coast around Caswell Bay. There are also a number of caves along the cliffs and relict cliffs on the north coast and a number inland, the most well known and accessible of which is probably Cathole in Green Cwm. It is the most important of the inland caves because of its Pleistocene fossils and human remains from the Bronze Age. The finest cave in Gower, however, is undoubtedly Llethrid Swallet, which lies a short distance to the north of Cathole. It includes a chamber 40 metres long, 30 metres wide and up to 10 metres high, known as 'The Great Hall'. The roof of the chamber is well decorated with stalactites, including one known as 'The Curtain' because of its extended shape (Fig. 156).

FIG 155. The 'hole at the Poynt of Worme heade', the Outer Head of the Worm, as described by John Leyland in the sixteenth century. It lies at the centre of the photograph. (Harold Grenfell)

FIG 156. The Llethrid Swallet 'Curtain', a spectacular stalactite formation. (Peter Francis)

Many books have been written about the Gower caves, and there is a whole publication devoted to every aspect of the most famous Gower cave, Goat's Hole, Paviland (Aldhouse-Green, 2000). As described in Chapter 4, the latter contained the 'Red Lady', the only Upper Palaeolithic ceremonial burial in the British Isles. The emphasis of all these publications, however, is either on archaeology and prehistoric animal remains or on recreational caving. In contrast to the vast amount of information that is available on the previous occupants of the caves, little is known about the wildlife present today.

THE ORIGIN OF THE CAVES

The present coastal caves are the remnants of once extensive systems, some parts of which have been removed by coastal erosion and some filled by debris from the last ice age. Generally glacial periods are times of cave infilling and degradation with many passages becoming completely choked by deposits. When the caves were first used by people the passages emerged from a cliff line south of the present-day coast and they would have overlooked wide coastal plains with the sea lower and more distant than at present. Primitive cave passages, formed by the limestone being dissolved by fresh water, almost certainly existed before the sea exposed them, but it is difficult to distinguish caves formed by the sea, and later modified by the penetration of fresh water, from existing passages altered by the erosion of the coast. A number of caves open in the coastal cliffs, however, such as Bacon Hole and Minchin Hole, are almost certainly very old solution-cave fragments, these two being now most notable for their extensive sequences of Pleistocene sediments and archaeological material. The inland caves such as those in Green Cwm owe their origins to groundwater penetrating suitable geological strata.

Although water cannot penetrate solid limestone it is able to flow through cracks in the rocks. It is these cracks that are the key to understanding the origin of most of the Gower caves. Caverns in the rock form principally by means of a simple chemical reaction in which hydrogen ions from groundwater, acidified with dissolved carbon dioxide, act on the relatively insoluble carbonate ions in the limestone to produce soluble bicarbonate ions, which are then washed away. It has been estimated that the process makes the limestone 25 times more soluble than it would be in pure water, and the result is holes in the rock.

This first stage of cave formation, known as 'initiation', creates the openings through the rock that permit the flow of groundwater. The main stage of cave development, however, is 'enlargement', when the small initial fissures are enlarged. This is followed by 'degradation', which is the terminal phase where the cave either collapses, is filled with sediment, or is removed by a lowering of the overlying surface. In a complex cave system all three processes take place simultaneously in passages at different depths and positions in the limestone. Enlargement and sediment infilling can also take place at the same time in a single passage. The timescales for cave formation are long and the initiation phase can take tens of millions of years while the enlargement of a cave passage to a metre in diameter can take up to ten thousand years.

While cave formation is determined totally by the geology, the flow of water starts to influence the development of the cave soon after the initial openings are created. As the limestone fissures are enlarged the permeability of the rock increases and the fissures and caves are drained so that they contain air-filled spaces and a water table is established. Below the water table the openings remain submerged and the cave therefore develops differently above and below the water level. In particular the water flow becomes more turbulent and there is increased erosion due to mechanical abrasion by sediment from the surface. As the cave system evolves it increases in complexity as individual passages are abandoned in favour of new routes at lower levels. Finally degradation and destruction of cave passages involve filling and choking by sediments, collapse and complete removal, in most cases after the cave has been abandoned by its formative stream.

Calcite deposition is common in caves where saturated percolation water issues from fissures, loses carbon dioxide to the cave air and deposits calcium carbonate to regain equilibrium. Or, as Isaac Hamon put it in respect of Bacon Hole, 'they say is a drop of water in the top or Rooffe thereof continually, by wch dropping there is a stone congealed.' Deposition on the cave floor creates tall stalagmites or rounded bosses, the profiles of which relate to saturation levels and drip rates. Formations such as stalactites and stalagmites are of considerable scientific value since caves are very long-lived landforms that preserve valuable evidence of past events on the earth's surface.

Wall and roof collapse is a widespread feature in caves; it modifies the profiles of passages and contributes to cave enlargement where fallen blocks expose new surfaces to attack by water. Major collapses ultimately block cave passages because the fallen material occupies a larger volume than the undisturbed rock. A related feature that occurs in the Bishopston Valley is the so-called 'Daw Pits' (Fig. 157). The word 'daw' is an old name for the jackdaw and the pits were once the haunt of nesting birds, though even by the 1930s this was only a distant memory. There are a number of such pits including Higher Daw Pit, Lower Daw Pit, Gulver Pit and Gwynspark Pit. These pits, which appear to be the result of a dramatic collapse of a cave chamber, are an unusual feature in limestone and occur as vertical-sided

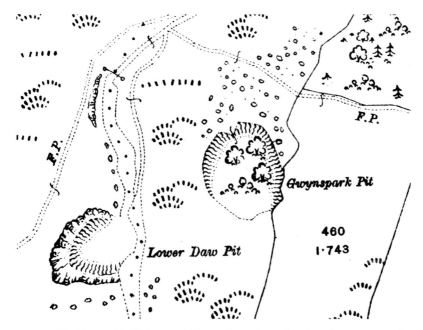

FIG 157. The 'daw pits' in Bishopston Valley, collapsed cave chambers that were once the haunt of jackdaws, as shown on the 1884 Ordnance Survey Map. (West Glamorgan Archive Service)

shafts some 24 metres deep and up to 30 metres in diameter. Gwynspark Pit is the deepest in the valley, being 30 to 35 metres deep with a boulder-strewn floor and steep sides. The collapse of these chambers is considered to be a relatively recent event, but it is not entirely clear how they were formed, and other suggested causes include the coalescing of drip pockets formed under an impermeable cap rock and the subsequent collapse of the cap. Further down the valley is Guzzle Hole, a partially abandoned resurgence where the Bishopston Pill can be seen flowing underground.

CAVE EXPLORATION

The caves of Gower have attracted the attention of naturalists and archaeologists since the beginning of the nineteenth century. Some of the earliest recorded finds were from Goat's Hole, the location of which had long been known to local people, and farmers were aware that the cave contained bones. In the summer of 1822,

Gower's first medical practitioner, Daniel Davies, was present at the first recorded discovery of the cave with the Reverend John Davies, who may have been his brother. During their exploration they discovered mammoth remains, which they reburied in the cave sediments for protection. News of the Davieses' discovery reached the Talbots of Penrice Castle when John deposited two Roman coins in the family museum. Lady Cole and her daughters had for some years corresponded with the Reverend William Buckland, being interested in natural history and geology, and were encouraged in their studies by Dillwyn, who was a family friend. It is not surprising therefore that Buckland was the first academic invited to undertake a thorough excavation of the rich deposits in Goat's Hole (Fig. 158). His book *Reliquiae Diluvianae; or, Observations on the Organic Remains Contained in Caves, Fissures and Diluvial Gravel and on Other Geological Phenomena Attesting to the Action of the Universal Deluge*, published immediately after the Gower excavations in 1823, attempted to address the occurrence of extinct fauna in caves. Buckland argued that the remains of animals found in caves afforded the means of judging of the inhabitants and character of the earth before the Great Flood recorded in Genesis. The book sold rapidly, and recognition of his achievement was widespread. His conclusions concerning Goat's Hole and the nearby Hound's Hole centred on the activities of hyenas, and although he considered

FIG 158. The Reverend William Buckland's plan showing the excavations in Goat's Hole, or Paviland Cave. (Department of Geology, National Museums and Galleries of Wales)

the 'Red Lady' burial remarkable he explained it away as intrusive. In the Upper Pleistocene many caves were used as permanent dens by many different species; the Gower caves are no exception, and as a result were often referred to as 'bone caves'. Similarly Sir Henry de la Beche followed the 'hyena's den' theory in his excavations at Spritsail Tor Cave in 1839, with little regard to the presence of human remains.

The most active early explorer of the caves was Colonel E. R. Wood, a local person with a deep interest in palaeontology. Beginning in 1848 he excavated vast quantities of cave deposits, only a few of which produced any traces of human occupation. He re-excavated Spritsail Tor Cave and investigated the famous group of caves at Pennard between Three Cliff Bay and Hunts Bay. At Bosco's Den in 1858 in the upper levels he excavated a large collection of teeth, bones and antlers. Particularly remarkable was the enormous collection of antlers belonging to over 1,100 reindeer. The mainly broken antlers, which belonged to young animals, had been naturally shed, but how they got there is not known. As well as reindeer the excavations in the cave deposits recovered the remains of animals such as cave bear *Ursus speloeus*, wolf and bison *Bison priscus* from the colder periods along with species like spotted hyena, soft-nosed rhinoceros, straight-tusked elephant and lion *Panthera leo* from the warmer periods. These animals are characteristic of the Gower bone caves and have been found in various combinations at the sites.

With the publication of Charles Darwin's *On the Origin of Species by Means of Natural Selection* in 1859 a more scientific approach began to be taken and a proper interpretation of all of the evidence from the exploration of the caves undertaken. Colonel Wood's analysis of his excavations of Deborah's Hole and Long Hole in 1861 reflected this important change in thinking and it soon became widely accepted that the flint implements found in the Gower caves were directly associated with an extinct fauna. Again in 1869 he found human remains associated with animal bones at the Mewslade Quarry Fissures. Despite advances in theory much valuable material was lost in these early excavations simply because it was not recognised for what it was.

It was therefore fortunate that following the 1869 excavations there was a gap of some forty years before the next major studies, during which only a few casual finds were recorded from the caves. If the excavations had continued at the same pace the value of the environmental record would have been greatly diminished. When Professor W. J. Solas re-excavated Goat's Hole in 1912 with the assistance of Henri-Édouard-Prosper Breuil, a French archaeologist better known as the Abbé Breuil, excavations had become more thorough and he was able to place the 'Red Lady' in its proper context as a rare example of 'stone-age' burial near the end of a long sequence of Upper Palaeolithic occupation of the caves.

Breuil was a notable authority on prehistoric cave paintings. Shortly after being ordained an abbé in 1897 he developed a strong interest in Palaeolithic art, and he devoted much of his life to studying the subject. He was the first to study the Lascaux cave in Southern France, which contains one of the most outstanding displays of prehistoric art yet discovered. The re-excavation of Goat's Hole was largely responsible for a controversy about some red streaks which were noticed the same year by Professor Solas and the Abbé Breuil on the wall of Bacon Hole (Fig. 159). In a recess at the back of the cave they discovered ten wide red bands, which were almost horizontal and roughly parallel. Given his interest, Breuil naturally claimed that they were cave paintings, similar to those found in the Dordogne. An iron screen and gate were therefore erected to protect them. Some years later this theory was discredited as it became apparent that the markings were slowly changing shape and were therefore natural, being caused by minerals seeping from the rock, but sections of the iron screen remain as a reminder of the hopes of a Gower Lascaux. Bacon Hole is so named because the red oxide streaks on its walls were thought to make it look like a slice of bacon.

A re-examination of Culver Hole, Llangennith, and of Spritsail Tor Cave by T. K. Penniman and others in 1931 led to the recognition that caves had been used as burial places in the later prehistoric period. At the same time a re-excavation of Port-Eynon Point Cave in 1931 and 1932 by the Reverend H. Arnold and his son produced a considerable quantity of animal remains, which they forwarded to the

FIG 159. Bacon Hole, with Pwlldu Head in the background. (Harold Grenfell)

TABLE 14. Animal remains from Port-Eynon Point Cave. (Adapted from various sources)

COMMON NAME	SCIENTIFIC NAME
Mole	*Talpa europaea*
Water shrew	*Neomys* spp.
Bear	*Ursus* spp.
Fox	*Vulpes vulpes*
Wolf	*Canis lupus*
Lion	*Panthera leo*
Roe deer	*Capreolus* spp.
Ox	*Bos* spp.
Horse	*Equus caballus*
Vole	*Microtus* spp.
Thrush	*Turdus* spp.
Gull	*Larus* spp.
Razorbill	*Alca torda*
Guillemot	*Uria aalge*
Puffin	*Fratercula arctica*

Natural History Museum in London (Table 14). One of the features of this second excavation was that the Arnolds were extremely thorough and they preserved every fragment of organic matter, including minute bones and teeth. The result is a much better picture of the fauna; too often the excavators of the Gower caves were only interested in the larger and more spectacular animal bones.

Towards the end of the 1930s the first serious exploration of the Gower caves took place following the formation of a Welsh group of the Mendip Exploration Society. Led by Brigadier E. A. Glennie, they visited numerous caves, until the outbreak of war in 1939 put a stop to their activities. A few years later, however, between 1943 and 1946, E. E. Allen and J. G. Rutter carried out the first thorough survey of the Gower caves. They visited and surveyed not only the bone caves, but also the lesser-known holes, 90 in all. The results of this work were published in two volumes (1946) and these still form an important reference source for those interested in the Gower caves.

Recreational caving in Gower really began in 1946 when the South Wales Caving Club was formed. During the 1950s a member of the club, Maurice Taylor, and his two sisters, Marjorie and Eileen, spent seven years searching Gower for new caves, finding quite a number of these and also reopening and lengthening

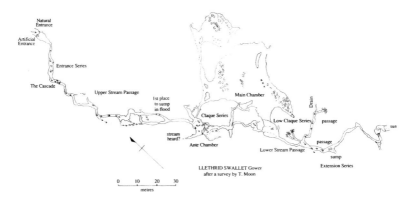

FIG 160. Map of Llethrid Swallet, showing the extensive nature of the caverns. (Joint Nature Conservation Committee)

other caves. The Club has played an important role in producing accurate surveys of many of the Gower caves, including Llethrid Swallet (Fig. 160). In the late 1980s Melvyn Davies, the warden for the former Nature Conservancy Council, who had a keen interest in caves, also spent much of his spare time exploring and recording holes. In total he found 95 cave sites where 'the hole was big enough for a human body'. Since then further explorations have extended the list and the total number of Gower caves, that is those large enough to admit people, is now an incredible 128, but it is unlikely that there are many more to be found.

CAVES AND THEIR WILDLIFE

Over a hundred species of invertebrate animals have been recorded as maintaining permanent populations in British caves, while other species such as bats and moths use caves regularly as temporary shelters. Animals using caves can therefore be divided into different categories depending on the use they make of the cave. Some animals spend only part of their lives in caves (trogloxenes), while others, although occurring elsewhere, are able to live in caves permanently (troglophiles) and some are only found underground (troglobites). In addition to the use they make of the cave it is also possible to categorise animals based on the type of habitat they occupy, the so-called 'threshold fauna' living in the zone between the entrance and the limit of light penetration and the 'dark-zone fauna' living where there is no natural light.

The main investigations of the animals of the Gower caves were carried out in the late 1970s and early 1980s by Geoff Jefferson from the Zoology Department of University College, Cardiff. Since then the observations have come mainly from cavers rather than biologists and there is a real need for further work.

ANIMALS OF THE THRESHOLD

The animals most frequently associated with caves, in the public mind at least, are bats. The peninsula is special as it is one of the few limestone areas with both species of horseshoe bats. Greater horseshoe bat and lesser horseshoe bat occur in a number of the caves and form an important link between the external and internal ecosystems. Usually present in the threshold area, they also penetrate into the dark zone. Lesser horseshoes are a particularly Welsh species, thriving in Gower as well as anywhere else in the world. Greater horseshoes, in contrast, are at the northwestern limit of their range here. They are, however, particularly faithful to suitable roosts and will continue to use them for many generations (Fig. 161). But seeing them in the same place, year after year, can create an air of familiarity that masks their rarity and vulnerability, and they are in fact probably the least abundant of the Gower bats. Winter monitoring suggests there may be less than fifty of these bats in Gower, but this figure may be misleading because, despite their large size, they can be very secretive. Bats using the caves are mainly adult

FIG 161. Greater horseshoe bat occurs in a number of the Gower caves. (Melvin Grey)

and immature bats less than four years old. The occasional record of younger bats suggests that they breed in the area, but no nursery site has yet been found. Some of the caves are 'male sites', where a bat may live alone for much of the year, although outside the breeding season they may be accompanied by non-breeding animals. Mating generally takes place in the autumn and winter, when the males are joined by females, who may mate with a number of individuals.

Although both species of horseshoe bats were originally cave dwellers, and the Gower caves are used as hibernation sites, few animals now use them in summer. Anecdotal reports from the middle of the last century suggest that some caves at that time had large populations of both greater and lesser horseshoes and may also have housed nursery clusters. These clusters were groups of females, numbering several hundred individuals, which gathered in caves where their combined body heat would raise the temperature high enough to rear their young. Due to the dramatic decline in the populations of British bats over the last fifty years, the numbers of bats are now too low for caves to be used as breeding sites. Summer colonies of lesser horseshoes are found instead in the roofs of the large houses and stable blocks, the breeding females choosing sites with large entrance holes that give access to open roof spaces warmed by the sun. The recent discovery of greater and lesser horseshoes in the underfloor area of a modern holiday chalet in the peninsula is an indication of the ability of bats to adapt to a changing world, if they are given the opportunity.

New studies have revealed a previously unknown use of caves by bats, known as swarming. Swarming occurs in late summer and early autumn and can involve large numbers, sometimes hundreds, of bats. They arrive at a cave after dark, enter it and disperse within it, and most are gone by the following morning. The phenomenon may be repeated the following night, but not necessarily by the same bats, which may have moved on to another cave. In some areas bats have been marked and have been found swarming at another site 30 miles (48 kilometres) away, and it is suspected that greater distances may be involved. The purpose of the behaviour is not yet understood, although the identification of hibernation sites and mating may be part of the answer. It would be worth surveying the Gower caves to check for this behaviour, as many caves elsewhere, previously dismissed as of little or no interest, have been found to have significant levels of bat activity when checked at the right time of year.

Lesser horseshoes are known to use at least eight buildings in Gower as nursery roosts, but there are likely to be a number of other sites that have not yet been discovered. There may be no more than 2,000 individuals in total. This is still quite a fragile population and the trend to convert outbuildings and barns into dwellings will increase the pressures on this species and limit population growth.

The greatest mystery regarding the bats is where the majority go when they are not in the nursery roosts. While they are frequently encountered in the caves, there are only small numbers and the majority of individuals examined are males. Perhaps the mild climate means that they remain active for much of the winter and only retreat to an underground location in extreme weather. Bats can be very active in the winter, feeding over the coastal slopes and in the sheltered valleys. Alternatively perhaps they leave the peninsula for more suitable hibernation sites. Several of the caves within the Parkmill and Llethrid valleys, such as Cathole, are nevertheless used as hibernation sites by Daubenton's bat *Myotis daubentonii*, whiskered bats and Natterer's bats. The presence of Daubenton's bat is particularly interesting as they are known as the water bat and feed almost exclusively on insects on the surface of the water. At first sight the peninsula would not appear to be an ideal location for this species, as there are relatively few lakes and ponds and many of the streams are well covered by vegetation.

Some exposed coastal caves are also frequented, surprisingly regularly, by bats of the genus *Myotis* that would normally be more associated with woodlands. Sea caves are under-surveyed and may prove more important for bat roosts than is presently realised. There are no hedges, or other obvious 'flight line' features, to the caves. Perhaps these sites are traditional locations that may have once had more suitable vegetated links, or bats are migrating along the coast using the peninsula as a landfall. Greater horseshoes will, however, cross open water and have been found on a number of islands. There has even been a report from a bird-ringer on Lundy of a horseshoe being caught in the nets there. Clearly a dependence on linear landscape features breaks down for some journeys. New species of bats do appear to be colonising Gower, and in the winter of 2000/01 an unusual bat was seen in a crevice on Great Tor, between Oxwich and Three Cliff Bay. It could not be extracted, but appeared to be a species of pipistrelle and was originally thought to be a Nathusius' pipistrelle *Pipistrellus nathusii*, a European migrant that has begun to colonise Britain and which has been found elsewhere in South Wales. Alternatively, it may have been a Savi's pipistrelle *Hypsugo savii*, which was recorded the same week elsewhere in Britain, and which has the same colour and proportions as the bat seen at Great Tor.

Many invertebrates, especially insects, use cave thresholds as overwintering sites. There are two moths in Britain that are particularly associated with caves, the tissue moth *Triphosa dubitata* and the herald moth *Scoliopteryx libatrix*, and they are often seen settled on the walls or roofs of cave thresholds in Gower (Fig. 162). The caterpillars feed on vegetation outside the cave, but soon after emerging from the chrysalis the adults fly into caves. Herald moths become very torpid and can often be seen high in the dark zone of the cave covered with beads of

FIG 162. Herald moth, a species particularly associated with caves and often seen in the threshold zone. (Harold Grenfell)

moisture, while tissue moths prefer to settle closer to the entrance and lower down. It appears that a period of suspended development is necessary before the ovaries of the female can produce eggs. Similarly large numbers of the common mosquito *Culex pipiens* can be seen in the caves from September to April. These are females of the autumn generation which have already mated, but which will not lay their eggs until they have left the cave in spring.

Another characteristic animal of the threshold zone is the large orb-web cave spider *Meta menardi*, which occupies the deeper part of cave entrances, trapping insects on their way in and out. It has only been officially recorded in Worms Head Cave, but as it is widely distributed elsewhere in South Wales it is likely to be present in many of the Gower caves. It feeds on virtually any prey and catches both flying and crawling invertebrates, feeding on woodlice and millipedes, among other animals. Spider eggs are roughly spherical and about 1 millimetre in diameter, being laid in a compact mass and covered with silk to form a sac. The number of eggs laid depends on the size of the female, with larger cave spiders laying more and sometimes larger eggs. Like lacewings, some spiders place their egg sacs on stalks to protect them from predators. The cave spider makes an exceptionally large sac with a small stalk.

The wild rock dove *Columba livia* has been extinct as a breeding species in Glamorgan since 1925, but its descendent the feral rock dove, the result of centuries of interbreeding with feral pigeons, is a common breeding resident and regularly nests in a number of the coastal caves close to the entrance. Badgers also use many of the smaller caves as ready-made setts and can penetrate considerable distances into the systems.

ANIMALS OF THE DARK

There are two significant factors in the ecology of the dark zone of caves, the absence of light and a remarkably constant environment. Temperature, for instance, usually stays constant at 8 or 9 degrees Celsius, although it may vary in the vicinity of active stream passages. The lack of light means that the cave community does not have a direct source of energy and that the food chain must generally start outside the cave, and it is noticeable that animals tend to be more numerous in parts of caves which are near the surface. This is particularly true of the fly *Heleomyza serrata*, which is common in many Gower caves, usually where the rock cover is thin. There are considerable populations of animals in parts of caves far from the surface, however, and where there are no obvious signs of any organic matter coming from the surface. In these cases the animals appear to be feeding on a floccular material present on the surfaces of stalagmites, which seems to consist largely of filamentous chlamydobacteria.

Jefferson found 30 species of invertebrates in the eight caves he explored, the richest cave being Llethrid Swallet with 16 species (Table 15). Cavers too have noted a 'healthy fauna such as freshwater shrimps and springtails' in the cave. The shrimps include the well-shrimp *Niphargus fontanus*, which has also been collected from the entrance of Ram Grove Exsurgence where a strong spring of fresh water rises near the foot of the cliff. This aquatic crustacean is a translucent eyeless animal totally adapted to underground life, whose main areas of distribution are the Mendips and South Wales. A related species, *N. aquilex*, has been recorded from the Red Chamber. Generally this species is only occasionally reported from caves, being found mainly in the gravel of riverbeds. Another shrimp found in Llethrid Cave and which is often abundant in caves is the freshwater shrimp *Gammarus pulex*, which is actually not a shrimp, but an amphipod. Some populations have reduced body pigmentation, showing an adaptation to cave life. The shrimp feeds on decaying organic debris and is known sometimes to be predatory; it is itself a major source of food for brown trout and other fish. The distribution of aquatic cave fauna such as the well-shrimp is affected by a variety of factors including

TABLE 15. The invertebrates of Llethrid Swallet. (Adapted from Ford, 1989)

COMMON NAME	SCIENTIFIC NAME
Enchytrachid worm	*Henlea nasuta*
Copepod	*Acanthocyclops vernalis*
Copepod	*Acanthocyclops viridis*
Shrimp	*Gammarus pulex*
Springtail	*Anurida granaria*
Springtail	*Isotoma notabilis*
Mayfly	*Habrophlebia fusca*
Meniscus midges	*Dixa* spp.
Empid fly	*Tachydromia* spp.
Water beetle	*Helophorus brevipalpis*
Water beetle	*Helophorus laticollis*
Water beetle	*Hydraena gracilis*
Rove beetle	*Atheta* spp.
Mite	*Parasitus* spp.
Mite	*Pergamasus crassipes*
Well-shrimp	*Niphargus fontanus*

sediment type, food supply, water currents and water temperature. The total
population of some cave species is very small and a few may even be restricted to
one or two individuals in a single cave. As a result they are very vulnerable to
extinction and collecting is not to be encouraged.

The crustacean isopod *Proasellus cavaticus*, recorded from Barland Sink at
the top of the Bishopston Valley, is a truly underground animal found usually in
the water film flowing over stalagmite slopes or on stones in streams. Like the
well-shrimp and a number of other inhabitants of the dark zone it is blind and
lacking pigmentation. Again it is also found mainly in Mendip and South Wales.
Guzzle Hole lower down the valley has produced records of a related species,
P. meridianus, which is not a confirmed cave dweller. Jefferson was intrigued by
this and thought that the underground stream warranted further study, but this
never occurred.

The association of the two typically cave-dwelling animals, the well-shrimp
and *Proasellus cavaticus*, in Mendip and South Wales seems to indicate that these
animals are survivors of a preglacial British underground fauna. As described in
Chapter 3, South Wales was subject to repeated glaciation and yet true cave-
dwelling crustaceans are commoner in this area than in any other part of Britain.
Two possible explanations have been put forward for this: either there has been
recolonisation since the last retreat of the glaciers or the animals survived beneath
the ice cover. The similarity of the Mendip and South Wales faunas suggests a
recolonisation from Mendip. The two areas are not far apart, and in immediate
postglacial times they were not separated by water, as the upper part of the Bristol
Channel was then dry land. There are some problems with the theory, however, as
the two faunas are not identical. The alternative explanation of survival beneath
the ice also raises further questions, although Gower was near the edge of the ice
sheet and this would probably have aided survival in that it allowed food from the
surface to reach the animals below.

The most important members of the terrestrial communities in the dark
zone are Collembola (springtails), several species of which are commonly found
on mud banks within the Gower caves. More than 70 species of Collembola have
been found in British caves, but only 15 are widespread, with the most frequently
recorded being *Tomocerus minor*. In the Gower caves this position is occupied by
the troglophile *Anurida granaria*. Almost nothing is known about the ecology of
springtails in British caves, although they appear to be 'base level' consumers
grazing on bacteria and microfungi in the sediments. In turn they are prey for
various carnivorous mites and beetles. It is not known whether the species found
underground are genetically the same as those species found outside the caves, or
whether some are isolated in caves and are de facto troglobites but unrecognisable

as such. Clearly much work is required, and genetic or molecular studies will be required to answer these questions.

The common cave gnat *Speolepta leptogaster* is particularly widespread and numerous in the caves. Like many animals that live permanently in caves, the gnat can be found in the deep threshold as well as in the dark zone, but it is only rarely recorded from outside caves and it may be a troglobite. The thin, translucent larvae, up to 14 millimetres long, live on damp cave walls and feed on micro-organisms and fungal material. Other species recorded include water beetles and non-biting midges *Dixa* spp., commonly known as 'meniscus midges' because the larvae of these aquatic insects live in the meniscus of the water. The water beetles include *Helophorus laticollis*, which is usually found in shallow, exposed, grassy pools on heathland. Many of these animals have obviously been carried into the caves by the various streams.

Fish may also enter the underground stretches of streams and the common brown trout is the species most often seen. Some animals appear pale and are often recorded as 'white fish', but although they are in a remarkably blanched condition they darken rapidly if brought into daylight. The dark spots, that in any case tend to be variable in trout, are reduced to almost nothing although the row of orange-red spots along the lateral line is often retained. The fish feed on invertebrates carried underground by the cave streams.

CAVE FLORA

In general caves are not known for their flora and the Gower caves are no exception. Plants in the cave threshold, however, show a marked zonation controlled by light intensity and the nature of the substrate. Flowering plants near the cave entrance are succeeded by ferns, then mosses, then liverworts and finally in the dim light green and blue-green algae. In the dark zone only fungi and moulds occur, although there are no species that are confined to underground habitats. There have been no studies of the Gower cave flora, but typical plants of cave entrances include herb Robert, dog's mercury and common nettle *Urtica dioica* (Fig. 163). Ferns recorded elsewhere from this location include hart's-tongue fern, maidenhair spleenwort *Asplenium trichomanes*, wall-rue and rustyback fern *Ceterach officinarum*. One of the commonest mosses is *Gymnostomum aerinosum*, which forms dense cushions in the damp areas and may become encrusted with calcite deposits. The liverwort *Conocephalum conicum* is also a very common species in cave entrances. These areas often accumulate deep layers of soil and organic material that can produce acid conditions.

FIG 163. Cathole Cave, showing typical flora at the cave entrance. (Harold Grenfell)

Studies of the microbiology of the Gower caves have been more extensive. Ogof Wyntog, a cave located north of the Knave, contains extensive deposits of a substance known as moonmilk. Moonmilk is a cheese-like mass, consisting of carbonate minerals and a microorganism, which is found sprouting from the cave ceiling or walls, usually near to an entrance. A large range of organisms has been isolated from this peculiar substance, including the bacterium *Macromonas* spp. (probably *M. bipunctata*), and various blue-green algae such as *Synechococcus elongatus* also occur. It is thought that in the darkness they feed by metabolic pathways quite different to the ones they use in the light. Curious encrusting growths known as 'wall-fungus' also occur frequently in the caves and investigation has shown that they consist of a complex bacterium on the borderline between bacteria and fungi, a species of *Streptomyces*, probably associated with a fungus, *Fusarium* spp.

NEW DISCOVERIES

Passages large enough to admit people, 'macrocaverns', form only a tiny proportion of the total cave habitat, the great majority being 'mesocaverns', that is holes with a diameter ranging from 1 to 200 millimetres. It has been estimated that the habitable surface area within limestone mesocaverns 'must run to at least two or three orders of magnitude more than that within explored caves' (Chapman, 1993). It is within these mesocaverns, which are for the most part completely inaccessible to the naturalist, that the majority of the specialised flora and fauna of the Gower caves resides, but to date there have been no studies of this habitat. The communities remain mysterious and under-recorded. However, judging by the studies of other cave habitats in Britain, it is likely that a wide range of species are present in the mesocaverns ranging from bacteria and fungi to flatworms, mites, polychaete worms and spiders. Important discoveries are also likely to be made in relation to microcrustacea such as copepods and cladocera. The study of cave ecosystems is still at an early stage and it is not unlikely that new species await discovery in the subterranean habitats of Gower.

CAVE MANAGEMENT

As with the wildlife of the Gower caves, there is also still surprisingly little information available on the factors that affect both the limestone caves and their wider surroundings, the so-called 'geoecosystem'. Such cave geoecosystems comprise the cave itself, the surrounding and interconnected system of smaller openings and the overlying soils and land surface. The three commonest activities which affect these systems are recreational activity, mineral extraction and agriculture. The most significant of these, certainly in Gower, are agriculture and recreation. Agriculture impacts on cave geoecosystems largely through its effect on the runoff that enters the area, although the roots of certain agricultural crops are known to weaken cave roofs, leading to 'blockfalls'. A change of vegetation cover from grazing pasture to arable land can also have a significant effect, as can pollutants such as organic chemicals, nitrate fertilisers and animal sewage. Cave systems receive inputs of water both from rainfall over the limestone area and from rain that falls onto adjacent non-limestone areas but feeds streams which run onto the limestone. Increased sedimentation following ground surface disturbance in cave catchments can result in the loss of invertebrate breeding sites. Indirect influences paradoxically probably have the most extensive impact and by their nature are the hardest to identify.

In Britain this 'whole catchment' approach to cave conservation has been extremely difficult to apply as there are problems in extending conservation measures to land which is not inherently valuable for conservation. Even quite small caves can have extremely large catchments, and though some activities may appear to have a relatively minor impact in the short term, consideration needs to be given to the cumulative impact over a longer period. In Gower it would be possible to modify the management prescriptions for those farms in agri-environment schemes that form part of cave catchments, but further research is needed, first to classify individual features of interest within the Gower caves and then to map their locations both within the caves and in relation to the surface.

There are no accurate figures for the number of cavers using the Gower caves each year, but given the profile of the peninsula in caving circles the total must be very high (Fig. 164). Some caves have been gridded to prevent access, particularly caves such as Cathole and Tooth Cave, which both provide winter roosts for the greater and lesser horseshoe bat, but unfortunately the locks on these grilles are often broken off. The majority of cavers are only interested in the sporting aspect, but a large part of the enjoyment obtained on a trip underground is derived from the type of passage being traversed and the features that can be seen while doing so. The maintenance of these features in as near a natural state as possible is what cave conservation is primarily concerned with. A national 'Adopt-A-Cave' scheme in which clubs volunteer their services to look after specific caves has been set up. The responsibilities include keeping the cave clean, as well as monitoring and reporting on damage, but the scheme is very informal. Lists of caves covered are

FIG 164. Caver admiring the stalactites in Llethrid Swallet. (Peter Francis)

regularly published in the magazine *Descent*, and clubs are invited to join by informing the editor of the sites they wish to look after. The Welsh Scout Council Caving Group has adopted Llethrid Swallet as part of this scheme.

THE FUTURE

There are few physical threats to the caves; they have evolved over many millions of years and will continue to exist for many more to come. The key issues, as described above, are possible changes to agricultural practices and recreational caving, both of which have the potential to damage the wildlife and the internal formations of these relatively unknown features of the Gower landscape.

PART IV

A New Future

CHAPTER 14

Protecting Gower

It is above all the spirit of Gower, in all its natural manifestations, that we have
ultimately to protect.

J. Mansel Thomas

OWER HAD BEEN well known and recognised as an important area for many years before its designation as an Area of Outstanding Natural Beauty, and this was reflected in a number of early acquisitions by the National Trust. The first was a donation of land at Thurba Head on the south Gower coast in 1933, followed by the donation of the nearby Pitton and Paviland Cliffs in 1939 (Fig. 165). The outbreak of the Second World War in September of that year, however, bought a sudden halt to conservation activity. It was not until 1953 that the next Gower property, Bishopston Valley and Pennard Cliffs East, was acquired by the Trust. Gower was also the site of the first purchase under the Enterprise Neptune campaign in 1965, when Whiteford Burrows was bought. Further properties were acquired under the same scheme in 1967. The Trust now actively manages 2,226 hectares of land in the peninsula, including 26 miles (42 kilometres) of coast, which is 75 per cent of the entire coastline. However, awareness of the Trust's role is considered to be low and a four-year project was set up in 2004 to address this.

Following the war, the National Parks and Access to the Countryside Act in 1949 led to the establishment of the National Parks Commission and the Nature Conservancy. In doing so it unfortunately created a fundamental and ultimately damaging division between recreation and nature conservation, which was not addressed in Wales until the creation of the Countryside Council for Wales in 1991. The Act did declare, however, that certain other areas, apart from the

FIG 165. Thurba Head, the first land acquired by the National Trust in Gower, in 1933. (Jonathan Mullard)

National Parks, should be preserved as Areas of Exceptional Natural Beauty, where 'public amenity should be of paramount concern'.

When the Nature Conservancy was set up it already had some extremely valuable reports upon which to base its policy. One of these was the Nature Reserves Investigation Committee's report. The Committee, which had been set up in 1942 as a result of the optimistically titled 'Conference on Nature Preservation in Post-war Reconstruction', organised by the Society for the Promotion of Nature Reserves the previous year, had the task of identifying places suitable for 'preservation' and collating information about them. The Society itself was the forerunner of the Wildlife Trust movement. The Committee's report listed nearly all the important areas for wildlife in Britain, some being termed 'Proposed National Nature Reserves' and some larger sites called 'Conservation Areas'. Most of Gower was listed as a Conservation Area and the committee regarded the peninsula as 'of such importance as to require safeguarding as a national possession'. The report went on to say that:

> The Gower peninsula contains a remarkable variety of types of vegetation all in a relatively unspoilt condition. It is also noteworthy for the wealth of its bird life. In general the area seems unlikely to suffer except from an extensive industrial or residential development or injudicious afforestation. It is therefore recommended (a) that the entire

*Peninsula west of a line – Llanmorlais–Brandy Cove – should be declared a Scheduled
Area and (b) that within this area the existing legal prohibitions against trapping
and egg-taking should be strictly enforced. Within the scheduled area four areas should
be preserved as Habitat Reserves: Burry Holm, Worms Head, Mead Moor and Oxwich
Marsh.*

Worms Head and Oxwich, as described previously, are now part of National
Nature Reserves, but Burry Holms, as related in Chapter 8, is one of the few
areas of Gower that has no specific designation. Mead Moor, once common land
enclosed in the late seventeenth century, had over some 260 years developed into
a rich mixed deciduous woodland and ranked, with the adjoining Millwood to
the east, as second only to Nicholaston Wood in its importance and landscape
value. Previously owned by the Penrice Estate, it was bought by a firm of timber
merchants and in 1952 a licence was granted by the Forestry Commission for the
selective felling of 'certain mature trees' in the woodland. It was promised that
the operation would 'in no way alter the external appearance of the wood'. Despite
assurances to the relevant government minister, Glamorgan County Council, the
National Parks Commission and the Gower Society, Mead Moor and Mill Wood
were destroyed and replaced by a 'a bald and scarred hillside'. Only a few stately
and ancient-looking oaks now remain, surrounded by birch and ash woodland
and deteriorating beech and conifer plantations, as a reminder of the past
richness of the area and the failure by government agencies to protect this
'national possession'.

The report also covered the geological importance of the peninsula and
recommended that the following Geological Reserves be scheduled: Worms Head,
Bishopston Valley with Pwlldu Head, Minchin Hole, Caswell Bay, Oystermouth
Old Quarry, Ilston Quarry. All of these sites are now protected by legislation.

THE GOWER SOCIETY

On 23 December 1947 four people – a forty-year-old doctor, Gwent Jones, an
architect of seventy, Ernest Morgan, a young teacher, Jim Rees, and a student at
college, David Bernard Rees – who had been for some months pursuing their
common passion, which was the study of Gower, held a meeting to propose the
formation of a public society 'to look for kindred spirits among the general
public'. The first public meeting of the Gower Society was held on 7 January 1948.
Around 125 people attended a lecture evening at the Royal Institution of South
Wales where Jim Rees and David Bernard Rees read papers on 'Invasions of

Gower' and 'Gower churches'. On Port-Eynon Point there is a memorial to two of
the early founders of the Society, Gwent Jones and Stephen Lee (Fig. 166).

The original aim of the Society was to 'encourage research and appreciation
of Gower', although this was not quite how it worked out. The fateful role of
protector of Gower and organiser of public opinion was thrust on the fledgling
society quite suddenly, and unexpectedly, by the Rhossili holiday-camp scare of
July 1948. It was proposed to build a holiday camp at Hillend, and a partial
levelling of the Burrows was planned. Gower by this time was a National Parks
'reservation area' and the scheme was eventually dropped, but the publicity
provided a great boost to the Gower Society, which soon had over 200 members.
Today it is one of the most active amenity societies in Britain. Other battles
successfully fought by the Society in those early days included the proposed siting
of a shell testing range in the Burry Estuary and a radar mast and 'large concrete
installation' on the top of Rhossili Down. The woods at Nicholaston, however,
were in particular danger in the early 1950s. They had been bought by a speculator
who was 'more interested in reducing the woods to timber than in re-planning
an over-mature landscape'. An Oxwich Bay Protection Fund was launched by the
Society and a public enquiry held. A compromise, which involved limited felling,
was the result, and the Forestry Commission was brought in to give advice on

FIG 166. Memorial to two of the early founders of the Gower Society, Stephen Lee and
Gwent Jones, on Port-Eynon Point. (Harold Grenfell)

replanting. The controversy eventually resulted in the Forestry Commission acquiring a lease over the site, following which the Nature Conservancy acquired the woods and brought them into the Oxwich National Nature Reserve. A proposal too was made in 1954 by the Swansea Corporation to set up a civil airport on part of the derelict RAF station on Fairwood Common. A parliamentary Bill was drafted 'to make provision for the extinguishment of certain common or commonable rights and other rights . . .' This was one battle that the Society did not win, and here again a compromise had to be accepted. A clause was inserted into the resulting Act, however, stating that 'if the enclosed area ceases to be used as an aerodrome, it shall revert to an open space'.

THE DESIGNATION OF THE AONB

During the early 1950s the Gower Society, together with Glamorgan County Council and the Gower Rural District Council, kept pressing the National Parks Commission to give special consideration to Gower. The Commission's first job, as reflected in its title, was the National Park designation programme, and it was not until that was largely out of the way in the middle of the decade that the Commission began to concentrate on AONBs, which were intended to complement the National Parks. In this climate lobbying by the local authorities and the Gower Society finally paid off and on 9 May 1956 Gower was designated as an Area of Outstanding Natural Beauty, the first of these 'miniature National Parks' in Britain.

There was concern from local people in Gower, once the area had been designated, about the availability of resources for the maintenance and improvement of the landscape. At the time, the National Parks Commission proposed an extensive series of grants for landscape management, which would be available to Gower farmers and landowners to enable them to conserve their part of the designated area. Sadly this aspiration was not realised and it was only in the 1990s that the Tir Cymen and Tir Gofal agri-environment schemes provided the type of widespread support for sustainable land management that was envisaged in the year of Gower's designation. In the intervening period many of the traditional field boundaries of hedges, stonefaced banks and stone walls had been neglected due to pressures on traditional farming, but this situation is not unique to Gower and thanks to these schemes much restoration work has now been carried out.

The designation of Gower as an AONB, despite its status, actually had limited effects. While it certainly meant that planning was tightened, it was essentially restrictive and did not ensure resources or a focus on priorities. To quote from the report of the Hobhouse Committee in 1947, 'There are many areas of fine country and coast in England and Wales which are not included in our selection of National Parks but yet possess outstanding landscape beauty, are often of great scientific interest and, in many cases important holiday areas.' Oddly, having noted these qualities and pressures, the report then goes on to say that these areas 'do not call for the degree of positive management required in National Parks, nor for the closer scientific control which may be necessary in National Nature Reserves', and in so doing sealed the fate of AONBs, which remained poorly funded and little known until the passing of the Countryside and Rights of Way Act in 2000.

THE VOLUNTARY APPROACH

The Gower Society was not the only voluntary organisation created as a result of concern about the area's future. The same year that the AONB was designated, 1956, also saw the formation of the Gower Ornithological Society, which was the beginning of systematic bird recording in Gower. It came into being because Norman Moore, then the Director of the Nature Conservancy, needed an organiser to undertake the census of buzzards in Gower as part of a national scheme. A local solicitor and naturalist, Neville Douglas-Jones, was asked to help and he soon recruited a network of volunteers. The Society has always been quite a small organisation, with current membership at around 100, but is very active, taking part in many surveys and playing an important role in the conservation of the area. An important ornithological milestone was reached in 1992 when the Society published *An Atlas of Breeding Birds in West Glamorgan.*

Five years later, in January 1961, the Glamorgan County Naturalists' Trust was founded by H. J. (Jo) Hambury and Neville Douglas-Jones with 'the aim of conserving areas of high scientific interest but at the same time not interfering with legitimate industrial development', a statement that reflected not only the social attitudes of the time, but also the current situation, Glamorgan being still a highly industrial county in this period. Hambury, an orthopaedic surgeon at Swansea Hospital and an active member of the Gower Ornithological Society, was Chairman for 10 years until 1971 and during that time built up and guided the Trust in its formative years, acquiring over twenty freehold nature reserves and a membership of over 1,000 people.

The organisation has been through many name changes over the years. It became the Glamorgan Trust for Nature Conservation in the 1980s, then the

Glamorgan Wildlife Trust and finally in April 2002 merged with the West Wales Trust and is now known as the Wildlife Trust of South and West Wales. The new organisation manages over 100 nature reserves including the Pembrokeshire islands of Skomer and Skokholm, Teifi Marshes and the Gower reserves, which represent by far the greatest concentration of properties. The combined Trust now has over 10,000 members and 32 staff.

A relative newcomer, in relation to the other organisations, is the Woodland Trust, which purchased Common Wood, on the northeast side of Cilifor Top, from the Forestry Commission in 1989. Another recent trend in voluntary conservation has been the setting up of individual specialist organisations for particular species or groups of species. Birds have always been well catered for, but there are now groups such as the Glamorgan Badger Group and the Glamorgan Bat Group available for naturalists with a specific interest.

STATUTORY NATURE CONSERVATION

The Gower Coast National Nature Reserve was the first National Nature Reserve in Gower, and only the second in Wales (the first was Cwm Idwal in Snowdonia in 1954). It was declared by the Nature Conservancy in 1958 and extended over some 47 hectares. It included a short stretch of mainland cliffs together with Worms Head (Fig. 167).

Oxwich Bay was declared a National Nature Reserve in 1963 when the Nature Conservancy entered into a nature reserve agreement with the Penrice Estate to manage the major part of the bay. Subsequently the reserve has been expanded twice, firstly to include Oxwich Wood, leased from another landowner, and then Crawley Wood, which was purchased in 1969. The reserve now covers over 260 hectares. In the same year the first Nature Conservancy Warden in Gower, R. H. S. (Pip) Hatton, was appointed (Fig. 168). Hatton also acted, in a voluntary capacity, as Scientific Officer for what was then the Glamorgan County Naturalists' Trust.

Two years later, in 1965, Whiteford Burrows was also declared as a National Nature Reserve. The purchase of the Burrows, although made by the National Trust under Enterprise Neptune, was facilitated by a consortium of the National Trust, the Nature Conservancy and the Naturalists' Trust. Because of this, and in order to manage the area, the Whiteford Burrows Advisory Committee was created, being comprised of members nominated by the constituent bodies. The Committee is still in being and meets regularly to oversee management of the area.

FIG 167. Worms Head from Tears Point. This stretch of coast was declared in 1958 as the second National Nature Reserve in Wales, after Snowdonia's Cwm Idwal. (Jonathan Mullard)

FIG 168. Oxwich Nature Trail, as shown in the *South Wales Evening Post* in 1966: 'All eyes on Mr Hatton (Gower Warden) as he explains the composition of sand.' (Countryside Council for Wales)

Following Pip Hatton's retirement in the late 1960s the Nature Conservancy located its Chief Warden for South Wales, Inigo Jones, in the peninsula to look after the three reserves. This presence was very soon supplemented by the appointment of an estate worker to undertake estate maintenance and practical conservation works on the reserves, and a warden to increase the resources in the wake of rapidly increasing public pressures and educational use. Increasing awareness of the importance of Gower's natural history led in 1972 to the Conservancy also locating the first Assistant Regional Officer for West Glamorgan, Iorrie Rees, in the peninsula, based first at Penmaen and then at the Oxwich Reserve Centre. The enlarged team was able to develop enhanced links with local naturalists, Swansea and Cardiff universities, and field educational users of the myriad of sites and natural history interests. In 1973 the Nature Conservancy was replaced by the Nature Conservancy Council, but this had little effect on activities.

During 1974 and 1975 the South Gower Coast Cooperative Management Group, involving the same organisations as the Whiteford Burrows Advisory Committee, was set up to coordinate the conservation and management of their respective properties along the coastline stretching from Worms Head to Port-Eynon. A Strategic Management Plan was agreed and this was a major step forward in the management of this significant section of coast. It was hoped to encourage the remaining private landowners to join in this approach. As with the Whiteford Committee, this group still meets today.

OXWICH RESERVE CENTRE

Despite its exceptional importance for wildlife and the high number of visitors, Gower has only ever had one purpose-designed interpretive centre, that at Oxwich, which was constructed by the Nature Conservancy during late 1972 and opened in the summer of 1973 (Fig. 169). There had been a Countryside Centre in the old school at Oxwich that was assisted in the early stages by the Naturalists' Trust, which provided exhibits and some funds, but it was felt that a new and more prominent centre was required.

At this time, as described in Chapter 7, the Oxwich reserve was under heavy public pressure as it was – and indeed still is – adjacent to a large privately run car park, with no dividing boundary between the two areas. This meant that there was open access to the dune areas. Regular assessments of the number of visitors to Oxwich consistently indicated levels in excess of 250,000 per year. In addition the dunes were regularly used for pony trekking. Oxwich was also becoming

FIG 169. The Oxwich Reserve Centre in the early 1970s. (Countryside Council for Wales)

increasingly popular as an educational resource. All this meant that the wardening resources, both permanent and seasonally recruited staff, were sometimes stretched to breaking point. The wardens did their best to 'educate' visitors about the sensible use of the reserve and how they could assist in the management and conservation of the area, but this was a hard job, as it required a wholesale change in the attitudes of the majority of visitors to wildlife and landscape conservation. The main aim of the Oxwich Reserve Centre was therefore to explain the importance of the area's wildlife to visitors, and it attempted to cater for a wide range of natural history knowledge. The Centre operated successfully until the early 1990s, when the lease on the site expired and could not be renewed.

VISITOR CENTRES

Following the demise of the Oxwich Centre, there were a number of feasibility studies for a Gower interpretive centre located at the airport site on Fairwood Common, but although substantial grant aid was available to build the centre the local authority, which coordinated the approach, was concerned about the annual running costs, and nothing materialised. There are three smaller visitor centres, however, at Rhossili, Blackpill and Bishop's Wood, that interpret specific areas of the peninsula, and in the absence of a comprehensive facility these have an important role. In addition, in Parkmill there is a commercial visitor facility, the Gower Heritage Centre, based around the working mill.

The former coastguard lookout building opposite Worms Head was once an information centre for the National Nature Reserve run by the Countryside Council for Wales, but it has recently been returned to its owners, the National Trust, and will be restored to its original condition. A short distance to the east, in Rhossili village, the Trust has a small shop and visitor centre in the coastguard cottages, which were erected in the 1930s (Fig. 170).

The Blackpill Wildlife Centre, situated on Swansea Bay, was opened in January 2001 by Robert Howells of the Gower Ornithological Society. A partnership between the Society, the West Glamorgan RSPB Members Group and the City and County of Swansea, the Centre's aim is to inform the public about the Site of Special Scientific Interest at Blackpill. Alongside his pioneering work in the inlet and estuary Howells has also identified and counted the visiting birds at Blackpill on a daily basis since 1958, long before it was recognised as an important site. In addition he has been instrumental in persuading the council to modify their beach-cleaning methods, so as not to damage the feeding area of the visiting waders. The centre is available for any group to visit and is open to the public on winter weekends.

FIG 170. The National Trust visitor centre and shop in the old coastguard cottages at Rhossili. (Harold Grenfell)

Bishop's Wood Countryside Centre is located adjacent to the Local Nature Reserve of the same name, in Caswell Bay. It is managed by the City and County of Swansea's Development Department to conserve and encourage wildlife diversity and provide access and information to visitors and schools. Also based at the reserve is the Caswell Wood Initiative, the aim of which is to encourage the conservation of woodlands, their proper management and the use of timber for traditional and contemporary crafts. This project has used local timber to construct a wooden roundhouse, which is intended as a venue for training events, promoting woodland crafts using local timber, and as an environmental educational base.

FIELD EDUCATION

Around 500 educational groups visit the peninsula every year. To many organisers of field study courses the important feature of Gower, when compared with many other parts of Britain, is the ease of access onto so many open areas of land, the extensive network of rights of way and the range of habitats. In order to cater for this demand, and to manage the use of sensitive areas, the Gower Field Education Project was set up in 1975 by the Nature Conservancy Council and West Glamorgan County Council Education Department. The remit of the Project was to advise and develop resource materials for West Glamorgan schools using the peninsula's important natural sites so that they were used in a manner and intensity which avoided damage whilst at the same time meeting the needs of the curriculum and pupils. This involved spreading field use to include 'lower grade' conservation sites, in order to lighten pressures on 'classic' sites. With the assistance of the County Adviser, the Project Teacher (first Greg Nuttgens and then Bob Burn) and Conservancy staff, teachers prepared resource materials. Schools from outside West Glamorgan visiting the peninsula for field studies were also encouraged to participate and practise the objectives of the Project, and very many did so (Fig. 171). The Education Project did not survive the closure of the Oxwich Centre, but advice on the suitability of sites for fieldwork is now available from the Countryside Council for Wales.

Residential field centres were established by Oxfordshire County Council at Kilvrough and by the London Borough of Merton at Stouthall. The latter was run as a Centre for Environmental Studies until 1998, when the Borough announced plans to close Stouthall in a cost-cutting measure. The centre was host to thousands of Merton schoolchildren over the years, providing them with a trip away from home and the opportunity to experience environmental studies at first

FIG 171. Bob Burn, Gower Field Education Project Officer, and visiting school group in 1985. (Countryside Council for Wales)

hand. In contrast Kilvrough Manor Outdoor Education Centre continues to be run by Oxfordshire County Council. The old school in Parkmill was opened by Glamorgan County Council in 1972 as a field centre and lasted until 1984, when it became a centre for Guides. Rhossili School was also once a local authority centre, but it is now a private outdoor pursuits centre, although some field studies take place. Of the centres funded by the local authority, only Borva House in Port-Eynon survives, and this is used mainly by local primary schools.

Despite all this activity there is very little evidence of lasting damage to any of the major habitats which can be ascribed to organised educational activity groups; especially when such activities are compared with general tourist activity or with commercial bait picking, crabbing, fishing, leisure sport climbing with bolts, scrambler bikes and four-wheel-drive vehicles. Since 1994, however, the cliffs and coastal inshore waters have seen an increase in the number of youth groups carrying out organised adventure and leisure activities, and this may have more serious impacts upon the area.

COUNTRYSIDE MANAGEMENT

An AONB Warden, the 'Gower Warden' so fondly remembered by older people, was appointed by the Gower Rural District Council in 1961 to implement small-scale projects and patrol the area, but, as described above, there was no strategic plan for Gower at this stage. The first Warden, Mr Guy, died after only a year and was succeeded in 1962 by Douglas Evans, a former water bailiff from the Brecon Beacons. According to a Gower Society report of the time Evans was 'an energetic, forthright bulldog of a man, dedicated to the countryside, who manages to remain undaunted in his unenviable position between officialdom and the public.' One of his achievements was the creation of the volunteer group known as the 'Gower Crusaders'. The group carried out practical conservation works, including litter picks, set up picnic sites at strategic points for visitors and helped other conservation organisations in undertaking conservation tasks. One such activity was the planting of marram grass at Oxwich as part of the measures undertaken to counteract the effects of thousands of visitors on the dunes. The post unfortunately lapsed on his retirement in the early 1970s and much of the early momentum was lost. There is a memorial plaque to Evans on a cairn at the picnic site and viewpoint on the south side of Cefn Bryn overlooking Penmaen.

As well as being the year of the Strategy for Gower, 1973 was also the year in which the importance of the peninsula's unspoilt coastline was further recognised by its definition as a Heritage Coast by the Countryside Commission. Heritage Coasts are a non-statutory landscape definition, unlike the formally designated AONBs and National Parks. They were identified in response to widespread concern about the loss of unspoiled coastlines to insensitive developments, including caravan sites, industry and urban expansion. Most Heritage Coasts, like Gower, simply extend along the shore between two named points. Their status carries no legal protection, but planning authorities must take the designation into account before taking decisions on matters that could affect the area. The responsibility for looking after Heritage Coasts normally lies with local authorities. Management plans are drawn up, and carried out by Heritage Coast Officers who often call on teams of volunteers to help with practical tasks.

The advent of the Heritage Coast therefore resulted in a Heritage Coast Warden, Roy Ladd, being appointed by Swansea City Council in the mid-1970s, and there were several initiatives on various degraded sand-dune systems around Gower, such as the successful work at Port-Eynon and Horton. By 1978 there were '12 labourers, 1 foreman, 1 trainee foreman, 1 clerical assistant and 1 Heritage Coast

Assistant' employed through the Manpower Services Commission as part of the Gower Heritage Coast Management Programme. The aim of the programme was to 'tackle the most pressing environmental problems along the Gower coast coordinating and utilising all possible sources of labour, materials and finance for that purpose'. In total there were ten projects that related to areas 'where public access and activity have degraded the environment and the emphasis has been placed on practical and effective projects which can be implemented quickly and by a relatively untrained workforce'. Project areas consisted of either 'fragile sand dunes' or very popular clifftop footpaths such as that between Rhossili village and Worms Head, which had become eroded.

The *Swansea District Plan* of 1981 noted that 'Some useful work on stabilising and protecting sand dunes has already been completed at Port Eynon using funds for the relief of unemployment. Although this is an example of what can be achieved wherever natural beauty is threatened, there is a need for wardens experienced in countryside matters to coordinate management initiatives and to provide a countryside educational service to both schools and the general public.' Despite all this activity there was no overall Heritage Coast management plan or any link to wider AONB initiatives. As with the previous AONB warden, when the Heritage Coast Warden retired in the late 1980s there was no direct replacement, although the City Council carried on with small-scale works on a number of coastal sites until the creation of the Gower Countryside Service in 1990.

The *Gower Management Plan* (Osborne, 1990) led to the author's appointment as the first senior AONB Officer in the UK, with the remit of acting as a coordinator and being a focus for action. One of the first tasks was to set up the Gower Countryside Forum, as the advisory committee for the designated area. As with the previous Special Area Sub Committee, this recognised the importance of the local authorities, statutory agencies and voluntary bodies having a coordinated approach to the designated area. The appointment of the AONB Officer was followed in 1992 by the appointment of a Project Officer, Steve Parry, whose role was to initiate practical conservation projects.

This work resulted in the designation of other important areas of the coastline owned by the local authority, at Mumbles Hill and Pwlldu Cliffs, as Local Nature Reserves, and pioneering approaches to the conservation of major sand-dune systems and common land. Particularly important was the management plan for Hillend and Broughton Burrows, which together represent the single largest stretch of the Heritage Coast in private ownership (Fig. 172). The plan for Cefn Bryn Common, the largest common-land unit in the peninsula, led to the signing of a Tir Cymen agri-environment scheme with the commons, the first such agreement in the country, and a number of important management

FIG 172. Conservation work on the dunes at Broughton by the Gower Countryside Service. (City and County of Swansea)

schemes. The built heritage was not neglected either, and a significant amount of time was spent on the consolidation of Port-Eynon Salthouse in a joint project with the Glamorgan–Gwent Archaeological Trust. This subsequently won the Heritage in Britain award. A jointly agreed interpretive strategy for the peninsula resulted in a coordinated approach to visitor information by all the relevant organisations, with joint information panels being produced and a number of local businesses being developed as Gower Information Points.

Following local government reorganisation in 1996, the Gower Countryside Service was incorporated into a wider countryside management group covering the whole of the new unitary authority area. This was a retrograde step as it removed the focus from the AONB and diluted the resources available. The final remnants of the Countryside Service were disbanded in 2000, and the first AONB to be designated is now the only one without a dedicated AONB unit.

One of the critical achievements of the Gower Countryside Service, however, was to set up the Gower Commons Initiative as part of the Tomorrow's Heathland Heritage programme. In the absence of a specific AONB unit this has continued vital work on the common land through a partnership of organisations. The programme is a national initiative that aims to revive lowland heathland and its wildlife, re-creating a landscape that benefits both people and wildlife. Led by

English Nature and supported by the Heritage Lottery Fund, the partnership is making substantial progress towards the national targets of restoring 58,000 hectares of heathland and re-creating a further 6,000 hectares.

The Gower Commons Initiative covers eight commons and brings together the National Trust, the City and County of Swansea, the Gower Commoners Association, the Countryside Council for Wales, Llangennith Manors, the Somerset Trust and the Gower Society. Much of the work is undertaken by the commoners working together with volunteers and using traditional skills alongside modern mechanical ones (Fig. 173). This has aided in the re-skilling and training of local people in traditional methods used to maintain the heathland. One important benefit of the project is that it has prompted a campaign to slow down traffic. Some cattle have also been fitted with reflective collars, in an attempt to reduce the number of road accidents and cattle deaths, many of which are caused by excessive speeds and the near-invisibility of black cattle at night. Much of the heathland has been restored successfully and rare habitats have been conserved, in addition to significant archaeological sites such as hut circles. Crucially, the project has successfully tackled the issue of burning and in an innovative partnership with the Fire Service has developed a management approach that will ensure the previous widespread and damaging burns are a thing of the past. This

FIG 173. Practical work being undertaken by the Gower Commons Initiative to conserve the lowland heathland on Pengwern Common. (Gower Commons Initiative)

FIG 174. Field at Middleton sown with barley, millet and sunflowers as a food source for overwintering birds. (Harold Grenfell)

has not, however, prevented serious damage caused by an illegal burn on the east slope of Rhossili Down, which will take years to recover.

There are also an increasing number of small-scale conservation initiatives in Gower. In 2003 the Gower Society, for example, grant-aided the planting of a field in Middleton with a mix of barley, common millet *Panicum miliaceum* and sunflowers *Helianthus annuus*, in order to attract yellowhammers and various finches during the winter (Fig. 174). This appears to have been extremely successful.

THE SITUATION TODAY

There are no direct threats to Gower today comparable to those of the past. Large holiday camps are unlikely to be built, and woods will not be clear-felled, unless the proposal is part of an approved management plan. Even the enormous visitor numbers of the 1960s and 1970s are unlikely to return, given the growth of low-cost airlines taking people abroad for holidays. Instead the quality of Gower is being gradually eroded by external pressures. Creeping suburbanisation through small-scale changes, together with unsuitable designs for new buildings, will, if left unchallenged, change the rural character of the area forever (Fig. 175). Gower is no place for pavements and streetlights, especially as the gradual reduction of dark skies and areas of tranquillity are a concern. Species such as glow-worms need darkness if they are to survive.

Offshore wind power stations, such as that now planned for Scarweather Sands in Swansea Bay, will blight the views out to sea, and the three proposed onshore developments at Mynydd y Gwair in the Lordship of Gower, Mynydd Bettws and Waunarllwydd, if built, may also be visible from the peninsula. Without doubt, however, the most significant changes to the Gower landscape will result from the reforms to the Common Agricultural Policy. The situation is complex and influenced by a number of factors, but as farmers begin to rely less on subsidies and start to make decisions based on the particular assets of their farm, the available incentives for environmental objectives and particular marketing opportunities, there will be some difficult decisions to take.

As far as direct resources for conservation initiatives are concerned, as this chapter shows, the history of such activities in Gower has been intermittent. Those initiatives dependent on external funding have rarely been made permanent and there is never enough long-term support from the organisations themselves, both the donors and the recipients, to make a permanent difference.

FIG 175. Looking north across Whiteford from the Bulwark, a view that encapsulates the variety and beauty of Gower. (Harold Grenfell)

The continually shifting priorities and fashions make it difficult to resource the basic work that is necessary to conserve the area. A large part of the problem, however, is that giving a local authority responsibility for managing a national landscape designation, and making it rely on grant aid from a range of countryside agencies, simply does not work. The people campaigning for Gower's designation fifty years ago recognised that the peninsula has 'National Park scale' problems without the equivalent resources, and this is still the case today. The five AONBs in Wales do not have the same level of financial support as those in England and despite small-scale grant schemes, such as the Sustainable Development Fund supported by the National Assembly, this problem still needs to be addressed. If the AONB designation is failing Gower, because of local politics, perhaps it is not too late to have the area designated as a National Park? That, after all, was the original aim of the Gower Society in the 1950s.

The Gower Flora of Isaac Hamon

The following list represents my interpretation of Hamon's list of 1697 and is based, in part, on comments in Emery (1965) and Wade *et al.* (1994) and knowledge of the current Gower flora. *Culpeper's Complete Herbal* (1653) has also been used for guidance, as the famous 'astrologer-physician' was almost a contemporary of Hamon and often uses the same common names. For obvious reasons the list can never be a definitive analysis. The majority of the current names are from Stace (1995).

Only one of Hamon's plants, 'botchwort', remains a complete mystery, although doubts remain about certain other species, and these are indicated by a question mark against the current common name in the table. In particular 'larks bill' may be either larkspur or monk's-hood and 'burnet' is likely to be either salad burnet or burnet rose.

HAMON'S NAME	PROBABLE SCIENTIFIC NAME	CURRENT COMMON NAME
'Sea hearbes'		
Scurvie grasse	*Cochlearia officinalis*	Scurvygrass
Sampir	*Crithmum maritimum*	Rock samphire
Lavar	*Porphyra umbilicalis*	Laver
'Rock herbs'		
Cetrack	*Asplenium ceterach*	Rustyback fern
Maiden hair	*Asplenium trichomanes*	Maidenhair spleenwort
Walrue	*Asplenium ruta-muraria*	Wall-rue

HAMON'S NAME	PROBABLE SCIENTIFIC NAME	CURRENT COMMON NAME
'Shrubs'		
Juniper	*Juniperus communis*	Common juniper
Buckthorn	*Rhamnus catharticus*	Buckthorn
'Field herbs'		
Agrimony	*Agrimonia eupatoria*	Agrimony
Wild carret	*Daucus carota*	Wild carrot
Mullein	*Verbascum thapsus*	Great mullein
Dandelyon	*Taraxacum officinale*	Dandelion
Pelamountain	*Thymus polytrichus*	Wild thyme
Mallows	*Malva* spp.	Mallow
Burdock	*Arctium minus*	Lesser burdock
Tutsan	*Hypericum androsaemum*	Tutsan
Eybright	*Euphrasia officinalis*	Eyebright
Bettony	*Stachys officinalis*	Betony
Elecampane	*Inula helenium*	Elecampane
Foxfingers	*Digitalis purpurea*	Foxglove
Yellow kay-roses	*Primula veris*	Cowslip?
Blue kay-roses	*Polyanthus* spp.	Polyanthus?
Rames or ramsey	*Allium ursinum*	Ramsons
Centry	*Centaurium erythraea*	Common centaury?
Yarrow	*Achillea millefolium*	Yarrow
Adders tongue	*Ophioglossum vulgatum*	Adder's tongue
Vervain	*Verbena officinalis*	Vervain
St John's wort	*Hypericum* spp.	St John's-wort
Cancker wort	*Papaver rhoeas*	Common poppy?
Devilles bit	*Succisa pratensis*	Devil's-bit scabious
Ragwort	*Senecio jacobaea*	Common ragwort
Mugwort	*Artemesia vulgaris*	Mugwort
Preakestone-psley	*Aphanes arvensis*	Parsley-piert
Larks bill	*Consolida ajacis*	Larkspur?
Plantane	*Plantago* spp.	Plantain
Pimpnell	*Anagallis arvensis*	Scarlet pimpernel?
Fumitory	*Fumaria* spp.	Fumitory
Burnet	*Sanguisorba minor*	Salad burnet?
Botchwort	?	?

HAMON'S NAME	PROBABLE SCIENTIFIC NAME	CURRENT COMMON NAME
'Hearbs in some waterie places'		
Water cresses	*Rorippa* spp.	Water-cress
Rosa solis	*Drosera rotundifolia*	Round-leaved sundew
Lungwort	*Pulmonaria officinalis*	Lungwort
Liver wort	Various	Liverwort

Local Names of Plants and Animals

Apart from the now archaic names for plants and animals listed by Isaac Hamon, the main source for the old Gower names of plants and animals is Horatio Tucker. In his book, published in 1951 by the Gower Society, he records that 'As a child I learned the local names of the birds and the flowers – the only names that my grandmother knew.' He is said to have compiled a list of over 400 words, but this appears to be lost. The names are of course English, as Gower is mainly an English-speaking area. In contrast, the Welsh names are standardised names and there appear to be none that are specific to the peninsula. Some of the names Tucker records covered more than one species and he notes, for instance, 'Lundibirds, which nested on Worms Head, in our language included not only puffins but also guillemots and razorbills.' The term 'lundibirds' must have originated from Lundy Island, which can be seen from Gower in clear weather, far out in the Bristol Channel. The island's emblem, the puffin, is unfortunately now reduced in numbers, but still occurs, together with guillemots and razorbills. Their presence on Lundy would have been well known to the Gowerians of old.

LOCAL NAME	TUCKER'S NAME	SCIENTIFIC NAME
Adders' meat	Lady smock	*Cardamine pratensis*
Angle touches	Worms	Various
Brims	Horseflies	Various
Bumba-goose or bumbagus	Bittern	*Botaurus stellaris*
Chatterpies	Magpies	*Pica pica*

LOCAL NAME	TUCKER'S NAME	SCIENTIFIC NAME
Dilly leaves	Coltsfoot	*Tussilago farfara*
Drushes	Thrushes	*Turdus* spp.
Fernowl	Nightjar	*Caprimulgus europaeus*
Foxes' tails	Purple orchid	Various
Guckoo-shoes	Violets	*Viola* spp.
Jack Phillip	Sandpiper	*Actitis hypoleucos*
Lady washdishes	Wagtails	*Motacilla* spp.
Lundibirds	Puffins, guillemots and razorbills	*Fratercula arctica/Uria aalge/Alca torda*
March	Wild celery	*Apium graveolens*
Oakwibs	Cockchafers	*Melolontha melolontha*
Pennywort	Penny royal	*Hydrocotyle vulgaris*
Rames	Wild garlic	*Allium ursinum*
Reremouses	Bats	Various
Ruddock	Robin	*Erithacus rubecula*
Sourgrobs	Sorrel	*Rumex acetosa*
Twinks	Chaffinches	*Fringilla coelebs*
Vildeveer	Fieldfare	*Turdus pilaris*
Wants	Moles	*Talpa europaea*
Witches	Moths	Various

Designated Sites

There are six different statutory wildlife designations in Gower, apart from the AONB: Sites of Special Scientific Interest (SSSI), National Nature Reserves (NNR), Local Nature Reserves (LNR), Special Areas of Conservation (SAC), Special Protection Areas (SPA) and one Ramsar Site (an international wetland).

The initial wildlife designation is always as an SSSI, which may result in a site being designated an NNR. The other designations are used to recognise a site's importance at a European level (SAC and SPA) or international level (Ramsar). It should be noted that SSSI, NNR, SAC, Ramsar and SPA designations cover overlapping areas, and are essentially subsets of each other. Two of the SACs in Gower are for the marine environment. In contrast, LNRs are usually designated by local authorities and do not necessarily overlap with other labels.

SSSIs represent the best wildlife habitats and geological features in Wales and cover more than 12 per cent of the land area, but an assessment of their condition suggests that while 47 per cent of sites are in a favourable or recovering condition, 52 per cent are in an unfavourable and worsening condition, with the remaining one per cent having been partially lost in recent years. The Countryside Council for Wales has therefore changed the emphasis of its work from designating new sites to bringing the existing ones into better condition. Some notifications will still go ahead, however, if the designation underpins the management of a site of international importance, an important site is threatened by unsympathetic development or management, or if SSSI notification is absolutely necessary for the sustainable long-term management of the site.

As at June 2004 there was a total of 37 statutory designations in the peninsula and by the time of publication further details of these should be available via the CCW website.

Sites of Special Scientific Interest (sssi)

Barland Common Stream Section

Berry Wood

Blackpill

Bracelet Bay

Burry Inlet and Loughor Estuary (part of Carmarthen Bay and Estuaries sac, Burry Inlet spa, Burry Inlet Ramsar Site)

Caswell Bay

Cefn Bryn Common (part of Gower Commons sac)

Cwm Ivy Marsh and Tor (part of Carmarthen Bay and Estuaries sac, Burry Inlet spa, Burry Inlet Ramsar Site)

Fairwood, Pengwern and Welshmoor Commons (part of Gower Commons sac)

Gower Coast: Rhossili to Port-Eynon (part of Gower Coast nnr and Limestone Coast of South West Wales sac)

Horton, Eastern and Western Slade

Ilston Quarry

Langland Bay (Rotherslade)

Llethrid Valley (part of Gower Ash Woods sac)

Mitchin Hole

Nicholaston Woods (part of Gower Ash Woods sac and Oxwich nnr)

Oxwich Bay (part of Oxwich nnr; part in Gower Ash Woods sac and part in Limestone Coast of South West Wales sac)

Pennard Valley (part in Gower Ash Woods sac)

Penrice Stables and Underhill Cottage

Pwll Du Head and Bishopston Valley (part in Limestone Coast of South West Wales and part in Gower Ash Woods sac)

Rhossili Down (part of Gower Commons sac)

Sluxton Marsh and Whitemoor (part of Gower Commons sac)

Whiteford Burrows, Landimore Marsh and Broughton Bay (part of Whiteford
NNR, Carmarthen Bay and Estuaries SAC and Carmarthen Bay Dunes SAC, Burry
Inlet SPA, Burry Inlet Ramsar Site)

Rose Cottage

Courthouse Grasslands (part of Gower Commons SAC)

National Nature Reserves (NNR)

Whiteford

Oxwich

Gower Coast

Local Nature Reserves (LNR)

Mumbles Hill

Pwlldu Cliffs

Special Protection Areas (SPA)

Burry Inlet

Ramsar Sites

Burry Inlet

Special Areas of Conservation (SAC)

Gower Commons

Gower Ash Woods

Limestone Coast of South West Wales

Marine Special Areas of Conservation (SAC)

Carmarthen Bay and Estuaries

Carmarthen Bay Dunes

Geological Conservation Review Sites

These are the key earth-science localities in Gower that are of national and international importance.

NAME	BLOCK	GRID REF (SS)
Bacon Hole	Quaternary of Wales	561 868
Bacon Hole	Pleistocene Vertebrata	561 868
Barland Common	Namurian of England & Wales	576 897
Bosco`s Den	Quaternary of Wales	559 868
Bosco`s Den	Pleistocene Vertebrata	559 868
Bracelet Bay	Variscan Structures of South Wales and the Mendips	629 872
Bracelet Bay	Dinantian of Southern England & South Wales	629 871
Broughton Bay	Quaternary of Wales	419 930
Burry Inlet	Coastal Geomorphology	445 945
Caswell Bay	Dinantian of Southern England & South Wales	594 877
Caswell Bay	Variscan Structures of South Wales and the Mendips	595 873
Cat Hole Cave	Pleistocene Vertebrata	538 900
Cat Hole Cave	Quaternary of Wales	538 900
Eastern & Western Slade	Quaternary of Wales	487 855
Horton	Quaternary of Wales	481 855
Hunts Bay	Quaternary of Wales	563 869

NAME	BLOCK	GRID REF (SS)
Ilston Quarry	Dinantian of Southern England & South Wales	555 906
Langland Bay	Quaternary of Wales	613 871
Llethrid Valley	Karst	535 900
Long Hole	Pleistocene Vertebrata	451 851
Long Hole Cave	Quaternary of Wales	452 851
Minchin Hole	Pleistocene Vertebrata	555 869
Minchin Hole	Quaternary of Wales	555 869
Oxwich Bay	Coastal Geomorphology	510 870
Oystermouth Old Quarry	Dinantian of Southern England & South Wales	615 883
Pwlldu	Coastal Geomorphology	575 870
Pwlldu Head	Dinantian of Southern England & South Wales	568 864
Rhossili Bay	Quaternary of Wales	416 892
Three Cliff Bay	Dinantian of Southern England & South Wales	529 877
Worms Head	Quaternary of Wales	394 874

Wildlife Trust Reserves

SITE	AREA (HA)	HABITAT	GRID REF (SS)
Berry Wood	6.80	Ancient woodland	474 884
Betty Church	2.22	Broadleaved woodland/pasture	440 937
Broad Pool	1.71	Pond on common land	510 910
Cwm Ivy Woods	11.1	Ancient woodland	443 939
Harding Reserve	9.66	Quarry/woodland/grassland	555 905
Gelli-hir	28.6	Broadleaved woodland/pond	562 925
Hambury Wood	4.79	Ancient woodland	472 929
Killay Marsh	10.00	Plantation/fen/wet woodland	595 928
Kilvrough Manor Woods	7.50	Ancient woodland	555 891
Llanrhidian Hill	3.09	Woodland/scrub on common land	495 922
The Lucas Reserve	1.10	Wet woodland	447 933
Peel Wood	1.10	Wooded quarry	607 883
Prior's Wood & Meadow	17.40	Broadleaved woodland/grassland	577 938
Redden Hill Wood	1.30	Limestone woodland	538 894
Redley Cliff	3.60	Wooded headland	589 875
Deborah's Hole	6.70	Maritime heath/limestone grassland	435 862
Long Hole Cliff	20.70	Maritime heath/limestone grassland	450 850
Overton Cliff	9.40	Maritime heath/limestone grassland	458 848

SITE	AREA (HA)	HABITAT	GRID REF (SS)
Overton Mere	11.60	Maritime heath/limestone grassland	462 848
Port-Eynon Point	13.40	Maritime heath/limestone grassland	465 845
Roydon's Corner	1.70	Limestone grassland	456 851
Sedger's Bank	35.10	Foreshore to low water mark	470 844

Organisations and Contacts

There are numerous organisations concerned with British natural history and the countryside in general. The following list highlights those relevant to Gower. Information on other organisations mentioned in the text can easily be found on the Internet. All details were correct at the time of publication, but it should be noted that small voluntary groups may change their contact address more frequently than some of the larger bodies and they may not be able to respond to enquiries as quickly.

Butterfly Conservation

10 Calvert Terrace, Swansea, SA1 5AR. Tel: 0870 7706153. www.butterfly-conservation.org

The organisation's purpose is to secure a lasting future for all native butterflies, moths and their habitats within the UK. The ultimate goal is to help restore a balanced countryside with butterflies and other wildlife restored to the profusion that they, and we, once enjoyed.

City and County of Swansea

Environment and Conservation Section, Planning Services, Environment Department, Guildhall, Swansea, SA1 4PH. Tel: 01792 635094. www.swansea.gov.uk

The Environment and Conservation Section plays a key role, both in its own right and in the work it carries out with partner organisations, in managing both the natural and built environment of the area. In partnership with many local groups and national agencies it is preparing a Biodiversity Action Plan for Swansea. It also manages the Bishop's Wood Countryside Centre. Formerly an old coach house, this is now run as an interpretive centre with displays and information about the nearby Local Nature Reserve.

Countryside Council for Wales

Llys Tawe, Kings Road, Swansea, SA1 8PG. Tel: 01792 763500. www.ccw.gov.uk

The Countryside Council for Wales is the Government's statutory adviser on sustaining natural beauty, wildlife and the opportunity for outdoor enjoyment in Wales and its inshore waters. Among other duties it manages the three National Nature Reserves in the peninsula, monitors the Sites of Special Scientific Interest and until recently ran the Tir Gofal agri-environment scheme.

Coed Cymru

Neath Port Talbot County Borough Council, Civic Centre, Neath, SA11 3QZ. www.coedcymru.org.uk

Coed Cymru is an all-Wales initiative to promote the management of broadleaf woodlands and the use of locally grown hardwood timber in Wales. The local officer advises on woodland management in both the Neath and Swansea areas.

Forestry Commission Wales

Coed y Cymoedd Forest District, Resolven, Neath, SA11 4DR. Tel: 01639 710221. www.forestry.gov.uk

The Forestry Commission looks after the woodlands and forests belonging to the National Assembly for Wales. It has teams of staff dedicated to specific areas to bring woodlands and communities closer together, and manages the woods in the Parkmill area.

Glamorgan Badger Group

Swansea Area, 37 Priors Way, Dunvant, Swansea, SA2 7OH. Tel: 01792 206686.

All badger groups are members of the National Federation of Badger Groups. Their aim is to enhance the welfare and conservation of badgers. This includes undertaking sett watches and protecting them against persecution.

Glamorgan Bat Group

32 Primrose Rd, Neath, SA11 2AP. Tel: 01639 638658.

There is a UK-wide network of over 90 local bat groups. Like the others the Glamorgan group organises meetings, surveys and training activities and supports the care, protection, study and conservation of bats. Members also lead guided walks, give talks and organise other activities to promote bat conservation.

Glamorgan Moth Recording Group

87 Coed Glas Road, Llanishen, Cardiff, CF14 5EL. Tel: 02920 762182.

The group was formed in 1995, in response to the growing number of naturalists interested in recording moths in South Wales. It runs a series of field meetings during the summer and is working towards a comprehensive publication on Lepidoptera in Glamorgan.

Gower Bird Hospital

Valetta, Sandy Lane, Pennard, Swansea, SA3 2EW. Tel: 01792 371630. www.gowerbirdhospital.org.uk

The hospital is a charitable organisation that rehabilitates wild birds and small mammals before releasing them back into the wild.

Gower Commoners Association

91 Heathfield, Swansea. Tel: 01792 652007.

The association exists to protect the rights and interests of all the commoners in Gower and acts a voice for the individual commons management associations. Its primary objective is to ensure that the commons are effectively managed.

Gower Ornithological Society

24 Hazel Road, Uplands, Swansea, SA2 0LX. Tel: 01792 298859. www.glamorganbirds.org.uk

The society produces an annual bird report *Gower Birds*, together with a regular newsletter, and holds monthly indoor and occasional field meetings. It has contributed to all the recent bird surveys organised by national organisations.

Gower Society

Swansea Museum, Victoria Road, Swansea, SA1 1SN.
www.gowersociety.welshnet.co.uk

The Gower Society is a group of over 1,500 people who consider that the Lordship of Gower, and especially the Area of Outstanding Natural Beauty, is a very special place. The society lobbies local and national organisations in its efforts to protect the area. It arranges a programme of more than a hundred events a year and publishes an annual journal, which includes articles on all aspects of the peninsula, past and present.

Irish Sea Leatherback Project

School of Biological Sciences, University of Wales Swansea, Singleton Park, Swansea, SA2 8PP. Tel: 01792 205678. www.swan.ac.uk/bs/turtle

The project is a joint initiative between the University of Wales Swansea and University College Cork. Its aim is to understand the populations, origins and behaviour of leatherback turtles in the Irish Sea.

National Trust

Little Reynoldston Farm, Reynoldston, Swansea, SA3 1AQ. Tel: 01792 390636.
www.nationaltrust.org.uk

The National Trust cares for over 248,000 hectares of countryside in England, Wales and Northern Ireland, plus almost 600 miles of coastline and more than 200 buildings and gardens of outstanding interest and importance. It has a visitor centre and shop in the old coastguard cottages at Rhossili.

National Wetlands Centre Wales

Penclacwydd, Llwynhendy, Llanelli, Carmarthenshire, SA14 9SH. Tel: 01554 741087.
www.wwt.org.uk

Located on the north side of the Burry Inlet and owned by the Wildfowl & Wetlands Trust, the centre is a focus for wetland conservation in Wales. Its newest feature is the Millennium Wetland complex.

South Wales Arachnid Group

Endsleigh, Blue Anchor Hill, Pen-clawdd, Gower, SA4 3LZ. Tel: 01792 850578.

The group produce a newsletter, *Cobwebs*, which includes additions to the Glamorgan checklist of spiders, harvestmen and pseudoscorpions and a key to the webs of British spiders.

South East Wales Biodiversity Records Centre

13 St Andrews Crescent, Cardiff, CF10 3DB. Tel: 02920 641110. www.sewbrec.org.uk

The Records Centre provides a mechanism for collating, sharing and utilising the wealth of biological data and knowledge that exists in Glamorgan and Gwent.

West Glamorgan RSPB Members Group

RSPB Wales, Sutherland House, Castlebridge, Cowbridge Road East, Cardiff, CF11 9AB. Tel: 02920 353000. www.rspb.org.uk

The aim of the group is to publicise the RSPB's conservation work in the West Glamorgan area, to hold educational events, to raise funds for the Society's conservation work, and to provide a programme of activities for local members

Wildlife Trust of South and West Wales

Fountain Road, Tondu, Bridgend, CF32 0EH. Tel: 01656 724100. www.wildlifetrust.org.uk/wtsww

The Trust promotes the enjoyment and protection of wildlife throughout south and west Wales. An important part of this work involves setting aside wild places to establish as nature reserves, where the conservation of wild plants and animals is a priority.

Woodland Trust Wales (Coed Cadw)

Yr Hen Orsaf, Llanidloes, Powys, SY18 6EB. Tel: 01686 412508. www.the-woodland-trust.org.uk

The Woodland Trust is dedicated to the protection of our native woodland heritage. It manages Common Wood near Llanrhidian.

References and Further Reading

The following references represent the main sources of information used in the writing of this book. For reasons of space, I have omitted articles from the *Gower Journal* and a large number of internet resources. A full bibliography for a book such as this, where much of the information has been drawn together for the first time, would be extremely large.

Abbot, A. (1992) *Reconnaissance Survey of Aculeate Hymenoptera Habitat on the South Gower Cliffs.* CCW Contract Science Report 19. Countryside Council for Wales, Bangor.

Abbot, R. H. R. (1981) A new opilionid to Great Britain. *Newsletter of the British Arachnological Society* **30**: 4.

Ajax-Lewis, N. & Bellamy, D. (1976) *An Integrated Botanical and Zoological Survey of Worms Head.* Nature Conservancy Council, Oxwich.

Ajax-Lewis, N. (1991) *Where to Go for Wildlife in Glamorgan.* Pisces Publications, Newbury.

Aldhouse-Green, S. (2000) *Paviland Cave and the 'Red Lady': a Definitive Report.* Western Academic and Specialist Press, Bristol.

Allen, E. E. & Rutter, J. G. (1946) *Gower Caves.* Vaughan Thomas, Swansea.

Anon. (1896) Second field meeting: Gower. *Caradoc and Severn Valley Field Club* Vol. 1, 1893–1896.

Anon. (1995) *A Water Level Management Plan for Llangennith Moors, North Gower, West Glamorgan.* National Rivers Authority.

Anon. (1998) *Good Practice Guide on Managing the Use of Common Land.* Department of the Environment, Transport and the Regions, London.

Atkins, J. (ed.) (1995) *Burry Inlet and Loughor Estuary Symposium: State of the Estuary Report Parts 1 and 2.* West Glamorgan County Council, Swansea.

Baines, M & Reichelt, M. (2003) *Sightings in Wales.* Issue 4. CCW/Sea Watch. Nekton, Bristol. [Cetacean sightings]

Baines, M., Pierpoint, C. & Earl, S. (1997) *A Cetacean Sightings Database for Wales and an Evaluation of Impacts on Cetaceans from the Sea Empress Oil Spill.* Countryside Council for Wales, Bangor.

Baker, A. R. H. & Butlin, R. A. (eds) (1973) *Studies of Field Systems in the British Isles.* Cambridge University Press, Cambridge.

Baker, C. & Francis, G. G. (1870) *Surveys of Gower and Kilvey*. T. Richards, London.

Balchin, W. V. G. (ed.) (1971) *Swansea and its Region*. University College of Swansea.

Barne, J. H., Robson, C. F., Kaznowska, S. S. & Doody, J. P. (1995) *Coasts and Seas of the United Kingdom. Region 12: Wales*. JNCC, Peterborough.

Barnett, L. K. & Warren, M. S. (1995) Species action plan: marsh fritillary. Unpublished report, Butterfly Conservation.

Barneveld, J. & Hamley, S. (1991) *Botanical Survey of the Ditches of Llangennith Moors*. CCW South Wales Report SW/6. Countryside Council for Wales, Bangor.

Barrett, J. & Yonge, C. M. (1973) *Collins Pocket Guide to the Sea Shore*. Collins, London.

Bate, C. S. (1850) Notes on the fauna of Swansea and the neighbourhood made during the summer of 1849. *Report of the Swansea Literary Society* **1850**: 23–35.

Beale, R. (2003) *Gower AONB Management Plan: State of the AONB Report*. City and County of Swansea Environment Department.

Bell, T. (1853) *British Stalk-eyed Crustacea*. Van Voorst, London.

Blacker, N. C. (1989) The Ants (Hymenoptera, Formicidae) of the Gower Peninsula, West Glamorgan, South Wales. *Entomologist's Record and Journal of Variation* **101**: 261–266.

Blower, J. G. (1987) Giant *Geophilus* from Gower. *Bulletin of the British Myriapod Group* **4**: 53.

Blower, J. G. (1989) The Myriapoda of Gower. *Bulletin of the British Myriapod Group* **6**: 15–22.

Bowen, D. Q. (1971) The Quaternary succession of South Gower. In: Bassett, D. A. & Bassett, M. G. (eds) *Geological Excursions in South Wales and the Forest of Dean*. Geologists' Association, Cardiff.

Bowen, D. Q. (1977) The coast of Wales. In: Kidson, C. & Tooley, M. J. (eds) *The Quaternary History of the Irish Sea*. Geological Journal Special Issue 7. Seel House Press, Liverpool, pp 223–256.

Bowen, D. Q., Sykes, G. A., Reeves, A., Miller, G. H., Andrews, J. T, Brew, J. S. & Hare, P. E. (1985) Amino acid geochronology of raised beaches in south-west Britain. *Quaternary Science Reviews* **4**: 279–318.

Bowen, E. J. (1930) A survey of the flora of the north Gower coast in relation to marine ecological conditions. *Proceedings of the Swansea Scientific and Field Naturalists' Society* **1** (4): 109–111.

Bridges, E. M. (ed.) (1979) *Problems of Common Land: the Example of West Glamorgan*. University College of Swansea.

Bridges, E. M. (1997) *Classic Landforms of the Gower Coast*. Geographical Association and British Geomorphological Research Group.

Bridson, G. D., Philips, V. C. & Harvey, A. P. (1980) *Natural History Manuscript Resources in the British Isles*. Mansell, London.

Bright, P. & Morris, P. (1989) *A Practical Guide to Dormouse Conservation*. Mammal Society, London.

Bright, P. W. (1999) *Status and Woodland Requirements of the Dormouse in Wales*. CCW Contract Science Report 406. Countryside Council for Wales, Bangor.

British Mycological Society (2003) *List of Recommended English Names for Fungi in the UK*. www.britmycolsoc.org.uk/files/ENGLISH_NAMES.pdf.

British Ornithologists' Union (2005). *The British List: Bird Species Recorded in Great Britain*. www.bou.org/recgen.html.

Buckland, W. (1823) *Reliquiae Diluvianae; or, Observations on the Organic Remains Contained in Caves, Fissures and Diluvial Gravel and on Other Geological Phenomena Attesting to the Action of the Universal Deluge*. John Murray, London.

Bunker, F. & Hart, S. (2002) *Gower Seasearch 1995.* CCW Contract Science Report 516. Countryside Council for Wales, Bangor.

Bunker, F. & Holt, R. (2003) *Survey of Sea Caves in Welsh Special Areas of Conservation 2000–2002.* CCW Marine Monitoring Report 6. Countryside Council for Wales, Bangor.

Burn, B. (1994) *The Gower Field Education Project.* Report for Countryside Council for Wales.

Cadw (1998) *Register of Landscapes of Outstanding Historic Interest in Wales.* Cadw Welsh Historic Monuments, Cardiff.

Cadw (2000) *Glamorgan: Register of Landscapes, Parks and Gardens of Special Scientific Interest in Wales. Part 1: Parks and Gardens.* Cadw Welsh Historic Monuments, Cardiff.

Camden, W. (1586) *Britannia.* Newbery, London.

Campbell, B. & Lack, E. (1985) *A Dictionary of Birds.* Poyser, Calton.

Carter, P. W. (1952) Some account of the history of botanical exploration in Glamorganshire. *Reports and Transactions of the Cardiff Naturalists' Society* **82**: 5–31.

Caseldine, S. (1990) *Environmental Archaeology in Wales.* Saint David's University College, Lampeter.

Castle, G. & Mileto, R. (2002) NVC *Survey of Woodland* PSSSI *for the Gower Ash Woods* CSAC. CCW South Area Report. Countryside Council for Wales, Bangor.

Chapman, P. (1993) *Caves and Cave Life.* New Naturalist 79. HarperCollins, London.

Chapman, T. A. (1869) *Aphodius porcus*, a cuckoo parasite on *Geotrupes stercorarius. Entomologists' Monthly Magazine* **5**: 273–276.

Chatfield, J. (1979) Marine Mollusca in Wales. *Journal of Conchology* **30**: 1–34.

Chinery, M. (1977) *A Field Guide to the Insects of Britain and Northern Europe.* Collins, London.

Christer, W. G. (1979) The breeding dispersion and feeding biology of the raven *Corvus corax* on the Gower peninsula. Unpublished BSc dissertation, University of Swansea.

Chuter Ede, J. (1948) *The Wild Birds Protection (Glamorganshire) Order 1948.* HMSO, London.

Clements, D. & Skidmore, P. (1998) *The Autecology of the Hornet Robberfly* Asilus crabroniformis *L. in Wales, 1997.* CCW Contract Science Report 263. Countryside Council for Wales, Bangor.

Clements, D., Skidmore, P. & Denton, J. S. (1999) *The Autecology of the Hornet Robberfly* Asilus crabroniformis *L. in Wales, 1998.* CCW Contract Science Report 344. Countryside Council for Wales, Bangor.

Cliffe, C. F. (1850) *The Book of South Wales.* Cardiff.

Condry, W. M. (1982) *The Natural History of Wales.* New Naturalist 66. Collins, London.

Cooke, J. A. L. & Cotton, M. J. (1961) Some observations on the ecology of spiders occurring on sand dunes at Whiteford Burrows, Gower peninsula, Glamorgan. *Entomologist's Monthly Magazine* **97**: 183–185.

Cooke, J. A. L., Duffey, E. & Merrett, P. (1968) The male of *Lasiargus gowerensis* (Araneae: Linyphiidae), a recently discovered British spider. *Journal of Zoology (London)* **154** (1).

Cooke, R. (2004) The secret life of cockles. *Observer Food Monthly* March edition.

Cooper, R. N. (1986) *A Dark and Pagan Place.* D. Brown & Sons, Cowbridge.

Cooper, R. N. (1998) *Higher and Lower.* Subboscus, Swansea.

Copeland, H. J. W. & Askew, R. R. (1977) An analysis of the chalcidoid (Hymenoptera) fauna of a sand dune system. *Ecological Entomology* **2**: 27–46.

Coppins, A. M. & Coppins, B. J. (2002). Nicholaston Burrows SSSI (VC 41

Glamorgan): lichen survey. Unpublished report, National Trust.

Cox, J. (1999) The nature conservation importance of dung. *British Wildlife* **11**: 28–36.

Crampton, C. B. & Webley, D. (1963) The correlation of prehistoric settlement and soils: Gower, South Wales. *Bulletin of the Board of Celtic Studies* **20**: 326–337.

Crampton, C. B. & Webley, D. (1964) Preliminary studies of the historic succession of plants and soils on selected archaeological sites in South Wales. *Bulletin of the Board of Celtic Studies* **20**: 440–449.

Crowder, L. (2000) Leatherback's survival will depend on an international effort. *Nature* 405: 881.

Culpeper, N. (1653) *Culpeper's Complete Herbal.* Reprinted by Foulsham, Slough.

Darbyshire, T., Mackie, A. S. Y., May, S. J. & Rostron, D. (2002) *A Macrofaunal Survey of Welsh Sandbanks.* CCW Contract Science Report No 539. Countryside Council for Wales, Bangor.

Dargie, T. C. D. (1995) *Sand Dune Vegetation Survey of Great Britain: a National Inventory. Part 3: Wales.* JNCC, Peterborough.

Davidson, A. (ed.) (2002) *The Coastal Archaeology of Wales.* CBA Research Report 131. Council of British Archaeology, York.

Davidson, A., Davidson J. E., Owen-John, H. S., & Toft, L. A. (1987) Excavations at the sand-covered mediaeval settlement at Rhossili, West Glamorgan. *Bulletin of the Board of Celtic Studies* **34**: 244–269.

Davies, J. A. (ed.) (1996) *A Swansea Anthology.* Seren, Bridgend.

Davies, J. A. (2000) *Dylan Thomas's Swansea, Gower and Laugharne.* University of Wales Press, Cardiff.

Davies, J. D. (1894) *Historical Notices of the Parishes of Penrice, Oxwich and Nicholaston in the Rural Deanery of West Gower, Glamorganshire.* Swansea.

Davies, L. (1928) *Pennard and West Gower.* W. Spurrell & Son, Carmarthen.

Davies, M. (1956) Rhosili open field and related South Wales field patterns. *Agricultural History Review* 4: 80–96.

Davies, M. (1989) The caves of Gower. Unpublished manuscript. Burry Green.

Davies, W. (1814–15) *General View of the Agriculture and Domestic Economy of South Wales: containing the counties of Brecon, Carmarthen, Cardigan, Glamorgan, Pembroke, Radnor etc.* Sherwood, Neely & Jones, London. 2 vols.

Day, M. C. (1991) *Towards the Conservation of Aculeate Hymenoptera in Europe.* Nature and Environment 51. Council of Europe, Strasbourg.

Deere-Jones, T. (2001) *A Review of Environmental Assessments & Coastal Impact Studies for the Aggregate Extraction Proposals at the Helwick and Nash Banks.* Gower Society, Swansea.

De la Beche, H. T. (1846) On the formation of the rocks of South Wales and South Western England. *Memoirs of the Geological Survey of Great Britain* **1**: 1–296

Dillwyn, L. W. (1829) *Memoranda Relating to Coleopterus Insects Found in the Neighbourhood of Swansea.* W. C. Murray and D. Rees, Swansea.

Dillwyn, L. W. (1840) *Contributions Towards a History of Swansea.* W. C. Murray and D. Rees, Swansea.

Dillwyn, L. W. (1848) *Materials for a Fauna and Flora of Swansea.* W. C. Murray and D. Rees, Swansea.

Dines, T. (2003) Nature at large: the vanishing flowers of the field. *Natur Cymru* 7: 43.

Donovan, E. (1805) *Descriptive Excursions Through South Wales and Monmouthshire in the Year 1804 and Four Preceding Summers.* F. & C. Rivington, London.

Duffy, E. (1970) Habitat selection by spiders

on a saltmarsh in Gower. *Nature in Wales* **12** (1).

Eales, H. T. (2000) *A Survey of the Insects to be Found on Juniper (*Juniper communis*) on Three Sites within Northumberland National Park.* Northumberland National Park Authority, Hexham.

Edlin, H. L. (1961) *Glamorgan Forests.* Forestry Commission Guide. HMSO, London.

Edwards, M. & Hodge, P. (2002) *A Preliminary Survey of Coastal Soft-rock Habitats in Selected Areas of South Wales.* CCW Contract Science Report 493. Countryside Council for Wales, Bangor.

Emery, F. V. (1956 & 1957) West Glamorgan farming, circa 1580–1620. *National Library of Wales Journal* **9** (4) & **10** (1).

Emery, F. V. (1964) A note on the age of Broad Pool, Cilibion, Gower. *Bulletin of the Glamorgan County Naturalists' Trust* **3**: 12–13.

Emery, F. V. (1965) Edward Lhuyd and some of his correspondents: a view of Gower in the 1690's. *Transactions of the Honourable Society of Cymmrodorian* **1**: 59–114.

Emery, F. V. (1971) The Norman Conquest and the medieval period. In: Balchin, W. G. V. (ed.) *Swansea and its Region.* University College of Swansea, pp 147–159.

Etherington, J. R. (1981) Limestone heaths in south-west Britain: their soils and the maintenance of their calcicole–calcifuge mixtures. *Journal of Ecology* **69**: 277–294.

Etherington, J. R. & Clarke, E. (1987) Impact of agriculture on the cliff vegetation of South Gower, West Glamorgan. Unpublished report for Nature Conservancy Council. Department of Plant Science, University College Cardiff.

Evans, C. J. O. (1953) *Glamorgan: Its History and Topography.* William Lewis, Cardiff.

Evans, E. & Gwent, M. (1952) *A Portrait of Gower.* Royal Institution of South Wales on behalf of the Gower Society, Swansea.

Fearn, G. M. (1972) The distribution of intraspecific chromosome races of *Hippocrepis comosa* L. and their phytogeographic significance. *New Phytologist* **71**: 1221–1225.

Field, J. P. & Foster, W. A. (1995). Nest co-occupation in the digger wasp *Cerceris arenaria*: co-operation or usurpation? *Animal Behaviour* **50**: 99–112.

Fonseca, E. C. M. d'Assis (1973) Diptera on the Gower. Unpublished report, Nature Conservancy Council.

Ford, T. D. (1989) *Limestones and Caves of Wales.* Cambridge University Press, Cambridge.

Fowles, A. (1994) Invertebrates of Wales: a review of important sites and species. JNCC, Peterborough.

Fowles, A. (1996) *A Provisional Checklist of the Invertebrates Recorded from Wales: 2. Aculeate Wasps, Bees and Ants (Hymenoptera: Aculeata).* Countryside Council for Wales, Bangor.

Fowles, A. (2003) *Guidance Notes for the Definition and Mapping of Habitat Quality for Marsh Fritillaries.* CCW Science Report 03/5/01. Countryside Council for Wales, Bangor.

Freytag, J. (1977) Survey of the marine flora and fauna of the Gower Coast National Nature Reserve. University College Swansea. Unpublished MSc thesis, University of Swansea.

Gabb, G. (1999) *Jubilee Swansea. 2: the Town and its People in the 1890s.* Gerald Gabb, Swansea.

Gabb, O. D. (1998) The distribution and feeding biology of the barn owl (*Tyto alba*) in the Gower peninsula. Unpublished MSc dissertation, Environmental Biology, University of Wales Swansea.

Gain, W. A. (1897) Conchological notes from South Wales. *Naturalists' Journal* **6**: 105–109.

Gamwell, S. C. (1880) *The Official Guide & Hand-book to Swansea and its District.* British Association, Swansea.

George, T. N. (1930) The submerged forest in Gower. *Proceedings of the Swansea Scientific and Field Naturalists' Society* **4**: 100–108.

George, T. N. (1933) The glacial deposits of Gower. *Geological Magazine* **70**: 208.

George, T. N. (1940) The structure of Gower. *Quarterly Journal of the Geological Society of London* **96**: 131–198.

George, T. N. (1970) *British Regional Geology: South Wales.* HMSO, London.

Gibbs, D. (1991) *Llangennith Moors Invertebrate Survey.* CCW contract survey. Countryside Council for Wales, Bangor.

Gilbert, O. L., Orange, A., & Fletcher, A. (1992) Field meeting in Gower, South Wales. *Lichenologist* **24**: 299–304.

Gillet, M. T. P. (1992) *Metoecus paradoxus* (L) (Rhipiphoridae): more parts to the puzzle. *Coleopterist* **1**: 4–5.

Gillham, M. E. (1964) The vegetation of local coastal gull colonies. *Transactions of the Cardiff Naturalists' Society* **91**: 23–33.

Gillham, M. E. (1977) *The Natural History of Gower.* D. Brown & Sons, Cowbridge.

Glading, P. R. (1984) Ecological studies upon carboniferous limestone vegetation in South Wales. Unpublished PhD thesis, University of Wales College Cardiff.

Goodman, G. T. (1975) *Plant Life in Gower.* Gower Society, Swansea.

Gower, J. (1991) Turning the tide: estuaries. *Birds (RSPB)* **13** (8).

Green, J. (2002) *Birds in Wales 1992–2000.* Welsh Ornithological Society, Cardigan.

Green, S. & Walker, E. (1991) *Ice Age Hunters: Neanderthals and Early Modern Hunters in Wales.* National Museum of Wales, Cardiff.

Groves, H. (1907) *Ononis reclinata* in Glamorgan. *Journal of Botany* **45**: 280–281.

Gutch, J. W. G. (1839) The medical topography, statistics, climatology and natural history of Swansea, Glamorganshire. *Transactions of The Provincial Medical and Surgical Association* **7**: 249–282.

Gutch, J. W. G. (1841) A list of plants met with in the neighbourhood of Swansea, Glamorganshire. *Phytologist* **1** (7): 104–108.

Gwynn, D. & Muxworthy, P. (1989) *A Pictorial Journey through Edwardian Gower.* Gomer Press, Llandysul.

Hall, C. & Williamson, K. (2003) In their element: coastal otters in North Wales. *Natur Cymru* **7**: 7–11.

Hall, J. (2003) An oyster fishery at the Mumbles. *Mollusc World* **1**: 10–11.

Harding, P. (1971) Notes on the occurrence of woodlice (Isopoda: Oniscoidea) on sand dunes at Whiteford Burrows, Glamorgan. *The Entomologist* Feb/April 1971: 98–103.

Hardwick, P. & Gunn, J. (1990) The impact of agricultural operations on the scientific interest of Cave SSSI. Unpublished report, Nature Conservancy Council and Limestone Research Group. Nature Conservancy Council, Peterborough.

Harper, E. M., Taylor, J. D. & Crame, J. A. (eds) (2000) *The Evolutionary Biology of the Bivalvia.* Geological Society, London.

Harris, W. (undated) Worms Head study: an investigation into zonation on the Causeway. Unpublished student thesis, University of Swansea.

Harvey, P. R., Nellist, D. R. & Telfer, M. G. (eds) (2002) *Provisional Atlas of British spiders (Arachnida, Araneae),* Vols 1 & 2. Biological Records Centre, Huntingdon.

Hatton, R. H. S. (1970) The acquisition of nature reserves and an analysis of reserves in Glamorgan. *Glamorgan County Naturalists' Trust Bulletin* **9**.

Hays G. C., Houghton J. D. R., Doyle T. &

Davenport J. (2003). Aircraft give a new view of jellyfish behaviour. *Nature* **426**: 383.

Hayward, P. J. (2004) *A Natural History of the Seashore*. New Naturalist 94. HarperCollins, London.

Healy, M. G. & Doody, J. P. (eds) (1995) *Directions in European Coastal Management*. Samara, Cardigan.

Higgins, L. S. (1933) An investigation into the problem of the sand dune areas on the South Wales coast. *Archaeologia Cambrensis* **139**: 26–67.

Hipkin, C. (2003) Putting our alien flora into perspective. *British Wildlife* **14**: 413–422.

Hiscock, K. (1979) *Field Surveys of Sublittoral Habitats and Species Along the Gower Coast*. Nature Conservancy Council, Huntingdon, and Field Studies Council Oil Pollution Research Unit, Orielton Field Centre, Pembroke.

Hogg, A. H. A. (1974) Excavations at Harding's Down West Fort, Gower. *Archaeologia Cambrensis* **122**: 55–68.

Holyoak, D. T. & Willing, M. J. *Survey for Vertigo angustior at Selected Localities in West Glamorgan*. CCW Contract Science Report 222. Countryside Council for Wales, Bangor.

Hoskins, W. G. & Stamp, L. D. (1963) *The Common Lands of England and Wales*. New Naturalist 45. Collins, London.

Howe, M. A. (2002a) *A Review of the Coastal Soft Cliff Resource in Wales, with Particular Reference to its Importance for Invertebrates*. CCW Natural Science Report 02/5/1. Countryside Council for Wales, Bangor.

Howe, M. A. (2002b) *A Provisional Checklist of the Invertebrates Recorded in Wales. 3. Brachyceran Flies (Diptera: Xylophagidae to Dolichopodidae)*. Countryside Council for Wales, Bangor.

Howe, M. A. (2003) Coastal soft cliffs and their importance for invertebrates. *British Wildlife* **14**: 323–331.

Howell, M. (1981) *Swansea District Plan. 2: Rural*. Draft written statement. Swansea City Council.

Howson, C. M. & Picton, B. E. (eds) (1997) *The Species Directory of the Marine Fauna and Flora of the British Isles and Surrounding Seas*. Ulster Museum and Marine Conservation Society, Belfast and Ross-on-Wye.

Hughes, M. R. (1983) National Nature Reserves in Wales: a systematic survey. 3. Oxwich National Nature Reserve, West Glamorgan. *Nature in Wales* (new series) **1**: 27–33.

Hughes, M. R. (1993) Life after the sand trap. *Enact* **1** (3): 12–14. English Nature, Peterborough.

Humphrys, G. (1982) *Geographical Excursions from Swansea. 1: Physical Environment*. Department of Geography, University College of Swansea.

Hurford, C. & Lansdown, P. (1995) *Birds of Glamorgan*. Cardiff Naturalists' Society and Countryside Council for Wales, Cardiff.

Ives, E. (1991) *Metoecus paradoxus* (L) (Rhipiphoridae): a puzzle. *Coleopterist's Newsletter* **44**: 9–10.

Ives, E. (1992) *Metoecus paradoxus* (L) (Rhipiphoridae): a further note. *Coleopterist's Newsletter* **45**: 17.

James, B. L. (1983) Rice Merrick. *Morganiae Archaiographia: a Book of the Antiquities of Glamorganshire*. South Wales Record Society, Barry.

Jeffreys, J. G. (1862–69) *British Conchology: or an Account of the Mollusca Which Now Inhabit the British Isles and the Surrounding Seas*. Van Voorst, London.

Jenkins, J. G. (1984) *Cockles and Mussels: Aspects of Shellfish-gathering in Wales*. National Museum of Wales, Cardiff. Originally published in *Folk Life*, 1977.

Jermyn, D. L., Messenger, J. E. & Birks, J. D. S. (2001) *The Distribution of the*

Hazel Dormouse Muscardinus avellanarius *in Wales*. Vincent Wildlife Trust, Ledbury.

Jewell, P. S. (1935) Field excursion to Bishopston Valley. *Proceedings of the Swansea Scientific and Field Naturalists' Society* 1 (9).

John, R. F. (1992) Genetic variation, reproductive biology and conservation in isolated populations of rare plant species. Unpublished PhD thesis, University of Wales, Swansea.

Jones, M. B. (1970) The distribution of *Pariambus typicus* var. *inermis* Mayer (Amphipoda, Caprellidae) on the common starfish *Asterias rubens* L. *Crustaceana* 19: 89–93.

Jones, P. S., Kay, Q. O. N. & Jones, A. (1995) The decline of rare plant species and community types in the sand dune systems of South Wales. In: Healy, M. G. & Doody, J. P. (eds) *Directions in European Coastal Management*. Samara Publishing, Cardigan, pp 547–555.

Jones, R. (1826) *Book of Plans of Commons and Wastes*. Report for the Beaufort Estate.

Joy, N. H. (1933) *British Beetles: Their Homes and Habits*. Frederick Warne, London.

Kay, Q. O. N. (1997a) *Arable Weed Communities and Wildlife: a Survey and Evaluation of the Effects of Arable Option Schemes*. Adplant Surveys.

Kay, Q. O. N. (1997b). A review of the taxonomy, biology, geographical distribution and European conservation status of *Asparagus prostratus* Dumort. (*A. officinalis* subsp. *prostratus*), Sea Asparagus. Unpublished report to the Countryside Council for Wales.

Kay, Q. O. N. (2001) The arable weed flora of the Viel, a medieval open field system at Rhossili in the western Gower peninsula. Unpublished report to the National Trust.

Kay, Q. O. N. & Ab-Shukor, N. A. (1988) *Trifolium occidentale* D. E. Coombe, new to Wales. *Watsonia* 17: 168–170.

Kay, Q. O. N. & John, R. F. (1995) *The Conservation of Scarce and Declining Plant Species in Lowland Wales: Population Genetics, Demographic Ecology and Recommendations for Future Conservation in 32 Species of Lowland Grassland and Related Habitats*. CCW Science Report No 110. Countryside Council for Wales, Bangor.

Kay, Q. O. N., Davies, E. W. & Rich, T. C G. (2001). Taxonomy of the western European endemic *Asparagus prostratus* (*A. officinalis* subsp. *prostratus*) (Asparagaceae). *Botanical Journal of the Linnean Society* 137: 127–137.

Keegan, B. F., Ceidigh, P. O. & Boaden, P. J. S. (1976) *Biology of Benthic Organisms*. Pergamon Press, Oxford.

Kierman, K. (1988) *The Management Of Soluble Rock Landscapes: an Australian Perspective*. Speleological Research Council, Sydney.

King P. E. & Copland M. J. W. (1969) The occurrence of *Metoecus paradoxus* L. (Col. : Rhipiphoridae) in Glamorgan. *Entomologist's Monthly Magazine* 105: 114.

Kirby, P. (1992) *Habitat Management for Invertebrates: a Practical Handbook*. RSPB, Sandy.

Larson, W. L., Matthes, U. & Kelly, P. E. (2000) *Cliff Ecology: Pattern and Process in Cliff Ecosystems*. Cambridge University Press, Cambridge.

Latham, J. (2004) How 'natural' is woodland nature? *Natur Cymru* 10 (Spring 2004): 4–6.

Lawrence, D. & Higgins, R. (1998) *Gower Hedgerow Report*. Wessex Ecological Consultancy.

Lees, E. (1842) *The Botanical Looker-out Among the Wild Flowers of the Fields, Woods, and Mountains of England and Wales*. London.

Lewis, J. (1851) *The Swansea Guide: compiled from the most authentic sources*. Swansea.

Liles, G. (2000) *An Audit of the Otter* (Lutra lutra) *on the Gower peninsula.* The Otter Consultancy, Carmarthenshire.

Linnard, W. (1982) *Welsh Woods and Forests: History and Utilization.* National Museum of Wales, Cardiff.

Llewellyn, P. J. & Shackley, S. E. (1996) The effects of mechanical beach cleaning on invertebrate populations. *British Wildlife* **7** (3).

Locket, G. H. (1965) A new species of Linyphiid spider. *Entomologist's Monthly Magazine* **101**: 48–50.

Lousley, J. E. (1950) *Wild Flowers of Chalk and Limestone.* New Naturalist 16. Collins, London.

Lovegrove, R., Williams, G. A. & Williams, I. (1994) *Birds in Wales.* Poyser, London.

Lowe, D. J. (1989) The Carboniferous Limestone of South Wales. In: Ford, T. D. (ed.) *Limestones and Caves of Wales.* Cambridge University Press, Cambridge, pp 10–11.

Mabey, R. (1996) *Flora Britannica.* Sinclair-Stevenson, London.

Macdonald, D. & Tattersall, F. (2003) *The State of Britain's Mammals 2003.* Mammals Trust and WildCRU, Oxford.

Mackie, A. (2003) Mapping seabed habitats around Wales. *Natur Cymru* **8** (Autumn 2003): 21–23.

Malloch, A. J. C. & Okusanya, O. T (1979). An experimental investigation into the ecology of some maritime cliff species. I. Field observations. *Journal of Ecology* **67**: 283–292.

Marshall, J. A. & Haes, E. C. M. (1990) *Grasshoppers and Allied Insects of Great Britain and Ireland.* Harley, Colchester.

McKie, R. (2004) Ships sabotage war on acid rain. *The Observer* 10 October 2004.

McLean, R. C. (1935) An ungrazed grassland on limestone in Wales. *Journal of Ecology* **23**: 436–442.

Mercer, T. (2002) *An Assessment of the Nature Conservation Value of Mussel Crumble in the Burry Inlet and the Effects of Dredging/Hand Gathering Operations.* CCW Research Report 526. Aquatic Environments. Countryside Council for Wales, Bangor.

Miskell, L. (2003) The making of a new 'Welsh metropolis': science, leisure and industry in early nineteenth-century Swansea. *History: the Journal of the Historical Association* **88**: 32–52.

Mitchell, P. I., Newton, S. F., Ratcliffe, N. & Dunn, T. E. (2004) *Seabird Populations of Britain and Ireland.* Poyser, London.

Mitchley, J. & Malloch, A. J. C. (1991) *Sea Cliff Management Handbook for Great Britain.* University of Lancaster / JNCC / National Trust.

Morgan, C. D. (1862) *Wanderings in Gower: a Perfect Guide to the Tourist and Lover of Nature.* Swansea.

Morgan, I. K. (1990) Notes on the ecology and British status of the opilionid *Sabacon viscayanum ramblaianum. Dyfed Invertebrate Group Newsletter* **19**: 15–18.

Morris, B. (2000) *Gabriel Powell's Survey of the Lordship of Gower 1764.* Gower Society, Swansea.

Morris, C. H. R. (undated) *A Gossiping Guide to Gower.* The Swansea National Eisteddfod Prize Book.

Mullard, J. D. (1990) *Mumbles Hill Local Nature Reserve Site Management Plan.* City of Swansea.

Mullard, J. D. (1992) *Cefn Bryn Common Draft Management Plan.* Gower Commoners Association, Swansea.

Mullard, J. D. (1993a) *Pwll Du Cliffs Site Management Plan.* City of Swansea.

Mullard, J. D. (1993b) Gower peninsula: coastal management in an AONB and Heritage Coast. In: *Planning for Coastal Areas and Inland Waterways.* Irish Planning Institute, Dublin.

Mullard, J. D. (1995) Gower: a case study in integrated coastal management initiatives in the UK. In: Healy, M. G. & Doody, J. P. (eds) *Directions in European Coastal Management.* Samara Publishing, Cardigan, pp 471–476.

Mullard, J. D. (ed.) (1996) AONBs *in the Landscape: the Area of Outstanding Natural Beauty 40th Anniversary Conference.* City and County of Swansea.

Mullard, J. D. (1998) *Gower Commons Initiative Business Plan.* Gower Heathlands Group / City and County of Swansea.

Nelson-Smith, A. & Bridges, E. M. (eds) (1977) *Problems of a Small Estuary.* University College of Swansea.

Nicholl, D. S. W. (1889) Notes on the rarer birds of Glamorganshire. *Zoologist* **3** (8): 166–174.

North, F. J. (1955) *The Evolution of the Bristol Channel.* National Museum of Wales, Cardiff.

Oldham, T. (2002) *The Caves of Gower.* Anne Oldham, Cardigan.

Oldisworth, J. (1802) *The Swansea Guide: containing such information as was deemed useful to the traveller, through the counties of Glamorgan & Monmouth, from the exemplifications of ancient and modern authors.* Z. B. Morris, Swansea.

Oldisworth, J. (1823) *The New Swansea Guide: containing a particular description of the town and its vicinity, together with a short history of the county.* H. Griffith, Swansea.

Orledge, G. M. and Smith, P. A. (1999) A survey of the black bog ant *Formica candida* on the Gower Peninsula, South Wales. Unpublished report, Environment Agency.

Orledge, G. M., Nash, D. R., Blanchard, G. B. & Conway, J. S. (1998) *Distribution of the Black Bog Ant* Formica candida *on Rhossili Down, Gower.* CCW Contract Science Report 266. Countryside Council for Wales, Bangor.

Osborne, T. (1990) *Gower Management Plan.* Swansea City Council.

Owen, T. R. (1973) *Geology Explained in South Wales.* David & Charles, Newton Abbot.

Packham, J. R., Randall, R. E., Barnes, R. S. K. & Neal, A. (2001) *Ecology and Geomorphology of Coastal Shingle.* Westbury Academic and Scientific Publishing, Otley.

Page, C. N. (1988) *Ferns.* New Naturalist 74. Collins, London.

Pavett, M. (1998) *Monitoring of Bumblebees and Other Aculeate Hymenoptera Populations on the South Gower Cliffs.* CCW Contract Science Report 328. Countryside Council for Wales, Bangor.

Penford, N., Francis, I. S., Hughes, E. J. & Aitchison, J. W. (1990) *Biological Survey of Common Land: a Survey of the Biological Characteristics and Management of Common Land. 13: West Glamorgan.* Nature Conservancy Council, Peterborough.

Penhallurick, R. (1994) *Gowerland and its Language.* Peter Lang, Frankfurt am Main.

Powell, H. T., Holme, N. A., Knight, S. J. T, Harvey, R., Bishop, G. & Bartrop, J. (1979). *Survey of the Littoral Zone of the Coast of Great Britain. 4: Report on the Shores of South West Wales.* CSD Report 269. Nature Conservancy Council, Peterborough.

Preston, C. D., Pearman, D. A. & Dines, T. D. (2002) *New Atlas of the British & Irish Flora* Oxford University Press, Oxford.

Prosser, M. V. & Wallace, H. L. (1998) *Lowland Heathland Survey of Wales: the Gower Commons 1997.* CCW Contract Science Report 310. Countryside Council for Wales, Bangor.

Prys-Jones, R. P., Howells, R. J. & Kirby, J. S. (1989) *The Abundance and Distribution of Wildfowl and Waders in the Burry Inlet.* BTO Research Report 43. British Trust for Ornithology, Tring.

Rackham, O. (1986) The *History of the Countryside.* Dent, London.

Ratcliffe, D. A. (1993) *The Peregrine Falcon.* 2nd edn. Poyser, London.

Rees, E. I. S. (2003) Aspects of the ecology and distribution of the hermit crab *Diogenes pugilator. Porcupine Marine Natural History Society Newsletter* **12**: 36–39.

Reid, J. (ed.) (2003) *Atlas of Cetacean Distribution in North-West European Waters.* JNCC, Peterborough.

Reiedl, R. (1996) *Biologie der Meereshöhlen: Topographie, Faunistik und Ökologie eines unterseeischen Lebensraumes.* Parey, Hamburg.

Rhind, P. (2002) The history, status and control of common cord grass in Wales. *Natur Cymru* **5** (Winter 2002): 32–34.

Rhind, P. & Robertson, J. (2003) The fungi of Welsh sand dunes *Natur Cymru* **9** (Winter 2003): 37–40.

Rhind, P. M., Blackstock, T. H. & Parr, S. J. (1997) *Welsh Islands: Ecology, Conservation and Land Use.* Proceedings of the Welsh Islands Conference. Countryside Council for Wales, Cardiff.

Rich, T. C. G., Bennallick, I. J., Cordrey, L., Kay, Q. O. N., Lockton, A. J. & Rich, L. K. (2002) Distribution and population sizes of *Asparagus prostratus* Dumort., wild asparagus, in Britain. *Watsonia* **24**: 183–192.

Riddelsdell, H. J. (1907). A flora of Glamorganshire. *Journal of Botany* (Supplement) 1907.

Riddelsdell, H. J. (1911) The flora of the Worms Head and the nativity of certain disputed species. *Journal of Botany* **49**: 89–92.

Roberts, A. (2001) *Estuary People.* Published by the author, Swansea.

Robinson, W. R. B. (1972) A petition from the Vicar of Pennard in Gower in 1535. *Archaeologia Cambrensis* **121**: 74–79. Cambrian Archaeological Association.

Royal Commission on Ancient and Historical Monuments in Wales (1976) *An Inventory of the Ancient Monuments in Glamorgan. Volume I: Pre-Norman. Part I: The Stone and Bronze Ages.* HMSO, Cardiff.

Rutter, J. G. (1948) *Prehistoric Gower. The Early Archaeology of West Glamorgan.* Welsh Guides, Swansea.

Sadler, J. (2003) *Exposed Riverine Sediments.* Biodiversity Technical Series 2. Environment Agency, Bristol.

Seed, R. (1996) Patterns of biodiversity in the macro-invertebrate fauna associated with mussel patches on rocky shores. *Journal of the Marine Biological Association of the United Kingdom* **76**: 203–210.

Sharp, R. (2002) Skates and rays around the Welsh coast: a declining resource. *Natur Cymru* **4** (Summer 2002): 31–34.

Sheail, J. (1998) *Nature Conservation in Britain: The Formative Years.* HMSO, London.

Shrubb, M. (2003) *Birds, Scythes and Combines: a History of Birds and Agricultural Change.* Cambridge University Press, Cambridge.

Smith, I. R. (1981) *Vegetation Survey and Monitoring on the Hard Coast Areas of the South Gower Coast NCR Site West Glamorgan.* Nature Conservancy Council, Peterborough.

Sneddon, P. & Randall, R. E. (1993a) *Coastal Vegetated Shingle Structures of Great Britain. Final Report.* JNCC, Peterborough.

Sneddon, P. & Randall, R. E. (1993b) *Coastal Vegetated Shingle Structures of Great Britain. Appendix 1: Wales.* JNCC, Peterborough.

Sowerby, J. (1790–1814) *English Botany: or, coloured figures of British plants, with their essential characters, synonyms and places of growth.* The author, London.

Spotila J. R., Reina R. D., Steyermark A. C., Plotkin, P. T. & Paladino, F. V. (2000) Pacific leatherback turtles face extinction. *Nature* **405**: 529–530.

Stace, C. (1995) *New Flora of the British Isles.* Cambridge University Press, Cambridge.

Step, E. (1932) *Bees, Wasps, Ants and Allied Insects of the British Isles*. Frederick Warne, London.

Stewart, B. & Grenfell, H. (2000) *The Butterflies of Gower*. Gower Society, Swansea.

Strawbridge, D. & Thomas, P. J. (1999) *A Guide to Gower*. Gower Society, Swansea.

Stubbs, A. & Drake, M. (2001) *British Soldierflies and Their Allies*. British Entomological and Natural History Society, Reading.

TACP Consultancy (1994) *Orchards in Wales*. CCW Policy Research Report 94/5. Countryside Council for Wales, Bangor.

Tallack, R. E. (1996) The rook population *Corvus frugilegus* in W. Glamorgan 1975–1996. *Gower Birds* 6 (5).

Tattersall, W. M (1936) *Glamorgan County History. Vol 1: Natural History*. William Lewis, Cardiff.

Thomas, D. K. (1992) *An Atlas of Breeding Birds in West Glamorgan*. Gower Ornithological Society, Swansea.

Thomas, D. M. (1982) *The Poems*. Dent, London.

Thomas, D. M. (1983) *The Collected Stories*. Dent, London.

Thomas, H. J. (1985) Iolo Morganwg vindicated: Glamorgan's first field archaeologist. *Glamorgan–Gwent Archaeological Trust Annual Report* 1983–1984 (2): 149–157.

Thomas, J. M. (1982) *Yesterday's Gower*. Gomer Press, Llandysul.

Thomas, N. L. (1978) *The Mumbles: Past and Present*. Gomer Press, Llandysul.

Toft, L. A. (1988) A study of coastal village abandonment in the Swansea Bay region, 1270–1540. *Morganwg* 32: 21–37.

Trow, A. H. (ed.) (1907–12) The flora of Glamorgan. Published in parts in the *Transactions of the Cardiff Naturalists' Society*. Published as a single volume in 1911.

Tucker, H. M. (1951) *Gower Gleanings*. The Gower Society, Swansea.

Tucker, H. M. (1957) *My Gower*. Rowlands, Neath.

Turner, D. & Dillwyn, L. W. (1805). *The Botanist's Guide through England and Wales*. Phillips & Fardon, London.

Tyler, J. (1994) *Glow-worms*. Tyler-Scagell, Sevenoaks.

Tyler, P. A. & Shackley, S. E. (1980) The benthic ecology of linear sandbanks: a modified *Spisula* sub-community. In: Collins, M. B., Banner, F. T., Tyler, P. A., Wakefield, S. J. & James, A. E. (eds) *Industrial Embayments and Their Environmental Problems: a Case Study of Swansea Bay*. Pergamon Press, Oxford, pp 539–551.

Vaughan-Thomas, W. (1983) *Portrait of Gower*. Robert Hales, London.

Vera, F. W. M. (2000) *Grazing Ecology and Forest History*. CABI Publishing, Wallingford.

Vickery, J. A., Tallowin, J. R., Feber, R. E., Asteraki, E. J., Atkinson, P. W., Fuller, R. J. & Brown, V. K. (2001) The management of lowland neutral grasslands in Britain: effects of agricultural practices on birds and their food resources. *Journal of Applied Ecology* 38: 647–664.

Wade, A. E., Kay, Q. O. N. & Ellis, R. G. (1994) *Flora of Glamorgan*. National Museum of Wales, HMSO, London.

Walker, A. R. (2003) The Dillwyns as naturalists: Lewis Weston Dillwyn (1778–1855). *Minerva (Journal of Swansea History)* 11: 20–42.

Waltham, A. C., Simms, M. J., Farrant, A. J. & Goldie, H. S. (1997) *Karst and caves of Great Britain*. JNCC, Peterborough.

Ward, A. H. (1987) Early agriculture on Rhossili Down, Gower, West Glamorgan. *Bulletin of the Board of Celtic Studies* 34: 220–227.

Ward, A. H. (1989) Cairns and cairnfields: evidence of very early agriculture on Cefn Bryn, Gower, West Glamorgan. *Landscape History* **11**: 5–18.

Warwick, R. M. & Davies, J. R. (1977) The distribution of sublittoral macrofauna communities in the Bristol Channel in relation to substrate. *Estuarine and Coastal Marine Science* **5**: 267–288.

Watkins, A. (1891) A survey of pigeon houses in Herefordshire and Gower. *Royal Archaeological Society Journal* **48**.

Webb, J. A. (1956) The flora of Gower. *Proceedings of the Swansea Scientific and Field Naturalists' Society* **3** (Supplement): 1–25.

Wells, S. M. & Chatfield, J. E. (1992) *Threatened Non-Marine Molluscs of Europe.* Nature and Environment No 64. Council of Europe, Strasbourg.

Whittle, A. & Wysocki, M. (1998) Parc le Breos Cwm transepted long cairn, Gower, West Glamorgan: date, contents and context. *Proceedings of the Prehistoric Society* **64**: 139–182.

Wilkinson, P. F., Locock, M. & Sell, S. (1998) A 16th-century saltworks at Port Eynon, Gower. *Post-Medieval Archaeology* **32**: 3–32.

Williams, D. (1998) *Gower: a Guide to Ancient and Historic Monuments on the Gower Peninsula.* Cadw Welsh Historic Monuments, Cardiff.

Williams, D. H. (1970) *The Welsh Cistercians.* Hughes and Son, Griffin Press, Pontypool.

Williams, D. H. (1990) *Atlas of Cistercian Lands in Wales.* University of Wales Press, Cardiff.

Williams, M. (1972) The linguistic and cultural frontier in Gower. *Archaeologia Cambrensis* **121**: 61–69.

Williams, P. W. (ed.) (1993) *Karst Terrains: Environmental Changes and Human Impact.* Catena Supplement 25. Catena, Cremlingen.

Wilson, P. & King, M. (eds) (2001) *Fields of Vision: a Future for Britain's Arable Plants.* Plantlife, Cambridge.

Wilson, P. & King, M. (2003) *Arable Plants: a Field Guide.* English Nature and WildGuides, Peterborough.

Withers, R. G. (1977) Soft-shore macrobenthos along the southwest coast of Wales. *Estuarine and Coastal Marine Science* **5**: 467–484.

Wood, E. S. (1973) *Collins Field Guide to Archaeology.* Collins, London.

Wood, P. J. & Gunn, J. (2000) The aquatic invertebrate fauna within a cave system in Derbyshire, England. *Internationale Vereinigung für Theoretische und Angewandte Limnologie* **27**: 901–905.

Woodman, J. (1998) A sample survey of arable weeds on farms with arable options under the Tir Cymen scheme, Gower. Unpublished report, Countryside Council for Wales.

Woolmer, A. P. (2003) The benthic ecology of Carmarthen Bay. Unpublished PhD thesis, University of Wales, Swansea.

Woolmore, R. (2005) Gower AONB: designation history series. Unpublished document, Countryside Agency.

Yalden, D. W. (1992) Changing distribution and status of small mammals in Britain. *Mammal Review* **22**: 97–106.

Yarwood, R. & Evans, N. (2002) *Agricultural Biodiversity Resources of Welsh Domestic Livestock.* CCW Contract Report. Countryside Council for Wales, Bangor.

Species Index

Ceratinopsis romana 186
Cerceris arenaria 118
Cereus pedunculatus (daisy anemone) 166
Ceropales maculata (coastal spider hunting wasp) 184
Certhia familiaris (treecreeper) 317
Cervus elaphus (red deer) 50, 63
cetaceans 160–2
Ceterach officinarium (rustyback fern) 352
Cetorhinus maximus (basking shark) 153
Cettia cetti (Cetti's warbler) 287, 290
Chaenorhinum minus (small toadflax) 175
chaffinch (*Fringilla coelebs*) 288
Chamelea gallina 149
Chamerion angustifolium (rosebay willow-herb) 331
channelled wrack (*Pelvetia canaliculata*) 134, 213
Charadrius hiaticula (ringed plover) 171–2
charlock (*Sinapis arvensis*) 63
Cheirocephalus diaphanus (fairy shrimp) 298
Chelon labrosus (mullet) 234
chicken 69
chickweed 206
chiffchaff (*Phylloscopus collybita*) 317
Chinese muntjac (*Muntiacus reevesi*) 77
Chondrus crispus (Irish moss) 141
Chordeuma proximum 314
chough (*Pyrrhocorax pyrrhocorax*) 124–6, **126**, 128
Chromatochlamys muscorum 92
Chrysanthemum segetum (corn marigold) 329, **330**
Chrysaora hysoscella (compass jellyfish) 156
Chrysomela populi (bright red leaf beetle) 195
Chthamalus
  C. montagui 134
  C. stellatus 134

Cicindela
  C. campestris (green tiger beetle) 214, **215**
  C. maritima (dune tiger beetle) 182–3
Cinara juniperi (juniper aphid) 120
Cinclus cinclus (dipper) 282
Circaea lutetiana (enchanter's nightingale) 312–13
Circus aeruginosus (marsh harrier) 287
Cirsium
  C. acaule (dwarf thistle) 104
  C. arvense (creeping thistle) 205, 208
  C. dissectum (meadow thistle) 332
  C. palustre (marsh thistle) 301
  C. vulgare (spear-thistle) 214
Cladonia impexa 174–5
Clavelina lepadiformis (light bulb sea squirt) 141, **141**, 142
cleaver (*Galium aparine*) 214
Clematis vitalba (wild clematis) 121
Clethrionomys glareolus (bank vole) 326
Clinopodium acinos (basil thyme) 105
Cliona 144
  C. celata 136
clouded yellow butterfly (*Colias croceus*) 214
clover (*Trifolium*) 175
Clupea
  C. alosa (shad) 236
  C. harengus (herring) 234–5
coastal spider hunting wasp (*Ceropales maculata*) 184
Cochlearia
  C. anglica (English scurvygrass) 224
  C. officinalis (common scurvygrass) 101, 206, 213
Cochlodina laminata (common (two-toothed door) snail) 314
cockle 226, 229–34, **230**
cock's comb (*Plocamium cartilagineum*) 141

cock's-foot (*Dactylis glomerata*) 111–12, 182, 214, 265
cod (*Gadus morhua*) 151
Coelodonta antiquitatis (woolly rhino) 45–6
Coenagrion
  C. mercuriale (southern damselfly) 266, **267**, 291
  C. puella (azure damselfly) 285
Coenonympha pamphilus (small heath butterfly) 269
Coenosia stigmatica 315
Coincya monensis (Isle of Man cabbage) 181
Coleophora ochrea 119
Colias croceus (clouded yellow butterfly) 214
Collembola (springtail) 351–2
Colletes cunicularis 195
Columba
  C. livia (wild rock dove) 349
  C. oenas (stock dove) 214
common banded snail (*Cepaea nemoralis*) 186
common bent (*Agrostis capillaris*) 269
common bird's-foot-trefoil (*Lotus corniculatus*) 112, 214
common blue butterfly (*Polyommatus icarus*) 183
common bottlenose dolphin (*Tursiops truncatus*) 160
common cave gnat (*Speolepta leptogaster*) 352
common centaury (*Centaurium erythraea*) 214, 305
common club-rush (*Schoenoplactus lacustris*) 225
common cockle (*Cerastoderma edule*) 166
common cord-grass (*Spartina anglica*) 223–4
common cottongrass (*Eriophorum angustifolium*) 258, **259**
common dog-violet (*Viola riviniana*) 106, 260, 269
common dolphin (*Delphinus delphinus*) 162
common dor beetle (*Geotrupes stercorarius*) 255, 257, 258

Geranium
  G. dissectum (cut-leaved crane's-bill) 115
  G. robertianum (herb Robert) 288, 352
  G. sanguineum (bloody crane's-bill) 105, 179–81, **180**, 203
germander speedwell (*Veronica chamaedrys*) 214
Gerris lacustris (pond skater) 195
ghost sea slug (*Okenia adspersa*) 143
giant lacewing (*Osmylus fulvicephalus*) 281
gipsywort (*Lycopus europaeus*) 288
Glamorgan Brown 252
glasswort (*Salicornia*) 223
glaucous gull (*Larus hyperboreus*) 172
glaucous sedge (*Carex flacca*) 106
Glaux maritima (sea milkwort) 224
Globiceps cruciatus 195
glow-worm (*Lampyris noctiluca*) 122–3, 379
Glycera convoluta 167
Glyohesis servulus 266
Gnathia maxilaris 137
goat 63, 69, 202
goldcrest (*Regulus regulus*) 317
golden pluver (*Pluvialis apricaria*) 305–6
golden samphire (*Inula crithmoides*) 101, **102**, 119, 213
golden-ringed dragonfly (*Cordulegaster boltonii*) 301–2, **302**
goldeneye (*Bucephala clangula*) 296
goldfinch (*Carduelis carduelis*) 268, 288
goldilocks aster (*Aster linosyris*) 27, **27**
golf ball sponge (*Tethya aurantium*) 141
goose 69
gorse (*Ulex*) 77, 106, **106**, 114–15, 131, 203, 205, 206, 249, 260–1, 271, 331
gorse spider mite (*Tetranychus lintearius*) 263

Gower money spider (*Baryphyma gowerense* formerly *Lasiargus gowerensis*) 227–9, **228**
Gracilaria gracilis (slender red filmanent weed) 142
Grampus griseus (Risso's dolphin) 162
Grantia compressa (purse sponge) 136
grass eggar moth (*Lasiocampa trifolii*) 183
grass snake (*Natrix natrix*) 123, 186, 285–6
grasshopper warbler (*Locustella naevia*) 286, 305
grasskelp (*Enteromorpha*) 136, 139
grassland puffball (*Lycoperdon lividum*) 187
grayling (*Hipparchia semele*) 122, 183
great black slug (*Arion ater*) 327
great black-headed gull (*Larus marinus*) 211, 239
great creseted newt (*Triturus cristatus*) 298
great green bush-cricket (*Tettigonia viridissima*) 183, **184**
great hammerhead shark (*Sphyrna mokarran*) 153
great spotted woodpecker (*Dendrocopos major*) 317, **318**
great willow herb (*Epilobium hirsutum*) 280
greater bird's-foot-trefoil (*Lotus uliginosus*) 291, 306
greater horseshoe bat (*Rhinolophus ferrumequinum*) 257–8, 345–6, **345**, 347, 355
greater knapweed (*Centaurea scabiosa*) 112
greater sea-spurrey (*Spergularia media*) 224
greater tussock-sedge (*Carex paniculata*) 291, 304
greater water-moss (*Fontinalis antipyretica*) 290
green hairstreak butterfly (*Callophyrys rubi*) 269
green tiger beetle (*Cicindela campestris*) 214, **215**

green woodpecker (*Picus viridis*) 130, 268
green-flowered helleborine (*Epipactis phyllanthes*) 192
grey bush cricket (*Platycleis albopunctata*) 121
grey heron (*Ardea cinerea*) 282, 287, 296
grey plover (*Pluvialis squatarola*) 172, 237
grey sea slug (*Aeolidia papillosa*) 144
grey seal (*Halichoerus grypus*) 158–9, **159**
grey wagtail (*Motacilla cinerea*) 282
grey willow (*Salix cinerea*) 312, 326
Griffithsides (trilobite) 36
guarded flask sponge (*Scypha ciliata*) 141
guillemot (*Uria aalge*) 124, 163, 208, 210–11, 384
Gymnostomum aerinosum 352

Haematobia irritans (horn fly) 254
Haematopus ostralegus (oystercatcher) 23–4, **23**, 171–2, 172, 231–2, 237, **238**, 240, 244
Haemopsis sanguisynga (large black horse leech) 296
hairy dragonfly (*Brachytron pratense*) 285
hairy snail (*Hygromia hispida*) 327
Halichoerus grypus (grey seal) 158–9, **159**
Halichondria panicea (breadcrumb sponge) 136, **137**
Halidrys siliquosa (sea oak) 139
Halurus equisetifolius (red bottlebrush weed) 142
Handkea
  H. excipuliformis (pestle-shaped puffball) 187
  H. utriformis (mosaic puffball) 187
Haplophilus subterraneus 314
harbour porpoise (*Phocoena phocoena*) 159–60
hard fern (*Blechnum spicant*) 280
hare 269

sea bindweed (*Calystegia soldanella*) 175, 179, 199
sea buckthorn (*Hippophae rhamnoides*) 198
sea campion (*Silene uniflora*) 19, 101, 174, 176, 206, 213
sea club-rush (*Bolboschoenus maritimus*) 225
sea holly (*Eryngium maritimum*) 175, 179, **180**
sea kale (*Crambe maritima*) 174
sea lamprey (*Petromyzon marinus*) 236
sea lettuce (*Ulva lactuca*) 139
sea mayweed (*Tripleurospermum maritimum*) 205, 206
sea milkwort (*Glaux maritima*) 224
sea mouse (*Aphrodite aculeata*) 167
sea oak (*Halidrys siliquosa*) 139
sea pea (*Lathyrus japonicus*) 174
sea plantain (*Plantago maritima*) 216, 224
sea rocket (*Cakile maritima*) 169
sea rush (*Juncus maritimus*) 57, 224, 244
sea sandwort (*Honkenya peploides*) 169, 175
sea slater (*Sphaeroma serratum*) 137
sea slug (*Fiona pinnata*) 155
sea spleenwort (*Asplenium marinum*) 101
sea spurge (*Euphorbia paralias*) 179, 199
sea stock (*Matthiola sinuata*) 108, 216
sea storksbill (*Erodium maritimum*) 206, 214
sea sturgeon (*Acipenser sturio*) 151–2
sea trout (*Salmo trutta*) 235
sea wormwood (*Serphidium maritima*) 224
sea-blite (*Suaeda maritima*) 223
sea-purslane (*Atriplex portulacoides*) 224
seaweed 134, 136, 137, 139, 140–1, 213
sedge (*Carex*) 192, 224, 304

sedge warbler (*Acrocephalus schoenobaenus*) 239, 286, 305
Sedum
S. album (white stonecrop) 326–7
S. telephium (orpine) 213
seedbug (*Macroplax preyssleri*) 120
Semibalanus balanoides 134
Senecio jacobaea (ragwort) 217
Sepia officinalis (cuttlefish) 150
serotine bat (*Eptesicus serotinus*) 257
Serphidium maritima (sea wormwood) 224
serrated wrack (*Fucus serratus*) 134
Serratula tinctoria (saw-wort) 263
Sertularia argentea 144
sessile oak (*Quercus petraea*) 258, 312
shad (*Clupea alosa*) 236
shag (*Phalacrocorax aristotelis*) 208
shanny (*Lipophrys pholis*) 139
shark 152–3
sharp rush (*Juncus acutus*) 306
sharp-flowered rush (*Juncus acutiflora*) 291, 295
sharp-leaved fluellen (*Kickxia elatine*) 329
sheep 63, 65, 68, 81, 94–5, 112, 113, 114–16, 177, 202–3, 205, **242**, 243, 248, 252–5, 264, 269, 271, 304
sheep's sorrel (*Rumex acetosa*) 206, 208, 214
sheep's-fescue (*Festuca ovina*) 111–12, 269, 291
shelduck (*Tadorna tadorna*) 237, **238**
shore bug (*Aepophilus bonnairei*) 137
short-eared owl (*Asio flammeus*) 242
short-tailed vole (*Microtus agrestis*) 214, 269
shoveler (*Anas clypeata*) 237, 286
Silene
S. gallica (small-flowered catchfly) 329

S. uniflora (sea campion) 19, 101, 174, 176, 206, 213
silky wave (*Idaea dilutaria*) 119–20, **120**
silver birch (*Betula pendula*) 50
silverweed (*Potentilla anserina*) 175
Sinapis
S. arvensis (charlock) 63
S. cheiranthus (wallflower cabbage) 22
siskin (*Carduelis spinus*) 288
Sitka spruce (*Picea sitchensis*) 313
Sitta europaea (nuthatch) 317
skate 153
skylark (*Alauda arvensis*) 214, 268, 305, 332
slender red filmanent weed (*Gracilaria gracilis*) 142
slow-worm (*Anguis fragilis*) 123, 186, 326
small cord-grass (*Spartina maritima*) 223
small heath butterfly (*Coenonympha pamphilus*) 269
small pearl-bordered fritillary (*Bolaria selene*) 122
small restharrow (*Ononis reclinata*) 18–19, 105
small scabious (*Scabiosa columbaria*) 112, 203
small toadflax (*Chaenorhinum minus*) 175
small white woodlouse (*Metatrichoniscoides celticus*) 134
small-flowered catchfly (*Silene gallica*) 329
small-leaved lime (*Tilia cordata*) 310, 312, 313
smooth cord-grass (*Spartina alterniflora*) 223
smooth ground beetle (*Broscus cephalotes*) 182
smooth meadow-grass (*Poa pratensis*) 182, 205
smooth-stalked sedge (*Carex laevigata*) 291
snake millipede (*Ophyiulus pilosus*) 314

water-pepper (*Polygonum hydropiper*) 305
water-stalwort (*Callitriche*) 305
waved carpet moth (*Hydrelia sylvata*) 315–16, **315**
waxcap (*Hygrocybe*) 187
weevil 116, 118
well-shrimp (*Niphargus fontanus*) 350–1
western clover (*Trifolium occidentale*) 29
western gorse (*Ulex gallii*) 107, 261, **262**
whale 160–1
wheat (*Triticum*) 83
wheatear (*Oenanthe oenanthe*) 214, 217
whinchat (*Saxicola rubetra*) 261
whiskered bat (*Myotis mystacinus*) 320, 347
white beak-sedge (*Rhynchospora alba*) 263
white clover (*Trifolium repens*) 29–30, 205, 255
white hedgehog sponge (*Polymastia mamillaris*) 141, 143
white horehound (*Marrubium vulgare*) 104
white horseshoe worm (*Phoronis hippocrepia*) 142
white spiky sponge (*Dysidea fragilis*) 141
white stonecrop (*Sedum album*) 326–7
white water-lily (*Nymphaea alba*) 295
white-sided dolphin (*Lagenorhynchus acutus*) 162
white-tailed bumblebee (*Bombus lucorum*) 110, 214
whiteletter hairstreak butterfly (*Satyrium w-album*) 316–17

whitethroat (*Sylvia communis*) 124, 268
whiting (*Merlangius merlangus*) 151
whooper swan (*Cygnus cygnus*) 296
whorled caraway (*Carum verticillatum*) 263, 332
wigeon (*Anas penelope*) 241
wild asparagus (*Asparagus prostratus*) 104
wild carrot (*Daucus carota*) 112, 182
wild cat (*Felis catus*) 63, 320
wild clematis (*Clematis vitalba*) 121
wild daffodil (*Narcissus pseudonarcissus* spp. *pseudonarcissus*) 313
wild horse (tarpan) (*Equus ferus*) 62
wild privet (*Ligustrum vulgare*) 310
wild radish (*Raphanus raphanistrum*) 329, 330
wild rock dove (*Columba livia*) 349
wild service tree (*Sorbus torminalis*) 312
wild thyme (*Thymus polytrichus*) 106, 112, 175
willow (*Salix*) 288, 290, 291
willow warbler (*Phylloscopus trochilus*) 288
winter-cress *Barbarea vulgaris* 280
wolf 341
wolf spider (*Arctosa perita*) 184
wood anemone (*Anemone nemorosa*) 312
wood horsetail (*Equisetum sylvaticum*) 312

wood meadow-grass (*Poa nemoralis*) 265
wood mouse (*Apodemus sylvaticus*) 269, 326
wood sage (*Teucrium scorodonia*) 107, 269
wood sandpiper **295**, 296
wood spurge (*Euphorbia amygdaloides*) 310
woodlouse 176
woodlouse spider (*Dysdera crocata*) 176
woolly rhino (*Coelodonta antiquitatis*) 45–6
wrack (*Fucus*) 213
wren (*Troglodytes troglodytes*) 288
wych elm (*Ulmus glabra*) 309–10, 316–17

Xanthoria aureola 101–2, **103**

yellow iris (*Iris pseudacorus*) 225, 284, 288, 301, **301**, 304, 305, 306
yellow loosestrife (*Lysimachia vulgaris*) 279, 305
yellow meadow ant (*Lasius flavus*) 128, 334
yellow whitlowgrass (*Draba aizoides*) 18, 22, 108–12, **109**
yellow-legged gull (*Larus cachinnans*) 172
yellow-winged darter (*Sympetrum flaveolum*) 302
yellowhammer (*Emberiza citrinella*) 124, 305, 378
Yorkshire-fog (*Holcus lanatus*) 107, 115, 182, 214, 260, 291, 305, 306

Zaphentis oystermouthensis 36
Zostera noltii (dwarf eelgrass) 223
Zygaena trifolii (crimson and black-spot burnet moth) 195

General Index